THE JAMES BEARD CELEBRATION COOKBOOK
MEMORIES AND RECIPES FROM HIS FRIENDS

The James Beard Foundation

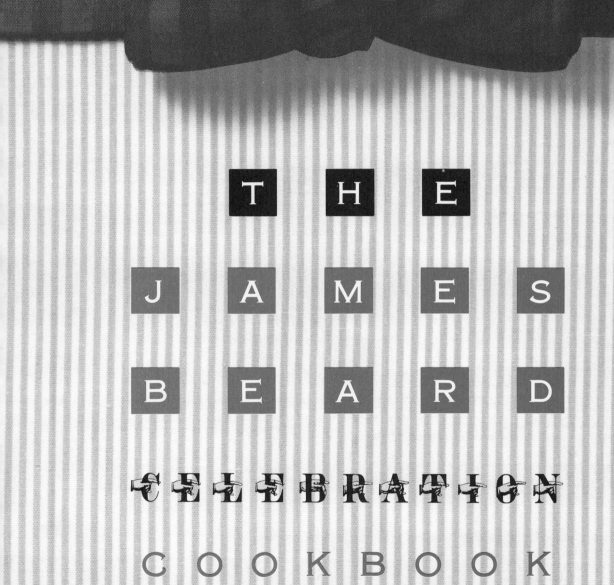

THE JAMES BEARD

CELEBRATION

COOKBOOK

William Morrow and Company, Inc. ▪ **New York**

Library of Congress Cataloging-in-Publication Data

The James Beard celebration cookbook : memories and recipes from his friends / The James Beard Foundation.
    p. cm.
    ISBN 0-688-07637-8
    1. Cookery.   I. James Beard Foundation.
TX714.J36 1990   90-41029
641.5—dc20   CIP

Printed in the United States of America

BOMC offers recordings and compact discs, cassettes and records. For information and catalog write to BOMR, Camp Hill, PA 17012.

Book Design by Stephanie Tevonian

ACKNOWLEDGMENTS. MORE EVEN THAN MOST BOOKS THIS ONE HAS BEEN MADE POSSIBLE BY THE GOODWILL AND ENERGIES OF NUMBERLESS PEOPLE. RECIPES HAVE BEEN GIVEN BY FRIENDS, ADMIRING WRITERS, COOKERY TEACHERS, AND RESTAURANT CHEFS. THEY HAVE ALSO WRITTEN WARM MEMORIES OF JAMES BEARD. RECIPES HAVE BEEN LOANED BY THE PUBLISHERS AND OWNERS OF COPYRIGHTS IN JAMES BEARD'S BOOKS.

THE RECIPES HAVE BEEN TESTED BY REBECCA MARSHALL, JOY HORSTMANN, AND ANNA BRANDENBURGER OF BARBARA KAFKA'S STAFF AS WELL AS BY LOYAL VOLUNTEERS:

FLO BRAKER, SANDY DUKE, JIM FOBEL, JUDY GERSTEIN, MARGERY HELD, LINDA HOWITT, URSULA KALISH, BARBARA KLION, LINDA LEIBERMAN, MICHELE LYSTER, BARBARA MELTSNER, CHRISTINE PASQUARIELLO, ELLIE PEACE, NANETTE PORCELLI, BETTY SANEHOLZ, LINDA SPEER, PHILIP STAFFORD, SHERLE TALLENT, PAM THOMAS, AND LORNA DE VRIES.

WE WISH TO THANK SUSAN LESCHER, WHO, WITHOUT PROFIT, UNDERTOOK THE REPRESENTATION OF THIS BOOK TO THE PUBLISHING WORLD, AND MARIA GUARNASCHELLI, THE EDITOR AT WILLIAM MORROW WHO PATIENTLY WAITED FOR THIS VOLUNTEER EFFORT BY MANY HANDS TO COME TOGETHER.

AS THE EDITOR, IT IS MY PRIVILEGE TO THANK ALL THESE PEOPLE AND TO WELCOME YOU TO THAT EXTRAORDINARY WORLD THAT JAMES BEARD CREATED BY BRINGING SO MANY PEOPLE TOGETHER IN HIS ENTHUSIASM FOR LIFE AND FOOD AND TO THANK THE LOYAL BOARD OF THE FOUNDATION WHICH HAS WORKED WITH SUCH LOVE

AND DEVOTION TO CONTINUE HIS DREAM:

JULIA CHILD, FOUNDER; PETER KUMP, PRESIDENT; NORMAN TANEN, VICE PRESIDENT; BERNARD PERRY, TREASURER; CAROLINE STUART, SECRETARY; ARTHUR ABELMAN; RUTH BAUM, WILLIAM T. BEATTY; ANNE BYRD; TIM JOHNSON; RICHARD LAVIN; JACQUES PÉPIN; AND LEN PICKELL.

THE DISTINGUISHED NATIONAL BOARD OF ADVISERS (SEE BELOW) HAS ALSO BEEN OF GREAT HELP.

FINALLY, I MUST CONFESS THAT YOU WILL MEET AN ''I'' ON SOME OF THESE PAGES. THERE SEEMED NO WAY OF WRITING ABOUT JAMES ANDREW BEARD, JAMES AND JIM, IMPERSONALLY.

Barbara Kafka, editor pro bono ✍
For the James Beard Foundation

C O N T E N T S

The bow ties pictured on the endpapers and part titles and the dishes, pots, etc., on the part title pages all belonged to James Beard. The bow ties were kindly lent by Larry Forgione, and the photographs of Beard's dishes and pots are courtesy of the William Doyle Galleries.

Contributors

Recipes from James Beard's books (62, 63, 167, 238, 239, 247, 264, 315, 316, 317, 318)

Barbara Kafka Recipes (125, 126, 130, 131, 137, 155, 161, 310, 323)

Contributors of remembrances, but not recipes:

M.F.K. Fisher (392) ▪ *Mary Homi (51)* ▪ *Mary Lyons (52)* ▪ *Jean Purvis (41)* ▪ *Clark Wolf (389)*

Contributors of recipes and remembrances:

Florence Aaron (68) ▪ *Sandra N. Allen (246)* ▪ *Lidia Bastianich (152, 153, 321, 376)* ▪ *Joe Baum (92)* ▪ *Simone Beck (362, 364)* ▪ *Rose Levy Beranbaum (66)* ▪ *Jan Birnbaum (322)* ▪ *Fritz Blank (375)* ▪ *Bobbi and Carole's Cooking School (211, 311)* ▪ *Flo Braker (282, 338, 339, 359)* ▪ *Ella Brennan (89, 219)* ▪ *Philip Brown (276)* ▪ *Anna Teresa Callen (160, 300, 301)* ▪ *Yannick Cam (94)* ▪ *Mark Caraluzzi (45, 119, 141, 326)* ▪ *John Carroll (203)* ▪ *Cecilia Chang (228)* ▪ *Julia Child (253, 256)* ▪ *Craig Claiborne (57)* ▪ *Elizabeth Clark (85, 269)* ▪ *Suzanne Corbett (113, 320)* ▪ *Helen Corbitt (65)* ▪ *Marion Cunningham (171, 355, 356, 357)* ▪ *Julie Dannenbaum (135, 144)* ▪ *John and Sally Darr (230)* ▪ *Elizabeth David (59)* ▪ *François Dionot (214)* ▪ *Dux/ Mike Kelly (347)* ▪ *Merle Ellis (242)* ▪ *Florence Fabricant (97)* ▪ *Barbara Fenzl (365)* ▪ *John Ferrone (257, 259, 379)* ▪ *Jim Fobel (107, 142, 150)* ▪ *Michael Foley (192, 294, 377)* ▪ *Larry Forgione (98, 100, 305)* ▪ *Pierre Franey (95, 96)* ▪ *Jane Freiman (374)* ▪ *Maggie Gin (195)* ▪ *Joyce Goldstein (178, 215, 349, 350)* ▪ *Richard Grausman (244)* ▪ *Gael Greene (265, 266)* ▪ *Jane Grigson (86, 88)* ▪ *Paul Grimes (61)* ▪ *Carol Guidice (183, 382)* ▪ *Mary Hamblet (220)* ▪ *Marcella Hazan (69)* ▪ *Prudence Hilburn (309)* ▪ *Suzanne Hoffman (201)* ▪ *Christopher Idone (216)* ▪ *Carl Jerome (306, 318)* ▪ *Judith and Evan Jones (274)* ▪ *Elaine Kaufman (112)* ▪ *Mike Kelly/Dux (347)* ▪ *Matt Kramer (383, 384)* ▪ *Diana Kennedy (82)* ▪ *Loni Kuhn (79, 296, 381, 391)* ▪ *Chris Kump (162)* ▪ *Peter Kump (145, 340)* ▪ *Jerry Lamb (263)* ▪ *George Lang (352, 353)* ▪ *Jane Lavine (188)* ▪ *Chicken Lea (190)* ▪ *Silvia Lehrer (148)* ▪ *Leon Lianides (187)* ▪ *Jimella Lucas (169, 337)* ▪ *Nick Malgieri (366)* ▪ *Jacqueline Mallorca (251)* ▪ *Abby Mandel (83, 84)* ▪ *Lydie Marshall (268)* ▪ *Michael McCarty (193, 213, 272, 293)* ▪ *Helen McCully (168)* ▪ *Bettina McNulty (218, 236)* ▪ *Mark Militello (186)* ▪ *Mark Miller (118, 273, 285, 390)* ▪ *Paul Minnillo (151)* ▪ *Maurice Moore-Betty (231, 319)* ▪ *Jane Montant (380)* ▪ *Karin Moser-Duftner (351)* ▪ *James Nassikas (184)* ▪ *Cornelius O'Donnell (121, 123, 204)* ▪ *Bradley Ogden (181)* ▪ *Elizabeth Lambert Ortiz (270)* ▪ *Jeanne Owen (64, 250)* ▪ *Jean-Louis Palladin (127)* ▪ *Jacques Pépin (283, 284)* ▪ *Kathleen Perry (80)* ▪ *Le Plaisir (140, 303)* ▪ *Jean-Paul Pradié and Alain Sinturel (90)* ▪ *Joanna Pruess (199)* ▪ *Wolfgang Puck (327, 328)* ▪ *Stephan Pyles (129, 210, 325, 336, 344)* ▪ *Hermann Reiner (172)* ▪ *Leslee Reis (226, 346)* ▪ *Seppi Renggli (157)* ▪ *Leslie Revsin (78)* ▪ *Bill Rice (116)* ▪ *Claudia Roden (354)* ▪

INTRODUCTION. *When James Beard died, his was the most famous food name in America and was known throughout the world. He personified American food. Many of his friends and students combined to retain his house as a center for American food—which it had been when Jim was alive. Culinary groups meet there; there is a library and an archive; there is a teaching kitchen and there are meals prepared by the foremost American chefs; there are events such as wine tastings and book signings. To accomplish all this a foundation was formed. Much money has been and continues to need to be raised to buy the house, to restore it, and to make all its functions possible.*

This book, a collaborative effort of the foundation and James's many friends, is both a gesture of love and a fund-raising activity. It is full of recipes that James liked or would have liked, some uncollected material of his own, and the warm and funny memories of a diversity of friends.

James Beard was one of the giants of American food. He was a big man who towered over most of us. He had large hands, a large mind, and a generous heart. His readers, the cooks in homes all over America, miss him and so do his food-world friends: the chefs in the restaurants, the writers of cookbooks and articles, the editors of books and magazines and newspapers. I miss him. I miss the talks about opera and the chats at 7:30 in the morning—late for him, early for me. I miss the sharing of seeming finds and inventions that were given a sure perspective by James's rich knowledge of food. I miss the gossip about friends and enemies and the anecdotes—often about food—interwoven with every conversation.

Tempting though it is to try, it is almost impossible to describe the magic web that James threw over friends, students, and readers. It is easy to say that he was larger than life-size, a sort of exaggerated father, or older brother, figure. Certainly, he was extraordinarily intelligent. Beyond a doubt, he had an unusually retentive memory, particularly when it came to dishes and flavors of the past. He had a Rabelaisian laugh and a fierce temper. He had the gift of enthusiasm in speech and writing. Every class he ever gave was always the best. He wanted everybody to cook, to make a life of cooking, to make cooking their work, and to involve each new friend in his large world of past and present friends.

This involvement with food was also an involvement with him. He had his doctor in class, a lady he met when signing books in the Middle West, his editors, and society ladies met at cocktail parties. James gave to everybody; but the bargain implied giving in return. People would do unbelievable things for Jim in work and in personal service, things he accepted with such ease and lack of self-consciousness that any notion of burden was eschewed.

In return, he promoted the interests of those he made his friends, getting this one a job, that one a book contract, and giving still another a book party to sponsor them in the food world.

Students became friends as well as acolytes. He had a fantastic way of involving them with the food, with the teaching, making them feel that they had accomplished something and that it was good. They waited eagerly for his comments on what they had cooked and took his words as a kind of benediction. ✍

MEMORIES

THIS WHOLE BOOK IS STUFFED WITH MEMORIES,
LIKE A CHRISTMAS GOOSE WITH BREAD AND SAGE, BUT THERE
ARE A FEW THAT DID NOT FIT WELL INTO ANY CHAPTER.

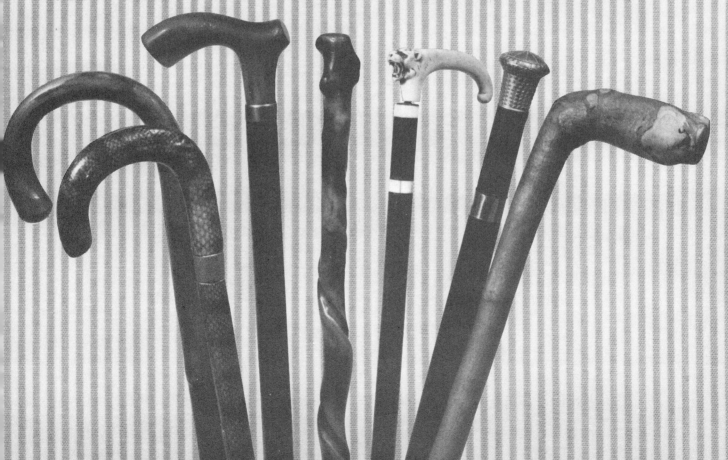

Some didn't fit because the writer provided no recipe. Others were simply too long. A few are by Jim and deserve to stand proudly on their own. Here they are, the gravy for the stuffing.

A JAMES BEARD MEMOIR.

Several years before James died, he decided that his next book was going to be a personal memoir; but he was having trouble getting started. For several years before this, he had had the habit of doing the first draft of his writing by dictating into a machine, but even this method wasn't working. We decided to try a new tack: We would write together and the starting point would be a series of tapes on which he would reminisce, goaded and supported by my questions. If nothing else, sitting down at a set time every week for several hours to do the tape would get him going.

After about five sessions, James had to go into the hospital during one of his many courageous bouts with disease. Afterward, the sessions ceased and the book never was completed, although he often talked of our going off to Lausanne—where he had finished writing a previous book—and completing the project . . . alas. . . .

In the tapes we did, he talked about his mother, his childhood, and his growing sense of self-awareness. Several themes were touched on that crop up throughout this book: his warm and long-continuing friendships, his interest in people and gossip, his vivid memories of food, his happy greediness, his temper, his attachment to Oregon (Portland and Gearhart), his series of involvements—probably based on his feelings about his mother—with England and English women, his love of houses and things, and his nascent recognition of his own homosexuality.

I have left out my questions. They were primarily promptings and guidelines for future questions, many of which never got answered on tape. I have added a scant amount of material from other interviews that were not taped, primarily where what is on the transcription would not make sense without it. The material has been edited only slightly to avoid the "Yes" that James, a positive man, used instead of "ah" or "um." I have also made complete sentences where the subject may have been given in my question. I feel that I am conveying his material and that he had every intention of publishing; but, of course, he did not live to edit it.

There will be real biographies of James, with all the dates and the spellings of names and the reality of events examined and verified. This is not one of those. It is the transcription of one side of an ongoing conversation. Jim had a remarkable memory for names, places, dates, telephone numbers, and the layout of any town in which he had spent time. He never got lost. This does not mean that what we recorded is gospel. Presumably there are factual elisions and errors, the tricks that even a good memory plays.

The memoir is not linear either, although it starts before James's birth with the life of his potent mother and less-present father. From there it weaves toward his adult life. The form is that of memory, with detours and asides, evocations of later times, and always the vivid memory of food, which seemed to frame Beard's past in much the way a musician might remember in terms of sounds and songs.

We sat at the street end of James's second-floor living room in pseudo-Oriental splendor, a sort of Victorian version. He would put his legs up—he had to—and I would perch on one of the many insubstantial chairs. We did not eat during our sessions; both of us drank soda and I ferried glasses up and down the narrow, circular iron staircase to the helpful Clay. After work, we would forage in the kitchen, picking on whatever was at hand, or I would go to Sixth Avenue to his favorite sandwich shop and pick up some interesting concoction—thin pumpernickel with chopped liver and rare roast beef was a favorite.

We didn't drink unless we went out to lunch. He had already given up wine, which—despite his insistence on wine for meals in classes and his long experience with wine experts—was never a major interest. He drank the Glenlivet on the rocks feeling like a child escaped from school.

We started our tapes by discussing his mother and her early life. She owned a hotel which was sold before James was born; but he speaks about her relationship with it as if it were something that he had seen. I got the impression that she retained a relationship with the hotel even after she sold it and that he saw her work there. However, she loved to reminisce and his visions of her may have been a reconstruction. ✍

My mother was a magnificent rustle; she never quite stopped at anything. She rustled and she rushed. She had eyes on four sides of her head and must have had the keenest sense of smell of anybody I ever knew. She could detect anything as she barged through any room or space. There was that feeling of whirl. She was about five foot eight and had a very good figure. She was full-busted and well corseted. I would say that she was very handsome.

She was almost two characters. I mean when she dressed she looked so slick you would think that she never touched anything with her fingers. When she was working she was another person. She worked in the kitchen at home. In the hotel, she never soiled her hands too much, but she got them in. She had the belief that if anything went wrong, she would be able to take over. She would never tell a cook or a chef what to do unless she knew how to do it herself. If it came to a side of beef being cut up, she could do it.

Father lived in another world. You see, before I was born, they came to a rather amicable agreement that they were not to interfere in each other's businesses. He, at one point, wanted to take over the business at the hotel, and that's why she eventually gave it up. She didn't tell him anything about. She sold it sort of in secret and announced to him that she had sold it and was going to have a child.

He was working for the government as an evaluation expert, an appraiser for the court. My liking for antiques probably came from him in some way. I have a friend who, in later life, was one of the major antique dealers in Portland, and she once said to me that my father could smell a dud at five hundred feet. I came in with one dud in my life. He picked it up. I argued with him, and

I found out it was no use. He just had a little ability about him.

He was about five foot ten; but my grandfather—my father's father—was six six. The Beards went through Kentucky to Missouri and through Iowa. Father was born in Iowa. After all, I'm one generation from the covered wagon. Grandfather was a soil tiller. In that part of Oregon where they settled, he grew fruit and truck farmed mostly. I was only there once, and by that time, he was about ready to give up. He then did nothing. They stayed in the town where they were, and he sort of enjoyed his children. I think they had money of their own. Some of the children pooled in. Father was one of sixteen children; but those aunts and uncles didn't like my mother at all. They had no truck with her, and she didn't want any truck with them.

They all thought when my father married my mother it was a cinch that they could all come to Portland and stay and never spend any money. The first ones came and they got a bill. Mother already had the hotel when she married. Oh, yes.

She was born in England, in Wiltshire. She had an aunt and uncle who were extremely successful people and they were childless. My mother was one of twelve children. This aunt and uncle came and picked her out and took her to live with them when my mother was about nine. She adored her own father, and I don't think she had much use for her uncle. My grandfather was a superintendent, first of Mr. Gladstone's estate. Then my mother lived with her family in Ireland when she was still quite young. She used to run away; she didn't like the food they were giving her. She used to run away and eat with the workers on the property because she loved potatoes. She was completely independent.

Then she went to live with the aunt and uncle. They lived quite lavishly in London—he was in shipping—but they were religious fanatics. They were deep into *modium sanctii* and so forth. She became increasingly fed up with all that. With her independent spirit, she was, or finally wormed her way into being, friends—shall we say?—of several of the people who sailed for her uncle. She finally bribed or persuaded one of them that she was going to run away and that he would give her passage to this or another country. She ran away from all that repression at sixteen, about 1885.

She knew one person in America. She knew a woman and her family in Toronto, knew them from England. They had left England and gone to Toronto. She went to them. She was determined that she was going to travel. She was really adventurous in her way.

She saw an advertisment in the paper of people who wanted a companion for their children to tour the United States. So, she went to answer the ad. The woman talked with her and said, "My dear, I'm so sad about this because I've just engaged someone and I like you so well." They were an army family and they had to travel and usually stayed with army people, and they wanted to put the children in a hotel with someone to take care of them and to do some touring.

As Mother left the house, the milkman tipped his hat and called her by name and said, "How do you do?" Mother knew the milkman because he also delivered milk to her house. Three days later he came to the house where she was living and said, "Miss Jones [mother], the people where you were the other day wondered if I knew where you lived; they would like to see you." That's better than the telephone, isn't it? Because there wasn't any telephone. She went back and the woman said, "I've dismissed the person I hired because I liked you so well."

Mother went off and they toured for three years, all through the United States. She adored it. They landed in Portland; someone died in the family and the family was recalled. Mother said, "I think I'm staying here." She really didn't know a soul there at that time. She just said, "I like this, and I think I'm staying." She was eighteen, or nineteen. She found various jobs. She knew she could take care of children, so she found a very interesting job with people who were to be her friends and backers the rest of her life, the Maxwells.

In about two years, she married very happily—not my father. Before she actually got married, she had gone back to England to visit and sort of push it down their throats. She just laid it on. She went to the old Grand Hotel, which is on Trafalger Square, and then took a carriage to visit the aunt and uncle. Of course, they were floored. They thought she was in the dregs. They probably would have preferred it had she been in the dregs: "We never speak of Aunt Clara." They disinherited her. Else I would have much more money. They gave it all to the church instead. That's what makes me such a good churchman.

She went to visit her father too. The funny part of it is that I never heard her talk about her mother at all. I only heard her talk about her father. Isn't that funny? I don't think she was terribly fond of the rest of her family either, because in later years she did only correspond with one of the twelve. I don't think she ever had any regard for them as relations.

The first time, she married a man I know very little about except that he was in business and had a shop of his own and he made very good money; but he developed what was then called consumption and died. He died, oh, about fourteen months after their marriage. I think they were about the same age. His name was Brennan. He must have left her with some money. She went to Europe again. Then she met some people who lived in the Middle West somewhere. She went to visit them and they had a tragedy there, in the household, and she stayed for about a year to hold the house together.

Finally, she went back to Portland and met—through the friends whose sick child she had taken care of—a woman from San Francisco named, I think, Curtis who had a hotel in San Francisco, a small one. In fact, she had two and she wanted to start one in Portland. So Mrs. Curtis built this thing and gave my mother a job as manager. Mother stayed there for about a year or so.

In the meantime Mrs. Curtis had decided to enlarge, to build a larger place; but my mother decided she was going to take a year away. She took more than a year because she met this great friend of hers who was quite a well known actress in New York. She came and lived in New York for about a year and a half. This is the woman who really remained a friend throughout her life and with whom she did a great deal of traveling later. Her name was Stella Chase-Haynesworth. My mother knew quite a lot of people in the theater at that time. Somewhere I've got her autograph album. There were people like Hamilton Bodil, the leading man, and Hobart Bosworth, afterward a big shot in the movies.

Bosworth wanted to marry her; but she said she didn't want any part of it at that time.

She went back to Mrs. Curtis again. All these people that she kept leaving kept accepting her back. She was efficient and had a great deal of charm. Then she went off on another holiday with Stella Chase-Haynesworth. They spent it at Lucky Baldwin's estate. That's when they suddenly thought it amazing to go down to Panama. There was a ship going down there. They were digging the canal. I don't know if

Stella knew somebody in the group that was going. Anyhow, they went down and just had the most fabulous time without bothering to tell Mrs. Curtis she was taking off.

She went back to New York and on to Europe. She was a voyager all her life. She got a cable from the Maxwells that Mrs. Maxwell was very ill. They asked her to come back and be with them as they had a daughter who was fragile—ill. So, she stayed with Ruth and the other children, who were pretty well grown by then, until Mrs. Maxwell was well. I don't know the exact dates. It was all part of her reminiscences. She talked about herself very often. She loved to reminisce.

Once she was back in Portland, she decided she wanted a place of her own. I think the Maxwells did some of the backing for her. She started the Gladstone.

Before I go off on the Gladstone years, I want to say a word or two about Ruth Maxwell—the ailing daughter—who grew up to be one of the most beautiful women I have ever known. She married an English cousin of hers who was consul general in Morocco. She went to live in Tangiers and lived out practically all of her life in Tangiers. She was a brilliant linguist. At the beginning of World War I, she lent her abilities to the government and became a very important person in the intelligence, in international intelligence. I adored her. I saw her in Tangiers, and she'd come to Portland.

She was a focal point in the famous Bernsdorf case. Count von Bernsdorf was one of the attachés to the German embassy who was involved in a tremendous spy racket. Ruth, with her linguistic ability and her beauty and her coming from a good family, caught him—good conversation and such. Her husband divorced her because he thought . . . she was a fallen woman. She really had the most glamorous career. She worked for the government all through the Spanish Civil War while living in Majorca and traveling back and forth.

She had two daughters, both of whom married brilliantly and live in Morocco. Ruth would come back to her home; she'd come back to go to her mother, who was a most fabulous woman. Ruth was always very devoted to my mother and she was very fond of me. The last time I saw her was, oh, I guess about 1960. Ruth was really the rule in Tangiers during the last ten years of her life. If you weren't accepted by Ruth, you didn't get into anything. She died about 1970, I think. Finally, she went into the real estate business. Old fortunes give out. She had several.

In any case, when my mother started the Gladstone, she got a great many of the people she had with Mrs. Curtis. The hotel was quite Victorian. It was a wood structure, about four stories, with a great deal of carpenter Gothic and loads of redwood inside that was varnished. That was very typical of the Northwest. Redwood was the thing. When she built her own house, it was the same thing—redwood, redwood, redwood. It was very beautiful. All the Portland houses had that same sort of glimmer.

She had an architect for the hotel. There were about forty bedrooms and a sort of lounge. It was constructed in the same style as the house. It was, strangely enough, on the corner opposite the Curtis. Mother liked rubbing it in. The Curtis didn't do too well after she started the Gladstone. Most of the people took pension, so meals were important. She had good menus. I had about five of them. She bought well. She knew how to throw little tidbits around. There was a lot of French wine and white from Seattle.

Mother had the hotel for about seven years. Jue Let, who later became our chef at home, was the sous chef there and Gib (also Chinese) was the pastry chef. Most of the

staff was Chinese except, occasionally, she would get someone who was from France or somewhere, who she knew would not stay. They would stay long enough to teach and then go on to San Francisco. Let was a very fine cook.

She met my father. She had known him off and on with friends of hers, my godfather, General Summers, and his wife, who were pulling the bow and shooting the arrow for about four years before she would have anything to do with him, because she didn't really like him—which I found out later. He had two daughters by a previous marriage. His wife had died, and then one of the daughters died, leaving him with one. The Summerses said to her, "Now, you must have a companion for your older years, and you must marry someone. It's not right to go on living alone." She wanted to live alone. Finally, I guess they talked her into it. So she did.

They went off on their honeymoon. While they were on their honeymoon, she found out that he was quite seriously in debt. She decided then and there that he had married her because she had money. It was sad in a way. That's when she began to think about selling out. He wanted to take over the business. He felt that he was great. She had the added problem of his daughter. She was about eighteen; she lived in the hotel and she felt that she was moving into another world.

She felt she was living in a dream. She used to do the most maddening things, like once, at the beginning of it, she went down with her laundry and took with her all the stockpots. She thought that they were for washing clothes because in those days one did boil one's laundry, Well, you can imagine the scene between Let and Lucille (my stepsister).

Then, she, my mother, always told the story of Lucille being very clothes conscious.

She was all her life. When she moved in, she said, "Now, I'll need an entirely new wardrobe for living here. I figure I'll need fourteen new dresses and so on and so forth." My mother didn't get them for her. One day Lucille snitched one of my mother's taffeta petticoats and wore it downtown. It fell off of her. She just stepped out and left it standing on the street.

So mother sold the hotel about three years before I was born. She took Let with her. Let came to her and said, "What about the money?" She said, "I have all my money." He said, "Then I go with you. If you didn't have all your money, I would have stayed until you had all your money." She sold the hotel to a very delightful woman named Mrs. Murphy and her sister, who was Mrs. Cornell. Frances Cornell, her daughter, is still one of my close friends. Isn't that funny?

I can still remember going to the hotel when I was quite young, and in the apartment that my mother had had and that Mrs. Murphy and Mrs. Cornell took over afterwards, there was this enormous bathtub, the most enormous I had ever seen. So Frances and I used to slide down the sides of the bathtub.

Even though my mother had this actress quality herself, she was a very rigid person with her routine. For the most part, she'd get up at five o'clock, put on her divided skirt, starched blouse, her fedora hat, and her boots—the correct attire for bicyclists—and go on a five-mile bicycle trip. When she got back, in the days when she was still at the hotel, she'd walk into the dining room at breakfast to greet everybody. Then she'd go off to the markets.

When she married my father, she said, "I'm going to build a house. You may live in it; but we're independent." She kept him because she was ashamed to admit she made a mistake. She told me about it years later.

I was born about three years after she had sold the hotel; but she had had a child the year before that had died. That was the child she told my father about when she sold the hotel. Then she had me. I was her only child, and she managed me. She didn't bring me up. She directed my life rather than paying any attention to it. She had Thema to take care of me, and she had her life, and my father had his life. It was always lonely. It left me with admiration for her, but not affection. My father only emerged as a character in my life much later when I began to realize that he was having his separate life.

I began to feel sorry for him and feel that she was as hard on him as she was on me. And I was, as I grew older, very much in accord with his having a mistress and having his own life.

Thema and Let, both Chinese, brought me up. I often wore Chinese suits that were not what we think of today. They were very simple little coats that had little frogs across them to the shoulder and then buttoned down the sides. There were short pants. The suits were sometimes linen, sometimes cotton. They were usually in shades of blue. Sometimes there was a white one. Other children didn't wear these; but Thema and my mother agreed.

I also wore what was then in vogue, as you can see in photographs, what was known as Buster Brown suits. Buster Brown was the great comic strip character. Everyone had a Buster Brown suit and a Buster Brown cut. You remember the cut, like a pageboy now.

When I was very little, I had a playhouse in the garden. There were about four neighbor children that I liked very much. There was a girl that lived next door to us that I was very fond of, and a boy across the street. I was not very nice to them. I had a lousy temper. I had, up until I was about

forty-five, I guess, a really violent temper, a Joe Baum temper. That's one reason I always got along with Joe. When I was little, oh, I was violent. I can remember when I was about five we very often had dinner in town. Strangely enough, my mother and father and me together. I can remember standing in the street and getting into a temper tantrum because I didn't want to go to the restaurant they were going to. I wanted to go to another one. Even then I had my own taste in restaurants.

There was one restaurant that we all loved very much. I suppose it was Viennese in origin and was run by a family. It was what I like to call a restaurant restaurant. You know, the menu is full of all the things you can find in the market at that time. It had a Chinese chef, a very good one. Every good chef was Chinese.

We had another, well, a friend of my mother's . . . her husband had a restaurant that I adored which was considered very fast by most people. Because people went there . . . um hum. There were private rooms upstairs. There were about three restaurants that had private rooms upstairs.

It was slightly risqué, but it was good food. They had marvelous seafood, for instance, wonderful oysters and fish and sauces. We had Eastern oysters and then there were tons of Olympias. Sometimes the Olympias came opened. There were a few places where they opened them and other places where they came in jars. Very rarely did you see them in their shells.

The dinner that Alice Waters had in honor of Mary Frances [M.F.K. Fisher] she started with six different oysters and the Olympias were in the shell, the first time I'd seen them in their shells for ages.

The Faults, who owned this restaurant, were very good friends of my mother's. We used to visit Mrs. Fault. She had a house way up the Columbia and we used to go out and visit her in the summer. My father never went with us.

When we were at home there were a few meals when everybody was together, sometimes Sunday breakfast.

Mainly, I ate by myself. At breakfast I always had fruit and tea and once in a while *congee,* and once in a while I'd have cured fish, Chinese cured fish or English cured fish. I adored kippers and you got wonderful ones in those days. Lunch . . . I remember going out for lunch more than I can remember eating at home.

At dinner, we had enormous quantities of game in the fall and in the winter. We had pheasant, duck, teal, wild goose, brant—a relative of the goose, all of them. I think you can only get it in the Northwest now. It's very good. It was all cooked in the European fashion, but when we had duck everybody in the family wanted it different. Let made it differently for everybody.

He never cooked Chinese food for dinner. Although sometimes he did make soups and wonderful noodle dishes. We had all those bowls and all the rest of the things for them. I had a selection of chopsticks. My Chinese godfather gave me some ivory ones when I was very young. Mostly we used the common ordinary wooden chopsticks, which are still the best chopsticks as far as I am concerned. I hate plastic ones. Everything slides off of them. We were all pretty deft with chopsticks. My father was as deft as my mother was.

My Chinese godfather was a friend of my father's and my mother's. We had a great many friends who were Chinese. I went to Honolulu a month ago. I got this note from a gal with a Xerox of something I had written. I forget if it was in *Delights and Prejudices* or whether it was in an introduction I did in Johnny Kan's cookbook. It said that I remembered when I had the Kan girls to my birthday party. She called up and asked, "Which Kan girls did you have?" We had quite a long chat. All three of them now live in Honolulu. The one I spoke to was married to a man named Cong, I think, Kan-Cong.

I don't think I've ever said this before, but, in my childhood and sometimes now, I wish I had been born Chinese. I was really brought up by the Chinese and I knew so many Chinese people. They were more understanding and appreciative. I was always fascinated going to their homes for food. There, of course, it would be Chinese food, except for one woman who wanted to experiment with European foods and American food. She sort of shunned her native Chinese food. She'd serve us all of these Chinese dishes filled with the European and American food.

It gave me the feeling that Chinese food was something you get in restaurants or that Chinese people cooked for you. I never cook it myself.

Even today, I have Chinese robes and furniture and artifacts. Of course, some of it is Victorian stuff influenced by the Chinese—bamboo and so forth. I often wear Chinese clothes. I think the greatest compliment I've had in years was when I came down the elevator at the Beverly Wilshire in a Chinese outfit. The little Chinese elevator operator said, "Oh, sir, you remind me of my grandfather." So, I've become an ancestor. I have a quadruple Chinese ancestor portrait over the fireplace.

I've always collected Chinese things. Our house when I was a child was completely Chinese. I sold all of that, stupidly enough, when my mother died. I think it was a release from the family; but I kept one thing. I regret selling now. We had lots of carton pierre [papier-mâché] and ebony, you know with marble inlays and mother-of-pearl inlays—Victorian Chinese as well as Victorian American. These things we had by the millions—the bamboo tables. I adore them; I just adore them.

I went to school at six. I adored it. It was another more secure world and there were people. Sometimes I went home for lunch. Sometimes I'd have lunch at school. There weren't school lunches in those days.

It was a bag lunch, and you took it.

It was a public school. Interestingly enough, the principal of the public school was a neighbor of ours. So I knew him and his son. There were nineteen children I knew who all started school on the same day. We went through all of grammar school together; we started high school together; we went all through our high school together, and twelve of us started our college together. Isn't that amazing? I still see those people. They became a sort of family.

We were treated well. We were all fairly brilliant students. We did nine years of grammar school in six years. I don't know anything else like it, ever. We shared so much together. We had parties together. There were birthday parties. You always

had creamed chicken in patty shells with creamed peas . . . always. That was children's food. You had little tiny rolls like Parker House rolls. You had enormous quantities of homemade ice cream and cakes, little cakes and big cakes: chocolate layer cake, coconut layer cakes, and moonshine cakes, which were egg yolk cakes with some whites beaten into it and a very light butter topping. It was a great treat. Then there were always loads of favors at the table. I can remember a birthday party when I was about six years old when everybody had a little basket—you'll laugh when I say it—a little basket with pansies growing in it and everybody took them home.

I was a large child and I was terrible

to the other children before I got to school; but by the time I got to school I got along with them very much all right.

My upbringing was different than other children's. By the time I was seven, I knew that I was gay. I think it's time to talk about that now. My mother's friends didn't have conventional life-styles. I think she was very curious about a child growing up. I must say she went to great lengths to find out things. Oregon was always a fairly liberal state. It's done some very interesting things. It was the second state to vote for women's suffrage. They had a bill where feeble-minded people had to be sterilized if they were put into an institution. Then, I think it was revolutionary, the health department had long treatises on sex of all forms which were distributed throughout the schools, even when I was in school which was far ahead of most places.

There were a lot of people with unusual sexual life-styles and my mother always seemed to attract them. You know, people would look down on certain people and talk about them and gossip. Mother started championing their cause, very much. We had one very attractive friend who just never seemed to be able to keep herself out of somebody's bed. She had a lovely time as a result. She got taken on wonderful trips and things like that. Well, my mother would talk about her very casually. She would often talk about such things. I can remember coming in once when she had people there and turning to one woman and saying, "Oh, I heard you were living with so and so. Is it true?" I was, of course, banished for a while.

She talked about her homosexual friends—women and men—openly. There was a great scandal in Portland. Two people we knew quite well were involved in it. She talked about it at great length, going into details about it. She was never bitter about it. I can remember her once talking to me

about masturbation and asked me if I had tried it yet. She told me that if people said I would grow hair on my hand not to believe them.

I'm sure she thought she was helping me in some way. She already saw me as having a different life of my own. She was completely accepting about it. Of course, she had her own life too, going off with her women friends on trips.

My father perceived it later because he didn't see me that much; but he was not thrilled. One or two of my school friends knew; but *no*, they were not critical. Some of the parents were a problem even when I was quite young. They knew my mother's attitude—not the people in the immediate neighborhood, but some of her other friends just didn't want their children to have any truck with me. I was always an individual, let's face it.

It never bothered me. Even when I was dressed differently I never felt bothered. I moved into blue serge suits from the lilliputian designs. I was different from the rest of them again, even though they were correct blue serge suits. The rest of them wore corduroys; but the blue serge was my choice, not my mother's. I didn't want to have blue serge all the time. I remember screaming at her for a tweed suit. The first one I got, I slipped the first time I wore it and tore the knee out. It was retribution.

I wasn't a greedy child. I loved food. I sometimes spent time in the kitchen, more at the beach than I did at home. I had a great curiosity about things; I wanted to taste everything . . . not just food, but especially food. In those days we had such fabulous fruit and vegetables; that was a great temptation. I remember being much more interested in fish and vegetables and fruit than I was in meat. I can't remember ever having that violent desire to sit down and eat a great chunk of meat. We did get very good

The James Beard Celebration Cookbook

locally bred meat. Mother always had things aged according to her desire. She had them hang it. Even though she didn't have the hotel anymore, she still had that kind of relationship with suppliers. They were scared to death of her.

There were other great food memories of Portland. New Year's was a great event for the Chinese in Portland and they closed all of their businesses for about a week. My father had many Chinese friends. You'd go from shop to office and they'd have out all their festive furniture and their great hangings of ancestors and the tables were set up with all the rare foods and the things. I mean the little mandarin oranges would come from China, all packed in wood boxes and rope. They were beautiful just to see. They'd bring candied kumquats, candied coconut, and melon seeds. They had sweetmeat boxes that fetch a great price now. They were round, usually lacquer or wood, sometimes painted. They had individual compartments. They had in them, in addition to the other things, lily root candy, lotus candy, all that sort of thing. The patterns were just beautiful.

Then there were always gifts to take home, usually food: sweetmeats and mandarins, ginger in jars—those beautiful jars that people buy in antique shops now, the blue-green ones, and the sort of drab gray ones, and some of them had beautiful patterns on them. You'd have those to use for everything. You'd take them to the beach and use them for flowers.

There was much formal greeting about all this, a sort of classic formality. One would bow and clasp hands. There would always be one or two great dinners during that week and there were two restaurants in Portland that had—well, one of them right across from the police station—about four floors. The furniture in it was astoundingly beautiful. It was all rosewood and teak and sometimes ebony with inlays. Different rooms had different decorations. They all had balconies where the doors could be thrown open. They were all handsome.

There was a great private room at the top of this restaurant and certain people would entertain there during the year and have their own wall hangings—great panels—sent down for these events.

A friend of mine who was only a child at the time went into the antique and decorating business in a flashy and incredible way. He had one of the houses that was going to be torn down moved to a piece of property that he bought. He bought and then sold all of the tables—octagonal and round tables with marble inserts and a sort of lazy Susan.

The lazy Susans of those days were big and the legs revolved too. They were very stunning. Some of the food was put on them. If you were eating family style, you could just reach in and take some from the center, which is the traditional way.

My earliest memory of food is crazy; I told it once to a doctor and he said it's incredible. I was born in 1903 and in 1905 they had the Lewis and Clark Exposition in Portland. I was taken to the exposition two or three times. The thing that remained in my mind above all others—I think it marked my life—was watching Triscuits and shredded wheat biscuits being made. Isn't that crazy? At two years old that memory was made. It intrigued the hell out of me. I can still smell it. Food is always associated with smell for me. What is smell but taste? Taste isn't in the mouth. Because you can give people blindfold tests and you can give them meat tests. Raw meat has no smell. If you blindfold them, they cannot tell which is which. Sometimes, blindfolded, they can smell the differences between cooked meats.

Even people like Frank Schoonmaker would get mixed up if he took a blindfold test with different liquors.

Foods were part of my earliest memories. Shopping is a memory, and certain foods. I mean the cherries that came off our trees were enormous Lamberts and the yellow-red Royal Annes. They had terrific visual appeal. I think that cherries are more beautiful to look at than taste. There were also the May Dukes and the Montmorencies and another one whose name I can't remember; the pits just slid out of them. It wasn't so crazy when you were told to pit cherries. I had one of those funny little old-fashioned machines.

There's a funny story about the first time I had a steamed bun, a Chinese steamed bun. I was with the amah and I said, "Do they kill ladies?" I thought they looked like a woman's breast with nipples and everything.

I began messing in the kitchen quite early. I began to steal in when no one was around. Somehow I always put onions in everything—except I was never interested in making desserts. I'm not that interested in them now. I'd always get onions; I guess it was the smell.

Another thing I had a passion for— and still do—is ham. We always had one raw ham and one cooked ham in the house at all times. That is security food. You could slice off a piece of raw ham and broil it or sauté it and use it for things. You could always have boiled or baked ham to do things with. I have used ham a great deal, and I did strange things with eggs. I didn't scramble them correctly as yet; but I would mix them with onions or ham and probably make a frittata. I still like that.

I didn't try Chinese food—still don't. It's something else, another procedure. It was also something done for me. That's it! Yes! It had its little place in the pigeonholes of my feeble mind of that time. I still only eat Chinese food when it's made for me even though when I'm sick I may have a craving for Chinese noodles or milk toast, which I adore.

There's something so satisfying about noodles and the fact that you very often have them with a strong chicken broth that entices you. I also love fried noodles. Noodles have a great place in my memory and I think of them Chinese, not Italian.

After Let left, Mother would cook and so would I, but not together. As I grew up— it's funny after talking about the noodles— I'd lean toward making pasta and do sauces for it. Especially when I'm at the beach I do these with clams, the razor clams. We always had good tinned razor clams, which work very well. It is very funny. I grew up with practically no tinned food. There were always sardines and anchovies and there might be occasional things like foie gras in the house.

Everything else was either fresh or it was canned at home. In those days, we used to get a great deal of white asparagus, beautiful big jumbos, because there can so much of it in California. There would always be at least one hundred jars of asparagus put up. There would be tomatoes. We never had tinned tomatoes in the house. Ours would be put in jars and kept for the winter because they were better tomatoes.

Preserving—jams, jellies, and so forth—began with strawberries and ended with quinces. It went through apricots and pineapples—loads of them from Hawaii. We had raspberries by the ton. We had raspberries in the garden and we'd load up with raspberry jam. There was one week in the year when the oranges were in from Spain, and that was marmalade week.

There were certain shops that had them. There were two beautiful food shops in Seattle and there was a man named Mayer, and he'd call to sell them saying the oranges would be in next week.

In the fall, we'd have oceans of game because both my mother and father had friends that hunted a great deal and who didn't care for what they got. So we had a line in the basement where they'd be hung. They'd come in and they'd just be hung and dated. I learned to clean them when I was four. There was much more aging of game then. Today, I think duck has to be aged two weeks. I have never liked high pheasant. I think there's nothing like grouse in England that comes in from the Queen's shoot in Scotland on the twelfth of August and is cooked fresh. In the old days, "21" used to fly in the grouse and have it on the day after the twelfth usually. Joe Baum did that too.

Nobody really needs a recipe today. Just take a little of that, a little of that, and it comes out. I used to think it was hard to teach. This last summer in Oregon, I changed my mind; that's why I like big classes. I can do a dish three times. If I have a dish and want three versions done of it, I ask, "Who wants to work on the recipe?" Then I can say, "All right, you've got the recipe. One of you follow that. Now, the other two can do something else with it. You'll have another flavor completely." It worked. They improvised.

The people I'm teaching are changing. They are learning to mess in the kitchen as I did when I was a child. This way of working brought something else out of them. At the end of the class, or when they'd sit down to eat, they'd say, "Well, we've got a lot of this left over. What shall we do with it tomorrow?"

That's the first sign of someone becoming a good cook, I think—to not waste. I've always said that the things you do the next day are often much more interesting than the thing you made in the first place.

I'm doing an article [never written] with that kind of class approach to chicken, with three different variations on a recipe and then three variations on each variation to show people. Working with chicken, I've found out something very interesting about it while doing a little research. Chicken basically needs pork, either a combination of butter and lard or bacon and butter, the two of them. You have the lard because it cooks well, and you have the butter to give it added flavor. That's true in the very earliest recipes. They even fried oysters in pork fat, but not always. They are pretty good in clarified butter. It's funny, but I am convinced butter doesn't have the flavor it used to have. I used to make it every week during one period of my life.

There are other things that don't taste the same anymore even though this summer I had apricots that tasted exactly the way they did when I grew up. I made apricot jam and everybody really went off their box about it. They were big ones, Tiltons. That memory for the names of varieties comes out of my childhood. That's how you went to the store and bought things.

If you were doing canning—peaches—everyone had a different variety they wanted. We always had Albertas and they had to be late Albertas.

This goes back to something I remember from Brazil, where you go up on the train and then you change to the cogwheel train at one of the stations on your way up to Petropolis. The boys would be around with great trays of bananas that they carried around on their heads. They didn't just have bananas. They would call out the variety they had. People would yell out, "*Banana d'oro, banana pronto.*" They had that sense about things when I was there during the war just as you might about having a Belon over a Portuguese oyster.

I have a book of apple varieties that were raised in New York State. It's fantastic, unbelievable. Of course, the great one that I adore, and it's almost extinct, is called Rambeau. It must have been a French apple originally. There is one little man near John Ferrone [friend and editor, see page 257] in Pennsylvania who has two Rambeau trees, and I got some last year. They are very flat and very round and beautifully shaped; but they have a heavenly taste when they are cooked.

When I was a child we had three Gravensteins in our garden. They were magnificent and grew very large. They were the best I have ever known. They are striped. They come in late summer and are very crisp. Then they mature and get very soft and the color changes completely. They're streaked when they come on; then they turn yellow. When they are crisp and new, no apple cooks as well; but they are so fragile. They can't ship them anywhere. We had friends who had Rambeau trees and my father would rob them. He loved to eat; but he had very different ideas about cooking.

We'd start with the Gravensteins. We'd go on to the Baldwins and the winter bananas and the Kings and the Spitzenbergs. The Spitzenbergs were my favorite; but I haven't seen a Spitzenberg in twenty years, I think. They were quite red and fairly large and they were luscious eating and fine for cooking. In those days when the Northern Pacific Railroad featured the great big baked potato, they also featured the big baked apple. They were Spitzenbergs. They were as luscious in their way as the baked potatoes.

The baked potatoes were incredible. They all weighed almost two pounds apiece. They came from Idaho, Oregon, and Washington. They were grown where they have lava soil; they were incredible. They based their whole dining service on that. I think if you had them they were fifteen cents on a dining car where everything else was expensive. That was their big advertisment.

Of all the ways of cooking apples, I

adore baked apples. I love apple sauce if it's correctly made. I think it should be cooked into a purée and then sweetened, because nine times out of ten it needs no sweetening—maybe a little butter. I cook it with the skins on, then purée it. I hate spices with apples; isn't that funny? I have never really liked apple pie. I usually like my baked apples with butter and very often brown sugar in the core and then basted.

One thing that I always love and still do are—the correct name is apples *bonnes femmes*—where you put sugar, a little butter, and a little vanilla in the apple and bake them on a piece of fried toast. All the flavorings go into the toast. When you take it out, it gets crispier and crispier. That is a really heavenly dessert. It's a Norman dessert by origin. I used to serve that sometimes when I had a sort of formal dinner party. People would love it. I served it warm. I think butter and apples have a great affinity. As you gather, I'm a pretty buttery boy.

Celery was better then too, almost pure white, blanched by dirt. There would be big heads. The markets would sell the little hearts all tied in bunches, maybe six little white hearts for eating raw. The big ones were for cooking. The markets had about five different grades of celery and they sold it like mad. The best market was owned by a Polish family; but they had changed ther name to Foltz. They were at the market and we became friendly.

Also in the market was a gal who was extremely beautiful. She was always around in rubber raincoat and high boots. Then suddenly I began going around to salons, as they might be called, and up she turns. She was a highly intellectual gal who worked at this thing all day. Then she ran around a great deal and expounded. She was ravishingly beautiful. She was part of the celery family. Her name was Xanthia Foltz.

She married somebody pretty glamorous and then went off somewhere. She was very politically minded and rather radical-minded. So was I.

At any rate, you could find 40 percent cream. The market went on for years. Then they put it under one top [roof]; it failed completely. We'd get morels in the spring. They still sell them. They sell them to restaurants and things. There is a girl out there now who makes a big business of selling mushrooms. She sells mainly chanterelles, and there's another one who sells morels.

I don't know why somebody doesn't sell cèpes [boletes]; they're so marvelous there. We would drive out on a Sunday afternoon, ten miles out of Portland. The mushrooms would cover a great big field. You could pick field mushrooms by the ton. There was a big vacant lot near our house. My mother would go out at 5:30 in the morning and bring back a ten-pound lard pail full of mushrooms. We'd have some of them for breakfast.

Today, people are scared of wild mushrooms in some parts of the country. I think that's been done by the columns and the columnists—just scared people. When I grew up, eating mushrooms was natural. Later, after I moved to New York, I used to go up to Cincinnati—a childhood friend of mine married one of the Lazaruses and went to live there with all that group. Elaine Mack and her husband, and sometimes Theodia Johnson would go too, and sometimes Denise Otis from *House & Garden*. We'd go out for one great weekend in the fall and everybody would hunt mushrooms all day. Then we'd go to the Lazaruses' house and cook them like mad. I've picked puffballs. People said, "You're not going to eat those."

We used to get all sorts of wild mushrooms in the public market. We'd get every grade of every vegetable that came in and small fruit. It was a great thing. The one in Seattle is very much like it. That one they have preserved by hard fighting by a group of people. The farmers come in still, the Japanese farmers who have the most beautiful vegetables. What is done in Seattle is to attract ethnic groups. There are a lot of ethnic shops in the Seattle market and it's great fun.

Portland is all gone. It's very funny; Portland has a strange attitude nowadays. Everyone used to go to the market in the morning. There was a French market called Mannings that was all over the place. They had a couple of places in the market. There were several other places where you could buy Danish pastry or donuts. It never had quite the feeling you get in the square in Grasse, a place where it was festive. No, Portland was much more a place where you took the car and parked and took your shopping bag and walked up and down. You saw your friends and chatted; but nobody ever participated. Portland was that kind of town. Everybody was too matter-of-fact. They probably thought it was not quite the thing to sit in a little stand in the market.

There are other things I remember from very early childhood. A new hotel opened, not the Benson. It was a very flashy hotel called the Multnomah. It's an Indian name. Portland is in Multnomah County. The hotel had a cabaret. Then they started to have tea and serve it in the lobby. I can remember going to tea. They had fruit tarts on the menu and brought them out all arranged on a plate. Mother looked at them and said, "What's that?" The waiter said, "Alligator pear, Madame." She said, "Alligator pear? Where does your chef come from?" He said, "I don't know." She said, "Doesn't he know anything?" So, she went back into the kitchen and told him what alligator pears were for.

The alligator pears we had then were purple; the skin was purple. You still find them in Mexico in some places. They were

beautiful with very thin, purple skins. Alligator pears hadn't been commercialized as yet.

That day in the Multnomah makes me think of another pastry story. We had three or four of what were known as candy shops, where they had candy and they had a soda fountain, a fairly good restaurant and snack bar sort of thing. In two of them the food was extraordinarily good. The third one had very good baked things, too. They were festive, fun. I remember going to a matinee on a Saturday and going across to one of them, the Cat 'n' Fiddle, where you always went for ice cream or pastry or hot chocolate, something like that. There were two women there, evidently from out of town, probably from eastern Oregon. They asked for French pastry. The waiter brought the tray. The women sat there drinking chocolate and went through the whole tray. The pastries they didn't eat they just sort of played with and then left. Finally, they got a bill for every one of the pastries and nearly fainted dead away.

Those places were a unique part of my living. One of them, Swetland's, was just beyond belief. It had a long marble counter of a sort of Pompeian design with bronze chairs and was quite handsome. They had fabulous candy. I don't eat candied flowers and I wouldn't eat the chocolate; but I did eat the wonderful ice cream, sandwiches, and certain little hot dishes like Welsh rarebit. It was my great haunt, way up in the heights.

These places were different from what we think of as restaurants. They looked different; they were like an early Schrafft's. You never thought of Schrafft's as a restaurant. Instead, it was a place to go to breakfast, or a place to have a light lunch. You never took it as a serious restaurant. Swetland's and Hazelwood both had a pretty full menu; but you had a different feeling than you would if you went to a formal restaurant.

People lost their taste for that sort of food, although there are ice cream freaks now. They want ice cream cones, or they want to eat en route somewhere. In those places, you had to go in and sit down and you had a hot fudge or caramel sundae with toasted almonds or a butterscotch sundae, and you were in heaven. It cost all of thirty-five cents for the best of them.

Even though the cooks were Chinese, the pastry makers were Italian. Portland had quite a lot of Italians. We had two—as our next-door neighbor used to call them—hucksters. They were Italians of good family. I mean they were an honest, thrifty family. They grew a lot of their own vegetables. They had property in town. They would grow vegetables on it and they'd buy more from other people. They would come around with a horse and wagon three times a week. They became great friends.

The first one we had was Galluzzo. He made a great deal of money. His children all went to school when I did and where I did. They all became useful citizens of Portland.

After that, we had another one who had the most fascinating personality. He adored the ground my mother walked on because they heckled each other. He would grow things I had never seen, like the first purple broccoli. He knew she would love things like that, so he would bring them. In those days, you had piles of leeks. You would use them in everything. He taught me my first frittata. He came in the kitchen and we made it with broccoli, onions, and Parmigiano.

He used to bring over a bottle of homemade wine every once in a while and leave it. He was really an extraordinary character with a great sense of humor. He taught me to heckle. He brought cardoons for the first time.

They grew very good, big artichokes in Portland. There were two or three great fields of artichokes in town. There was a lot of [undeveloped] property in those days—all gone now. I grew up with those things. They were everyday food, artichokes and cardoons and leeks. That afforded me an enormous privilege in its own way. I had a great love for this guy. He excited me with his love of food. His name was Delfinio Antrozzi.

We also had a wonderful creamery. That goes back. That's the place where they had chickens, ducks, and quail. Then they had hams and bacon and an enormous selection of cheeses. We had Brie and Rouge et Noir Camembert from California. We had Emmenthaler and Gruyère. We had Edam in the days when it was good Edam and pineapple cheese and wonderful Cheddar, always wonderful Cheddar, Oregon Cheddar and some Canadian. We also had some Roquefort.

My father had his own way of eating mince pie. He wanted it hot. Then he lifted the lid and buttered it very well and put a great slab of Roquefort cheese on it. It was sweet mince; but it had a lot of meat in it.

That creamery is where I once went to pick up some chicken. Someone I didn't know waited on me. When I said the chicken should be charged to Mrs. Beard, another man grabbed the chicken away and said, "Don't send that to Mrs. Beard. She'll come back and throw it in your face." That man always saved the chicken hearts and gizzards for me. I had a great passion for gizzards which has remained with me forever. He'd save two huge handfuls and I'd make a meal.

I could draw a chicken or a turkey and never break the gall. You know, I don't think one out of twenty persons could draw a chicken today if you asked them to, or singe it. I was never frightened by seeing chickens killed. We'd wring their necks, which was much more Oriental than chopping their heads off. It didn't bother me. I used to drown kittens when I was a child. I hated cats from the time I could remember. I still have that. I can bear them in a room with me; but I never had any use for them. If they touch me, I have to send everything I had on to the cleaner. Maybe I was allergic. I was very susceptible to sinus.

Even living in Portland, it was a sort of rural childhood. Our back neighbors had quite a collection of chickens. Maybe that contact with things growing and the frontier is why I have stayed so involved with American food.

My mother had a friend who had a place about twelve miles outside of Portland, in a very beautiful suburban area. They had cows, chickens, turkeys, and a great vegetable garden. In fact, Mrs. Harris was a very independent woman who was married to a bastard. Mrs. Harris used to sell eggs and sweet butter to her friends. She'd come in twice a week.

Baking bread was a disgrace. When I wanted to, everybody at home sort of threw up their hands. We could get very good Italian bread. There were two bakeries. They called them French, but they were Italian. Thinking of the Italians reminds me we had a very amusing Italian trattoria (I suppose you'd call it). It was in a less attractive part of town. They cooked very well. You'd go and have either a big platter of antipasto or you'd have egg soup and, usually, a pasta and a main dish, no dessert, for fifty cents. It was family style. You ate off of oil-cloth. They put down a big platter and you'd eat.

This was a place I went to later with my friends. Mother wasn't that informal. We went on the streetcar. The streetcar I adored.

In those public markets, a lot of people made sausage, all kinds. We had a man in the country and my mother would have him raise a couple of pigs for us every year and then he'd kill those and make sausages and smoke them. The hams came from him too. Sometimes he'd bring half a hog— butchered—and we'd make head cheese and faggots. Faggots are little sausages without casings, almost like scrapple, only better. All the little bits and ends we'd make up with oatmeal.

We even got pretty good cheese at the beach. We didn't get the variety. However, just down the coast from Gearhart was Tillamook, where they made cheese for generations and then they aged cheese. You had stronger-tasting cheese then. Once, Helen and Philip Brown and I went through twelve western states on a cheese, fish, and wine trip which was fascinating. We went up the coast into Oregon, Washington, Idaho, Montana, and Utah. We learned a great deal about domestic cheeses at that time.

There were still lots of Indians, particularly at the beach in the summer. There was a whole group who worked the oyster beds in the winter and then made a pretty good living out of baskets and doing odd jobs. They were independent—no reservation—part of the community. There was one local family who had a large piece of property. They gave this Indian group part of it for their summer home. They were different from the Indians I met later in the Southwest. They had a much more Oriental quality about them.

When my father crossed the plains, he was still shooting Indians—at five.

The first two years we went to the beach, my parents rented a house. Then we built, about 1907. I still go to Gearhart. It's still the same. The house is still there. I don't know who lives in it now. I have more of a fondness for the beach than I do for that house. It was quite a small house. It was shingle and tongue-in-groove fir and natural finish. It was never painted inside. It was always natural wood.

It was never hot at the beach. Later I got to like hot weather. From the time I can remember, whenever I saw a snowflake I wanted to hide. I hated snow. There was very little in Oregon. We're on the right side of the Cascades, warmed by the Japanese current.

This summer we had a meeting in Gearhart with the new Gearhart Preservation Society. It seems terrible to be part of something like that. It feels as if you are being preserved like an antique yourself. Most of the people who were at this meeting I had known for at least sixty-five, and some seventy, years. We always spent three months there in the summer and usually a stretch at Christmas time and usually spring vacation.

My father worked and he didn't usually come. We'd get him occasionally. He was active and I don't think he enjoyed it too much. We had no help at the beach. Let had left by then—when I was seven or eight. He went back to China.

We ate lots of seafood. I love the razor clams and the Dungeness crab. No crab has ever taken its place in my taste buds. There's still loads of it. The vegetables and fruits aren't what they were then unless you get the fruit that's ripened there, the raspberries, strawberries, cherries, and peaches which we used to have.

In high school, I worked with the stock company and I worked with a musical comedy stock company as well. I played rebellious children. In the last year of high school, I played Silent Murphy, the central role in Jerome Kern's musical called *Leave It to Jane*. I was already singing then. I had a high baritone, which would have become a heldentenor; it was a nice voice. It had charm in it. I didn't study voice until later. While I was at Reed, there wasn't much the-

ater. I already knew the theater and I liked it. Mother knew a lot of theater people.

After Let left, I cooked if mother wasn't around. I think mother got a great deal of pleasure out of cooking. When Let was there, she just let him do it. Then when he left, she cooked. When I cooked, I varied a great deal. I might do something like tournedos one day. The next day I might do something as complicated as pasta. Hamburgers were for the beach. I cooked fairly seriously by the time I was fourteen and fifteen. I never really learned. I had a funny feeling that I could take something I ate and reproduce it—like a musician with music. I wasn't drawn to cookbooks until much later.

There was a great influence on my cooking. One of my close friends who went through my school period was Chester Benson, the son of Simon Benson who was the great lumberman of the Northwest and made an enormous fortune. Chester and his brother were sons of the second marriage. Among Simon's investments in Portland was the building of a hotel for people who owned a successful hotel that was already there. When the new hotel was built, the people for whom it was built couldn't afford to take it over.

God knows how Simon managed to get people, but he decided to open up the hotel himself and call it the Hotel Benson. His son-in-law (husband of a daughter from the first marriage) was at that point an art director in Hollywood. He did the decoration. This was about 1911 or '12; the hotel is sixty years old now. The hotel opened just at the beginning of World War I, I guess, when we were in high school.

Simon got a very good chef. It was the first time that anyone in Portland put in a chef who was featured as a chef. He was Swiss. The food was extraordinarily good. Among the funny things that happened was that we boys were given carte blanche to go and sign checks whenever we wanted to. That kept up for a long time and I learned a great many things from Henri Thiele, who was the chef.

Imagine, we used to go there for dinner and have a table d'hôte dinner for $1.25, which was considered horribly expensive. We'd get an hors d'oeuvre that might vary according to the French Victorian idea of an hors d'oeuvre—might be a smoked fish or a vegetable à la greque. There was always a soup—consommé or cream—a fish course, a main course with vegetables, and dessert. À la carte was much better. I found that out quickly. That had a great influence on my life.

Strangely enough, it's still the best hotel in Portland and it's still called the Hotel Benson; but the Bensons don't run it anymore. I don't stay there when I go to Portland. I stay in an awfully old hotel about a block away from my mother's place that was started after she sold to a rival. It's a hotel, The Mallory, in Portland that everybody loves. It's like staying in that crazy hotel in Marseilles that Mary Frances [M.F.K. Fisher] writes about. It's been going for a thousand years and you stay there. The Mallory now has the most awful bright red bedspreads and yellow towels; but you stay there because it's got some qualityyou love.

Anyhow, I graduated from high school very early—we were all pushed along—at fifteen. I went to Reed College. All my friends went with me. I left home when I went to Reed. Then I began to be a rebel. I had always been in a way, but I became a more obvious and political rebel. Well, I became a great liberal and a friend of labor. Later I became much more of a red than now.

I got kicked out of Reed for politics and because sex had reared its lovely head. There was an attachment to one of the male professors. They didn't kick the professor

out. I went home to live. Even then my father wasn't aware of my sexual life. That came later.

There was nothing confining about being at home. I mean, we were all so independent. You could have your comings and goings. I had a nice big room where I had privacy and I had a telephone. I started doing a lot of cooking then, more in other people's houses than I did in my own. It was sort of a social passport. I knew two or three people who liked to cook and we'd do a sort of joint dinner. It was a sort of pleasant social occasion. We'd try out new dishes and the market provided a great many exciting things. There was a marvelous span of time with vegetables and small fruit that we wanted to immediately take home and cook. If you didn't know how to cook them, you wanted to experiment with them.

I began to study music; I played the piano and I studied singing a bit. I worked more and more with theater companies. I spent a great deal of the time at the beach one year trying to decide what I wanted definitely to do. Of course, everybody was criticizing me about not earning my living, living off my family, and not doing anything worthwhile. All of which I raised my finger to my nose about.

Then I began to be serious about acting and singing. I was working with somebody who had been at it a long time. He'd been in the musical comedy stock company where I played originally. He gave up and started a studio for theater and singing, and I worked with him a good deal. I can remember that there were a great many people around then in the group that my teacher, George Namison, pulled together who were to become great people in the theater. There was Ruth Taylor, who afterwards became the first Lorelei Lee in the movies, in *Gentlemen Prefer Blondes*. There was Bill Gable, who later became Clark Gable;

Earl Larrimore, who became the great star of the Theatre Guild. He died only a few years ago and was one of the best actors in America. We were in all these little things together. [Unfortunately, the annals of the theater don't record all the names, so some may be approximate.]

I was always lucky finding people. There were two or three people who became very prominent in radio. We did little productions outside of Portland in small towns and whatnot. We had a repertoire that was appalling. We had *What Happened to Jones? Meet the Wife, Nothing but the Truth,* and *Hedda Gabler.* We had *Hedda Gabler* because we knew we were going to hit some intellectuals.

I was very independent during this period, as was everybody in the family. Mother was very active with quite a few things. She and Chester Benson's mother were very close. Camelia Benson felt that she had been very badly treated by Simon, who had divorced her and married a third time. Camelia sort of perambulated around. My mother went off on trips with her very often. Mother also went off on trips with one or two other people. She was busy all the time.

My father was working or with his mistress. I was about twenty when I became aware that he had a mistress. He didn't hide it at all. I met her and got to know her very well. She was wonderful for him. She looked like my mother; she was the spitting image of my mother, in a way, but she was a warm personality. He had a child by her. When he died, I gave that child all of his jewelry. The child, a boy, looked a little bit like me.

This was where the tapes ended. With Jim there was never an end to reminiscence. When he finally left Portland, he spent time in California and then went to England to study singing; but he had problems with his vocal cords and his career ended. He went to New York and taught in a rather leftist school in New Jersey. He met the Rhodeses, started the hors d'oeuvre business, and wrote his first books. When the war came he went into the army, in which he did not fit. Released from the army, he took a job in which he may have been happier than any other—with the merchant marine, providing food and services in the various ports of call. First he was in Puerto Rico, where he had vivid memories of trying to get the hookers certified so his boys wouldn't get sick picking up women in the bars. Then he was in Brazil, where he got a cook from the local whorehouse. His tour of duty ended in the south of France.

The war over, he returned to New York, where he got a job with the Aarons at Sherry selling wine. Jack Aaron had a special fondness for Jim and sent him to France to learn about wine. When he came back he returned to writing books and wrote articles and taught. He also appeared on radio, television, and as a syndicated newspaper columnist.

Hints of what happened and the people he knew will appear throughout this book, called forth by the reminiscences of many friends. ✍

Before we launch into recipes there is another interview with Jim and a longish memoir on a remarkable cooking class, as well as some of Jim's own notes on a restaurant in formation that I thought might be a pleasure for you. Jim Fobel, who conducted the next interview, is an American cookery expert in his own right (see pages 107, 142, 150) and kindly contributed this interview with Jim to this book. ✍

AN INTERVIEW WITH JAMES BEARD BY JIM FOBEL

JF: Is there a *new* regional American cuisine?

JB: No, and I am so sick of hearing that term. No. There's American cooking. People think that they want to make a *nouvelle cuisine* over here and they can't do it.

JF: What's all the hoopla about?

JB: I think that people are trying to find a label for something and they can't do it. They're afraid to be simple.

JF: Is ours a cuisine that's been evolving?

JB: Let's call it cookery. I don't think that it's a cuisine *per se* yet because it's too all-engrossing. It's everything; still, it's American.

JF: So, it's eclectic?

JB: Yes.

JF: When Time-Life devoted eight volumes of their twenty-seven–volume series, *Foods of the World,* to American cooking (more than fifteen years ago), did they foresee the current popularity of regional American cooking, or has it always been popular?

JB: I think it's been popular. However, I think that Time-Life did a great service. I worked with them very closely and I know that they brought to light a great many facts about our life in this country that no one had ever done before, awakened the spirit of the people. But, of course, we've had wonderful people during the eighteenth and nineteenth centuries, and the twentieth century, who wrote about food, and wrote extremely well and were the background of American living. Like Fannie Farmer. We had Mrs. Lincoln. We had Eliza Leslie and Mrs. Hale. And we had Mrs. Child; not Julia, but another Mrs. Child. We had Katherine Beecher, sister of Harriet Beecher Stowe, who wrote a great deal about food in the nineteenth century. Mrs. Randolph, who wrote *The Virginia Housewife,* was as modern as today.

JF: You once said that "we are barely beginning to sift down into a cuisine of our own."

JB: Well, that's it. I think we're trying to amalgamate. But, again, it shouldn't be called something new. It's something we're pulling together that's always been with us.

JF: What do you think of all the high-quality American ingredients that are suddenly so readily available? There are all sorts of oils and vinegars coming out of California. . . .

JB: That's right. Of course this has always happened out there. You see, it seems new to many people, but I remember using California oils for forty years, I suppose. And, we've had a trend towards flavored vinegars and things like that during the last decade. But, I don't think our production methods have changed. We have always made some good cheeses. We had good cured meats. We had wonderful hams and bacon. We *created* smoked turkey. We created many smoked birds in this country. And now all this is beginning to take shape and come into one central thing, you see.

JF: Yes. What do you think about the new domesticated truffles from Oregon?

JB: They've got a long way to go. I've been in since the birth. They know it too. I mean, they know that they're just begin-

ning. But the fact that they have begun, and that the interest was great enough to create this thing, is tremendous. I happened to have been at the first mycological conference where they brought in some of the Oregon truffles and I knew that they were a far cry from the foreign truffles right from the start.

JF: Are the truffles white?

JB: Yup.

JF: Do they use pigs or dogs to harvest them?

JB: I think they probably use dogs now. They pretty well have an idea where they are. It's in the sheer infancy—really in swaddling clothes.

JF: Are any popular cooks or chefs using American ingredients exclusively?

JB: Yup. Several are coming in. Larry Forgione of the River Café [this was in 1983] is an example of someone who really goes out of his way to find things. And, he's discovered a great many things. That doesn't necessarily mean that he's cooking traditional American food. But, he's using domestic ingredients.

JF: One of your books, *James Beard's American Cookery,* is a fine example of an eclectic assortment of American recipes. How did you decide what to include as American?

JB: Well, that was kind of a job. I mean, you did copious reading of American books, the earlier books, and then decided who you wanted to talk about. Someone who was particularly pertinent to the subject, or who was farseeing enough to be ahead of her period, Mrs. Crowan, had extraordinarily modern ideas about a great deal of cookery. And Miss Leslie, who not only wrote a great deal about American food but translated the first French cookbook into American terminology—and found fault with an awful lot of French recipes. She didn't believe that any prosperous country would ever eat anything like liver and kidneys. She utterly damned those. And then you have people like Mrs. Randolph, who had an amazing knowledge of food. In the 1830s she gave a recipe for gazpacho—which no one dreamed of doing for a long time. Miss Leslie gave the first recipe for anything with curry in it. And it went on that way. There's been a great deal that's creative here.

Memories

JF: You included Oriental and Italian recipes; all of the ethnic....

JB: Well, there weren't many Oriental recipes. There were some things with curry but there weren't Oriental recipes. The Italian things came in, and Czech things and Scandinavian. But Oriental recipes lagged because of the fact that in China there were never written cookbooks. There was no written record. Recipes were handed down. And, as we come along, there have been enough Chinese recipes and cookbooks written to supply the needs of the past twenty-five centuries, I think.

JF: You said something very interesting in the book, that you have "experienced the glories of native cookery in the early years of this country, the decline of good cooking that followed the disappearance of hired help from the American households, and, since the mid-1940s, a renaissance of interest in food." Is our cooking getting better?

JB: I hope so. It must be, with all that's written about it and all the classes that people attend and the pursuit of American food, and other foods, throughout the country. It must be.

JF: Where do you think it's leading? Do you think we will eventually develop a cuisine?

JB: Well, I don't think that's necessary. I think we can stay as we are. I think we have good food and we don't have to label

it. We have one important thing that grew up in this country and that is the definition of regional cooking, which, as we became a more-traveled country and expanded, and the feeling of regional living disappeared to a greater extent, that regional cuisine spread itself. I think there are very few places where you find tightly knit regional cuisine. Period, if you know what I mean. Everybody eats gumbo. Everybody eats fried chicken. Everybody eats chili. Everybody eats other things that are part of our cuisine.

JF: It seems to me that in America we have more freedom than any other country in the world when it comes to cooking. We're allowed to claim any food that we want and cook it right here. In some countries the cuisine is more rigid.

JB: I think you're right; we have a breadth of view and understanding.

JF: Off the top of your head, are there some American classics that originated here?

JB: Certainly. Things like our method of curing and smoking ham and bacon. And, we mentioned smoked turkey before. That was an original thing. And so was succotash. It has many diversified variations on it. And, I think, most of our cooking with cornmeal. One European country picked up our love for cornmeal and that was Italy, with polenta. But cornbread and hushpuppies and such things as that certainly were ours. We became

masters of grilling. Especially with charcoal. I think that's a great American acquisition. I'm not sure a great deal of fish cookery is native to us. There are some things that are always classified as American which aren't. Apple pies and apple tarts were made in England and Scotland and Austria before we started making them here. As a matter of fact—fried chicken *per se*—what we do is a variation on a theme but there was German or Austrian fried chicken. They didn't call it fried. It had another name. Every country has had its own fish stew, it seems to me. In France you have several of them. [In this country] we created clam chowder and fish chowder and cioppino. In the South you've got court bouillon and other things that are purely our development in that field. And I think that gumbo probably goes in there too. Although that was part of the move that came out of Creole cooking.

JF: Earlier, you mentioned smoked ham. In your book *Beard on Pasta,* you include a recipe for Spaghetti Carbonara that is made with Smithfield ham. Would that exemplify a contemporary approach to American cooking?

JB: I suppose. Interestingly enough, there is an old theory that a man brought back the secret of Smithfield ham from China and Chinese ham and Smithfield ham are exactly alike.

JF: Yünnan ham?

JB: Yes. Of course you can't call anything a Smithfield ham unless it's cured and smoked in Smithfield [Virginia], and it's different from any other. But, I see no reason why we can't use it with fruit—the way people have prosciutto and melon or prosciutto and pears—thinly sliced. As a matter of fact, the restaurant down at the Vista Hotel, American Harvest, uses Smithfield for an hors d'oeuvre with fruit. It's very good.

JF: In the book, you also include a recipe for Angel Hair with Golden Caviar. Golden caviar is American, isn't it?

JB: Yeah.

JF: I tried the recipe and it's fabulous!

JB: That's a beautiful dish.

JF: It's so simple. I know that you love simply prepared foods.

JB: That's a whole secret of the development of food in this country. The fact that people have done unusual things with what we have—and applied European recipes to what was in the markets here and in doing so developed dishes that people hadn't created before.

JF: You also mention corn pasta in your book. I haven't tried it yet. Is it made from corn meal?

JB: Yes. It's not very common. I think it's made by only one or two producers in this country. The result is interesting.

JF: You go on to say that "we are going through

an especially lively period in the history of cooking." Is that because there are so many ingredients available?

JB: Yes, and so many people are experimenting. I think that's very important.

JF: I find it exciting.

JB: That's true. You know yourself.

JF: What commercially prepared or convenience foods do you use? If something was not available fresh would you substitute?

JB: Oh, yes. I use canned tomatoes. You're bound to use certain things.

JF: I think that America has done a terrible thing to the fresh tomato. Now, I'm finding that the domestic canned tomatoes are different than they used to be.

JB: Well, yes, you've got to shop around. You can find some very good ones. But, they'll take advantage wherever they can.

JF: I used to buy domestic canned tomatoes but now I find myself buying imported ones.

JB: I buy those and sometimes I buy Redpack [brand], which are whole tomatoes. They're, for the most part, packed in tomato purée. I like them very much. I use a great deal; they have a very good flavor. But, you can't trust any one thing for certain.

JF: Jim, if you were all by yourself and it wasn't a question of politeness, is there anything you wouldn't eat?

JB: Well, there are certain things I never eat.

JF: Such as?

JB: Oh, chicken livers. And I'm not very fond of broccoli. It's nice to look at. I don't seem to eat nearly as much beef as I used to. But I think that's a growing thing with many people. Of course, I'm an experimenter too. I once spent two weeks eating nothing but horsemeat in France just because I wanted to try every cut there was.

JF: Was one part better than the others?

JB: Yes. The tenderloin was exquisite, either cut into steaks or roasted whole.

JF: What did it taste like?

JB: Well, it's not gamey but rather on the sweet side, without much fat. I'll tell you this, it makes the most wonderful steak tartare in the world.

JF: I read that you are a bullfight afficionado. Have they ever asked you to cook a bull?

JB: After the fight? I had some beef the other night that I thought had been through a couple of fights. The way that we are starving the poor steers, so they don't have any fat, it's not to my palate. I defy, you see. Everybody says you mustn't do this, you mustn't do that. I just think: Give us the days of good fat on meat and we'll be much better off. Happier with our teeth anyway.

As you can tell from what she writes, Jean Purvis and her husband Bob were loyal students of Jim's, returning—as many did—year after year for more classes. While it may have been the only time in her life that Jean was called upon to cook like a professional, it was typical of the way James threw challenges at people, and they rose to meet his expectations. ✍

Bob and I returned to Gearhart for our fifth year of classes. We were amazed at James's undefeated attitude, his indomitable spirit, and unlimited energy. Last year in San Francisco he went in the hospital and wasn't expected to live. It was said it was the first doctor he had ever seen except over the dinner table. He had canceled his late spring classes because he was rushed to a New York hospital at 3:00 A.M. with a gallstone. He recovered from that and immediately made final plans for his Seaside classes in late June. When we arrived he was in a wheelchair with his foot elevated.

Marion Cunningham, since our first class together, had become his personal assistant. She made all arrangements and traveled with him wherever he had cooking classes. She also took on the enormous job of rewriting and modernizing Fannie Farmer's cookbook. Marion is a wonderful, cheerful, nice person. Her happy personality never failed, even with all her duties as well as perfecting Fannie Farmer's recipes whenever she had an extra minute. When James became so ill in San Francisco, Marion said she envied his lying down in the hospital, as she was exhausted from the errands he thought up for her to do.

After that hospitalization, he did lose about a hundred pounds by going on a strict diet with no salt, butter, cream, or Champagne. He said, "I look on it as a challenge."

Originally he had scheduled three weeks of classes each with twelve to fifteen students. Instead, he combined them into two classes with twenty to twenty-four students. He had a week's rest in between. After those classes he and Marion flew to London and then on to Bologna to give a week's class. His enthusiasm was amazing.

That year Richard Nimmo, who helped run his New York cooking school in Greenwich Vil-

lage, came to Seaside. Dick Nelson, who had a Portland cooking school, was his West Coast assistant.

Again our class was of advanced students and we immediately found the reason. We were scheduled to cook for a Gala Benefit at the Astoria Country Club for two hundred people ($20 per person) on Friday, July 1st. This was a benefit for the Seaside High School home economics department. James had used the school's facilities for six years and wanted to say thank you by remodeling and equipping the kitchen.

Other years we came at 10:00 and left at 2:00. This year we came earlier and earlier and left at 3:30 or 4:00.

For lunch the first day, we had homemade pasta with three kinds of sauces. Chuck Williams of Williams-Sonoma supervised the pasta. He inspired us because he said he could come home from work and make pasta in twenty minutes. We all made pasta and more pasta. The sewing room resembled a noodle factory. There was pasta in long strands spread out on the cutting tables, and shorter strands draped over the sewing machines. For salad each student made his favorite vinaigrette dressing. We had large bowls of the freshest mixed greens to use.

For dessert we had three kinds of custards, each differently flavored. One was flavored with mace, another with a bay leaf, and a third had rose geranium leaves. Our lunch was superb.

After lunch Beard would evaluate the food. One student was chastised for adding clams too soon to a pasta sauce, which made the clams tough. James asked another about a mistake in cooking the pasta. Before he could answer, all the cooks in his group began confessing to their mistakes. Soon everyone was laughing (and happy they weren't in the spotlight). "Take heart," sympathized Beard, "cooks everywhere have failures."

At Seaside, the quantities made often resulted in failures. Not every recipe can be tripled or more with success. Sometimes the recipes were wrong. Marion Cunningham and her group were assigned to make twelve dacquoises for the Gala that week. The first day they made four meringues. They were too brown and chewy. They baked four more. They were as bad. (These, however, did not go to waste. All extra food and all failures were put on the long center table. They appeared and quickly disappeared as they were snatched and eaten.) After many consultations with James, each other, and anyone walking by, the consensus was that the dacquoise recipe was wrong. Again four more dacquoises were made. A great cheer went up when they came out of the ovens—lovely crisp white meringues. The following morning the group came in at 8:30 to catch up by baking more and more meringues. (The next week, after the class was over, Maryon Greenough found six meringues in an oven where they had been left to dry.)

To practice, one day we were all asked to poach eggs. Later we discovered why: Eight hundred quail eggs had to be cooked for the Gala. We had far from perfect results. There were all shapes and sizes and degree of doneness. Some had brown yolks, some were tough. Two of mine disintegrated.

I was trying to sneak them into the garbage. James and his wheelchair were between me and the garbage. I turned to avoid his elevated foot, spilled the egg water, and immediately had his full attention with no way to dispose of those miserable eggs.

Often dishes were overdone or underdone, such as a lovely looking baked clam pie with a raw crust. One group made an apple dessert but thought it was so terrible that they threw it out and decided to make a raspberry shortcake instead. They doubled the recipe, but when they took it out of the oven it was underdone. The enterprising cooks took off the raw part and puréed raspberries over the crust. Two people made the same

soufflé recipe and cooked them in the same oven. One was fine, the other was dry and tasteless because the whites had been overbeaten. Someone who needed an oven, and didn't look inside, turned the oven to a high temperature. The cheesecakes boiled for fifteen minutes before the wrong temperature was noticed. So we all made mistakes but learned to improvise to make many things edible even if a failure. For the Gala each group was assigned specific dishes to make, plus helping where needed.

The first morning James told me to make two hazelnut cheesecakes. I did. He inspected them and said, "Fine, now make ten more by Friday." The cheesecake was no problem, but skinning the hazelnuts was. Every morning I would roast the hazelnuts and rub them between towels to skin them. Anyone with spare time could help rub the hazelnuts.

Another activity shared by all was poaching and peeling quail eggs. We received two hundred quails, shipped from New Jersey, along with twenty layers of eggs—eight hundred! A hundred and forty-four of them were poached (1 minute, 30 seconds) and the rest hard-boiled and soaked in vinegar water to remove the spots. The poached eggs were served in brioche croustades with Mornay sauce. The coddled ones were served with a dip. So, every morning all week, anyone with spare time would rub hazelnuts or peel quail eggs or both. We all came in earlier and earlier each morning until we were working eight to ten hours a day. No one expected this kind of work. We expected some work, some fun, beach time, et cetera. I'm afraid not everyone appreciated paying a fee and working such long, hard hours.

Beard was in his glory overseeing everyone and everything and keeping everyone hopping. His patience was never-ending as everyone asked him questions and constantly consulted him. He would send his assistants on errands, demonstrate techniques, and beam on students so enthusiastic to learn. He loved it all and we loved him.

We cooked quantities of vegetables,

eggplant, potatoes, boiling onions, beets, and refrigerated them for Friday. Peppers had to be charred in the oven, skinned, and julienned. Tiny onions—with short stems left on so they wouldn't separate—had to be peeled and blanched. The quantities of food staggered us: sixty cups of lentils, pounds of beef and sausage. One day there were four thirty-pound silvery Chinook salmons, one for gravlax, one for tartare, and two for poaching to be served with aspic. Veal breast was boned, fish filleted, beef marinated. We chopped, diced, minced, and made quantities of sauces. We made salami slices into cones and filled them with seasoned sour cream. Beard showed us how to keep their cone shapes. We stuck them into coarse chicken-wire trays to keep. The school had huge refrigerators but we couldn't ever have found the food again except for Maryon Greenough. Each day she would inventory the contents for us.

We did our best and Beard encouraged us, but we wasted materials with unworkable quantities and there was much to be done with many people. Dick Nelson went to the store every hour. How could so much butter, milk, cream, and mayonnaise disappear so fast? What happened to the dozens of spatulas and measuring cups we had?

Friday morning finally came. We were astounded when Beard blithely left us to be photographed at the Klingbergs' house in Astoria. We even had to do without Robin Klingberg's help. She had stayed up late to have her house spotless. Then she was Beard's stand-in for many pictures. When they returned, it was 2:00 and Robin was exhausted. Beard was full of energy and ready to go. We made more potato salad, lots of mayonnaise, peeled the rest of the quail eggs, washed greens, made garnishes, cut vegetables, and covered two huge salmon with aspic and decorations—a beautiful job by Judd Klingberg.

At 4:30, Beard said we could go home and get ready, "But be back at 5:30." By then there were station wagons, pickups, and cars, and food, food, food. There were dozens of borrowed silver platters and beautiful serving dishes which had to be carefully handled. We had pans for baking,

knives for cutting, and produce for last-minute preparations and garnishing.

The young staff at the kitchen of the Astoria Country Club was astonished at the invasion of twenty-two middle-aged cooks that suddenly descended on them and feverishly started working. We put food and dishes everywhere—on counters, tables, grocery shelves, broom closets, anyplace and everywhere. We filled the hall with tables of food and we squeezed between them chopping, arranging, and garnishing. As soon as the dish was ready, it was whisked to the buffet tables.

Beard had guided us to this point and he was out in front meeting old friends. We were glad he wasn't in the kitchen with us, as his wheelchair could never have fit anyplace in the kitchen.

As soon as the buffet dishes were ready, we started on the desserts. We needed to whip cream for the Strawberry Romanoff. We used the professional giant mixer in the kitchen. It worked so fast that our cream almost turned to butter. It looked curdled but it was all we had. We had to use it. We had learned to improvise, so we took out some of the whole berries from the Romanoff, washed them off, and sliced them over the bumpy cream. It looked fine.

Again Beard was posing for pictures by his favorite photographer, Dan Wynn, from New York. He took Irene Jue and a young slim blond girl to pose with him and trays laden with beautiful food. The blond girl held a small round tray but poor Irene had a huge ornate silver one that was very heavy when empty. Of course, picture after picture was taken, with poor Irene almost collapsing under the weight. We did help her hold it between pictures. Beard, who loved having his picture taken, was oblivious to all this. He would pose, flash his famous grin again and again while comfortably seated in his wheelchair.

He visited with his many friends and basked in their compliments with much hearty laughing. By 11:30, when we were through, we were too exhausted to eat—we just tasted, sat down for a glass of wine, and staggered home after fourteen hours on our feet. (A wife reported later that her husband slept twelve hours.)

We met the next day and heard that the Gala had raised enough money for a new home economics department for Seaside High School. Later Maryon Greenough sent us aprons made by her students. They were blue-striped, and embroidered at the top was "James Beard's Banquet Brigade 1977."

This was a great class, praised by Beard and approved by all. We had great camaraderie, much fun and expertise. We helped each other or else the Gala could not have happened. As Beard said, "Now you know how it feels to be professional cooks. You did professional work and very well."

MARK CARALUZZI *has contributed recipes to this book (see pages 119, 141, 326), but he also sent us the following that I think needs some introduction and comment. Mark came to class at Jim's house on 12th Street just before or after opening his American restaurant in Washington, D.C. At that and other times, Jim spun some tales. I even heard some of them. I would not want to stake my or James's honor on their absolute veracity. Some may have even been extravaganzas to startle the impressionable. On the other hand, James was very complex and they may have been gospel. I think you can read them and decide for yourselves what to accept as unvarnished truth. ✍*

Below are some of the memorable conversations I remember having with Jim. I remember asking him what were the most unusual things or meals he had eaten through his career, and he recounted two in particular which definitely qualify as unusual.

The first he said took place in Shanghai or Hong Kong, I can't remember, but as he explained he was taken to a restaurant that specialized in monkey brains, which was a delicacy at this particular establishment. He was the guest of honor and was sitting around a special table where the top of a small monkey's head had popped up through a small hole in the center of the table, and a skilled butcher of sorts sliced off the top of the head to expose the brains and all present were given small spoons to enjoy the "delicacy."

The second tale he recounted took place again, I think, in Shanghai, where he was taken to a restaurant that served skillet-fried duck feet of live ducks that were forced to stand on a hot flat grill surface.

I was a little horrified about both these stories and asked how could you have eaten the brains or watched the ducks without becoming ill, and he explained that he had devoted his life to searching and trying food and cuisines from all over the world and if these dishes were a delicacy or custom of that particular region or country and were looked on as a local speciality, then it was his interest, commitment, and duty to try all things no matter how foreign or strange they might happen to be. Needless to say, I never forgot that discussion or story.

On a more conservative note, one of the lessons I will always remember from Jim was his attitude of not following the crowd and being his own person, both personally and strongly so with his food philosophies. During the 1970s into the '80s there was such a tremendous increase in the attention to food, dining, and cuisine, and many of the so-called experts involved in writing or teaching about all that was happening on occasion preached about things in a very strict manner, leading people to believe theirs was the only way to do things. On countless occasions in various discussions Jim always said to "damn what other people think—find out for yourself and do not be influenced by their opinions." There were many examples of this—for instance, where he found frozen products to be of the same quality as fresh he was not afraid to say so.

JAMES BEARD. *Earlier in his career, Jim had spent a fair amount of time as a consultant to restaurants. I believe he started with the Bird and Bottle in Garrison, New York. He worked with Chillingsworth on the Cape and recommended both John Clancy and Paula Wolfert to work there.*

As you will see on page 92, James Beard had a long association with Joe Baum, one of America's foremost restaurateurs. They worked together on many restaurants. As James got older, he sometimes just sent in tapes outlining his ideas. The following notes were made after a series of tastings to develop the menu for The Market Bar and Dining Rooms in the bottom of the World Trade Center. It was just the kind of restaurant that James loved, with lots of grills and hearty foods. In his comments, we can hear—as always—the richness of the past informing the present.

Not everything that James said was applicable or practical; but much of it found its way onto the menu or into the style. In the end, everybody loved this restaurant.

The notes were funneled through me, as I was working for Joe Baum at the time and was a natural link to Jim. Again, I have cut out my own voice. In these notes, you will perceive Jim circling an idea in a sort of stream of consciousness. Sometimes a truly startling adjective will crop up. Although Jim is thought of, rightly, as a quintessentially American voice, he often refers to European dishes—predominantly French—that structure his idea of a market restaurant. He sees nothing incongruous in having them in an essentially American market context.

James's mode was opinionated, but never one of cloture. It was much more a musing, internal or with others, on the lines of what if . . . ? He also approached the repertoire for classes this way. What if we did lamb?—rare lamb, lamb with cucumbers, Chuck Williams's wonderful Irish stew. . . . Then we would flesh it out, develop recipes. With earlier restaurants, Jim spent more time in the kitchen. Here, he is more of a taster, resource, and free associator. ✍

The James Beard Celebration Cookbook

NOTES ON THE MARKET BAR AND DINING ROOMS MENU.

I think that a great deal of attention has to be paid to the menu again and again and again. It is not right! Nothing comes out looking the way that it should look. I talked yesterday about the fillet that we had for lunch with the marrow. It looked like a stewed piece of beef on an airline with some marrow on top of it. That is not the right way. If the fillet is to be sautéed, it should look as if it came right out of the pan and have the sauce underneath it, the marrow on top—not in globs—in nice little pieces. I think we are lost. Why give people a sirloin steak with nothing on the plate but a few onions? It should have a little glaze, or we should offer a sauce. Something should relieve it. It should look luscious and big. Even if the prices have to go up, it should look as if it were worth twice as much as you are paying for it.

I think that the whole structure of market cuts has to be reviewed. I think that we should not just have a boneless strip steak—a New York cut—or whatever you want to call it. We should have a good bone-in sirloin and we should have a T-bone, or we should have a pin-bone sirloin. We should have things that look magnificent. We should see how thick we can get something, rather than how much space it will cover on the plate. I would like to see a couple of steaks done in a cocotte—I mean to be seared and then tossed in with a sauce and put in the oven for a couple of minutes to let the steak and the sauce meld together, like the old sons-of-roast-beef steak, or the three-inch-thick sirloins that used to be served on the West Coast that were so wonderful. They had a sort of pseudo–barbecue sauce put into the cocottes and then the steak was lowered into them and they were thrown into the oven. They came out teeming with the sauce, not overcooked. They were excellent steaks. Nobody has had a Beef Steak Stanley on a menu for ages—with grilled banana—and nobody has had a carpetbag steak [split and stuffed with oysters]. All these things belong in this restaurant if it is ever going to be a steak house.

As I have said before, it's got to have good lamb items. It's got to have a good thick lamb chop. It's got to have small lamb chops. I would eschew a lamb steak. It has got to have a grilled leg of lamb. It's got to have a feeling for things. It has got to have a grill with kidney and liver. It has got to have a mixed grill sort of thing, a lamb chop mixed grill.

The menu still has no variety in meats. I would like to play with a sauté veal chop that might be put under the broiler for the last two or three minutes with something on it that would give it a glaze, but not toughen it. My objection to most broiled veal chops and pork chops is that they are tough when they are served. I think that here again we can have marvelous sautéed pork chops with creamed gravy. The place screams for things like that! We have the skirt steak, which, as far as I'm concerned, was the most flavorful steak I've had in the restaurant yet; but I think we have to think of another way to do it. I think we can have flank steak for two; but these things almost have to be carved at the table—just like porterhouse has to be carved at the table.

I'd like to see us have a good shallot sauce that was really more of a glaze than a sauce, that had white wine, a little vinegar, and some sort of herb that would give it zest. Then I think that we ought to have a *sauce maison*, which would be a sauce to be served with something—like the old "21" Club *sauce maison*. I think we should also work out a decent barbecue sauce and use it on pork, beef, and perhaps lamb. There would be a slight difference in these sauces; but they would not be smeary, but instead good, flavorful barbecue sauces. I once had in a restaurant somewhere a most delicious, thinly cut pork steak off the ham that was superb. It was sautéed very well and served with thinly sliced sautéed apples. It was a beautiful dish.

Then I think I would get into the poultry department. I think that we should have chicken sautés that are almost done to order. They can be done to order if you are really at it. They could be done with fresh herbs, chicken sauté with eggplant, for instance, a chicken sauté with oysters, a chicken sauté flambéed in Armagnac, a chicken Vallée d'Auge, which has the apple and the cream and the Calvados. I think we should do a sort of quick chicken paprikás by doing a sauté of chicken with paprika and giving a sour cream or smitane sauce. I think we should do a numberous group of sautés, and I see absolutely nothing wrong with our doing—from time to time—a chicken à la Maryland (with corn fritters and a good cream gravy). This could be a superbly good and authentic dish for us to serve, and it certainly is market-y.

I can even see a great, wonderful dish from time to time of ham with red-eye gravy, or ham and eggs among the made dishes. If I could have a good ham sliced and cooked, I would love it for dinner sometimes. That doesn't mean we have to go into the grits department.

I would like to see us do a number of things with oxtails, like the one we talked about the other day, the one that Elizabeth David has with black olives, which is great, or just a good heavy ragout of oxtail that sticks to your lips. There's another dish where the pieces of oxtail are taken out after poaching and rolled in crumbs and browned under the grill—like grilled beef bones are done. I think that all these things can count in.

I think a good brown chicken fricassee with dumplings—with a nice brown sauce that has cream added to it at the last minute. Even a white fricassee with a creamy sauce and dumplings and good chicken could fit. All of these should go as made dishes—not all of them every day, but picking and choosing from them.

I think we could do the New Mexican pork chops with pinto beans from time to time. I see no objection to our having an extraordinarily good chili. I think perhaps we can delve into game a little bit more. I would like to see us have fresh quail. I'd like to see us have baby pheasant when we can. Not every day, but so many days a week. I'd like to see good squab. These are all dishes that we're deprived of and it would be welcome to have them here.

There is no reason we couldn't have a perfectly great bollito [misto] as good if not better than the one Quo Vadis [for many years a classic New York restaurant where Sam Aaron (page 68) lunched almost daily and where Jim and I once ran into Mary Livingston, Jack Benny's wife, who had been a student of Jim's]. It would be sensational, and naturally a pot-au-feu from time to time, and a *poule au pot*.

I would like to see us play with broiled mallard duck breasts, and use the rest of the mallard for pâtés. I would like to see us do any number of game dishes if we could. I think frogs' legs done in various and sundry fashions belong down here. I certainly think that we should do some spectacularly good broiled fish and baked fish. I think, at night, that comes as a necessity.

If this restaurant is ever going to build up, it is going to build up because of freakish things that we do. I think we have to take meat restaurants as an example and outdo them. I can see doing the steak with Roquefort that we did at the Four Seasons. I can see just once in a while a luscious roast sirloin of beef with oven-roasted potatoes and maybe a very good bubble-and-squeak. We've neglected spareribs in this place, and they belong sometimes. They belong either with something, or by themselves. Do them perfectly simply with salt and pepper, or do them with a good glaze—and do not try and give a sticky, icky, gooey barbecued sparerib.

I think we can do a wonderful leg of pork that has been marinating in red wine for a week or so and then is roasted and served with a raisin and pine-nut sauce. I think we can do the mock venison. I think we can do a world of these things. We can do a fine coq au vin. We might do it sometimes under a brioche crust, which is a superbly good dish. We haven't touched those things. They should be dishes that make you salivate on sight and continue salivating until you are through eating them. Just the thought of them as you order them should make you salivate probably. I think a daube of beef is a part of our scheme. Things are endless that can work in here.

Things have got to be so good that people talk about food rather than the restaurant. I think our old chicken with forty cloves of garlic would go here, and I think some good pasta dishes. I think that in the pasta dishes I have tasted so far, the pasta was too well done and the vegetables were too well done, and nothing came together. They were thick and gooey and not what I call crisp, well-tailored, brisk pasta dishes.

I would like very much also to see us do some interesting and good things with a duck dish, like that one we had at Alliance that has that thick black sauce [*civet*—"with blood"]. I think once in a while a mass of pigs' tails and sauerkraut—maybe barbecued pigs' tails. I think grilled pigs' feet would be a good idea with a sauce diable. I think we should really have a fine cassoulet, but not too often. Let's do it with *confit d'oie* and good beans so that it sort of takes you

for a ride in the sky as you eat it.

I see absolutely nothing wrong with *pièce de boeuf à la Bourguignonne*, if it is good beef, carved perfectly, and has a good bourguignonne sauce with a garniture that is proper. I can see a very good sauerbräten from time to time with potato dumplings that don't need to be as heavy as most potato dumplings seem to be. They should seem to have some lightness about them.

I would be very, very happy to have, in addition to awfully good grilled lamb, to have a good rare *gigot* once in a while, and, in the days when baby lamb comes in, to have baby lamb for people. I can also see having poached lamb and braised lamb. I think the seven-hour braised lamb might be a very interesting dish, as well as the Italian dish where they cut the shoulder into thick chops and braise it with a few vegetables and some white wine.

I think we could have venison hamburger sometimes and some venison sausage and maybe little tenderloins of venison from time to time. If we can find other game animals that are easy to bring in, then why not try them out. We could certainly get wild boar. We might even do a wild boar head cheese if we can get a wild boar's head. Failing that, I don't know why we don't do a regular head cheese that is just so deliciously good that it is impossible to pass it by.

I remember years ago in the old caviar restaurant when Dadone ran it, there were the most beautiful, small, four- and five-pound broiled turkeys that were cooked to order and were superb when they came out. Why can't we do this? It has to be done for two or three or four persons, but, what the hell! It's part of this set-up. It's the market speaking again. It's everything that is an adventure in eating that comes into the market that is to be served at these tables, and until that happens, it is never going to be a market restaurant. It may be far afield from anything you've planned so far, but it is still part of what the market affords, and that is the important thing to keep in your mind and never loose sight of.

I wonder if we can get real scampi? For a time, some of the Italian restaurants were getting them flown in from Italy. If you could have real scampi once in a while and not big shrimp pretending to be scampi, it would be a great, great help to the world. I think we ought to have lobster once in a while in one way or another. I don't think we should make a daily feature of lobster; but I think we should have it. That is the nearest I can come to it—it should be! I can't see broiled lobster very much; but I can see having the most wonderful poached lobster and lobster *à la nage* and cold lobster in creation. I'm not sure I can't see a sort of a lobster Mornay with a good Mornay sauce. I think that we could have saddle of lamb and saddles of veal, if we ever have a place to carve. I think those things need the attention of being carved to add to their interest; but if we have a place to carve, they should be part of our food picture.

I haven't gone into stews because they are more luncheon dishes. I do think that we have got to develop some that are extraordinarily good and full of interest for people— no matter what they are made from they can be good stews. I think we should have that wonderful old goulash of Albert's [Albert Stockli was the eccentric, but wonderful, original chef of the Four Seasons restaurant in New York] that had the lemon and garlic and caraway seeds thrown into the blender just before it was served, which made it more interesting than any other goulash I've ever eaten. I think we should do a Székely goulash with the sauerkraut and the pork and the cream. All these things I think are of tremendous importance to this place now. I can see things as lowly as fried apples and bacon—if we had good bacon being served to people.

For desserts I think we could go into things like great rolled pancakes flambéed— not necessarily the Luchow pancake [the late, great, German restaurant's huge puffy apple pancake], but different ones. Not crêpes either, but good thin pancakes fruited and flamed and interestingly presented. I see no reason why we can't have good homely things like apple crisp and blueberry grunt—things like that on the menu from time to time—not every day! I also think that we can do much more exciting things with fruit. I think salad should be something to order except with certain dishes where it belongs; but it could be much more interesting were it done almost as a *specialité de la maison*.

The scope of this restaurant is unbelievable. It is endless what can be put there, and if these few suggestions help, I will come up with more because I believe that if anything is going to move that place it has got to be a startler of a menu. So let me know what you think about these things, and we will discuss them.

I wish we still could. ✍

MARY HOMI *has been for many years one of the foremost publicists in this country for European hotels, as well as a warm caring friend. She is one of the many people whom Helen McCully (page 168) and Jim shared.* ✍

I first met James A. Beard in 1962 when I was invited to a dinner party given by my friend Helen McCully not long after I arrived in the United States from England. I was in awe of this jolly giant of the food world. He loved England and we had fun discussing "real English food"; he also loved to travel, especially to Europe. From then on we became good friends; there was not a week that passed that we did not either talk by phone or visit with each other, the only interruptions being our travels—Jim with his teaching and demonstration appearances around the States, and my visiting clients.

Several years later, I asked Jim if he would ever consider giving classes in Europe. He thought the idea was grand, so I began to organize very special Jim Beard Cooking Courses in European hotels such as the Gritti Palace in Venice; Le Grand, Rome; Brenner's Park, Baden Baden; et cetera. These courses were so successful that many of Jim's friends, such as Julia Child, Simone Beck, Richard Olney, et cetera, asked me if it would be possible to run a series of these courses, which we did for many years.

Jim not only loved to cook, he loved to eat. It always gave me great pleasure when I made jams, jellies, and chutneys to give Jim a pot or two. He tried many times to convince me to open my own gourmet store; but I never seemed to get organized.

MARY LYONS *is the fabulous woman who has run*
Foods from France for many years. She was in part responsible for one of the truly joyous moments in
James's later life, a happiness to tears, when he got the Ordre du Mérite Agricole, whose ribbon he wore
forever after. To know more about Helen McCully, see page 168; Clay Triplette is on page 209. ✍

I can't remember when—1966 perhaps—or exactly where I was introduced to James Andrew Beard. Helen McCully had me in tow. We were going to some sort of reception, the debut of a cookbook, to welcome a visiting food luminary, a sampling of caviar, or something of that order. From Helen, I already "knew" Jim. He and she talked by phone early every morning to hash over what they had done the day before, what they planned to do that day, items in the newspapers, what Scotty Reston had to say—they agreed/ disagreed, gossip columns ... you get the picture. Helen always had something amusing to pass on to me. And of course, I knew what Jim looked like; but I never before had been face-to-face with him.

There he was. Seated in one of those dramatic Dragon Lady fan-backed rattan chairs. Pink-cheeked, jaunty bow tie slightly askew, not only filling the chair, but filling the room. He looked so ... so swell! I do recall Helen's introduction: "Jim, here's Mary Lyons." All he said was, "It's about time." After that, conversation between them rattled on just as though they had never covered the world that very morning on the telephone.

A few years later, I moved to an apartment just a few blocks away from Jim in the village, so that I was often in his house. Either for dinner with a close friend or two, Helen, José Wilson, John Ferrone, Eleanor Lowenstein, Leon Lianides, et al. Sometimes dropping by for an after-work tête-à-tête over a Scotch on the rocks. Many times with a houseful of friends from all over the country, even abroad, gathered in the kitchen drinking Champagne, munching, filling plates, joshing with Clay. How Jim loved having people about. His sense of theater—grand-operatic the-

James Beard's Greenwich Village townhouse

The James Beard Celebration Cookbook

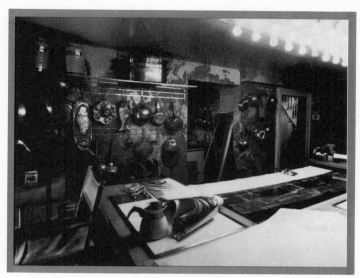

The Beard kitchen

ater—was second nature to him. Whenever he arrived at a restaurant, he made an "entrance," knowing that all heads would be turned his way. I can still picture his arrival at Lutèce one cold winter day, alighting from the taxi in his enormous fur coat which Mme. Soltner graciously *débarrassed* and then, staggering only slightly, headed to the checkroom. Even swathed in bandages in his splendid room at New York Hospital, recovering from yet another operation, he was the munificent host, offering friends a glass of Champagne and a nibble of something exotic.

In his townhouse on 12th Street our little chats, lubricated by the aged Scotch, eventually came around to France. Jim always wanted every detail from my most recent trip, which restaurants were "up," which "on the slip," how Paris looked, which wines I had discovered, which year, my opinion of such and such a chef.... And he knew France well. Toward the end of the war, Jim had been sent to the south of France, Antibes, I think, by the United Seamen's Service to organize restaurant facilities for American servicemen on R and R in that area. In 1954, he coauthored *Paris Cuisine* with Alexander Watt, a Scotsman who spent twenty-five years living in Paris and was well known at the time as a connoisseur of food and wine. On frequent vacations abroad,

after checking out Paris, Jim always spent a few days along the Mediterranean coast.

Certainly France was an important influence on his life, and he often expressed the wish that he and I could plan a trip together. Alas, our schedules never coincided but in lieu of what would have been for me an unforgettable experience, I did the next best thing. I proposed to the French Embassy that Jim be awarded the prestigious honor of the Ordre du Mérite Agricole. Jim was immensely flattered by the idea, but in those days the wheels of the French government did not roll in TGV [superfast train] style. Almost fifteen months later, Jim was informed that he had been designated a chevalier of the order. On March 23, 1978, in the suite of Robert Lemercier, commercial counselor to the French Embassy in New York, the ceremony took place.

In addition to M. Lemercier, representing the French government were his *adjoint*, Jean-Pierre Gachelin, and André Baeyens, Attaché de Presse to the French Embassy [currently French ambassador to Austria], and a group of Jim's closest friends: Judith Jones [his editor; see page 274], Barbara Kafka, José Wilson [his long-time associate, now sadly dead], Sam Aaron [see page 68], Eleanor Lowenstein [the owner of The Corner Bookstore, authority on American cookbooks, and his bibliographic resource], Emily Gilder [his secretary for many years], John Ferrone [see page 257], Jane Becker [now the publisher of Knopf], Margaret Stern [a wine expert], and Richard Nimmo [his last secretary]. Robert Lemercier, a delightful and personable white-haired gentleman, very obviously was full of pride that it was he to so honor Jim—and he played his role with the perfect Gallic air of the dramatic. Among other things in the official citation he read was this statement: "Every century had its gastronomes: Carême, Brillat-Savarin, Escoffier. This is the century of James Beard."

To conclude, the ceremony was conducted in French and ended with pinning the impressive medal on Jim's lapel, presentation of the certificate of the order, and—de rigueur—a kiss on each cheek. Throughout this historic fifteen minutes, Jim was very quiet—even retiring—and, to our surprise, his eyes filled with tears. He replied very briefly, thanking M. Lemercier appropriately yet amazingly at a loss for words. The spell was broken when Barbara Kafka rushed up to him, wiped away the tears, and kissed him soundly. We all followed suit and Champagne was served to toast the new chevalier. Jim's words to me were, "If only Helen were here." (Helen McCully had died six months before.)

Then we all filed off to the Four Seasons for a splendid luncheon which Tom Margittai and Seppi Rengli masterminded to match this milestone in Jim's life.

I have so many more memories I'd like to share, but just one more short one, important to me. One Christmas present from Jim is certainly the most inspired I ever received. A case of twenty-four half bottles of champagne, twelve different brands. The message was, "*One* at a time please, and not all at *one* time. . . . Love, Jim." Every Christmas Eve since then I reserve a half bottle of Champagne to personally toast a wonderful man and a singular friend.

HORS D'OEUVRE & CANAPES

By the happy coincidence of meal arrangement—
book following meal—the title of this chapter is
also that of James's first book. In this book, there

ARE MORE FIRST COURSES, APPETIZERS, THAN IN HIS AND FEWER CANAPÉS. ONE QUOTATION FROM JIM'S BOOK WILL SHOW THAT HOWEVER CONTEMPORARY IT MAY FEEL TODAY, IT REFERS IN PART TO A PAST WORLD, A WORLD THAT JIM ENJOYED IN EUROPE BEFORE THE SECOND WORLD WAR. TALKING ABOUT OPEN-FACE SANDWICHES, HE WROTE: "GREAT PLATTERS OF OPEN-FACE SLICES COME INTO THE DINING ROOM OR DRAWING ROOM EVERY NIGHT TO TEMPT THE APPETITE AND TO ADD POUNDS TO THE GIRTH—HOW SAD THAT FOOD SHOULD DO THAT TO SOME OF US WHO LOVE IT SO WELL!"

JAMES'S BOOK GREW OUT OF THE BUSINESS THAT HE WAS IN WITH THE RHODESES. AS WITH A NUMBER OF JIM'S PROJECTS, THERE WAS CONTROVERSY SURROUNDING THE BOOK. BILL RHODES FELT CHEATED, FELT THAT THE MATERIAL WAS IN PART HIS. HE AND JIM BECAME ESTRANGED, ALTHOUGH JIM REMAINED FRIENDLY WITH IRMA. SHE AND JIM BOTH WENT ON TO WRITE GOOD BOOKS. BILL DID NOT.

CRAIG CLAIBORNE *gives a recipe below that illustrates the interweaving. Jim really did love the recipe and used it in different versions in several books. In one, he credits the recipe to a Parisian hostess. I don't think we will ever know. The recipe was so much a part of Jim's life that it followed him to his San Francisco home-away-from-home, the Stanford Court when Jim Nassikas was in charge.*

Jim had a room in a corner of the hotel that was most easily reached from the service elevator. He and I used to go up to it from Fournou's Ovens in the basement when we had finished giving a class. If the timing was right, we would make a brief pause on the main floor. There, in a sort of pantry, just beyond the elevator doors, would be standing the tea cart that had just made its exit from the front of the house. If we were lucky, the silver épergnes would still bear a few leftover onion sandwiches which we would hastily stuff in our mouths before continuing our ascension. I always felt a little guilty—not Jim.

If you look on page 323, you will find a brioche recipe of my own that I find does very well in these sandwiches. However, I have had them made with close-grained, from-the-market white bread and they were very good. There are some who contend that mayonnaise out of a jar is the real secret of these morsels; the parsley clings better. Do see what you like.

Craig Claiborne is no longer at The New York Times; *but the food world will long remember him as the man who made restaurant reviewing respectable. He also made it and his food columns, and continues to make his books vastly interesting as well as authoritative. His many readers attest to that.* ✍

During Jim Beard's lifetime, I spent many a glorious hour around his table feasting on foods worthy of Apicius and drinking wines worthy of Bacchus. Curiously, however, the one food that comes to my mind most distinctly when I think of visiting Jim's home is a bit of trivia which he loved and for which I harbor some small passion. It is a raw onion sandwich made of round cutouts of bread, smeared with homemade mayonnaise, and the rims wholly flecked with finely chopped parsley.

Jim always gave credit to Irma Rhodes as the creator of these sandwiches. She had collaborated with Jim and her brother, Bill, in opening a catering establishment known as Hors d'Oeuvre, Inc. And, Irma informed me a few years ago, it was Bill who brought that sandwich idea to New York. She told me that in the 1920s Bill had visited a Parisian bordello and the madame had served irresistible morsels of food made with thin rounds of bread cut from a brioche loaf. As indicated, they were spread with mayonnaise and filled with crisp raw onion rings. The idea of coating the outer rim with chopped parsley came out of the trio's imagination.

Irma Rhodes's Onion Sandwiches

24 thin slices firm-textured bread, such as challah or brioche
6 tablespoons mayonnaise (recipe follows)
12 wafer-thin onion slices
Salt to taste
Freshly ground black pepper to taste
1 cup finely chopped parsley

Using a 1¾-inch (about) cookie cutter, cut out rounds from the centers of the bread slices (the number may vary from one to three, depending on the size of the cookie cutter and the size of the bread slices).

Spread mayonnaise on each of the bread rounds with a small spatula. The diameter of the onion slices should approximate that of the bread rounds. Sprinkle each with salt and pepper. Place one onion slice each on half the rounds. Cover each one with another bread round, mayonnaise-side down, on top of the onion.

Using the spatula, smear the outside rim of the sandwich with mayonnaise, coating fairly liberally with the mayonnaise. Roll the rim of each sandwich in parsley to coat the outside rim generously. Continue until all the sandwiches are coated, adding more ingredients as necessary. Cover and chill for 1 hour.

✘ *Makes 12 or more sandwiches*

Mayonnaise

1 egg yolk
1 teaspoon imported mustard, such as Dijon
1 teaspoon white wine vinegar or fresh lemon
    juice
1 cup peanut, vegetable, or olive oil
Salt to taste
Freshly ground black pepper to taste

Place the egg yolk, mustard, and vinegar in a mixing bowl. Beat vigorously with a wire whisk or an electric beater until combined.

Start adding the oil gradually, beating continuously with a whisk or electric beater. Continue beating and adding oil until all of it is used. Add salt and pepper to taste. If the mayonnaise is not to be used immediately, beat in a tablespoon of water. This will help stabilize the mayonnaise and retard its turning when stored in the refrigerator. ✘ *Makes about 1 cup*

ELIZABETH DAVID *is the lady who rescued English food from postwar despair with a vision of the foods of the warm Mediterranean. She has written brilliantly on bread and Italian food and spices in books, magazines, and newspapers. She is a beauty who has a life even more extraordinary than her enduringly popular books. She and Jim shared passions for food and for food books. When I first visited her, her books all had little paper slips sticking out of them, notes and references for past and future writings.* ✍

In the '50s, '60s, and '70s Jim spent two or three weeks every summer in London. We had some good times, lunching at the Capitol Hotel or at the Dorchester, where Jim always stayed. Sometimes we would hire a car and drive down to lunch at the Bell at Aston Clinton in Buckinghamshire, where Gerard Harris, the landlord, had built up a wine list renowned throughout the country. His food was excellent too—roast duck was one of the specialities—and Jim especially loved the friendly, informal atmosphere of a country pub.

Another place Jim enjoyed was the Connaught. It was at a luncheon there that I first met him, along with Helen Evans Brown, who also became a much-loved friend. In those days the hotel was managed by Rudolf, who was a Swiss, a real charmer, and a great friend of mine, and a great hôtelier, now alas dead. The chef was French—I'm afraid I've forgotten his name—and very good, but much of the food was high-class English and quite plain. Every day there was a roast, there were steak and kidney pies, and there were English puddings—the Connaught's bread and butter pudding was a favourite there long before Anton Mosimann of the Dorchester made his own version famous on Britain's television screens—the magnificent English Cheddar and Stilton cheeses. It has to be remembered that in Britain rationing had ended only in 1956, so to me the sight of those beautiful cheeses, not to mention the whole hams on the cold buffet, and the jugs of cream offered with the desserts, were feasts in themselves, and of course to Jim all of them were rare treats not to be resisted.

In the late autumn of 1965 I opened a kitchen utensil shop in Pimlico, a corner of southwest London not far from Chelsea. Jim found this new diversion great entertainment. He would sit for hours in our stockroom watching the comings and goings of the staff, sometimes offering advice to the less clued-up of the young girls—"There's a woman asking for a soufflé dish large enough to serve six people, which one shall I give her?"— and occasionally emerging to talk to a delighted customer. In my small, low-ceilinged, plain little shop, Jim's huge frame was a memorable sight.

Early the following year, I think it was February or March 1966, another American called on me in the shop and introduced himself. He had been sent by Jim Beard. His name was Chuck Williams, of the famous Williams-Sonoma kitchen shop in San Francisco. With Chuck I had so many common interests that we quickly became firm friends. I saw him year after year when he came on buying trips; he gave me much help and advice about my shop, and I hope that I was sometimes able to reciprocate with information useful to him. It was Chuck who accompanied me on my first flight to San Francisco—I found the prospect of that eleven hours in the air terribly daunting, and still do, although I have faced it many times since—and of course I still see him with joy every time I visit that much-loved city. So Jim's legacy of shared friendship is still very much with me.

One summer Jim was loaned an apartment in London, so instead of going to restaurants we would eat there, or sometimes in my own Chelsea home. We talked a lot about cookbooks and our mutual favorites. One of them was the magnificent collection of recipes made by the Scottish Lady Clark of Tillypronie, published in 1909. I was putting together a small book mainly concerned with the extensive use of spices and herbs in British traditional cooking. In 1970 the book appeared in Penguin paperback under the title

Spices, Salt and Aromatics in the English Kitchen. One of the recipes I included was from that same book of Lady Clark's, a neat little formula for what in England we call biscuits, little shortbread cookies flavored with cheese, admirable with the wine we used to drink before luncheon. Here is the recipe.

Thick Parmesan Biscuits

For a dozen biscuits: ¼ pound plain [all-purpose] flour, 2 ounces each of butter and grated Parmesan, the yolk of one egg, salt, cayenne pepper.

Rub the butter into the flour, add the cheese, egg, and seasonings. Moisten with a little water if necessary. Roll out the dough to the thickness of half an inch. Cut into 1-inch-diameter rounds. Arrange on a baking sheet. Bake in the centre of a very moderate oven, gas No. 2, or 310 to 330° F., for just on 20 minutes. Serve hot.

Lady Clark makes the point that it is the *thickness* of these biscuits that gives them their character. The Parmesan is also essential. English cheese will not do.

The biscuits can be stored in a tin and heated up when wanted. ✕ *Makes about 1 dozen biscuits*

PAUL GRIMES *teaches cooking classes, some of which are at Peter Kump's Cooking School. He styles food for photography and also writes articles. As you can see, his idea is not unrelated to Elizabeth David's. Think Sherry as well as Champagne, or add the cookies to a dessert that can use sharpening, such as ice cream, frozen yogurt, and/or fruit.* ✍

These small cookies come from a dinner I prepared at the Beard House in December of 1986. I served them as an hors d'oeuvre with a glass of Champagne.

A Spicy Shortbread

■■■■■■■■■■■■■■■■■■■■■■■■■

12 ounces (3 sticks) unsalted butter, at room
    temperature
⅔ cup sugar
3 cups all-purpose flour
1½ teaspoons curry powder
1 teaspoon paprika
¼ teaspoon chili powder
1 teaspoon tumeric
¼ teaspoon cayenne pepper

Preheat oven to 350° F.

Place butter in large bowl and beat either by hand or with an electric hand mixer until it is light in texture. Add sugar and whip together until light and fluffy.

Sift flour together with spices. Stir into butter and mix thoroughly.

Roll the dough out between two sheets of plastic wrap to about ½-inch thick and roughly 12″ × 16″ in size. Place in the freezer for about 30 minutes.

Either cut dough into shapes with a 2-inch cookie cutter and place on a cookie sheet, or press dough into the bottom of a baking sheet. Bake for about 30 minutes, or until shortbread firms to the touch and is a golden color.

Remove from the oven and allow to cool on a wire rack. Remove cookies from sheet with a spatula or break large piece of shortbread into serving pieces. ✘ *Makes about 2 dozen cookies*

JAMES BEARD. *This is not a book of James Beard's recipes, but a few have been included. Some are just typical; others are recipes that he published but are really the work of his friends and thus permit us to hear their voices and include their work in a book to which they certainly would have wanted to contribute.*

It is due to the graciousness of various publishers and the inheritors of James's royalties that we have been able to include these recipes. Their generosity permits the inclusion of friends who were dear to Jim, an important part of his life and work even though they are no longer alive. Let's hope that they are all at a big party somewhere together.

I never worked on a project with Jim when he didn't mention Louis Dressing, and sure enough it turns up in his first book, Hors d'Oeuvre and Canapés. It turns up again in James Beard's New Fish Cookery on top of crab. You will notice that James's early recipes come from a period before the formal recipe writing style of today was established. ✍

This is another dish that comes from the Pacific Coast. The late Helen Evans Brown said it was served at Solari's in San Francisco in 1914. If I'm not mistaken, the father of the late West Coast writer Richard L. Neuberger served it in his Bohemian Restaurant in Portland, Oregon, at that time too. At any rate, the old Bohemian served the finest Louis I have ever eaten. [*JB*]

Crab Louis

It is very easy to make this superb dish. Begin with a bed of finely shredded lettuce. Heap plenty of crabmeat on top and garnish with quartered hard-cooked eggs and quartered tomatoes. Pour a Louis Dressing (see below) over all.

Louis Dressing

Two cupfuls of mayonnaise, one tablespoonful each of pickle, egg, olive, onion, green pepper, and parsley, all finely chopped. Add two tablespoonfuls of chili sauce.

A variation of this sauce is to add one half cupful of stiffly whipped cream to the dressing.

JAMES BEARD. *In* <u>*Menus for Entertaining,*</u> *Jim gave menus for "light breakfast" that give a nostalgic feel. Jim loved breakfast. One of the last television shows we did was shot in his kitchen in New York with Jim as the voice and me as the prompting questioner and hands at the stove. When I asked him what we should do, he said, "Breakfast." His ideas were more varied, more English, heartier, and more interesting than today's typical breakfast. Today, we would probably serve this as a first course at dinner, as I know Jim sometimes did, or it could be an unusual canapé. Jim and I once had a long talk about "under glass," the recipe description that indicated that a dish—often mushrooms, sometimes pheasant—would come to the diner its heat held in by a glass dome with a knob handle, known as a bell.*

James suggested this for breakfast along with bacon strips, fresh coffee cake, and butter. He didn't say how many it would serve. I guess he thought it was up to you to know your guests. I would guess at four for breakfast, six as a first course, and many canapés; but Jim served more amply than I do. ✍

Sautéed Mushrooms on Toast
■■■■■■■■■■■■■■■■■■■■■■■■■

6 tablespoons unsalted butter
1½ pounds mushrooms (small caps)
1 teaspoon salt
½ teaspoon freshly ground black pepper
Dash Worcestershire sauce
Buttered toast, as needed
Chopped chives and parsley
Bacon

Melt butter in a heavy skillet, add the mushrooms, and sauté over medium heat. Stir and shake the pan from time to time. Cook until mushrooms are lightly browned and still crisp. Do not overcook. Add seasonings.

Serve on buttered toast with chopped herbs and crisp bacon.

Jim's early books are studded with references to and recipes by Jeanne Owen. The Broiled Oysters and Bacon comes from Hors d'Oeuvre and Canapés, *along with Jeanne's Anchovies.*

Jeanne Owen was French, despite her name. She was small, dynamic, and had been an actress. It's not clear how, other than being French, she got so involved with food, but she held imperious sway over the Wine and Food Society in New York for many years. At some point, Jim met her and they became very close friends. He much admired her knowledge and flair with tastings. He would often bring up a tasting that she had done of a plethora of hams. That was food after Jim's heart. He would recall with pleasure the rich scent of ham that pervaded the room. I think that this tasting may have set the tone for the tasting classes that Jim and I later taught, where many kinds of a basic ingredient would be tasted, discussed, and worked with.

Later both Jeanne's and Jim's formidable angers wreaked havoc with the relationship and they didn't talk for many years. Jim missed the friendship and was very relieved that they had made up a few years before her death. ✍

Jeanne Owen serves this delicious oyster hors d'oeuvre very often and the demand usually far exceeds the supply. Of course you'll need oyster forks and small plates. [*JB*]

Broiled Oysters and Bacon

For a dozen freshly opened oysters that are left on the half shell, you will need the following: Put three tablespoonfuls of Escoffier Sauce Diable in a small skillet with a minced and crushed garlic clove and three tablespoonfuls of chopped parsley. Heat this very slowly over a low flame.

On each oyster, place about one teaspoonful of pulverized crisp bacon, a small spoonful of the sauce, and a tiny strip of raw bacon. Place under the broiler till the bacon has cooked and the oysters are heated through. Serve at once.

Jeanne's Anchovies

For years this dish has been a great favorite with guests of Jeanne Owen. More than one person who had never liked anchovies has become a true devotee after trying them this way once.

Open a large-size can of anchovy fillets, drain the oil into a bowl, and place the fillets on a plate. Mix the oil with enough chopped parsley to make a thick paste. Add a chopped shallot or two according to taste and about a tablespoon of tarragon vinegar. Arrange the anchovies in an oblong dish and pour the sauce over them so that just a tip of each fillet shows. Serve with a fork and have plenty of Melba toast at hand for foundations. These are really a sensational dish and one everyone will like. [*JB*]

was the queen of the ladies' lunch both at Neiman-Marcus and at The Greenhouse Spa. She formulated recipes that were light but advanced for their time, like the Roquefort Mousse in Theory & Practice of Good Cooking. *There, it is filled with a seafood salad and served as a luncheon dish. I like it better on its own with celery or crackers as a first course. Raw vegetable strips can be put in the center of the ring. ✍*

This delicious mousse, which I have often used in my classes, was the inspiration of Helen Corbitt, Director of Restaurants of Neiman-Marcus in Dallas. [*JB*]

Roquefort Mousse

1 tablespoon vegetable oil
¼ cup freshly squeezed, strained lemon juice
1 envelope unflavored gelatin
1 cup boiling water
¼ pound Roquefort cheese, left at room
    temperature for about 1 hour
1 medium cucumber, peeled, seeded, and grated
    (about 1 cup)
4 tablespoons finely chopped parsley
2 tablespoons finely chopped pimiento
1 tablespoon finely chopped capers
1 teaspoon grated onion
1 teaspoon salt
½ teaspoon or more freshly ground black pepper
1 cup chilled heavy cream

Place a large mixing bowl (in which you will whip the heavy cream later) and balloon whisk in the freezer. Brush the inside base and sides of a 6-cup ring mold with the vegetable oil. Turn mold upside down and place on a piece of paper towel to allow any excess oil to drain off.

Place lemon juice in a small bowl and sprinkle gelatin over. Allow to stand for about a minute to soften the gelatin. Add boiling water and stir until gelatin is completely dissolved. Reserve.

Place cheese in a food processor, and process until smooth. Wrap grated cucumber in a dish towel and squeeze out all the water. Spread it out onto paper towels and pat dry of any excess water. Add to the cheese with chopped parsley,

pimiento, capers, onion, salt, and pepper. Process to combine. With the motor running, add the dissolved gelatin through the feed tube. Scrape down the sides of the work bowl and process for 1 minute longer.

Refrigerate the mixture for about 20 minutes, or until it has become slightly thickened.

Remove the bowl and whisk from the freezer. Pour in heavy cream. Whisk until it has almost doubled in volume and soft peaks form when whisk is lifted from the bowl.

Fold whisked cream into chilled mousse mixture gently with a rubber spatula. Without deflating the mixture too much, be sure to blend in the cream thoroughly.

Pour mixture into prepared mold and refrigerate for at least 4 hours, or until completely set firm.

To unmold the mousse, run the tip of a small sharp knife around the edges of the mousse to loosen the sides. Place serving platter on top and invert mousse out onto it. Shake slightly to release the mousse from the mold. If the mousse will still not come out, with the mold still inverted onto the plate, rub the top of the mold with a warm sponge.

Hors d'Oeuvre & Canapés

ROSE LEVY BERANBAUM *has become famous as the*
author of <u>The Cake Bible</u>. *She is a great baker, had a cooking school for quite a few years, and has written*
numerous articles. She continues with a book on chocolate and another on pastry. She is a student Jim could
well be proud of. 🖎

Twenty years ago my first job in the food profession was at Reynolds Metals Company, developing recipes for use with aluminum foil. My boss, Eleanor Lynch, decided that for inspiration, she would send me to a series of classes given by her friend James Beard.

It was my first cooking class and afterward, as I walked the five blocks between James Beard's house and mine, I felt as if I were flying. I will always remember that feeling. My life was changed.

One of the most memorable images of Jim was his demonstration of a soufflé. He made it look so easy to whisk egg whites—the large copper bowl perched securely against his portly belly as his powerful wrist rhythmically wielded the balloon whisk. But what astonished and impressed us all most was the unabashed use of his hand to fold the beaten egg whites into the base. This was the 1960s. People didn't come into such direct contact with food. But Jim told us it was right, it was good, in fact it was necessary to feel for little lumps of undissolved flour. So we did it, feeling a little strange and quite daring.

Using my fingers worked so well, in fact, that I decided to demonstrate the technique at Anna Mulfetto's Cordon Bleu Cooking School, where I had just become an assistant. Everyone was very impressed; the soufflé was delicious, and I was feeling a little smug at the success of my very first cooking demonstration when suddenly I discovered that my 18-carat-gold pinky ring was missing! The slippery egg whites and small joint of the little finger had evidently conspired in its disappearance. I knew it had to be somewhere in that soufflé. It was my last pinky ring but not my last soufflé addition.

I still have all the recipes I learned in those unforgettable four classes at the James Beard Cooking School. The one that strikes me as the best to represent the essence of Jim's unique spirit is Crêpes aux Duxelles. It is impressively elegant, yet at the same time hearty and generously fulfilling.

Jim taught us to chop the mushrooms using an enormous knife. The process took about 15 minutes. The food processor, of course, does a beautiful and speedy job.

Jim's Crêpes aux Duxelles

6 ounces (1½ sticks) unsalted butter
2 pounds mushrooms, wiped clean and chopped
  very fine
1 clove garlic, smashed, peeled, and crushed
½ teaspoon salt
Freshly ground black pepper to taste
7 Crêpes (recipe follows)
1 tablespoon melted unsalted butter, optional

Melt butter in a large heavy skillet (not cast-iron) over moderate heat. Stir in mushrooms, garlic, salt, and pepper. Reduce heat to low and cook for about 1 hour and 15 minutes, stirring occasionally. The liquid from the mushrooms should evaporate and the mushrooms will turn dark brown. This thick, dark mixture is *duxelles*. It may be prepared in advance, cooled, and stored in a tightly covered container, refrigerated, for up to one week, or frozen for up to one month.

Preheat oven to 350° F.

Place one crêpe on a baking sheet and spread evenly with one sixth of the duxelles. Repeat layering, ending with a crêpe on top. Either brush top crêpe with melted butter or cover with aluminum foil to prevent drying.

Bake in the center of the oven for about 7 minutes, or until heated through. Remove from oven and transfer to a serving platter. Cut into 8 wedges and garnish with additional mushroom slices if desired. ✘ *Serves 8*

Jim's Basic Crêpes

3 large eggs
1¼ cups milk
2 tablespoons butter, melted
1 cup unsifted all-purpose flour
⅛ teaspoon salt
1 tablespoon clarified butter

Place all ingredients except clarified butter in a blender and process until thoroughly mixed and smooth, stopping the motor occasionally and scraping down the sides of the container with a rubber spatula. Let batter rest for 2 hours at room temperature, or cover and refrigerate overnight before using.

When ready to make crêpes, heat a 7½-inch crêpe pan over moderate to high heat until hot enough to sizzle a drop of water. Brush pan lightly with the clarified butter. Pour a scant 2 tablespoons of the batter into center of the pan, immediately tilt the pan to the left and then down and around to the right so that the batter moves in a counterclockwise direction, covering the entire pan.

Cook crêpe until the top starts to dull and the edges begin to brown (about 20 seconds, depending on the heat of the pan). Use a small metal spatula to lift the edge and see if the crêpe is golden brown. Then, grasping the edge of the crêpe with your fingers, flip it over and cook for 10 to 20 seconds, or just until lightly browned. Slide the crêpe out on to wax paper. Cover with another piece of wax paper and continue making and layering the crêpes between the paper.

The extra crêpes can be covered tightly with plastic wrap and stored in the refrigerator or freezer. ✘ *Makes about 18 7½-inch crêpes*

Florence and Sam Aaron were friends of Jim's for many, many years. Sam's older brother, Jack, owned one of New York's preeminent wine and liquor stores, Sherry's, which today is Sherry-Lehmann. He was a supporter of Jim's in the late forties after Jim returned from the war jobless. First, Jim worked selling wine—who could resist? Then Jack decided that it was time for Jim to go to France and learn about the wine trade. He lived in Paris, traveled, and became good friends with both Frank Schoonmaker—the ex-correspondent who, in his time, wrote some of America's most important wine books—and Alexis Lichine—négociant, vineyard owner, and wine writer. Later, Beard was to travel with them to California and get in on the rebirth of the California wine industry.

Sam Aaron had also been away at war. When he came back, he gave up his work in clinical psychology and went into the wine business. Over the years, he came to know James very well and even wrote the wine section of an updated edition of one of Jim's books with him, <u>How to Eat Better for Less Money</u>. It was edited by José Wilson, who became a friend of James's while she was an editor at <u>House & Garden</u>; she later worked with Dione Lucas and then she came to work with Jim on his cooking school and some of his writing.

She was an Englishwoman with a peppery character and great loyalty and knowledge, who unfortunately loved a drink a little too well. When José died, Jim wrote a very moving piece about her instead of his usual column. He said, "For several seasons José directed and taught in my cooking school. Together we created the book that I think best represents me and is most faithful to my current views on food, <u>James Beard's Theory & Practice of Good Cooking</u>. Previously we had published our book based on these columns, <u>Beard on Food</u>. . . . She gave me friendship such as one seldom finds in a lifetime. Her presence affected the course of my life." How sad that the years had made them slightly remote. This is certainly the warmest tribute James ever gave.

Florence Aaron, Sam's wife, is one of the great ladies, and she and Sam took one of Jim's early classes given at the then brand-new Lutèce in New York. Jim taught there along with André Surmain, at that time the owner of Lutèce and today the owner of an excellent restaurant in Mougins in the hills above the Riviera.

Florence says of this recipe, "This is actually a variation on a Paula Peck recipe. She was Jim's star pupil."

Paula Peck later became a fine cookery writer on her own and her book, on baking, is still a classic. It was one that Jim referred to often. ✍

Marinated Hard-Cooked Eggs and Nova Scotia with Onion Rings

■■■■■■■■■■■■■■■■■■■■■■■■■■

10 hard-cooked eggs, peeled and cooled

12 ounces sliced Nova Scotia salmon, cut into
    1-inch squares

1 medium red onion (about 4 ounces), peeled and
    cut into very thin rings

⅓ cup olive oil

⅓ cup white wine vinegar

Salt and freshly ground black pepper to taste

¼ cup chopped fresh dill

Cut eggs across into ¼-inch thick slices and arrange in a single layer on a 12- to 14-inch oval platter. Arrange pieces of salmon over eggs and scatter slices of onion on top.

In a small bowl whisk together oil, vinegar, salt, and pepper. Pour over ingredients on platter. Cover with plastic wrap and refrigerate for at least 2 hours.

Remove from refrigerator, and uncover. Before serving, sprinkle with chopped dill.

✖ *Serves 6 as a first course*

MARCELLA HAZAN. *It took Jim a while to adopt new people; but he was more flexible about this than most people his age. He taught me the great lesson that one of the secrets of happiness as one gets older is to keep including younger people in one's circle. There were always younger people around Jim. I think they were so comfortable because age per se meant very little to Jim—his own or anyone else's.*

He could put you to the test when he met you, though. My first meeting with Jim was almost a disaster and my last. I had been brought in by Burt Wolf to take over the Cook's Catalogue *project. José Wilson had started editing it, but it wasn't going along terribly well. I didn't know it at the time, but this proposed change in editors threatened Jim's basic loyalties. All five foot two inches of me was shaking and was virtually propelled downtown by Burt. We went into the house on 12th Street—this was in the days before Jim put in the circular staircase that later connected the office and the living area above, and Jim, or visitors if admitted to the upstairs, had to go out into the hall that served all the apartments and go up the common stairs.*

Uncomfortable with the idea of being looked over for possible approval or rejection, I suppose I began to chatter and show off. We were talking about fats for pâtés. We began to disagree about the uses of kidney fat—a disagreement we kept as long as we cooked. Abruptly, Jim rose to his feet apoplectic—literally purple—with rage and trod heavily out of the office and halfway up the stairs while flinging over his shoulder, "I cannot work with this woman." Burt and I stayed in our places transfixed by shock. Gradually, we got our coats, if not our nerves, back and went toward the hall, only to hear the steps stop about halfway up the stairs. Very slowly, Jim came back to where we stood on the landing. He stuck out his enormous hand and apologized, saying that he guessed he was having a bad day.

From that time forward, we became good friends—even if we didn't always agree.

Marcella and Victor Hazan suffered none of these trials. As soon as he saw Marcella's first book, Classic Italian Cooking, *James adopted her as his Italian expert and forever afterward looked a little suspiciously at the work of other writers on Italian cooking. As he saw it, her work was authoritative, but direct and relatively simple. It didn't complicate matters needlessly. People would cook the foods. Since these were the hallmarks of his own writing, it followed that he liked these qualities in Marcella's work.* ✍

Jim Beard was my own living food encyclopedia. Whenever I was at a loss for the English equivalent of some ingredient or technique, whenever I came across a food reference that baffled me, for which I had found no explanation in print, or which I may have been too lazy to track down, I telephoned Jim. He could unfailingly tell me what I needed to know. Sometimes I called him even when I was reasonably certain I had discovered the answer, simply to be reassured by his sonorous explanations which, on fortunate occasions, might be strung out with episodes from his unrivaled cooking and eating life. To these last I listened as raptly as children listen to fairy tales.

Sometimes, however, it was Jim who called me. One of these calls I remember particularly well. He had been immobilized by bad circulation in his legs and he had been passing time looking through a stack of Italian food magazines. "Marcella?" It was a wailful, querulous voice he had when he was exasperated by the contrariness of nature and events. "I am looking at a recipe with an ingredient I have never heard of. And it isn't even in the dictionary! What in the world is *rubra?*" "*Rubra?*" I giggled, "*Rubra* is ketchup." It must have struck him as the funniest thing he'd heard in days. His mood suddenly changed and he exploded into laughter he made no effort to cut short, "Ho ho ho, ho ho ho," thunderclap after thunderclap of *basso profundo,* gargantuan laughter.

This recipe was for a cocktail sauce to use with shrimp that had become extremely popular in Italian restaurants in the '70s, a popularity it has held on to. Because of its lovely pale pink color, it is sometimes called *salsa aurora*.

This is enough sauce for 1 pound of boiled and peeled shrimp, which is 4 to 5 portions.

Shrimp with Salsa Aurora

1 egg yolk, at room temperature
Salt to taste
½ cup extra virgin olive oil
1 tablespoon fresh lemon juice
1 teaspoon Cognac
⅛ teaspoon hot red pepper flakes
1 tablespoon tomato ketchup
1 tablespoon chopped fresh chives

Whisk egg yolk and salt together in a small mixing bowl until it becomes light in color and foamy. While whisking, add oil in a thin stream.

When all of the oil is fully incorporated, whisk in lemon juice. With a spatula fold in remaining ingredients.

To serve, place the cooked, shelled shrimp in a bowl with two thirds of the sauce; gently toss together to coat the shrimp thoroughly. Divide the shrimp into 4 or 5 serving cups. Top with the remaining sauce. ✗ *Makes ¾ cup*

BILL WILKINSON. *For many of the years that Jim lived for part of the year as Jimmy Nassikas's guest at the Stanford Court hotel, Bill Wilkinson was Nassikas's able right hand. When Bill left to start the Campton Place, also in San Francisco, he and James remained friendly. In the Stanford Court days, it was with Bill that Jim and I often made nighttime raids on the kitchen to assemble ingredients for the kind of cold salad that Jim loved, with bay shrimp and avocado and bacon or whatever looked appealing. He would surely have liked this unusually seasoned cured salmon.* ✍

When I think of James, I think of the most simple foods. I really believe the simplest things gave him the greatest pleasure.

Years ago at Stanford Court we had some wonderful roasts on the menu at Fournou's. We had a beef loin with a Périgourdine sauce, we had a roast duckling with a kumquat sauce. Jim much preferred his duck grilled plain. . . . He loved the heels of our very crusty sourdough bread.

The items which I like tend to be the same idea, mostly simple, a cured salmon, grilled lamb, a good fruit pie, basic bread.

Cinnamon-Sage–Cured Salmon

2 ounces cinnamon sticks (about 14 sticks)

1½ ounces white peppercorns (½ cup)

¾ head garlic, cloves smashed and peeled

5 ounces kosher salt

4 ounces granulated sugar

3 ounces light brown sugar

1 small bunch of fresh sage

1 3½- to 4-pound salmon fillet with skin (side of salmon from a 9-pound fish)

Cheesecloth

☐ *Vinaigrette*

1 large shallot, peeled and finely chopped

½ bunch parsley, preferably Italian, stemmed and finely chopped

¼ cup fresh lemon juice

¼ cup Champagne vinegar

1 cup virgin olive oil

1 cup mild olive oil

Kosher salt to taste

Freshly ground black pepper to taste

□ *Garnish for 6 servings*

1 English cucumber, washed and thinly sliced

6 to 10 assorted radishes, washed and thinly sliced

1 bunch watercress or peppercress, washed

Break cinnamon into small pieces. Place in a large spice grinder or blender along with white peppercorns and grind. This may need to be done in batches. Place garlic in a food processor and process until finely chopped. Add ground cinnamon and peppercorns, salt, sugars, and sage and process until well combined.

Remove all pin bones from fish with your fingers or a needle-nosed plier.

Choose a large baking dish for curing the fish and place a rack inside dish to allow liquid from fish to drain off.

Place a large piece of cheesecloth on rack. Spread half of the cure on the cheesecloth. Lay fillet over, skin-side down, on cure. Spread remaining cure over top of fish. Cover with plastic wrap and refrigerate, weighted, for 10 to 12 hours, or longer.

Whisk together vinaigrette ingredients.

When ready to serve, unwrap salmon and scrape off all of the cure. Slice salmon on the diagonal into ⅛-inch-thick slices, making pieces as large as possible. Arrange in the center of a plate or platter and place vegetables around, or arrange salmon and garnish on individual serving plates. If placing on a platter, serve sauce separately. If plating, spoon 3 tablespoons vinaigrette over each portion and serve. ✖ *Serves 20*

One charm of food people is that they always have something to eat. Jim Beard could be relied upon for a substantial snack at any hour, declaring with a belly laugh that his own generous bulk must be properly maintained. I well remember a buxom cheese brioche, which he was testing for *Beard on Bread*. We demolished practically the whole loaf along with a bottle of wine as Jim recounted stories about New York foodies, then fixed me with his beady gaze awaiting my contribution.

Not to be outdone, when he visited us in Washington I whipped up my favorite little cheese soufflés. They take only about ten minutes to bake.

Little Cheese Soufflés with Marinated Shrimp

⅓ cup unsalted butter
¼ cup flour
1½ cups milk
Salt to taste
Freshly ground black pepper to taste
Pinch freshly grated nutmeg
5 eggs, separated
1 cup grated Gruyère cheese
½ cup cooked, peeled baby shrimp
1 tablespoon Pernod or other anise liqueur
3 egg whites
8 ramekins (each 1 cup capacity)

Make the soufflé base: Melt the butter in a medium saucepan. Whisk in flour and cook until foaming. Whisk in milk and bring to a boil, stirring constantly, until the sauce thickens. Season with salt, pepper, and nutmeg and simmer for 2 minutes.

Remove from heat. Whisk egg yolks into hot sauce so they cook and thicken slightly. Stir in cheese, reserving 1 tablespoon for the top of the soufflés. Taste for seasoning; the mixture should be highly seasoned. Rub a piece of butter on top to prevent a skin from forming. Mixture can be kept at room temperature for up to 6 hours.

Preheat oven to 425° F. Generously butter ramekins. Mix shrimp with Pernod and spread in bottom of ramekins, dividing shrimp evenly among the ramekins. Place cheese mixture over low heat to warm. Add a pinch of salt to the egg whites and beat until stiff peaks form. Fold a quarter of the egg whites into the cheese mixture to lighten it and fold back into the egg whites. Spoon into prepared ramekins. Sprinkle reserved cheese on top of each. Soufflés can be refrigerated at this point for up to 1 hour.

Bake in preheated oven until puffed and brown, about 10 to 12 minutes. Serve at once.

✖ *Serves 8*

assistants, and he writes about the relationship on page 109. Jim always felt that Felipe could make food look more beautiful and enticing than anyone else Jim knew. Felipe does that nightly on his tapas bar at his restaurant in New York, The Ballroom, which often includes the dishes that follow. While he makes about thirty tapas nightly, you could have quite a satisfactory party with just these three. ✍

This classical dish, which is quite popular throughout Spain, is made not only with potatoes, but also with a variety of other vegetables. The most delicious tortillas are the ones made exclusively with potatoes, as in this recipe; they are also referred to as *tortillas de papas*.

When selecting potatoes for this tortilla, the best to use are the simple and common all-purpose potatoes. Baking potatoes, although they are tasty and can be used, have a tendency to fall apart during cooking. What you are looking for in a tortilla, besides good flavor, is texture, produced by thinly sliced potatoes still holding their shape.

Freshly made tortillas are heavenly and make great appetizers or side dishes. They are a colorful and a wonderfully tasty addition to a buffet table. They keep well, tightly covered, in the refrigerator for about one week.

Tortilla Española

■■■■■■■■■■■■■■■■■■■■■■■■■■■

3½ pounds all-purpose potatoes
½ cup plus 1 tablespoon olive oil
1 tablespoon coarse salt
1 large onion, peeled and thinly sliced (about 2 cups)
8 large eggs

Peel, quarter, and thinly slice the potatoes.

Heat ½ cup of the oil in a 12-inch skillet over moderate heat. Add the potato slices and toss to coat evenly with the oil. Cook, covered with a lid, stirring occasionally, for 10 to 15 minutes or until the potatoes are semi-cooked.

Stir in salt and onion slices, cover, and cook until the onions are soft and the potatoes are fully cooked but not collapsing.

Remove skillet from heat and transfer potato and onion mixture to a bowl. Allow to cool.

In a separate bowl, beat the eggs. Add to the cooled potatoes and mix together thoroughly.

Heat remaining oil in a 10½-inch skillet over moderate heat until the oil coats the base and sides of the skillet and is almost to the point of smoking. Pour in the potato and egg mixture and allow it to set over high heat for 1 to 2 minutes.

Reduce the heat to low and cook for about 15 minutes or until the tortilla is set enough to turn.

Place a large pot cover or large plate over the skillet and carefully flip the tortilla over on to it. Slide the tortilla back into the skillet and cook over very low heat for about 15 minutes or until set. To see if the tortilla is properly cooked, press your fingertips over the top. It should feel firm.

Place serving dish over the skillet and gently flip the tortilla onto it. Serve hot or at room temperature. ✖ *Serves 6 to 8*

Red kidney beans are ideal for this luscious dish. *Caracoles* is the Spanish term for snails; the kidney beans not only complement the texture of the caracoles but also bring out their subtle, meaty flavor beautifully. Besides kidney beans, other types such as pinto or black beans are quite suitable.

When selecting snails for this recipe, choose snails that are whole, firm, and especially of a handsome size. It is a good idea to rinse them under cold running water before using them; this process will take out the unpleasant briny taste.

This dish can be served as a tapa along with a glass of chilled dry sherry, or as an appetizer. It also makes a great item for lunch served over lettuce leaves and accompanied by warm crusty French bread and a good glass of wine.

Caracoles and Red Beans

½ pound (1⅓ cups) dry red kidney beans, or
    2½ cups canned red kidney beans, drained
1 tablespoon plus 1 teaspoon kosher salt
1 7-ounce can snails, rinsed and well drained
4 tablespoons olive oil
1 small clove garlic, smashed, peeled, and finely
    chopped
½ medium onion, peeled and finely chopped
    (1 cup)
2 tablespoons dry white wine
Pinch ground cloves
½ teaspoon paprika
Pinch cayenne pepper
1½ tablespoons flour
1¼ cups Beef Stock (page 111), or canned beef
    broth
1 tablespoon balsamic vinegar
¼ cup chopped parsley (preferably Italian)

If using dry beans, soak overnight in a pot large enough to hold the beans and 3 quarts of cold water. Place the pot with the beans, soaking liquid, and 1 tablespoon of the salt over high heat. Bring to the boil, lower heat, and simmer for 30 to 40 minutes or until beans are tender but not falling apart. Drain in a colander and reserve.

Place 3 tablespoons of the oil in a skillet over medium heat. Add the garlic and onion and sauté until the onion is translucent. Add the wine and cook until liquid has evaporated. Add the cloves, paprika, cayenne, and flour. Stir well and stir in stock. Stir with a whisk until smooth. Bring to a boil over medium heat, stirring often. Turn heat down and simmer for 10 minutes, stirring occasionally. Add snails and cook over low heat for 20 to 30 minutes, stirring occasionally. Remove from heat and let cool.

In a serving bowl, combine drained beans and snails. Add the remaining oil, vinegar, and chopped parsley. Correct seasoning with remaining salt if necessary. Toss gently and serve.
✖ *Serves 4*

oasted vegetables are extremely tasty—especially eggplants. The roasting process brings out the best of these vegetables; it emphasizes their bouquet and gives them a marvelous smoky flavor, which makes them irresistible.

This way of roasting and serving eggplants is very common throughout the Iberian Peninsula. As a matter of fact, a popular Catalonian dish called *escalivida* is no more than plainly roasted and peeled eggplants, as in the recipe below, served sprinkled with olive oil and garnished with a few whole anchovy fillets.

What makes this Moroccan eggplant so interestingly delicious is not only the roasting of the eggplant but also the sauce of Moorish origin. Fresh coriander leaves, or *cilantro* in Spanish, make this aromatic sauce unique in taste and bouquet. The sauce and the eggplant make an exquisite marriage. A good substitute for the cilantro sauce is a basil sauce, pesto.

Moroccan Eggplant

■■■■■■■■■■■■■■■■■■■■■■■■■■■■

3 eggplants (about 1 pound each)
½ cup plus 2 tablespoons olive oil
2 cloves garlic, smashed and peeled
½-inch-long piece fresh ginger, peeled and cut into chunks
1 fresh jalapeño pepper, seeded and cut into chunks
2 teaspoons ground cumin
7 cups tightly packed fresh coriander leaves, rinsed, drained, and patted dry
2 tablespoons fresh lemon juice
1 tablespoon kosher salt
2 lemons, thinly sliced, for garnish
Sprigs of fresh coriander for garnish

Preheat oven to 450° F.

Prick the skin of each eggplant several times with a fork. Rub the eggplants with 1 tablespoon of the oil and place them on a rack set on a shallow baking sheet. Roast for about 1 hour, or until they are soft. Remove from oven and set aside to cool.

Place ¼ cup of the oil in a food processor along with the garlic, ginger, jalapeño pepper, and cumin. Process until smooth. With machine running, add 4 cups of the coriander through the feed tube, one cup at a time. Add lemon juice, salt, and another ¼ cup of the oil. Scrape down sides of processor bowl and add remaining coriander. Process until smooth. Correct seasoning and scrape into a serving bowl.

Preheat the broiler.

When eggplants are cool, peel with a paring knife; start from the stem and peel skin downward, leaving the stem attached. Slice each lengthwise into thirds, keeping the stem ends intact. Fan out the eggplants and, using a teaspoon, carefully remove most of the seeds. Place the fanned-out eggplants on a baking sheet and broil until the slices are golden and slightly charred around the edges. Brush with remaining tablespoon of oil and serve with sauce.

✘ *Serves 6 to 8*

Jim never stopped being intrigued by new culinary talents. It must be clear by now that he didn't condescend to women in any way. In fact, he admired them and was one of the first champions of new women chefs, not because they were women, but because he found their presence in professional kitchens normal. His mother had clearly taught him something.

One of the young women chefs he admired was Leslie Revsin. When she was the chef at One Fifth Avenue, she also had the virtue of being in the neighborhood. Jim went there often and wrote about her in his column. This recipe of hers could be used at home at cocktail parties as a passed hors d'oeuvre. Chickpea flour is available in Near Eastern and Indian stores. ✍

Spicy Potato Fritters with Two Sauces

¼ cup chick-pea flour
¼ teaspoon baking soda
5 tablespoons cold water
¾ cup thinly sliced onion
½ cup finely chopped, peeled raw potato
3 tablespoons chopped fresh cilantro
½ teaspoon ground roasted cumin seed
½ teaspoon cayenne pepper
½ teaspoon ground turmeric
½ teaspoon salt
Vegetable oil for frying
Avocado Sauce (recipe follows)
Yogurt-Mint Sauce (recipe follows)

In a medium bowl, blend the chick-pea flour, baking soda, and water. Set this batter aside.

In another medium bowl, combine the onion, potato, cilantro, and ground cumin seed. In a small dish, stir together the cayenne pepper, turmeric, and salt; sprinkle this over the onion mixture and toss to coat it evenly with the spices.

Add the onion mixture to the reserved chick-pea batter and stir to coat the vegetables thoroughly.

Pour enough vegetable oil into a large heavy skillet to cover the bottom well. Put the skillet over high heat. When the oil is hot, push teaspoonful-sized dollops of the fritter mixture into the oil. Fry the fritters on all sides until they are a deep golden brown and cooked through. (Test them occasionally with a toothpick to see if they are cooked in the center; if the toothpick comes out wet, fry for a little longer.) Add a little more oil to the skillet if it is needed, and reduce the heat if the fritters are frying too quickly.

Remove the cooked fritters with a slotted spoon to drain on paper toweling. Serve with Avocado Sauce and Yogurt-Mint Sauce, passed separately. ✘ *24 small or 12 large fritters*

Avocado Sauce

1 ripe avocado (about 8 ounces), preferably Haas
3 tablespoons plain yogurt
¼ teaspoon roasted ground cumin seed
4 teaspoons fresh lime juice
½ teaspoon salt, or to taste

Place all of the ingredients in the work bowl of a food processor. Process to a very smooth mixture.

Taste the sauce for seasoning and add more salt if necessary. Serve the sauce very cold. ✘ *Makes 1 cup*

Yogurt-Mint Sauce

1½ tablespoons chopped fresh mint (from about ½ of a large bunch, about ¼ cup tightly packed leaves)
1½ tablespoons minced onion
½ teaspoon peeled and chopped roasted jalapeño pepper (1 medium jalapeño)
½ cup plain yogurt
Pinch cayenne pepper, or to taste
⅛ teaspoon salt, or to taste

In a small bowl, combine all the ingredients and stir until they are well blended. Adjust the seasoning if necessary. Serve the sauce very cold. ✘ *Makes ⅔ cup*

LONI KUHN. *Although Jim made his home in New York, he always returned to the West Coast—the beaches in Washington and San Francisco—and flirted with the idea of someday going back there to live.*

He had many San Francisco friends from a myriad of groups. He was close to Denise Hale and to the old-guard San Francisco socialites as well as to a number of ex-movie people who had settled down in San Francisco. He was involved with the numerous San Francisco restaurants, the shops (there were classes to provision), and the cooking teachers. One of his favorite teachers, and a warm supporter, was Loni Kuhn. To show how the Jim-fallout works, recently I was in San Francisco doing a television program that had a live audience. Whom should I see in the audience but Loni with her friends, come to cheer me on. The dividends of warmth and friendship continue. ✍

Green Mango Appetizer

2 large green mangoes
1 cup cold water
2 cloves garlic, smashed, peeled, and minced
½ teaspoon salt
Freshly ground black pepper to taste
1 to 2 jalapeño peppers, stemmed, seeded, and
    minced
⅓ cup fresh lime juice

Peel mangoes, remove pits, and cut into bite-size pieces. Place in a medium bowl and mix with remaining ingredients.

Allow to marinate for about 30 minutes, but not any longer or the mangoes will start to fall apart. Serve skewered with toothpicks. ✖ *Serves 4*

Before there was a James Beard Foundation, there was a moving moment at an International Association of Cooking Professionals meeting. Julia Child was speaking—it was shortly after Jim Beard's death—and, visibly moved, she declared that his house should be preserved as a center for American cooking. A young cooking teacher who had never met Jim was sitting in the audience and she responded deeply to the message. She enlisted her husband, Bernard. Together, with both money and work, Kathleen and Bernard Perry have been as responsible for the possibilities of the James Beard Foundation as anyone. ✍️

My professional career as "the everyday gourmet" has centered on bringing simplified and affordable cooking techniques and menus to the American public. My work has relied heavily on the awareness of, and interest in, American and European cuisine pioneered in this country by Jim Beard and Julia Child. The contributions of these two formidable personalities in popularizing cooking in kitchens throughout America with print, video, and television presentations certainly has made the efforts of all of us now pursuing such a career easier and more successful.

For these reasons, and because it just seemed to be the right thing to do, I answered Julia's call four years ago to help preserve the Beard property and his memory. I have been happy to join the legion of dedicated lay and professional people she has mobilized to help make the Foundation what it is today.

A slice of this elegant vegetable terrine is stunning on a dinner plate. But it's easily made in a loaf pan with a simple batter and layers of colorful everyday vegetables. Serve it with Hollandaise Sauce or a cheddar cheese sauce or just with a pat of butter.

The terrine can be made a day or two ahead and refrigerated. To serve, cut the loaf into 1-inch slices and place on a baking sheet. Cover loosely with buttered wax paper or aluminum foil and place in a preheated 350° F. oven for 8 to 10 minutes, until hot.

Vegetable Terrine

3 eggs
1 cup milk
½ cup flour
2 teaspoons salt
2 tablespoons butter
2 tablespoons chopped onion
2 10-ounce packages frozen chopped spinach, defrosted and all water squeezed out
12 ounces whole carrots, peeled and trimmed
12 ounces cauliflower, cored and separated into medium-size florets
Butter for greasing loaf pan and foil

Preheat oven to 400° F.

In a blender or food processor, combine eggs, milk, flour, and salt and process until smooth. Reserve.

Melt butter in a medium skillet over moderate heat. Add onion and cook, stirring, until softened. Remove from heat, and stir in spinach and about a third of the reserved batter. Reserve.

Bring a medium pan of water to a boil and cook whole carrots for about 6 minutes, depending on their thickness, until tender but still crisp. With a slotted spoon, remove to a plate and allow to cool. Add cauliflower florets to the water and cook for about 3 minutes. Remove with a slotted spoon and allow to cool slightly.

Butter a 2-quart loaf pan, then butter a piece of aluminum foil large enough to line it with a slight overhang. Line the pan with the foil, fitting it into the corners and allowing it to hang over the edges.

Place half the cauliflower in the base of the pan and pour over half of the remaining batter.

Next, spread half of spinach mixture over the cauliflower in an even layer. Lay the carrots next to each other lengthwise in the pan. Spread the remaining spinach over the carrots, then the remaining cauliflower, and press down gently. Pour over the remaining batter.

Butter a piece of aluminum foil large enough to cover the pan. Place over the vegetables, seal with the overhanging foil, and gently press down the foil.

Place pan in a larger roasting pan and place in oven. Pour enough boiling water into the larger pan so that it reaches about halfway up the sides of the loaf pan. Bake for 1 hour.

Remove from the oven and remove loaf pan from the water. Allow to cool for at least an hour. Remove foil from the top and invert on to a plate. Carefully peel off the foil and cut across into 1-inch slices. ✖ *Serves 6 to 8*

DIANA KENNEDY. *Even though James remained fiercely loyal to his friends, he could from time to time appreciate the work of a newcomer in what he considered a friend's field. Although he had long been a supporter of Elizabeth Lambert Ortiz—one of his collection of Englishwomen food-friends—when the work of Diana Kennedy began to appear, he immediately recognized the extraordinary virtues of yet another English food authority. She has graciously shared this recipe from* The Art of Mexican Cooking, *which James so liked.* ✍

I barely knew Jim except for his writings, when he, Danny Kaye, Jacques Pépin, and I were all gathered in San Diego for a cancer benefit. Somehow it happened that I was to cook dinner for everyone.

I can't now remember the details of the menu, but I know we started with a *botana* [snack] of guacamole and corn tortillas. Peter [Kump] told me sometime later that Jim, when asked about the dinner, simply said it was one of the finest Mexican meals of his life and added, "I *thought* I had eaten guacamole before." That was praise indeed.

The word *guacamole* derives from the Nahuatl words *ahuacatl* ("avocado") and *molli* ("mixture" or "concoction").

Guacamole is best eaten as a *botana* of tacos with freshly made corn tortillas, and how good it is will depend very much on the quality of the avocados. Even if you leave the pit sitting in it or add lime juice—which spoils the balance of flavors—it will not keep for long, so make it at the last moment. Bring out your *molcajete* and make a show in front of your guests as they brilliantly do in Rosa Mexicano in New York. If you don't have one, resort to the blender for the base only and mash the avocados with a wooden spoon or, as they did in the old days, with your hands. It should be lumpy, not smooth.

Guacamole

3 tablespoons finely chopped onion
4 serrano chilies, finely chopped
2 rounded tablespoons finely chopped cilantro
Sea salt to taste
3 large avocados (a little more than 1½ pounds)
⅔ cup finely chopped unpeeled tomato

☐ *The Topping*
2 tablespoons finely chopped onion
1 heaped tablespoon finely chopped cilantro
2 tablespoons finely chopped tomato

If possible, use a *molcajete*. Grind the fresh chilies, cilantro, and salt to a rough paste.

Cut the avocados in half, remove pits (do not discard), and scoop out the flesh with a wooden spoon. Mash the flesh roughly into the base, turning the mixture over so that the seasoning is well distributed. Stir in the chopped tomato and sprinkle the top of the guacamole with the extra onion, cilantro, and tomato.

Place the pits back into it for a nice effect and serve immediately, or within 15 minutes, in the *molcajete*. If you are using a blender, blend the base, turn it into a dish and continue as above.
✖ *Makes 2 cups*

It is easy to tell from the memory of Abby Mandel, a fine Chicago cooking teacher and writer of books and articles on food-processor cooking, how James pressed friends and acquaintances into service on the task at hand. The remarkable thing is that they all seem to remember the hysteria with affection. ✍

When I last saw Neil O'Donnell (from Corning Glass Works), we began to reminisce hilariously about the cooking mayhem that developed on the stage during Jim's cooking demonstration back in 1975 at the Pick Congress Hotel in Chicago. Neil and I ended up having a wild time, helping frantically with the preparations at the back of the stage, coaxing many ingredients in water to come to a rolling boil for Jim's Bollito Misto, in an old, battered, round-bottomed hotel stockpot.

In the middle of this, Carl Jerome was ignoring all the chaos and calmly assisting Jim up front in his wonderfully relaxed demonstration. That day, Jim made a simple pizza with rosemary, garlic, and oil, and it made a lasting impact then. I had long loved eating pizza, still one of my favorite foods. Jim, always ahead of the times, is the one who introduced me to the pleasures of making them! This simple, clean-flavored grilled pizza has been the source of much enjoyment in my kitchen.

Grilled Tomato and Cheese Pizza with Fresh Herbs

□ *Herbed Oil*
5 large fresh basil leaves
3 fresh sage leaves
2 tablespoon fresh oregano leaves
1 medium garlic clove
¼ cup olive oil
¼ teaspoon salt

□ *Topping*
1 medium tomato (about 7 ounces)
1 small onion (about 2 ounces)
4 ounces Mozzarella cheese, thinly sliced
1 ounce grated Parmesan cheese, preferably imported
Fresh basil leaves for garnish
Two 8-inch circles Pizza Dough (recipe follows; freeze remainder for later use)

To make the herbed oil: Mince the herbs and garlic in a food processor or by hand. Mix with the oil and the salt. The oil can be made a day in advance and refrigerated.

For the topping: Remove the seeds and all membrane from the tomato and cut the outer shell into ¼-inch dice. Toss with 2 teaspoons of the herbed oil and reserve. Cut the onion into paper-thin slices.

For the pizzas: Grill the rolled-out dough over a hot wood fire, with the cover on, until they are browned on the underside. Remove from the grill and put them on a piece of foil with the grilled sides facing up.

Stir the herbed oil and spoon 1 tablespoon onto each round of dough; then brush it evenly over the surface. Arrange one half of remaining ingredients over each crust in this order: onions, mozzarella, tomatoes, and Parmesan.

Return to the grill, cover, and cook just

Hors d'Oeuvre & Canapés

until bottoms are browned and cheese is melted.
Dab tops and edges lightly with herbed oil and
snip fresh basil over the tops. Serve immediately.
✗ *Makes 2 8-inch pizzas*

Pizza Dough

1 package active dry yeast
1 teaspoon granulated sugar
1 cup warm water (105° to 115° F.)
3 to 3¼ cups all-purpose flour
2 tablespoons olive oil
1 teaspoon salt

Stir the yeast and sugar into the water and
let stand until foamy, about 5 minutes.

Put 3 cups of the flour, oil, and salt in the
work bowl of a food processor and turn the
machine on. Pour the yeast mixture through the
feed tube and process until the dough is still moist
but cleans the sides of the work bowl. If it is too
sticky, add more flour, by the tablespoon,
processing each addition before adding more. If it
is too dry, add more water, by the teaspoon,
processing each addition before adding more.
Once the consistency is right, process dough until
it is supple and elastic, about 40 seconds.

Transfer dough to a large plastic food bag,
squeeze out air, and seal at the top. Let rise in a
warm spot until it has doubled, about 1 hour.
Dough can be used immediately or refrigerated
for up to 5 days. To refrigerate, open the bag and
punch the dough down. Reseal the bag and
refrigerate.

Divide the dough into 5 equal portions. Roll
each piece on a floured board to an 8-inch circle.
Stack between oiled sheets of waxed paper. Dough
can be rolled in advance and refrigerated
overnight or frozen. Bake as directed in recipe
above. ✗ *Makes 5 8-inch pizzas*

ELIZABETH CLARK. *Born on an Iowa farm between the Des Moines and Mississippi rivers, Liz Clark settled down after school and archeological travel to teach, first in Davenport and then in Keokuk. In 1971, she got deeply involved with her three loves: an 1852 house on a bluff above the Mississippi, cooking, and travel. She opened a restaurant in the house as well as a cooking school and took classes in France and Bangkok. She also did a benefit for the Foundation, and this was one of the recipes she used.* ✍

Snail-Stuffed Cherry Tomatoes with Basil Cream Sauce

48 large cherry tomatoes
Salt
4 tablespoons unsalted butter
2 medium shallots, peeled and minced (about ⅓ cup)
2 tablespoons brandy
1 cup heavy cream
¾ cup packed fresh basil leaves (reserve 24 large, perfect leaves for serving; shred remaining leaves)
1 can California *petit-gris* snails (36 snails), drained, rinsed, and coarsely chopped
1 teaspoon tarragon wine vinegar
Freshly ground black pepper

Cut off and discard the top of each tomato. Using a grapefruit knife, hollow out the tomatoes and cut a tiny slice from the bottom of each one so that it will sit upright. Sprinkle the insides of the tomatoes with salt and place them upside down on paper toweling to drain for 30 minutes. Shred all basil but 24 reserved leaves.

In a heavy enameled saucepan, melt the butter over medium heat. Add the shallots and sauté until they are transparent; do not let them brown. Stir in the brandy and cream, bring the mixture to a boil, and reduce the mixture until it is thick enough to coat the back of a spoon. Stir in the shredded basil, snails, and vinegar, and remove the saucepan from the heat. Season to taste with salt and pepper.

In a steaming basket set over simmering water, steam the reserved whole basil leaves for 1 minute. Immediately refresh them under cold running water and blot them dry with paper toweling. Arrange 4 leaves, spoke-fashion, on each of 6 small plates. Fill each tomato with some of the chopped snails and sauce. Spread a spoonful of the sauce in the center of each plate, and place 8 stuffed tomatoes on the sauce. ✗ *Serves 6*

JANE GRIGSON *was a warm, wonderful, wise, and cultured Englishwoman who has written brilliantly on cookery—her native British cookery and its ingredients, as well as the cookery of the France she knew, lives in from time to time, and loved so well. It is clear that she and James were fated to become friends. Her late husband, Geoffrey, figures in this account as a food writer; it should be noted that he was also a professor, a poet, and an art historian. Their daughter, Sophie, is also a food writer. ✍*

It was quite by chance, an odd chance, that we first met James Beard in the wilds of Wiltshire one dark night. Geoffrey, my husband, had been working at the BBC in Bristol all day. We were on our way home by twisty and sodden roads—no motorway in those days—encumbered here and there by falling branches blown down by the gale. Rain fought with the windscreen wipers. I suppose it must have been the autumn of 1964, or early in 1965.

About fourteen miles from home Geoffrey said, "I've had enough of this. Let's stop and have a decent dinner," as he drove extravagantly into the yard of the Bell Inn at Sutton Benger.

At the time, and for some years afterwards, it was the only good restaurant between London and Bath, where George Perry Smith reigned in glory at the Hole in the Wall (three sittings every night for dinner, people happy to perch on the stairs and wait for a table). The Bell was an oasis in a prolonged gastronomic wilderness. The proprietors were the Strattons: Madeleine, the wife, was French and a most delicious cook. We were not well-off in those days—the Bell was a rare treat—but I suppose that with the appalling drive and a BBC cheque in his pocket Geoffrey sensed that dinner was going to be a special occasion. As indeed it turned out to be.

We parked and ran to the door. Warmth engulfed us, and a sudden silence out of the storm. In the bar a fire sparkled and glowed on rows of bottles. The lighting was discreet to our tired eyes. Only one other person was there, a great mountain of a man with the most amiable, rubicund expression. He was studying the wine list and menu with a serenity that combined anticipation with an air of deliberate choice. We ordered a drink, sat down a

couple of tables away, ostensibly discussing the weather, but covertly wondering who this magnificent person might be.

Suddenly Mr. Stratton forgot his English reserve. "I must introduce you," he said from behind the bar. We all looked up politely. "This is James Beard, the famous food writer from New York—he's a great reader of *Country Life*! And this is Geoffrey Grigson, who writes and reviews for *Country Life*, and his wife Jane. They live a few miles away."

At that stage I had barely begun work on a book about charcuterie, knew little of any cookery world, and had no more than a glimmer of James Beard's importance. Geoffrey was better placed. He had just reviewed the English edition of his *Delights and Prejudices*, an autobiography with recipes, for *Country Life*. Instead of selling the review copy, according to normal practice, he had given it to me but I'd barely had time to skim through it. Whether the review had already appeared in print, I do not now recall. Most likely not. I would guess James Beard was in England at such an unpleasant season of the year to help launch his book, his first on the English market.

Cocooned from the storm, and from the likelihood of any other clients, we sat and talked for half an hour. It was an encounter out of time. Perhaps because we were out of the racket of the storm, we all spoke much more freely than is usual on a first acquaintance. James Beard discoursed at length on *Country Life*. Each week, he said, he selected a house from that glorious front section of property advertisements in which all that is most attractive in British domestic architecture comes up for sale at one time or another. Then he contemplated the young English Rose who appears always on the first page of the magazine proper, wearing pearls, often in misty focus, celebrating her engagement or recent marriage (I am told that the editor alone makes the weekly choice of upper-crust pulchritude).

Finally he would settle down to the articles and a prolonged study of the English psyche, which never ceased to puzzle and amaze him. The sensation of that particular epoch in most of the media were two couples, Armand and Michaela Dennis and George and Joy Adamson, who—quite separately—were working in Africa to save lions, tigers, and other large animals. One or the other of the four had recently published a book with a curious title, *Leopards in My Bed* I think it was. This led to fantasies of some ribaldry.

Eventually we sat down to eat. In case Mr. Beard had had enough of the natives, Mr. Stratton placed him at one end of the long restaurant and ourselves at the other. Too distant for more than an occasional remark, but not too far for observation. "Watch him!" said Geoffrey. "You'll learn a lot." So I did. I'd much to learn about my new trade, and here was one of its monuments.

The first course passed without incident. The main course was brought in by a waitress. James Beard had chosen chicken in Champagne, and the girl started ladling it on to his plate, all generous and Wiltshire fashion. Up went a genial but imperious hand. "Stop!" he said. "You are crowding my plate. Please help me to a little, and leave the dish on the table so that I can take some more—if I want it."

This made an enormous impression on us both. The war had been over almost twenty years, but restaurant judgments were still being made by the quantity they gave, as much as and sometimes more than by the quality. Indeed, for many years afterwards the *Good Food Guide* went on commending places for their "generous portions," as if we were still rationed and barely fed. That gesture and remark of James Beard's made us realize just why the standard of English food was often so unsatisfactory, in spite of Elizabeth David's books and the new enthusiasm for good cooking. Madeleine Stratton, French though she was, had had to bow

to the desire for too-muchness—though, on her menu, there was a high level of French quality, too. "Of course," said Geoffrey. "That's what's wrong. We pile our plates like troughs in this country as if we were a nation of pigs!" We'd just bought a tiny house in France—no running water, no electricity—and were beginning to make friends. When they invited us to a meal, we recalled that everyone took a little of the proffered food—just as James Beard had done. The serving dish was rearranged in the kitchen and brought back for second helpings.

Once he managed to tame the service, James Beard enjoyed his dinner. He sat well back from the table and addressed the food with an agreeable smile. Delicate forkfuls were raised to his lips in a steady and appreciative manner. He really savoured the food and the excellent wine. It was a pleasure to watch him eat, to see how the serving around him became milder, the movements of waiters and waitress more dignified and respectful.

When the *Art of Charcuterie* came out in New York, in 1968, including James Beard's recipe for a pâté for picnics, from *Delights and Prejudices,* I don't imagine he remembered our meeting at Sutton Benger, though he did everything he could to smooth my path, in his generous way. Later on I met him again in London. Then he organized a party in his extraordinary house in Greenwich Village for the American publication of a subsequent book of mine. All the same, I think the greatest service he ever did me, at just the right moment, was that first unconscious lesson in the civilization of eating. From him I caught a sense of pride: He knew that what keeps us alive is worthy of all our attention and care—and of a lifetime's study.

As a recipe I have chosen not chicken but oysters in Champagne, because it was in *Delights and Prejudices* that I first read about those delicate little Olympia oysters that are now my favourites. And only in New York have I been able to eat a large variety of oysters. For this dish, however, use round flat oysters [Belon] for the best result.

Oysters in Champagne Sauce

48 round flat oysters
½ bottle Champagne
3 tablespoons chopped shallot
4 large egg yolks
½ pound unsalted butter, cut into cubes
1 cup heavy cream, whipped
Salt and pepper to taste

Open the oysters, tipping them with their juice into a large sauté pan. Place the 48 deeper shells on baking trays. Discard the flat shells.

Stiffen the oysters briefly over medium heat. Drain them and put one into each shell. Reserve 6 tablespoons of the liquid.

Preheat broiler.

Boil Champagne, shallot, and reserved oyster liquid in a shallow pan until reduced to a couple of tablespoons of moist purée. Cool to tepid. Beat in the yolks. Return pan to a low heat (or use a bain-marie [or double boiler]) and add butter to make a Hollandaise sauce. Do not overheat. Strain, mix in the cream, and add salt and pepper to taste. Spoon over the oysters and brown under the broiler. Serve with bread to mop up the sauce. ✕ *Serves 8*

ELLA BRENNAN *says she isn't comfortable writing. She is comfortable with food, as a member of the famous Brennan family of New Orleans with a restaurant in Texas as well, so she has made recipes her contribution to this book. Her restaurant in New Orleans is called the Commander's Palace and ranks on all the lists of the best in New Orleans. It was in her kitchens that Paul Prudhomme got his start. Ella and Jim were friends, large people with a love of food, a party, and a hearty laugh. ✍*

This can be served as an appetizer in shallow au gratin dishes accompanied by sliced French bread or garlic bread to sop up the savory sauce.

Oysters Marinière

1 pint heavy cream
24 fresh oysters
4 tablespoons unsalted butter
8 shallots, peeled and minced
3 cloves garlic, smashed, peeled, and minced
1 cup chopped fresh parsley
½ cup dry white wine
¼ teaspoon freshly ground black pepper
Salt to taste

Place cream in a medium saucepan and bring to a boil over moderate heat. Reduce heat to low and simmer until cream has reduced to about ½ cup. Remove from heat and reserve.

Shuck the oysters and drain them of any liquid. Reserve oysters in a bowl.

Melt butter in a medium saucepan over moderate heat. Add shallots and garlic and cook, stirring, until they become transparent.

Stir in the reserved oysters, parsley, wine, pepper, and reserved heavy cream. Allow mixture to come to a boil, reduce heat to low, and simmer for about a minute, or until the edges of the oysters begin to curl.

Remove from heat, season to taste with salt, and serve. ✖ *Serves 4*

One
morning James's call was filled with enthusiasm for the tiny charcuterie that he had found when out for a
walk on East 13th Street. He wrote about Les Trois Petits Cochons, recommended it to friends, and used it.
Today a huge success, it is a wholesale pâté business located in Tribeca, and the remaining two little pigs,
chefs Alain Sinturel and Jean-Pierre Pradié, sell their products all over the country. ✍

Left to right: Chefs Alain Sinturel and Jean-Pierre Pradié

Tricolor Terrine of Scallops

■■■■■■■■■■■■■■■■■■■■■■■■■■■

1½ pounds bay or sea scallops

3 small cloves garlic

3 small shallots

Salt to taste

Freshly ground white pepper to taste

Pinch of nutmeg

3 tablespoons Cognac

Pinch of saffron

3 eggs

3 cups heavy cream

1 large bunch stemmed parsley (about 3 packed
  cups), blanched

1 tablespoon tomato paste

About 1 teaspoon unsalted butter

Beurre à l'Échalote Sauce (recipe follows)

All ingredients should be very cold.

Divide scallops into three ½-pound portions and place each on foil. Add 1 clove garlic and 1 shallot to each portion. Season each portion with salt, pepper, and nutmeg. Wrap each portion in the foil and place in freezer to chill.

Heat 1 tablespoon of the Cognac in a small saucepan. Stir in saffron, pour into a small bowl, and chill in the refrigerator.

Put a small pot of water on to boil for cooking and tasting the scallop mixtures.

Remove 1 portion of the scallops from freezer. Place in a food processor. Add 1 egg and 1 tablespoon of Cognac and process until smooth. With machine running, add 1 cup of the cream and process until ingredients are puréed and thoroughly blended. Drop a teaspoon of the mixture into boiling water; allow to cook for 1 minute; remove with a slotted spoon and taste for

The James Beard Celebration Cookbook

seasoning. Adjust seasoning of scallop purée, spoon into a metal bowl, and refrigerate.

Remove second portion of scallops from freezer and, using food processor, blend with blanched parsley leaves, 1 egg, and remaining tablespoon Cognac. With machine running, add 1 cup of the cream and process until puréed and thoroughly blended. Drop a teaspoon into boiling water and taste for seasoning. Adjust seasoning, spoon into another metal bowl, and refrigerate.

Remove last portion of scallops from freezer and place in the food processor along with remaining egg, Cognac-saffron mixture, and tomato paste. Process until smooth. Gradually add last cup of cream and process until ingredients are puréed and thoroughly blended. Drop a teaspoon into boiling water and taste for seasoning. Adjust seasoning; spoon mixture into a metal bowl, and refrigerate.

Preheat oven to 250° F. Boil about 5 cups of water for the bain-marie.

Butter a 9″ × 5″ × 3″ loaf pan or a 2-quart terrine with the unsalted butter. Spoon in the first portion of scallop purée and smooth the top with a spatula. Spoon in the scallop-parsley purée and smooth the top with a spatula. Top with last scallop mixture and smooth with a spatula. Generously butter a piece of foil and place over terrine, buttered side down. Place in a large roasting pan and pour in boiling water to come about halfway up the sides of the pan. Bake for 2½ hours or until a thin skewer comes out clean after piercing center of terrine. Serve warm or cold with Beurre à l'Échalote Sauce.

✘ *Serves 8 to 12*

Beurre à l'Échalote Sauce

1 teaspoon finely chopped shallots
1 tablespoon dry white wine
½ cup heavy cream
Pinch of saffron
¼ pound unsalted butter, cut into 1-inch dice
Salt to taste
Freshly ground white pepper to taste

Combine shallots and white wine in a small saucepan and reduce over low heat until liquid has completely evaporated.

Stir in cream and saffron. Cook, stirring, over low heat until mixture is reduced by half.

Add all the butter at one time and continue cooking, stirring, until butter is completely absorbed by the cream. Season to taste with salt and pepper and keep warm on top of a double boiler until ready to serve.

✘ *Makes 1 cup*

JOSEPH BAUM. *The relationship of Joseph Baum and James Beard was rich and complicated, and it continued from 1953 until James's death. Both men were strong medicine, hard-driving and opinionated, and yet it would be fair to say that they loved each other and served each other well. It may be that the potential for rage that was in both of them kept the perilous balance; neither would push the other too far. They also shared a keen belief in the attainability of perfection and a love of good food.*

Joseph Baum is one of the most brilliant restaurateurs in America. He arrived in New York City after attending Cornell and working in Florida to produce the Newarker at Newark Airport for Restaurant Associates, of which he eventually became president, building on the way many restaurants that America will not forget: The Forum of the Twelve Caesars, The Tower Suite, the Four Seasons, the Brasserie, Charley O's, La Fonda del Sol (a breakthrough South American restaurant with a brilliant decor by Alexander Girard), and an extraordinary semi–fast-food chain filled with the sausages that he and Jim loved, Zum Zum. After Joe left R.A., he created all the restaurants at the World Trade Center, including Windows on the World, as well as Aurora and the newly refurbished Rainbow Room. During these later years, Joe also served as consultant to many major restaurant projects.

Right up until Aurora and the Rainbow Room, by which time James's energy was no longer at peak, Beard was a consultant on each and every project, providing Joe with a touchstone of quality and history. While Jim only rarely went into the kitchen, he provided ideas from his rich repertoire and tasted, criticized, and corrected the preparation of dishes.

Jim and Joe met when Joe was working on the Newarker. Jim was brought by the publicity agents, who no doubt thought that Jim's fame could put a seal of approval on this restaurant, which—although in an unlikely spot—did succeed. What happened instead was a close and personal bond between two difficult men who learned to work together. Joe thinks that it worked so well because he had the ability to ask Jim the proper question, the one that would get the memories and ideas flowing. ✍

The James Beard Celebration Cookbook

I like to say he cooked the way he dressed. He'd combine plaids, stripes, and prints, and it worked—and he'd do the same with food. He had a sense of style and ineffable taste, so that he virtually personified the distinction between style and fashion.

Onion and Mussel Tarts with Curry and Apple Sauce

■■■■■■■■■■■■■■■■■■■■■■■■■

½ ounce unsalted butter
½ pound onions, coarsely chopped in the food
    processor
1 tablespoon honey
48 mussels, scrubbed and debearded
½ cup white wine
1 shallot, chopped
4 5-inch circles puff pastry, cut from 1 sheet of
    defrosted frozen puff pastry
1 teaspoon curry powder
1 cup heavy cream
1 green apple, peeled and diced
1 tomato, diced
Chopped fresh chervil for garnish, if desired

   Melt butter in a deep 6- to 8-inch skillet. Add onions and honey and cook over very low heat, using a flame tamer if necessary, for one hour or until golden. Check them often to make sure they don't burn.
   Preheat oven to 400° F.
   Place mussels in a large pot with wine and shallot. Cook just until mussels open. Remove from pot with a slotted spoon, leaving liquid in pot. Remove meat from shells. Reserve meat and discard shells.
   Place puff pastry circles on a baking sheet and divide onion mixture evenly among them. Bake for 23 to 25 minutes or until pastry is light brown.
   While pastry is cooking, add curry to mussel liquid and reduce to ¼ cup. Add cream, strain through a fine sieve, and return to pot. Just before serving, return mussels to sauce briefly to warm. Spoon mussels over the top of the tarts. Add apple and tomato to sauce and spoon around tarts. Garnish with chervil and serve immediately.
✖ *Serves 4*

Chefs who never knew James Beard, chefs from different backgrounds—like the French Yannick Cam—have a deep sense of a debt to Jim and an admiration for him that make them want to help raise funds for the Beard Foundation and to contribute to this book. Yannick owns Le Pavillon restaurant in Washington, D.C., which is one of the best and most elegant in the country. ✍

Homard Rôti au Sauternes au Gingembre, Pamplemousse
■■■■■■■■■■■■■■■■■■■■■■■■■■

(Roasted Lobster with Sauternes and Ginger Sauce, Grapefruit Zest)

2 live Maine lobsters (about 1½ pounds each)
10 tablespoons light olive oil (not virgin, which will burn)
1 tablespoon safflower oil
2 tablespoons finely julienned peeled ginger root
1 tablespoon finely julienned grapefruit zest
1 scant cup Sauternes wine (fine-quality wine must be used for the correct balance of flavor and acidity)
4 tablespoons chilled unsalted butter, cut into small pieces, optional

Preheat oven to 450° F.

Pith lobsters, separate claws and tails from bodies, and reserve. Discard bodies or save for another use. Place olive oil in a large oven-proof skillet. Heat over moderate heat just until oil begins to smoke.

With long-handled tongs, carefully add lobster tails and claws to the oil. This will sputter and sizzle loudly, so stand back. As the sputtering dies down, turn the lobster pieces to cook evenly; when they have turned a light red color, transfer the pan to the oven. Cook for 6 minutes.

Remove from the oven and allow to rest for about 6 minutes. Carefully crack the shells, remove the meat, and reserve.

Pour off all the oil from the pan and wipe clean with a paper towel. Add safflower oil to the pan and place over moderate to low heat. Stir in ginger and grapefruit zest and cook for 1 minute. Add wine and simmer, stirring occasionally, for about 4 minutes, or until the mixture has reduced in volume by about three quarters.

Remove the pan from the heat and, if desired, stir the pieces of butter into the reduction until fully incorporated.

To serve, slice each lobster tail into 6 medallions. Arrange 3 medallions in the center of each plate, with one claw and one elbow. Spoon sauce over the lobster meat.

✖ *Serves 4 as an appetizer*

PIERRE FRANEY *may be America's most famous chef.*
He came to America with the French Pavillion at the 1939 World's Fair. Caught here by the war, he became
the chef at Henri Soulé's Pavillon, the restaurant that dominated the fine food scene in America as long as it
existed. Pierre became known to the general public when he went to The New York Times. *His regular*
column and his books have spread his fame and food across America. He first met Jim Beard when chef at
Le Pavillon. ✍

Left to right: Barbara Kafka, James Beard, Ferdinand Metz, and Pierre Franey

Salmon Mousse with Sauce Américaine (Lobster Sauce)

∎∎∎∎∎∎∎∎∎∎∎∎∎∎∎∎∎∎∎∎∎∎∎∎∎

1½ pounds skinless, boneless salmon fillets
  (reserve the head, gills, and bones for the
  broth), cut into 2-inch cubes and chilled
Salt and freshly ground black pepper to taste
⅛ teaspoon freshly grated nutmeg
Pinch cayenne pepper
2 egg whites
1 cup cold Salmon Broth (recipe follows)
1 cup heavy cream
2 teaspoons butter, softened
Sauce Américaine (recipe follows)

Preheat oven to 375° F. Butter a 6-cup mold
(either a charlotte ring, fluted ring mold, or loaf
pan).

Place cubed salmon in work bowl of food
processor with salt, pepper, nutmeg, cayenne, and
egg whites. Process for 10 seconds. Scrape down
the sides of the container. With machine running,
add fish broth and heavy cream through the feed
tube, processing just until smooth, about 45
seconds. Scrape mixture into prepared mold and
smooth the top with a spatula. Cover tightly with
aluminum foil.

Place mold in a roasting pan and add
enough boiling water to reach 1½ inches up the
sides of the mold. Place the pan in the oven and
bake for 45 minutes, or until the internal
temperature reaches about 104° F. on an instant-
read thermometer.

Remove from oven and invert mousse onto
warmed serving platter. Serve with Sauce
Américaine. ✖ *Serves 6 as an appetizer or 4 as a*
main course

Salmon Broth

2 pounds reserved salmon bones and head
½ cup coarsely chopped onions
¼ cup chopped celery
2 parsley sprigs
½ cup dry white wine
3 cups water

Rinse fish bones and head and chop to fit into a large saucepan. Add remaining ingredients to the pan. Place over high heat and bring to a boil. Reduce heat to moderate and simmer, uncovered, for 20 minutes.

Strain broth through a fine strainer into a smaller pan and return to moderate heat. Simmer broth until reduced to about 1 ½ cups. Remove from the heat and allow to cool. Store, refrigerated, until ready to use. ✖ *Makes 1½ cups*

Sauce Américaine (Lobster Sauce)

1 lobster, about 1 pound
1 tablespoon olive oil
2 tablespoons unsalted butter
Salt to taste
Freshly ground white pepper to taste
Pinch cayenne pepper
2 tablespoons finely chopped onions
2 tablespoons chopped shallots
½ teaspoon minced garlic
2 tablespoons Cognac
¼ cup dry white wine
½ cup crushed tomatoes, either fresh and peeled, or drained canned
2 tablespoons tomato paste
1 sprig fresh tarragon, or ½ teaspoon dried
1 sprig fresh thyme, or ¼ teaspoon dried
1 bay leaf
½ cup Salmon Broth

Cut the tail from the body of the lobster using a cleaver or a heavy knife. Cut off the claws. Split the body in half lengthwise and remove and discard the sac near the eyes. Remove the liver and coral and refrigerate. Chop the body into small pieces.

Heat oil and 1 tablespoon of the butter in a heavy saucepan over moderate heat. Stir in lobster head, pincers, tail, and claws. Increase heat to high and cook, stirring, for about 3 minutes. Stir in salt, pepper, and cayenne. Add onions, shallots, and garlic and cook, stirring, for 3 minutes.

Stir in 1 tablespoon Cognac, the wine, tomatoes, tomato paste, tarragon, thyme, bay leaf, and fish broth. Bring mixture to a boil and cover with a lid. Reduce heat to low and simmer for 7 minutes.

Remove lobster claws and tail; reserve. Pour remaining mixture through a fine strainer and press to extract as much liquid as possible from the mixture. Return liquid to the pan and discard the solids. Place pan over moderate heat and bring liquid to a simmer.

In a small bowl blend together 1 tablespoon of the butter with the reserved lobster coral and liver. Stir into the simmering liquid. Remove from the heat.

Transfer sauce to a blender or food processor and blend until smooth and silky. Season to taste if necessary.

When the claws and tail are cool enough to handle, crack the shells and remove the meat. Cut meat into small pieces and add to the sauce with any liquid that may have accumulated with them.

Blend in remaining tablespoon of Cognac and serve piping hot over the mousse. Reheat sauce if necessary.

"An onion stuck with cloves" has stuck in my mind. And it always makes me think about James Beard. When I bought my first copy of *The James Beard Cookbook* in the late 1950s and began cooking from it, I dutifully stuck my onions with cloves before making soups, stews, and stocks, just as the book demanded. Years later when I asked Jim about it, he said the cloves enhanced the flavor of a stock "providing you don't overdo it" and sticking them in the onion meant they were simply easier to fish out.

Had it not been for Jim, I would never have added the ground cloves, which contribute a pleasant hint of spice to this recipe.

Warm Salad of Chanterelles and Corn
■ ■

½ cup extra virgin olive oil
1 large red onion (about 10 ounces), peeled and
    thinly sliced into rings
2 shallots, peeled and minced
12 ounces fresh chanterelles, wiped clean, any
    large ones cut in half
7 ears fresh corn, yellow and white mixed, kernels
    removed and reserved
3 tablespoons sherry vinegar

½ teaspoon ground cloves
Salt and freshly ground black pepper to taste
1 bunch arugula, stemmed, washed, and dried

Place 2 tablespoons of the oil in a large heavy skillet and place over moderate heat. When oil is hot, add the onion rings and cook, stirring so that they cook evenly, for about 5 minutes. Increase heat to high and cook, stirring, for about 5 minutes longer until they turn nut brown and begin to crisp. Transfer to paper towels to drain off any fat. If you like them very crisp, transfer to a cookie sheet and place under a preheated broiler for about 3 minutes, being careful not to allow them to burn. Reserve.

Add the remaining oil with the shallots to the pan. Cook, stirring, over moderate heat until the shallots are soft but not brown. Stir in the chanterelles, increase the heat to moderate-high, and cook, stirring, for about 4 minutes, until they begin to sear. Stir in corn kernels and cook for 2 minutes longer. Stir in sherry vinegar and cloves. Season to taste with salt and pepper. Remove the pan from the heat.

To serve, line 6 salad plates with arugula and spoon warm salad over with the pan juices. Scatter the reserved onion rings over each portion and serve at once. ✖ *Serves 6*

In the last years of Jim's life and during his final illness, he had no more devoted friend and disciple than Larry Forgione. When they first met, Larry was the chef at the River Café and had already started on his search for the best of American ingredients. He also had a fierce desire to meet Jim Beard, his notion of the epitome of American food. Today, Larry has his own restaurant, now in its second location, An American Place; is a partner in American Spoon Foods, a specialty food—preserves and sauces—company in Michigan; and will shortly have his own book. ✍

In 1980, I was working as chef at The River Café. I wanted to meet James Beard, but I couldn't quite figure out how. Someone suggested that I look in the telephone book and, to my surprise, he was listed. I called and told him what I was doing and asked him to come in. He was friendly but vague. That was in the early days of my hunt for the best American ingredients. When I would find something new or exceptional, I would send over a taste—a basket of cèpes, a bowl of wild huckleberries. After about two months of this wooing, he made a reservation to come to the restaurant.

Unfortunately, the public relations person of the time wanted to make Jim's visit into a media event and Jim became very angry. When I called him, he said, "The next time I talk to you I'll talk through your PR director." I had no idea what he meant. When I found out, after about two weeks, I called to apologize. Jim became friendly and came to The River Café often. I continued to send him baskets of new foods. He would call to tell me how he cooked them, to share his pleasure, which then became mine.

After a year or so, I was deep into old cookbooks doing research on recipes. When I had a question, "What are rice birds?" I would call to ask Jim. He always knew. Sometimes I would go to see him and we would talk ardently for an hour and a half about things like apple pandowdy and he would tell me about all the different kinds he had ever had.

I started my own restaurant in 1983, with the backing and in the building of a friend who also turned out to be a friend of Jim's, Stephen Spector. One day, Stephen and I were sitting around trying to find a name for the restaurant. Stephen suggested that I call Jim. Jim said, "Why not An American Place?"

Before the opening of the restaurant and during its early years, Jim was, as always, generous with his knowledge and his time. We would talk about the menu. After I had devised a group of possible items, he would taste and help me chose. When he came into the restaurant, the staff and the customers buzzed. He would usually stop in the kitchen to say hello and sometimes just watch. As his walk got slower, his departure from the restaurant would get more majestic, and his progress would be stopped a dozen times by customers coming over to say hello. They felt they knew him and wanted to tell him how this or that recipe had pleased them. One man said he had been up on Nantucket when Jim was cooking in a restaurant there and he had run into Jim one breakfast at a diner. The man had said he had once had a recipe of Jim's for cranberry muffins, but didn't any longer and missed it. Jim had scribbled the recipe on a paper napkin. Now, the man wanted to thank him again.

As Jim went out less, I went to him more. I tried to get there on every holiday just to say hello. Usually I would bring one of my children along. Jim didn't really seem to know what to do with children, so they would go out in the garden with Clay and play. Even so, they sensed his aura of greatness. One who was four years old at the time loved the *Star Wars* movies. As we left Jim at the hospital during one of his many stays, my son said, "Let's call him Grandpa Yoda." I guess he was my third grandfather.

When I went to Jim's, he would often point me to books that he thought that I ought to read. He was generous about recommending other authors, from Helen Evans Brown to Mrs. Lincoln and Mrs. Gillette. Jim had a great pride in American food and always thought the tide would turn in its favor. Where chefs would tell me to use Nor-

mandy butter, he would suggest that I compare it with Iowa butter and tell me at what store I could find it.

Now that he's gone, I miss his warmth, knowledge, and generosity; but if there is one thing I remember for my work it is his repeated question after tasting complex dishes that I had labored on: "Was it fun?" It took a while to realize what he meant. He would usually drop the comment and then go on to talk about something like great, homey potato dishes— mashed and hashed brown. What he meant, I realize, was that food should be fun, that it shouldn't seem labored. I still test my new dishes with that question and I still have lots of potatoes on the menu.

Baby White Asparagus and Oregon Morels in Ambush

1½ tablespoons unsalted butter

1 tablespoon finely chopped scallions (from 1 small scallion)

3 ounces fresh morels, thinly sliced

2 tablespoons dry sherry

¼ cup heavy cream

Salt to taste

Freshly ground black pepper to taste

½ pound baby white asparagus

Parsley Sauce (recipe follows)

6 slices Pepper Brioche Bread (page 323), about ¼ inch thick, toasted

6 slices country ham, about ⅛ inch thick

6 slices Colby cheese, about ¼ inch thick

Melt 1 tablespoon butter in a small sauté pan over moderate heat. Stir in scallions and morels. Cook for about 2 minutes, until morels are softened. Add sherry and cook until almost completely evaporated. Stir in heavy cream, simmer for 3 minutes, and season with salt and pepper to taste. Remove from heat and reserve.

Bring about 2 inches water to a boil in a wide skillet. Poach asparagus in the boiling water for 3 to 4 minutes (depending on the size of the asparagus), until tender. Drain through a strainer, reserving the liquid. Place the remaining butter in the pan and melt over low heat. Remove from heat, add asparagus, and toss to coat in the butter. Reserve.

Make Parsley Sauce.

Preheat broiler. Place slices of toast on a cookie sheet. Cover each with a slice of ham and mound asparagus on each piece. Spoon morel mixture over, leaving the asparagus tips uncovered. Lay a slice of cheese on top of each portion. Place under broiler for about 2 minutes, just until the cheese is melted.

Place each portion on a plate and spoon over Parsley Sauce. Do not reheat sauce or it will separate. ✗ *Serves 6*

Parsley Sauce

½ cup reserved asparagus poaching water

2 tablespoons heavy cream

4 ounces unsalted butter, cut in small pieces

2 tablespoons lemon juice

¼ teaspoon Worcestershire sauce

¼ teaspoon hot pepper sauce

Salt to taste

2 tablespoons chopped fresh parsley

Bring asparagus water to a boil in a small pan, and boil until it has reduced to about 2 tablespoons (i.e., just covering the base of the pan). Add heavy cream and return to a boil. Reduce heat to low and whisk in butter. Stir in remaining ingredients. Remove from heat and keep warm until needed; do not reheat sauce, or it will separate.

**One of James's closest friends for
many years was his neighbor Alfredo Viazzi, the owner of many Greenwich Village restaurants, notably
Trattoria d'Alfredo on Hudson, just a short walk from Jim's house. Jim and Alfredo had food in common,
but equally profoundly they loved the theater. Often, Alfredo would make money with restaurants and lose it
in theater. He himself was a handsome theatrical man, born in Italy, who made food theater, not with fancy
presentation but with gusto.**

 **Unfortunately, Alfredo died not very long after Jim. Fortunately, he left us with two excellent books
from which these recipes come. After talking to Jane White [Viazzi], Alfredo's widow and a fabulous actress,
whose nearby house was a warm spot of welcome for Jim, I selected two recipes that Jim and I enjoyed
together at Alfredo's. They are first courses; but less robust eaters than Jim and Alfredo might choose to
have them as the center of a meal.**

 **As Jane says, "How they used to laugh together! I got such a kick out of their shared joy in life, in
food, and in their own celebrity. . . . How Jim, sitting always at the big window table in the old Bank
Street Trattoria, gave so fully of his allure to real and potential customers; and how Alfredo, showman
that he was, brought his own special commedia plus his loving chef's genius to the whole scene! After
those two, they've thrown away the mold!"** ✍

The word *stronzata* in the Roman dialect has many connotations, but it is mostly used to mean "a mess," "a pile of this and that," or "a foolish action." In this case, the name is a whim of mine. This dish has gained the acclaim of half a dozen food magazines and is the number-one seller at my restaurant.

Stronzata di Verdure con Salsa Verde

(A Mess of Vegetables)

1 cotechino (about 1 pound)
Salt
1½ pounds fresh asparagus
1½ bunches fresh broccoli, cut into florets with
  about 1-inch stems attached
1 small head cauliflower, cut into florets, stems
  and outer leaves removed
1 pound string beans, tipped and tailed
¾ cup chicken consommé
1 cup grated Parmesan cheese
1½ cups Salsa Verde (recipe follows)

 Bring a large pot of water to a boil over
moderate heat. Prick the cotechino a few times
with a fork and cook, whole, in the water for about
1½ hours. Remove from the water and reserve.
When cool enough to handle, cut across into 12
slices, about ½-inch thick.

 Add a little salt to the water and return to
the boil. Cook the remaining vegetables in the
salted water, cooking the asparagus for 5 minutes;
the broccoli for 4 to 5 minutes; the cauliflower for
10 minutes; the string beans for 8 minutes. When

each of the vegetables is cooked, remove with a slotted spoon to a bowl of iced water, return the water to a boil, and add the next vegetable.

Pour the consommé into a large oven-proof casserole. Place over low heat. Add vegetables, keeping them in separate piles. Sprinkle them with about half of the cheese. Place cotechino slices over cheese. Cover with lid and cook for a few minutes, until vegetables are thoroughly hot.

Preheat broiler. Remove casserole from heat and remove lid. Place casserole under broiler for about 3 minutes. Remove from broiler and sprinkle over remaining cheese. Serve hot with Salsa Verde on the side. ✕ *Serves 6*

Salsa Verde

2 hard-boiled eggs, peeled
1 large bunch fresh parsley
8 anchovy fillets
1 small onion, peeled
2 pieces whole red pimiento
1 tablespoon chopped garlic
1½ tablespoons medium-sized capers
Freshly ground black pepper to taste
¾ cup olive oil
½ cup red wine vinegar

Place eggs, parsley, anchovies, onion, and pimiento either in a grinder or food processor and coarsely chop. Transfer mixture to a deep bowl. Stir in garlic, capers, and pepper. When fully mixed together, stir in oil and vinegar. The sauce should have a distinctive vinaigrette flavor; if it seems too mild, add more vinegar.

Serve on the side with hot vegetables.
✕ *Makes 2 cups*

Il Ristorante Biffi has been located in the Galleria Vittorio Emanuele II in Milan since the latter part of the nineteenth century. Until the 1950s it was a first-class restaurant, and its patrons were the glittering superstars of the nearby La Scala, eminent composers, writers, movie directors, the beautiful soubrettes of the *varietá* houses, and the inevitable motley groups of hangers-on.

The menu always featured a most elaborate buffet that included Peperoni Stile Biffi. Unfortunately, Biffi's has now been converted into a sort of self-service restaurant, featuring such fare as pizza, hot dogs, and packaged potato chips. The famous peperoni are no longer to be found, but their memory is well worth preserving.

The James Beard Celebration Cookbook

Peperoni Stile Biffi

■■■■■■■■■■■■■■■■■■■■■■■■■

(Stuffed Peppers Biffi)

¼ loaf Italian bread, in rough hunks
1 pint heavy cream
6 medium to large sweet red peppers (or green, if
    red are not available)
8 fillets of anchovy
3 pieces whole red pimiento
¼ cup medium-sized capers
⅓ cup chopped parsley
3 3-½-ounce cans Genova tuna, flaked, undrained
    (drain if using American tuna)
½ cup pitted black olives, roughly chopped
Pinch oregano
Pinch nutmeg
Pepper to taste
1 cup grated Parmesan cheese
¼ cup olive oil
1 cup beef or chicken consommé

Soak bread in cream. Cut off tops of peppers and clean insides of all seeds and fibers; shave bottoms slightly so that peppers will stand up in baking pan. Wash peppers well under running cold water and dry.

Preheat oven to 400° F.

Prepare stuffing: coarsely grind anchovies, pimiento, capers, and soaked bread. Place mixture in mixing bowl and add parsley, tuna, olives, oregano, nutmeg, pepper, and all but 4 tablespoons of the cheese. Mix thoroughly, then stuff peppers with mixture.

Put olive oil and consommé in a deep baking pan. Carefully stand peppers in pan and cover with aluminum foil. Bake for 15 minutes; then uncover and bake about 5 to 8 minutes until a firm crust is formed on the tops.

Before serving, sprinkle remaining grated cheese over tops and place under broiler for 2 minutes. Serve hot. ✗ *Serves 6*

S O U P S

JIM LOVED A BOWL OF SOUP, GOOD STOCKS, AND
SUBSTANTIAL SOUPS. HE WOULD HAVE LOVED THIS CHAPTER.
AS YOU CAN SEE FROM THE RECIPES CONTRIBUTED BY MANY

PEOPLE WHO KNEW JIM VERY WELL, HE LOVED CHOWDERS AND BEAN SOUPS, THINGS THAT WERE HEARTY AND FILLING AND COULD MAKE A MEAL.

JIM FOBEL *has had an active life of writing and testing for a myriad of food magazines. He is the author of two books,* Jim Fobel's Old-Fashioned Baking Book (Recipes from an American Childhood) *and* Jim Fobel's Diet Feasts. *Both are books James would have loved—particularly those very American layer cakes. The two Jims became Village friends.* ✍

The first time that Jim Beard tasted this broth he told me that it was the best he'd ever had in his life! Now, I must confess that there was a little more to it than just the recipe. I collect Mexican wooden spoons and I had accidentally left the one made of mesquite in the broth as it cooled, and it imparted an amazingly good flavor (not smoked, of course, but exotic). So, if you have one of those spoons (mine was from Oaxaca) you might try the same thing. I guarantee you, even without the spoon, that this broth will be superb.

Superior Chicken Broth

2 whole chickens, about 3 to 4 pounds each, cut into quarters (or equal weight of chicken parts)

4 ounces smoked country ham, in one slice

3 quarts cold water (depending on size of chickens and pot you may need more in order to cover the chickens)

3 ribs celery, cut across into thin slices

2 medium onions, peeled and sliced

1 large sprig parsley

2 cloves garlic, smashed and peeled

8 cloves

2 bay leaves

1 tablespoon dried basil

1 teaspoon dried thyme

1 teaspoon dried tarragon

Salt to taste

Make slashes in the chicken with a heavy knife. Place in a large stock pot. Add remaining ingredients. (If desired, you can make a bouquet garni of the cloves, bay leaf, basil, thyme, and tarragon.) Bring to a simmer over moderate heat. Skim the surface of fat and scum as needed. Reduce heat to very low and simmer, partially covered, for 10 to 12 hours (or overnight).

Remove the largest ingredients from the broth, place in a colander, and press down to extract liquid. Discard the solids and pour the rest of the broth through the colander. Strain the broth again through a fine strainer. Skim any fat from the surface. If you have more than 2 quarts broth, place in a smaller pot and simmer over medium heat until broth has reduced to about 2 quarts. Season to taste.

If not using immediately, pour into plastic containers and store either in the refrigerator or freezer. ✕ *Makes about 2 quarts*

FELIPE ROJAS-LOMBARDI *met James many years ago. The common feeling they had for the foods of Peru was based on a trip that James made to Peru for Joe Baum when he was at Restaurant Associates and research was being done on the foods of South America before the opening of La Fonda del Sol.*

Felipe gave this recipe to the book because he uses it in his recipe for Caracoles and Red Beans (page 76), but it is such a splendid broth you may want to use it for many things. It does make a large amount. You can halve it, but it is well worth making it all and freezing some. ✍

It seems as if I knew James Beard all my life. Which is strange, since I grew up in Peru. Come to think of it, though, Jim had been to Peru and was one of the few people I've ever met who actually had a great knowledge about the food of Peru.

Let's face it. Jim Beard had a great knowledge about the food of everywhere! He found every place, every food, every taste, and most people fascinating. He was a man who loved life so fully and enjoyed every succulent moment of it.

I went to a party, oh so many years ago, knowing I would leave in a few minutes. Unless I'm actually making the food and serving it, I really don't enjoy parties all that much. That night I was certain I'd be home and in bed early. Wrong!

That was the night I met Jim Beard, and it changed my life. We met, naturally enough, over a buffet table. He stacked his plate neatly with an assortment of good things to eat and invited me to join him over in a corner for a little talk. I had no idea when I sat down that I would remain in the corner with Jim, talking, talking, talking, mixed with some eating, for three hours, or until the host invited us to leave.

If you knew Jim, or even met him only once, you know that one word above all summed him up: charm. He was certainly the most charming person I have ever known, and our conversation that fateful evening ended with his welcome invitation to come and visit him at his school.

Which I did. Not only did I visit, I stayed

for five years as his assistant and fellow traveler. I traveled throughout the United States and Europe with Jim, assisting him in his teaching, his demonstrations and television appearances, his consulting work, his books . . . and the testing and the testing and the testing of the recipes. It was exciting, and for someone who loved food, who wanted to make food his life, there was no experience like it. Jim Beard was my college, my post-graduate work, my doctorate. I like to think I graduated with flying colors.

My memories of Jim are as large as he was, and he was a big man—not only heavy, but very tall, someone who was physically as well as intellectually and creatively larger than life. I remember so many trips with Jim, so many demonstrations.

There was the time we were to "perform" with a demonstration in poaching fish for a very large women's group in the Midwest. The auditorium must have been filled with some two thousand women that afternoon. The stage had been beautifully outfitted with a sink and stove and wonderful worktable. Since we were to show the skill and technique of poaching a large whole flounder, I brought with us one of Jim's beautiful, large, tin-lined, copper poachers easily capable of holding a ten- to fifteen-pound fish, which we anticipated would be about the size of a whole flounder.

We arrived and inspected our setting. Everything seemed in place, but we were missing the flounder. "Call the chairwoman," Jim said. I did. "Where's our flounder?" I asked. "Why, it's right there on the counter wrapped up," came the reply.

I looked around. Sure enough, there was a tiny package which, when opened, revealed two tiny frozen fillets of flounder. Jim's comment not only summed up the event, but summed up his wonderful approach to life. Laughing, he said to me, "Well, Felipe, you're really going to have to make those fillets dance."

Another time, another demonstration, and one of my proud moments with Jim. We were to show the perfect way to cook an omelette, and there, at our stage worktable, were twin burners. We had arrived for a run-through that afternoon, for the evening show.

Testing the equipment, we quickly discovered that the burners didn't work, wouldn't heat up. We were stuck. You can't cook an omelette without heat. Suddenly it hit me. Backstage I found an old steam iron that must have been left there from some other show. I brought it on stage and inverted it, keeping it jammed between the two defunct hot plates. I turned it on; it heated up; and I put the pan on the iron; we had our heat. It worked. Then came the accolade that I obviously have always cherished: "Ah, ha, Felipe! Pure genius," came that wonderful rumbling voice.

When I became involved in The Ballroom, the Chelsea restaurant that has been my home for the past seven years, Jim was told that "Felipe is going to have a tapas bar." Jim misheard the word *tapas* and, like so many others during the early days, thought he heard the word *topless;* he simply sighed his gentle and kind sigh and said, "Well, if that's what Felipe wants." That was all. No condemnation, no shock, just his wonderful, good self, and his desire to see his disciples pursue those things that interested them . . . even if it was a topless bar!

I'm pleased to be able to say that Jim loved The Ballroom, and whenever a supply of really young suckling piglets arrived, I would call him up and just say, "They're in." He'd be over that night. Jim loved that sweet tender young pig meat and especially the pig's crisp skin—he always wanted extra skin. [See recipe on page 279.]

He loved the Caracoles and Red Beans [page 76], and thought the Tortilla Española [page 75] was the "best possible tribute to Spain." But it was the Moroccan Eggplant [page 77] that seemed to really turn him on. "Ah," he would comment. "Now eggplant, that's a very sexy dish." Who but Jim Beard would think of food as sexy?

Felipe's Beef Stock

4 large onions with skins (about 3½ pounds), each cut into eighths

2 to 3 leeks, trimmed, washed, and each cut into 3 pieces

1 whole head garlic, unpeeled, cut in half crosswise

8 stalks celery with tops, washed and cut into pieces

2 small carrots (about 8 ounces), unpeeled and each cut into four pieces

6 pounds beef bones (preferably marrow and knuckle bones)

8 pounds veal bones (preferably shin, knuckle, and feet or a combination of them)

1 large oxtail, cut into small pieces, or several small oxtails

3 gallons cold water

8 whole cloves

2 bay leaves

1 bunch fresh thyme

24 black peppercorns

2 to 3 fresh hot peppers, jalapeño or árbol, or 1 to 2 dried red hot chili peppers, optional

Preheat oven to 500° F.

In a very large deep roasting pan, place all the vegetables, covering the bottom of the pan. Arrange the bones over the vegetables and roast in the upper third of the oven for 1 hour.

Remove from oven and, with a slotted spoon, transfer all the bones and vegetables to a large stockpot. Pour off the fat from the roasting pan and deglaze pan with 1 quart water. Pour this into the stockpot. Add the rest of the water, cloves, bay leaves, thyme, peppercorns, and hot peppers. Bring to a boil, skimming the scum as it rises to the surface. Lower the heat, stir, cover, and simmer for about 5 hours.

Remove the stock from the heat and let cool undisturbed. Strain through a fine sieve or a strainer lined with a double thickness of cheesecloth. Discard bones, vegetables, and herbs and let stock rest for 15 minutes to allow fat to rise to the surface. Degrease stock and use immediately or refrigerate or freeze. ✗ *Makes 6 to 8 quarts*

ELAINE KAUFMAN *is known to a large segment of the creative world as Elaine of Elaine's Restaurant in New York. It is on the Upper East Side in the Eighties. She and Jim first knew each other when she was working with Alfredo Viazzi in Greenwich Village. Jim adored garlic. One of his favorite recipes, as Julia Child reminds us, was for Forty Cloves of Garlic Chicken, also a Spanish dish. He loved this soup.* 🖎

Garlic Soup

■■■■■■■■■■■■■■■■■■■■■■■■

¼ cup olive oil
½ cup smashed, peeled, and sliced garlic (about
    10 large cloves)
½ cup finely chopped prosciutto
2 tablespoons finely chopped pimiento (1 whole)
1 quart chicken stock, homemade or canned
5 to 7 slices toasted Italian, French, or sourdough
    bread
4 eggs, well beaten
Salt
Freshly ground black pepper

In a large saucepan or medium stockpot, warm the oil over medium-high heat. Sauté the garlic until golden brown. Add the prosciutto and pimiento and stir well. Add the broth and the toast, and bring the soup to a boil. Keep the soup hot until it is served.

Just before serving the soup, whisk in the beaten eggs. Season with salt and pepper to taste.
✗ *Serves 4 to 6*

SUZANNE CORBETT *is the founder of her own company, Suzanne Corbett/Culinary Concepts, Inc., where she focuses on food marketing, communications, and American food history—a love she shared with Jim. She has published her writing in magazines such as Bon Appétit and Victoria Magazine, as well as many local newspapers and journals in St. Louis, Missouri, where she lives. Ms. Corbett has also contributed recipes to several books, including Good Old Food, A Taste from the Past by Irena Chalmers.*

For a thinner soup, increase the amount of chicken stock by ½ to 1 cup. This is especially delicious and comforting when served with Herbed Wheat Bread (page 320).

Spinach Potato Soup

4 cups peeled and diced potatoes (1¾ pounds unpeeled potatoes)
½ cup chopped onions (1 smallish onion)
2 cups chicken stock, homemade or canned
1 tablespoon salt, or less if using canned stock
1 clove garlic, smashed and peeled
Freshly ground black pepper
10 ounces frozen spinach, cooked and squeezed of excess moisture
3 cups heavy cream
2 tablespoons unsalted butter
Chopped fresh parsley for garnish
Hot paprika for garnish

In a large soup pot, combine the potatoes, onions, and stock over medium-high heat. Let this simmer until the potatoes are very tender, almost soft. Add the salt, garlic, and pepper to taste.

Pour the mixture into the work bowl of a food processor or a blender and process until it is smooth. Return the mixture to the soup pot over medium-high heat and stir in the spinach. Let the mixture simmer for several minutes, then add the cream and butter. Heat the soup thoroughly and garnish each serving with a sprinkle of parsley and hot paprika. ✕ *Serves 6*

RICHARD SAX *has worked as a magazine editor and a writer of culinary articles and books. He shared with Jim a love of the best basic ingredients. Richard Nimmo, who is referred to below, was the last of Jim's assistants. He transcribed tapes that Jim dictated to be made into articles, he helped develop recipes, and he helped with classes.* ✍

I remember well one day Jim Beard and Richard Nimmo came over for lunch. Beard's house isn't far (although they drove, as it was hard for Beard to get around), so, on that sunny Friday afternoon, it seemed like a leisurely, neighborly get-together, something I didn't often stop to do in the middle of a workday.

Naturally, when you have James Beard to lunch, you wonder, "What will I serve?" What do you feed a man who's eaten everything? But I felt I wanted to thank him somehow—he had given my entire generation so much feeling for food, and, especially, pride in our own American cooking—remember, this was before American cooking became "American cuisine." So I wanted to make something he'd enjoy.

I quickly rejected doing an all-out, multi-course, "fancy" luncheon. Instead, I'd serve the kind of simple foods I love to eat and love to cook. We started out with some appetizers like a little stew of wild and fresh mushrooms with garlic; some fresh fava beans, lightly dressed; and something else I can't remember. It was all set out on the table, and everyone helped himself to whatever he wanted.

As a main course, a big pot of chowder, which I brought right to the table. I was going to bake biscuits with it, but we got so wrapped up in conversation that I said, "The hell with it," so we had a big round loaf of sourdough bread I had bought (luckily). Plenty of white wine, though Jim sipped a single-malt Scotch, just a little bit. For dessert, homemade chocolate pudding in big, clunky bowls with whipped cream. I figured, "Why not? He probably hasn't had it homemade in ages." I think there might have been cookies with it, too. (Obviously, I spent a little time on this lunch.)

One thing a lot of people mention, remembering James Beard, is his total recall. Some days, I'd sit with him and ask him about food, and he'd remember the most amazing things from thirty years before. One time, he was talking about a dream he had, in which his mother appeared. Suddenly, he looked up at me and said, "It's a lot like dreaming, working with food, don't you think?"

At that lunch, Jim ate a little of the chowder, smiled and said quietly, "I love this," and finished a big bowlful. Other than that, we didn't talk about food at all.

Corn and Shrimp Chowder with Tomatoes

■■■■■■■■■■■■■■■■■■■■■■■■■■■

1 teaspoon vegetable oil

6 ounces bacon, sliced thick and cut into ½-inch-wide strips lengths

1½ medium-large onions, peeled and coarsely chopped

2½ small carrots, peeled, trimmed, and cut on the diagonal into ¼-inch slices

1½ slender celery ribs, peeled, trimmed, and cut on the diagonal

½ pound new or boiling potatoes, peeled, quartered lengthwise, and cut crosswise ½-inch thick

14 ounces chicken stock, homemade or canned

¾ cup water, or as needed

1½ fresh thyme sprigs, or ¼ teaspoon dried

3½ cups corn kernels (with milky pulp, cut and scraped from 5 to 10 ears), 2 or 3 cobs reserved, or 2 12-ounce cans corn niblets

1¼ cups whole milk, or more as needed

Salt to taste

Freshly ground black pepper to taste

¾ pound small-medium shrimp, peeled and deveined

1½ large ripe tomatoes, peeled, cored, seeded, and cut in large dice (if time allows, place diced tomatoes in a colander, sprinkle with kosher salt, and let drain for a few minutes)

3 tablespoons fresh chives, snipped into ½-inch lengths

Place the oil and bacon in a large heavy saucepan or casserole over medium heat. Cook slowly, stirring frequently and pouring off excess fat once or twice, until bacon pieces are lightly golden but not yet crisp, 5 to 7 minutes. With a slotted spoon, transfer bacon to paper towels to drain; set aside. Pour off all but 2 tablespoons fat from pan.

Add the onions, carrots, and celery to pan, tossing to coat. Sauté over medium heat, tossing frequently, until vegetables have softened slightly but are not brown, about 5 minutes. Add the potatoes, chicken stock, water (only enough to partially cover solids), and thyme. Break or cut the reserved corn cobs in half; tuck into mixture. Cover and simmer the mixture gently until the potatoes are tender but not mushy, about 15 minutes.

Uncover the soup and set aside to cool to room temperature for about an hour. Remove and discard thyme sprigs, if used. Remove corn cobs and, using a small knife, scrape all possible pulp and liquid from each cob back into soup; discard cobs. Skim fat and froth from surface.

Return pan to medium heat, stir in corn kernels with their liquid, and simmer for 3 minutes. With a skimmer, transfer about 3½ cups of the solids to a food processor and process until coarsely puréed. Stir purée back into soup, along with 1¼ cups milk. Return to a simmer (do not boil, or milk may curdle). Adjust consistency if necessary so soup is just lightly thickened—purée more solids and stir into soup, or stir in more milk. Season to taste with salt and a generous grinding of pepper. Recipe can be made ahead up to this point. Chowder improves upon standing.

When ready to serve, return chowder to a simmer. Stir in the reserved bacon and scatter shrimp over surface. Cover and simmer just until shrimp turn pink, about 3 minutes. Correct seasonings and stir in tomatoes and half of the chives. Cook just to heat tomatoes. Serve in wide soup bowls, sprinkling each portion with remaining chives. Pass crackers alongside if desired. ✖ *Serves 8*

BILL RICE *is one of America's foremost food reporters and editors, with a keen interest in wine. Today, he is in Chicago at the* Tribune. *Before this he was in Washington, D.C., and then in New York as the editor of* Food & Wine. *His bean soup has a refinement that many lack.* ✍

One of the many admirable traits James Beard possessed was extraordinary adaptability. He seemed to fit in anywhere, and with almost anyone. His interest ranged so far beyond the confines of food and cooking that it was rare, in my experience, that he couldn't find a rapport with people he met in all walks of life.

When he came to Washington, D.C., during my time there with the *Washington Post,* I delighted in introducing him to political journalists and people in the theater. On one occasion, an actress friend volunteered to host a small party for Jim, whom she had never met.

He and I arrived a bit early. She called down from upstairs that we should help ourselves to something to drink. Jim asked for wine. I found some easily, even found a corkscrew, but I couldn't locate any wineglasses. In desperation I picked out two small, curiously shaped glasses, filled them, and returned to the living room.

Moments later, my friend Sally Jane swept down the stairs, making an actress's entrance until she caught sight of the glasses on the table before us. A look of consternation came over her face and she began to blush.

"Mr. Beard," she stammered. "I'm so sorry. Your wine is in a jam jar." Then I received one of those "if looks could kill" looks.

Jim chuckled, wrapped his huge hand around the tiny glass vessel, toasted his hostess and saved my life.

"The wine tastes fine," he said, "and there's nothing wrong with the glass, either."

Everyone survived, the guests soon arrived, and, with proper wineglasses in hand, we had a delightfully convivial party.

My undeserved reward came in the form of a memorable scene late in the evening: At everyone's urging, Sally Jane sang numbers from vintage musical comedies as Jim, who knew all the lyrics to every song, sat beside her at the piano and acted as prompter.

James Beard's adaptability also applied to food. He was remarkably receptive to almost any dish, no matter how simple, as long as the food was cooked with respect to the ingredients and had flavor. When I'm cooking, I often ask myself, "Does this have enough gusto for Jim?" If the answer is no, I will rethink a recipe or alter the seasoning.

My Best Bean Soup

4 carrots, peeled and thinly sliced (about 2 cups)

2 onions, peeled and thinly sliced (about 2 cups)

2 medium ribs celery, thinly sliced and leaves
    reserved (about 1 cup)

3 tablespoons vegetable oil

4 cloves garlic

4 allspice berries

1 teaspoon dried thyme

1 bay leaf

6 to 8 sprigs parsley, washed

1 pound great northern beans, covered with
    boiling water, soaked for 1 hour, and drained

2 ham hocks

8 cups chicken stock (approximately), homemade
    or canned

2 teaspoons Worcestershire sauce

1 teaspoon salt, or to taste

Freshly ground black pepper

4 smoked sausages, cut into chunks, or 1 to 2 cups
    cubed leftover roast pork, optional

In a large pot, sauté carrot, onion, and celery in vegetable oil until soft, about 10 minutes.

Tie the garlic, allspice, thyme, bay leaf, parsley, and celery leaves in a cheesecloth bag. Add it to the pot along with the beans and the ham hocks. Pour in chicken broth, adding more broth or water if necessary to cover the beans by 2 inches. Bring liquid to a boil, lower heat to a simmer, and cook the beans, partially covered, for 2 hours or until soft. Skim any fat that rises to the top during the first half hour of cooking.

Remove the cheesecloth bag and discard. Remove the ham hocks. Cut the meat from the bones and chop it. Remove 1½ cups of the beans and broth and purée in a food processor or blender. Return to the pot along with the chopped ham. Add the Worcestershire, salt, and pepper. Taste and adjust seasoning as desired. Soup may be prepared ahead and refrigerated overnight.

Reheat soup with optional sausage or pork and serve with plenty of bread and mugs of beer.

✗ *Serves 12 to 16*

Soups

MARK MILLER. *I met Mark Miller the first time Jim and I went out to San Francisco to give two weeks of class together. For some odd reason, we had a day free; it must have been the weekend between weeks, and we drove out to Berkeley to have lunch at the restaurant of a young man whose culinary talents Jim extolled all the way out. Mark, a former anthropologist, is one more of the fine young cooks who are the academic world's loss. Even then, he was experimenting with Southwestern ingredients and flavors, grilled dishes, invented dishes, and traditional dishes, all with deep flavors and often with a spicy kick. Today, Mark Miller is a great success at Coyote Café in Santa Fe and has written a cookbook as well.* ✍

Black Bean Soup

1 pound dry black beans
1 teaspoon cumin seed
1 teaspoon coriander seed
1 teaspoon Mexican oregano
½ large onion (about 6 ounces), peeled, with root
    fibers still attached
4 cloves garlic, smashed and peeled
2 fresh jalapeños, cut in half lengthwise
1 bunch fresh cilantro, tied together
½ cup tomato purée
2 bay leaves
½ teaspoon dried thyme
1½ teaspoons peppercorns
1½ teaspoons salt
6 quarts water

Pour black beans into a strainer and pick out any foreign particles or small rocks (rocky beans are not related to Rocky Road ice cream). Rinse under cold running water and drain.

Combine cumin, coriander, and oregano in a dry skillet and place over moderate heat. Cook for about 3 minutes, shaking the pan constantly so that the spices are toasted but do not burn. Remove from heat and allow to cool for a few minutes. Transfer to a spice mill and grind together.

In a large pan combine beans, onion, garlic, jalapeños, cilantro, tomato purée, bay leaves, thyme, peppercorns, salt, spice mixture, and water. Bring mixture to a boil over moderate to high heat. Reduce heat to low and simmer, uncovered, for 2 hours, stirring occasionally.

Remove the cilantro bunch. If soup has reduced a lot at this point, replenish with more cold water. Simmer for about 1 hour longer. Remove from the heat.

Remove the onion, garlic, jalapeños, and bay leaves and serve. ✕ *Serves 8*

MARK CARALUZZI. *When Mark Caraluzzi was going to open The American Café, he and his partner came to a course that Jim and I were giving in New York, to imbibe Americana from the fount. He and Jim remained friends. On page 45, you can see how Jim loved to spin a tale and how Mark drank it in.*

Lentil Soup

■ ■

10 ounces brown lentils (1½ cups)

2 tablespoons unsalted butter

2 tablespoons olive oil

2 ounces slab bacon, cut across into ½-inch-long strips

2 ounces pancetta, finely chopped

3 ounces onion, peeled and coarsely chopped (about ¾ cup)

4 ounces carrot, peeled and coarsely chopped (about ¾ cup)

1 rib celery, trimmed and coarsely chopped (about ½ cup)

¼ cup all-purpose flour

12 ounces canned Italian plum tomatoes, coarsely chopped

5 cups veal stock

¾ pound smoked ham hocks

¼ teaspoon dried thyme

1 small bay leaf

1½ teaspoon salt

½ teaspoon freshly ground black pepper

¾ pound Italian sausage, cut into ½-inch slices

2 cloves garlic

2 tablespoons olive oil

2 tablespoons red wine vinegar

2 tablespoons chopped fresh parsley

Place lentils in a large pan and cover with cold water. Bring to a boil over high heat. Reduce heat to low and simmer, partially covered, for 45 minutes. Remove from heat, drain, and reserve.

In the same pan, melt butter and oil over moderate heat. Stir in bacon and pancetta, reduce heat to low, and cook for about 10 minutes, stirring occasionally.

Stir in onion, carrot, and celery. Cook for 5 minutes longer. Stir in flour and cook for about 20 minutes, stirring frequently, until mixture becomes a rich brown color. Add tomatoes, veal stock, ham hocks, thyme, bay leaf, salt, and pepper. Bring soup to a boil over high heat, reduce heat to low, and simmer, uncovered, for about 30 minutes, skimming the surface occasionally. Add sausage and simmer for 20 minutes longer.

While soup is simmering, place garlic, oil, and vinegar in a blender and purée until smooth.

Stir garlic emulsion into the soup. Remove from heat. With a slotted spoon remove ham hocks; cut meat from the bone and return meat to the soup. Add parsley and serve.

✖ *Makes 9 cups*

Untermann, see page 180. Even if you cannot get geoducks, don't bypass this recipe. Your local clams can be substituted. James always declared that clam chowder should only be made with razor clams, and he even allowed for the use of canned. Those of us from the Eastern seaboard are happy to use our quahogs. I guess it's a question of where you were raised. ✍

We were the shaken beneficiaries of James Beard's enthusiasm for new restaurants. Shortly after we opened, James visited the restaurant and wrote a nationally syndicated column about the Hayes Street Grill. It was our first mention in the national press and it encouraged us no end.

We were trying to serve only Pacific Coast fish and seafood then, which was nine years ago. Sometimes we didn't have much on our blackboards. Now, we're getting all sorts from the Pacific that James would have appreciated, growing up as he did in the Pacific Northwest. If he were alive today, I'd dearly love to serve him some of this geoduck clam chowder. The geoducks make the best clam chowder I've ever tasted.

Get your hands on one or two geoduck clams. (Try a Chinese fish market.) Run very hot water on them. Their shells will open and their outer skin will loosen. Peel off and throw away the belly. Slit the whole clam down the center, lengthwise; cut off the tip of the siphon and wash the whole clam well under water. Then, put the clams through the coarsest blade of a meat grinder. You should have about 2 pounds of clam meat.

Geoduck Clam Chowder

2 pounds ground clam meat
2 quarts cold water
2 medium onions, peeled and cut into quarters
4 ribs of celery, cut into big chunks
2 carrots, peeled and cut into big chunks
5 sprigs fresh thyme
4 tablespoons unsalted butter
4 slices bacon, finely julienned
1 large onion, peeled and finely diced
2 red or green bell peppers, stemmed, seeded, and finely diced
6 small red new potatoes, finely diced
1 cup half-and-half
Salt and freshly ground black pepper, to taste
Pinch chopped fresh thyme

In a large stockpot combine clam meat, water, onion quarters, celery, carrots, and thyme sprigs. Place over moderate heat and bring to a boil. Reduce heat to low and simmer for about 45 minutes.

With a slotted spoon remove vegetables and thyme and discard. Reserve broth and clam meat.

Place butter in a heavy pot and melt over moderate heat; add bacon and cook, stirring, until golden brown. Stir in diced onion and peppers. Reduce heat, cover, and cook until vegetables are just tender.

Pour in reserved clam broth and clams; add diced potatoes. Bring mixture to a boil over moderate heat, reduce heat to low, and simmer for 10 to 15 minutes.

Stir in half-and-half and season to taste with salt, pepper, and thyme. ✖ *Serves 8 to 10*

CORNELIUS O'DONNELL. *Neil O'Donnell was one of Jim's favorites, a hearty, generous man who has roamed the country for many years working for Corning Glass and doing charity events. Both roles brought him together with Jim, as Jim was for many years a spokesperson for Corning and appeared in their ads.* ✍

It was in the Bahamas at our annual sales meeting—the first one in years that included spouses. Jim had done a couple of print ads as well as two television spots promoting the new Corning smoothtop ranges. We thought it would be a good idea to have Jim attend the meeting and prepare a couple of recipes.

At least a month before, I began pestering Jim for the recipe to be sure we would have the ingredients on hand. He said he needed to be "inspired by the moment" and not to worry. Well, that inspiration took the form of an early morning visit to the native market the day of the cooking demonstration. Unfortunately, it was also the anniversary of some (now vague to me) national political victory, so the *la mañana* mentality was particularly evident. The marketing trip went well, and James thoroughly charmed the produce sellers.

Just imagine that imposing figure striding, stopping, inspecting, and buying whatever appealed. In his wake came three Corning executives

schlepping cartons of the freshest vegetables and herbs James could find—as well as enough finger bananas to feed the Bahamian Army and then some.

Back at the hotel all of us peeled, chopped, and sliced a small mountain of those vegetables, and Jim made the most delicious sauté any of us had ever eaten. I spoke to the waiter, who I suspected had celebrated hard the night before, and repeated our instructions about having the largest bowl of vanilla ice cream this very classy resort hotel could supply rushed to the meeting room at exactly half past twelve. Jim, knowing this plan, started sautéing and sugaring the bananas, with dark rum at the ready for flaming, at precisely 12:24. I remember him glowing as he added at least a pound of unsalted Land O' Lakes butter to the pan. At the collective intake of breath, he peered over his glasses and murmured, jowls aquiver, "I'm a Butter Boy!"

I kept glancing nervously at the service elevator some acres of carpet away. Yes, we had the bananas but no ice cream. I bolted, caught the elevator in seconds, and pushed blindly at one of the buttons. Mercifully, seconds later, I found myself in the bowels of the kitchen. "ICE CREAM!" I screamed, and suddenly three people who had been catatonically staring at their inner lids began frantically heaving ice cream balls into the largest stainless bowl I'd ever seen. Within a minute I staggered back to the elevator with my burden. Blind luck led me to push the right button, for the doors opened and there, fifty feet away, was Jim, match in hand, igniting the banana-sugar-rum concoction. He looked up at the disheveled figure bearing down on him and calmly said, "... of course, you'd serve this over ice cream you've scooped into balls. And in this climate, that has to be done at the *VERY* last minute."

It was at the Music Academy of the West in Santa Barbara. James and that fine gentleman Philip Brown were cooking together for the benefit of the scholarship fund (or something). Corning was happy to supply one of our brand-new smoothtop ranges. James had just become our spokesman and had done print and television ads for the product, and we had installed some in his new kitchen on West 12th Street. On the other hand, Philip had never used anything that didn't have burners, coils, or a glow to indicate the presence of heat.

I was standing in the rear of the auditorium watching the goings-on in the large mirror which clearly reflected the rangetop—and taking great pride in all this wonderful publicity. Philip proceeded to begin *his* recipe by putting one of our snow-white pans on a still-hot burner that James had just finished using. He took the longest time to describe what he was about to do, so that when he added three tablespoons of butter to the by-now overheated pan, the butter incinerated. I froze. Jim looked at the pot and Philip's astonished face and, without missing a beat, said, "You forgot to tell them you're using beurre noir for this recipe."

Ever aware of authenticity, Jim showed that he could be an opportunist too.

In doing photography for an ad, we found we couldn't get back far enough to shoot what we wanted in his kitchen (then on 9th Street). So, when we recreated his kitchen in a photo studio, he agreed to lend at least four cartons of his kitchen bibelots (the Guerlain bottles, majolica, etc.).

This stirred Corning to be equally authentic and assure he had a backdrop of his famous black-and-white pineapple wallpaper. It had been discontinued years before, but we succeeded in ordering a special run.

After the shoot, Jim had enough to paper the foyer of his new digs on 12th Street.

I couldn't resist the title. The soup is so *efficient* to put together, with no wasted motion, and it takes half an hour or less. Start by setting out the basic chowder base ingredients. First chop the bacon, then start to cook. While that is happening you have time to chop leeks or garlic. When they are in the pot, chop celery and add pepper. Then open the tomatoes and shred the carrot. Well, you get the point. Now get cooking!

This is a meal in itself, or serve it with a lemon sorbet and cookies or fresh fruit.

The James Beard Celebration Cookbook

E-fish-ent Chowder

½ pound medium shrimp

2 8-ounce bottles clam juice or broth

3 slices bacon, cut across into ¼-inch strips

2 tablespoons olive oil

3 medium leeks (about 4 ounces each), white and
   light green parts cleaned and coarsely
   chopped

1 clove garlic, smashed, peeled, and minced

1 red pepper (about 6 ounces), stemmed, seeded,
   deribbed, and finely chopped

2 ribs celery, peeled and cut across into thin strips

1 32-ounce can Italian plum tomatoes, coarsely
   chopped, with liquid

1 carrot (about 3 ounces), peeled and shredded

1½ cups chicken stock, homemade or canned

½ cup white wine

3 medium potatoes (about 6 ounces each), peeled
   and cut into ½-inch pieces (about 2 cups)

1 teaspoon dried thyme, crumbled, or
   ½ teaspoon each dried oregano and basil (for
   the Italian touch)

1 bay leaf

Freshly ground black pepper to taste

2 tablespoons tomato paste

1 pound scrod fillets, cut into 1-inch pieces

½ pound bay scallops, cleaned (or sea scallops, cut
   into small pieces)

¼ cup chopped fresh parsley

Peel and devein shrimp. Reserve shrimp
and place shells in a small pan with clam broth.
Over medium heat bring to a boil and simmer for
3 minutes. Strain broth and reserve; discard shells.

Place bacon in a 5-quart saucepan and cook,
stirring over high heat until just crisp. Remove
with a slotted spoon and reserve.

Add olive oil, leeks, and garlic to the fat in
the pan, lower heat, and cook, stirring, for 2
minutes. Stir in red pepper and celery and cook
for 3 minutes.

Stir in tomatoes with their liquid, carrot,
reserved clam broth, chicken stock, and wine.
Increase the heat and bring mixture to a boil. Stir
in potatoes, dried herbs, bay leaf, pepper, and
tomato paste. Lower heat and simmer, uncovered,
for about 20 minutes, or until potatoes are cooked
through.

Stir in the scrod pieces and cook for 2
minutes. Stir in shrimp and cook for 2 minutes,
then stir in scallops and reserved bacon and cook
for 2 minutes longer.

Remove from heat and stir in fresh parsley.

✖ *Makes 13 cups*

BARBARA KAFKA. *In the previous chapter, I described Jim and me at the perilous start of our relationship. This recipe belongs to a time just after that when, with a lightning turn about, he had adopted me as one of his circle. Being in his circle meant his total faith that you could do anything and he sometimes set challenges which you yourself were far less convinced than he that you could master. At that time, Jim was running a full-time cooking school rather than, as he did later, teaching sporadic classes in various parts of the country. He was going out of town and decided that the week should be filled with classes for each of the five days by his discoveries. I know that Madhur Jaffrey also taught one of the classes.*

I was to teach an evening class and then repeat it the following midday for another group. The evening class was filled with high-powered New York experts come to see the new kids on the block. The midday class was filled by home cooks from all over the country who had waited eagerly for an opening at one of the week-long series.

I decided to do a bouillabaisse, a dish I was reasonably sure of and had served at home to acclaim. I took the precaution of going down to Jim's several days before the class because I had never worked on the Corning Cook Tops that he had had installed in his kitchen. I took a big pot, put it on the burner, and checked to see that the oil would get really hot; it did. It turned out that that was an insufficient check. When I tremblingly began the class, I immediately ran into a problem.

I started the rouille, which I was making in the then-new food processor. As the editor of a little magazine called Cooking, *published by Carl Sontheimer of Cuisinarts, I was thoroughly familiar with the food processor and used it regularly to make mayonnaise and mayonnaise-type sauces, of which rouille is one. However, I got so busy talking to the class that I overprocessed the rouille and the machine got warm and the sauce so thick it wouldn't accept all the oil. The sauce broke—twice—before I got it to work. I was losing the audience.*

Rouille finally made, I moved to the cook top, and everything was going fine until the point in the recipe where it says, "Bring to a rolling boil." What I hadn't realized was that the burner had a sensor and while it would heat a small amount beautifully, it wouldn't bring a large pot of liquid to a rolling boil. Additionally, when it came time to add the white wine, I discovered that members of the class had been quietly nipping it during the overly long class. Poor Clay (see page 209) had to run down to the cellar to get more wine. I was out of control.

Finally, the fish stew got made and people seemed to eat it with pleasure, and the students—some of whom have since become friends—don't seem to hold it against me. I was shattered.

The next day with the out-of-towners went much better. I broke the rouille once, but they they seemed relieved to find out that even "experts" could make mistakes, and the rest of the class was a modest triumph.

When Jim came back, I shamefacedly confessed my problems. He simply laughed boomingly and expressed his confidence in me. I was relieved. Later, we taught many classes together so he can't have held a grudge. I owe Jim a vast debt of gratitude. Without him I would never have taught or gone on to do many of the things that I have. It wasn't recipes that I learned but courage and a sharing of the whole world of food—information and friends.

You should have no problem with the recipe. Just don't put it on a self-adjusting burner. ✍

This is a French Mediterranean soup that turns any evening into a party. It is the soup that my son always asks for for his birthday. Put the rouille around in bowls so that people can add it as they eat. Also have bowls of thinly sliced French bread croutons that have been sautéed in olive oil. For a really authentic note, add bowls of peeled cloves of garlic and encourage your guests to rub their croutons with the garlic. This is not food for picky eaters or the dainty of fingers. Set out oyster forks and large soup spoons. Use very large soup bowls and have extra bowls around for shells. Jim and I both had enormous white footed French soup bowls that we bought on a trip to San Francisco. Oh yes, supply extra napkins.

Bouillabaisse

☐ *Rouille with Pastis*

  4 egg yolks

  ½ teaspoon kosher salt

  ¼ teaspoon dry mustard

  2 cups olive oil

  6 cloves garlic, cut into pieces

  3 small dried red peppers, crumbled

  1 teaspoon white wine vinegar

  1 gram (small test-tube container) stem saffron, dissolved in 2 tablespoons white wine and allowed to stand for at least an hour

  ½ teaspoon pastis or Pernod

☐ *Bouillabaisse*

  1 cup green virgin olive oil

  4 large onions, peeled and finely chopped

  ½ cup chopped fresh parsley

  2 eels (preferably sea), about 1½ pounds, skinned, cut into 1½-inch lengths, heads and tails reserved for later use in stock

  2 pounds cod fillets, cut into 2- by 4-inch pieces

  2 pounds mackerel, hake, or whiting fillets, or a mixture, cut into 2- by 4-inch pieces

  ¾ cup pastis or Pernod

8 good-size ripe tomatoes, cored, peeled, and
    chopped
2 quarts fish stock (your own recipe, or see below)
3 grams stem saffron, dissolved in ½ cup dry white
    wine
¾ cup white wine
8 large cloves garlic, smashed, peeled, and
    chopped
3 tablespoons kosher salt
¼ cup fennel greens, finely chopped
1½ tablespoons chili powder
Cayenne pepper
4 pounds red snapper or striped bass fillets, cut
    into large pieces
30 medium hard-shelled clams, scrubbed
30 mussels, scrubbed and debearded
30 medium shrimp, in their shells

French bread, cut across into ¼-inch slices,
    brushed with olive oil, and toasted

For the Rouille: Place egg yolks, salt, and
mustard in work bowl of a food processor and
process for a full 2 minutes. With the motor still
running, gradually add the oil in a thin steady
stream until the mixture thickens; then add the oil
faster. Add garlic and peppers and process to
combine, then add vinegar, saffron wine, and
pastis. Scrape into a bowl and reserve until ready
to use.

For the Bouillabaisse: Place ½ cup olive oil in
a large pot and place over low heat. Stir in onions
and cook, stirring occasionally, until they are soft
but not brown. Stir in parsley and eel and cook
until eel is lightly browned.

Add cod and the 2 pounds assorted fish to
the pot. Pour the pastis into a small pan and set
over low heat. Carefully set a match to it to ignite.
Pour the flaming liquid over the fish. When the
flames subside, stir in tomatoes, fish stock, saffron
wine, white wine, garlic, salt, fennel greens, chili
powder, cayenne, and remaining ½ cup oil.

Bring the soup to a rolling boil over high
heat. Cook, uncovered, for about 7 minutes. Stir in
red snapper and cook for about 3 minutes longer.

Add clams, cover, and cook for about 3

minutes. Add mussels and shrimp, recover pot,
and cook until the mussels open.

Remove the fish and shellfish to a serving
platter. Let the soup continue boiling until it has
amalgamated. Stir 3 tablespoons of it into the
rouille. Strain the soup.

To serve: Spread 2 slices of toast per person
with a little rouille. Place toasts in the bottom of
each huge soup bowl and ladle soup over. Serve
the fish and extra bowls of rouille on the side.
✖ *Serves at least 12*

Fish Stock

6 pounds nonoily fish and bones such as cod and
    whiting (not flatfish)
4 quarts water

Wash the fish heads and bones very well to
eliminate all traces of blood. Cut out the blood-
rich gills with scissors. Put the fish heads and
bones in a pot and cover with the water. Place the
pot over high heat and bring to a boil. Skim off the
scum that rises to the top. Lower the heat, and
simmer the stock for 4 to 6 hours, or until
approximately 8 cups of broth remain. Skim as
necessary. Refrigerate, freeze, use, or reduce to
make a glaze, as needed. ✖ *Makes 2 quarts*

The James Beard Celebration Cookbook

JEAN-LOUIS PALLADIN. *Jim seemed to be known wherever he went in the world, and chefs from every country respected him. Many of them have created events to raise money for the Foundation. Jean-Louis Palladin, originally from France, but for several years now from his own restaurant at the Watergate in Washington, D.C., is such a chef. He submits this elegant, lobster-gilded recipe worthy of the most elegant dinner in Jim's honor.* ✍

Cold Pea Soup with Mint

■■■■■■■■■■■■■■■■■■■■■■■■■■■■

☐ *For lobster broth*

4 cups water

1 cup white wine

1 medium onion (about 6 ounces), peeled and
  quartered

2 cloves garlic, smashed and peeled

10 black peppercorns

1 sprig thyme or ¼ teaspoon dried thyme

1 bay leaf

Salt to taste

1 live lobster (about 1¼ pounds)

☐ *For the soup base*

5 cups water

2 teaspoons salt, or more to taste

1½ cups green split peas, washed and picked over

1 sprig fresh mint

1½ cups heavy cream

Freshly ground black pepper to taste

2 tablespoons chopped fresh mint

4 ounces fresh peas

Place all broth ingredients except the lobster in a large pot with a lid. Cover and bring to a boil over high heat. Add lobster and boil for 2 minutes, uncovered. Remove pan from the heat, cover, and allow to stand for 10 minutes.

Remove lobster from broth, shell, and cut flesh into thin medallions. Place in small bowl, cover, and refrigerate. Strain broth (there should be 4 cups) and reserve.

Place 4 cups water, 1 teaspoon salt, and split peas in a pan. Cover with lid and bring to a boil over medium heat. Reduce heat and simmer, uncovered, for 5 minutes. Remove from heat and let stand, uncovered, for 1 hour.

Drain peas, return to pan, and add lobster broth. Bring to a boil; add mint sprig and 1 teaspoon salt. Reduce heat, cover, and simmer for 30 minutes. Add 1 cup water and simmer 15 minutes longer.

Remove from heat. Discard mint. With a slotted spoon, transfer peas to work bowl of food processor. Add a little of the broth and process until smooth. Pour into a bowl with the remaining broth. Cover and refrigerate until cold, or overnight.

When ready to serve, stir in heavy cream and season to taste. Serve soup in iced bowls or cups. Sprinkle with chopped mint and garnish with reserved lobster medallions and fresh peas.

✖ *Serves 6*

PAMELA WISCHKAEMPER *was one of those helpful San Franciscans who started as a student and ended up as an assistant in Jim's classes. Today, she is food editor of* San Diego Home/Garden *magazine and she still remembers Jim fondly.* ✍

Tomato Soup with Orange
■■■■■■■■■■■■■■■■■■■■■■■■■

3 tablespoons unsalted butter
4 ounces yellow onion, peeled and finely chopped
    (about ¾ cup)
6 medium-large ripe tomatoes (about 8 ounces
    each), peeled, seeded, and chopped (about
    4 cups)
¼ teaspoon baking soda
¼ teaspoon dried thyme
1 cup heavy cream
½ cup chicken stock, homemade or canned
3 tablespoons concentrated orange juice
1 teaspoon fresh lemon juice
Salt to taste
Freshly ground black pepper to taste
Sour cream for garnish
Chopped parsley for garnish

Melt butter in a saucepan over moderate heat. Stir in onions and cook until soft and translucent. Stir in tomatoes, baking soda, and thyme. Cook, stirring, for about 20 minutes until mixture has thickened.

Remove from heat and stir in cream, chicken stock, and orange and lemon juices. Season to taste with salt and pepper.

To serve hot, reheat over low heat; or serve cold. Garnish with a spoonful of sour cream and chopped parsley. ✗ *Serves 4*

Amazingly, Jim kept learning and evolving throughout his life. His last book, <u>The New James Beard,</u> *really was new and incorporated much of the seasoning and lighter style of the young chefs whom he was constantly meeting and enjoying. Stephan Pyles is brilliantly such a chef. He has two restaurants in Dallas, Routh Street and Baby Routh's. He also has two in Minneapolis. This elegant cold soup is typical of his light, inventive Southwestern style.* ✍

Golden Gazpacho with Bay Scallops

■■■■■■■■■■■■■■■■■■■■■■

5 to 6 golden tomatoes, or 3 pints yellow cherry tomatoes (about 1½ pounds), seeded and diced

2 ounces yellow bell pepper, stemmed, seeded, and finely chopped

3 ounces cantaloupe, skinned, seeded, and finely chopped

3 ounces papaya, skinned, seeded, and finely chopped

3 ounces mango, skinned, pitted, and finely chopped

1 medium cucumber (about 10 ounces), peeled, seeded, and chopped

2 ounces jícama, peeled and diced

6 scallions, white parts finely sliced

3 serrano chilies, stemmed, seeded, and finely chopped

¾ cup chicken stock, homemade or canned

¼ teaspoon saffron threads

2 tablespoons fresh lime juice, or more to taste

Salt to taste

Aromatic Poaching Broth (recipe follows)

8 ounces bay scallops

Combine tomatoes, yellow pepper, cantaloupe, papaya, mango, cucumber, jícama, and scallions in a medium bowl. Reserve.

Place serrano chilies, chicken stock, and saffron in a blender and process to combine well. Allow to stand for about 10 minutes. Pass liquid through a strainer. Return liquid to blender and discard solids. Add about three quarters of the reserved tomato mixture to the liquid and process until smooth. Pour into a bowl and stir in remaining tomato mixture, lime juice, and salt.

Cover with plastic wrap and refrigerate until chilled, about 2 hours.

Meanwhile, bring Aromatic Poaching Liquid to a boil in a medium pan. Add scallops and cook for 1½ to 2 minutes, until just opaque. Strain scallops and let stand until cool.

Divide cold soup among 4 chilled soup bowls. Garnish with scallops. ✗ *Serves 4*

This is a just-to-keep-things-moving recipe that can be used in the above recipe or any time you need a very simple poaching liquid. Half of the water can be replaced by white wine if you wish. The liquid can be reused. After several batches of fish or seafood have been poached in it, it becomes an excellent fish broth for use in soups.

Aromatic Poaching Broth

BARBARA KAFKA

4 cups cold water
1 large carrot, peeled and cut into 2-inch pieces
1 rib celery, peeled and cut into 2-inch pieces
2 cloves garlic, peeled and halved
1 medium yellow onion, peeled and quartered

Place all ingredients in a medium pan. Bring to a boil over high heat. Reduce heat to moderate and simmer for 20 minutes. Strain broth through sieve. Discard vegetables; use immediately or cool, cover, and store in the refrigerator.

BARBARA KAFKA. *A few years after* The Cook's
Catalogue *was published, James became involved as a consultant to Carl Sontheimer, who brought the food*
processor to America as the Cuisinart. We had had very good things to say about the new machine in the
catalogue. Among other things that Jim did for Carl was the writing of Recipes with a Cuisinart Food
Processor, *which showed just how to use the food processor. Jim asked me to contribute a recipe, which I*
gladly did. Along with the roast chicken in Food for Friends *and the recipes in* Microwave Gourmet *and*
Microwave Gourmet Healthstyle Cookbook, *it may be the most often prepared of my recipes. So here it is,*
once more again for Jim. ✍

Gazpacho
■■■■■■■■■■■■■■■■■■■■■■■■■

½ medium Bermuda or other sweet white onion,
    peeled and quartered
1½ firm, medium cucumbers, peeled and cut into
    chunks
2 small green peppers, stemmed, seeded, and cut
    into eighths
6 medium to large ripe tomatoes, cored, peeled,
    and cut into eighths
5 cloves garlic, smashed and peeled
1 cup tomato juice
½ cup light olive oil
¾ teaspoon chili powder or 1 small piece fresh
    chili pepper
1 tablespoon kosher salt, or to taste

Place onion in work bowl of food processor
and process until finely chopped, stopping
occasionally to scrape down the sides. Scrape into
a large bowl.

Repeat process with cucumbers and then
with green pepper, adding each to the onions in
the bowl.

Process 5 of the tomatoes until finely
chopped but not puréed. Add to the other
chopped vegetables.

Process the remaining tomato with garlic,
tomato juice, oil, and chili powder until a smooth
liquid has formed. Combine with chopped
vegetables, cover, and refrigerate until chilled.

Before serving, season to taste with salt. If
the soup is too thick, more tomato juice or a
combination of tomato juice and beef broth may
be added. ✕ *Makes 1½ quarts*

PASTA & RISOTTO

Jim loved pasta and noodles, rice, beans, potatoes, bread, and all sorts of starchy foods. One of his last books was Beard on Pasta. It seems only fitting and in line with the current overwhelming popularity of pasta that so many of

Jim's friends have contributed pasta recipes. Risotto was another favorite. Jim introduced me to Olympia oysters, those lovely, tiny, briny dollops of flavor from Washington State. We used to gobble them at the Stanford Court in San Francisco in James Nassikas's heyday. I developed a risotto using them for class and later printed it in American Food and California Wine. For another class, I did the buckwheat pasta that appeared in the same book. Jim paid me the ultimate compliment by using that recipe in his own pasta book.

When we ate out, pasta often seemed like just the dish, and working with it gave Jim an inspiration to branch out into culinary cultures he hadn't done much with before.

JULIE DANNENBAUM. *One of Jim's great food-friends was Julie Dannenbaum. She taught in his cooking school and he in hers. When he went to Venice to start cooking classes (see page 51) at the Gritti, Julie went with him, and she has been teaching there ever since. Out of her familiarity with Italian cooking, she has contributed several recipes to this chapter. We start with her basic egg pasta recipe, which can be used in many of the recipes that follow.* ✍

There are so many anecdotes I can remember about Jim, but the one that stands out most is when we were doing a demo together in Allentown, Pennsylvania, a long time ago (in the '60s). He had turned out his famous spinach roll onto the counter and had forgotten to put paper under it for rolling. He looked at it, roared with laughter, filled it, and put his very large hands around it and rolled it up to perfection. I adored him and I miss him as I know you do.

Basic Pasta Dough

1 egg
2 teaspoons olive oil
2 to 3 tablespoons cold water
2 cups unsifted all-purpose flour

Place egg, oil, and water in the work bowl of food processor. Process briefly to combine. Add ½ cup flour and process 3 seconds, add remaining flour, and pulse to combine. Remove from work bowl, knead together with hands, and form into a ball. Cover with plastic wrap and let rest for 40 minutes at room temperature.

IRENE SAX. *Rene Sax is a staff writer for the Wednesday section of* New York Newsday. *Before doing that she wrote books of her own and helped some of us write our cookbooks. She helped me with* The Cook's Catalogue *and Marion Cunningham with the revision of* The Fannie Farmer Cookbook. *She also worked with Jim on* Beard on Pasta. ✍

Jim, who wrote so many recipes in his life, taught me not to rely on them: that spontaneity was the fun of cooking. Once, when we had been making pasta all morning and his funny wooden drying-tree was hung with ribbons of noodles, it turned out that there was nothing to sauce them with at lunchtime. Jim just opened a jar of very undistinguished tomato sauce, heated it with the juice of half an orange, a dash of Tabasco, and a good splash of cream, and we had a marvelous lunch.

This sauce is one that has evolved in my family over the years, changing according to what I find in the pantry when it's time for supper. The amount given here is enough for 1½ pounds of pasta; cut the recipe in half and you have a nice sauce to spoon over grilled chicken or fish.

Pasta Sauce

■■■■■■■■■■■■■■■■■■■■■■■■■

½ cup olive oil

2 cloves garlic, peeled, sliced, and smashed

4 ounces yellow onion, peeled and finely chopped (about 1 cup)

2 3½-ounce cans anchovy fillets, drained, rinsed, and coarsely chopped

1 16-ounce can Italian plum tomatoes with their liquid, coarsely chopped

¼ teaspoon dried oregano

Freshly ground black pepper to taste

8 ounces black olives, pitted and coarsely chopped (about 1 cup)

¼ cup chopped parsley

Heat the oil in a heavy skillet over moderate heat. Stir in the garlic, onion, and anchovies and cook for 4 minutes. Stir in the tomatoes, oregano, and pepper and simmer for 10 minutes.

A few minutes before ready to serve, stir in olives and parsley and cook for 2 minutes. Pour over cooked pasta. ✖ *Makes 3 cups*

I got my first microwave oven because of Jim. He loved new equipment and had just gotten a microwave. Since, at that time, we frequently taught together and I often developed the recipes for our classes after discussion with him, it was essential that I get a microwave oven as well. Neither one of us mastered the oven at that time. Jim did master and use other new technologies as soon as they came his way, and I like to think that he would have been pleased that that original microwave oven set me off on my most recent books.

This recipe gives instructions for a simple basic tomato sauce that can be used as is or doctored with dried or fresh herbs and spices or other ingredients—basil, fennel seed, thyme, oregano, dried mushrooms, onion—to your taste. I like the sauce to stay a little chunky; but if you like a smoother, seedless sauce, by all means put it through a food mill after it is cooked. You may then want to put it back in the microwave oven, uncovered, to reduce somewhat.

The better the tomatoes, the better the sauce and the less time needed for cooking; but this will even make a quite good sauce with winter's pink almost-tomatoes. While it is hardly an instant sauce, it is cleaner and quicker than stove-top cooking and you avoid any risk of scorching.

Simple Tomato Sauce in the Microwave Oven

5 pounds of tomatoes, cored and cut in 1-inch
    pieces (usually eighths)
12 large cloves garlic, peeled and smashed
1 cup fruity olive oil (or less if preferred)
Salt and freshly ground black pepper to taste

Stir together tomatoes, garlic, and olive oil in a 5-quart casserole with a tightly fitting lid. Cover and cook in 650- to 700-watt microwave oven at 100 percent power for 15 minutes. Stir; replace lid and cook for 10 minutes longer. Uncover; stir and cook from 15 to 35 minutes longer, until you have evaporated as much liquid as you want.

Purée by putting through a food mill with the medium disk in place if a smoother texture is desired. Salt and pepper to taste. Use immediately or freeze in small quantities for future use.
✖ *Makes 6 cups when puréed, 7 cups when left chunky*

This is about as basic as pesto gets. It can be varied by changing the nuts—walnuts are nice—or the cheese; a little goat cheese or Gorgonzola adds a different flavor. The recipe is here mainly to be used in other recipes; but can be used on its own with linguine, gnocchi, or simple tortellini.

Pesto

2 cups packed fresh basil leaves
2 cloves garlic, peeled and smashed
¼ cup olive oil
3 tablespoons freshly grated Parmesan cheese
2 tablespoons toasted pine nuts

Place the basil and garlic in the work bowl of a food processor. Process until finely chopped. Gradually pour in the olive oil. Add the cheese and pine nuts. Process until fairly smooth in texture. ✖ *Makes about ¾ cup*

MIMI SHERATON *is one of America's best-known food reporters and cookbook authors. There is almost no area of the food world in which she has not been brilliantly active. While she probably became most visible to the general public as a reporter for New York and a restaurant critic for The New York Times and Time, she had already had a career as a home furnishings writer, first for an advertising agency and then at Good Housekeeping, Seventeen, and House Beautiful. While at Seventeen, she had begun writing about food. After leaving the magazines, she worked as a consultant, doing food-related gallery shows and restaurant consulting. When she went back to writing for the consumer, she gave up the consulting, feeling it was a conflict of interest.*

She has traveled widely by inclination and in connection with her writing. She has written books both as charming as From My Mother's Kitchen and as comprehensive and authoritative as The German Cookbook and her restaurant guides, now called New York's Best Restaurants. Today, she continues to write: her guides, a New York restaurant newsletter, Mimi Sheraton's Taste, and as food editor for Condé Nast Traveler. ✍

Jim Beard and I were more colleagues and neighbors than close friends and, as such, I worked with him on several projects at Restaurant Associates and met him often in food markets in Greenwich Village. I remember Jim best from those meetings, because his presence at Balducci's or at the Jefferson Market meat counter always created a festive atmosphere for all shoppers. It also satisfied them because they felt justified in their choice of markets. How could they not, when America's leading gourmand and bon vivant made the same choice? Other than that, I remember Jim from his early days as a consultant and showman who did projects for the public relations firm of Lynn Farnol, then representing the Presto Company that made electrical cooking appliances such as a deep-fryer. I was a junior editor then, about twenty-three, and was taken by my editor to the demonstration luncheon at the old Café Brittany. Snails were served and I had never eaten them, but watching Jim, I followed suit, never with a single regret. I still get a brief mental flashback of Jim digging in whenever I pick up snail clamps and set to on a dozen or so.

For me, Jim Beard's strong point was his appreciation of the simplest and most humble dishes and the way in which he accorded them the respect of using only the best ingredients and handling them with care. In that same spirit, I offer this recipe for meatballs with sausages and riga-toni, the kind of dish I would have served to Jim had he ever come to dinner. It is also very good with polenta instead of pasta.

Italian Meatballs and Sausages with Rigatoni

2½ pounds lean ground chuck
2 eggs
Grated rind of 2 lemons
1 clove garlic, crushed in garlic press
2 tablespoons grated Parmesan cheese
2 tablespoons finely minced parsley
3 tablespoons unseasoned bread crumbs
Salt and pepper
1½ pounds hot Italian sausage
1½ pounds sweet Italian sausage with fennel
2 to 4 tablespoons olive oil
4 cloves garlic, thinly sliced
3 large cans Italian plum tomatoes (each 2 pounds
    3 ounces), drained and chopped, with liquid
    reserved
1 large onion studded with 8 cloves
5 or 6 sprigs of parsley
Tomato paste to taste, optional
1 tablespoon dried oregano, or to taste
5 or 6 leaves fresh basil
2½ pounds dry rigatoni cooked al dente in boiling,
    well-salted water
Optional garnishes: minced parsley, grated
    Parmesan cheese, and Italian hot red pepper
    flakes

In a large bowl, using a fork, combine room-temperature ground beef with eggs, lemon rind, crushed garlic, cheese, minced parsley, bread crumbs, and salt and pepper to taste. Mix well but do not make mixture too dense and compact. Lightly shape into 10 or 12 large meatballs and set aside.

Cut sausage into 1-inch lengths. Heat 2 or 3 tablespoons olive oil in a large heavy skillet and in it fry sliced garlic for a few seconds until it is pale golden. Remove with a slotted spoon and place in a large Dutch oven or similar pot. Add sausages to pan and brown well on all sides, adding oil if needed, and turning pieces so they brown evenly. Place sausages in pot with garlic.

Brown meatballs in skillet, adding only as many as will fit without touching each other. Turn gently with a wooden spatula until brown on all sides. Place meatballs in pot with sausages. Pour excess oil out of skillet and add chopped, drained tomatoes. Simmer and scrape in all bits of browned meat. Pour tomatoes over meatballs.

Add clove-studded onion to pot, along with sprigs of parsley and oregano. Simmer gently, half-covered, for 1 hour, shaking pot frequently to prevent scorching. Gradually add salt and pepper as cooking progresses. If sauce is thinner than you want it to be, gradually stir in tomato paste, a teaspoon at a time, simmering for 5 minutes between additions, until you have the right consistency. If sauce is too thick, thin gradually with reserved tomato liquid. Add basil leaves for the last 5 minutes of cooking time.

Before serving, remove onion and cloves, along with sprigs of parsley and basil leaves.

Divide hot, cooked rigatoni into individual bowls (I use old-fashioned wide soup plates) and top each with one meatball and a few pieces of sausage. This amount allows for seconds for the hungry. Sprinkle with parsley and pass grated cheese and hot pepper. ✖ *Serves 6 to 8*

Once upon a time there was a restaurant in New York called Le Plaisir, which everyone remembers with awe, and Stephen Spector—along with Peter Josten—was its parent and owner. When it closed, its chef was Massa, who went to California and became fabled there. Stephen first met James over the quail Stephen was raising at his Griggstown Farm and selling to restaurants.

Stephen and James became close—daily telephone calls—friends. They both had vast spheres of knowledge. Stephen had been a dealer in drawings and collected American naïve antiques and Oriental porcelains. They both wanted to know everything that was going on in any field that interested them. They had wit. They loved to gossip. They had superb and individual taste and adored good food.

This recipe from the heyday of Le Plaisir was in constant demand. Whenever it was taken off the menu, customers complained. So for Stephen and Jim and Massa, here it is. ✍

Le Plaisir's Truffled Pasta

1½ teaspoons chopped shallots
1 ounce canned truffle pieces
1½ cups Madeira
1 cup chicken stock
1 cup heavy cream
Salt and pepper to taste
¾ pound fresh linguine
4 truffle slices for garnish

Combine shallots, truffles with their liquid, and Madeira in a pan. Place over high heat and cook, stirring occasionally, until reduced to a glaze.

Stir in the stock and reduce to about half. Stir in cream and cook until reduced to half again. The sauce should be quite thick. Season to taste with salt and pepper.

Bring a large pot of salted water to the boil and cook pasta until al dente. Drain well.

Toss pasta with the sauce and divide among four salad plates. Garnish with a slice of truffle.

✗ *Serves 4*

Smoked Chicken with Pasta in Mustard Cream Sauce

1 tablespoon plus ¼ teaspoon salt

8 tablespoons unsalted butter

1 small clove garlic, peeled, smashed, and finely chopped

1 small shallot, peeled and finely chopped

6 ounces heavy cream

1 tablespoon Dijon or Creole mustard

⅛ teaspoon freshly ground black pepper

1 pound fettucine or linguine

1 whole smoked chicken (about 2¼ pounds), boned and cut into small pieces (about 3½ cups)

4 ounces plum tomatoes, cut into small pieces and excess juice drained (about ½ cup tomato flesh)

2 tablespoons fresh basil, cut across into chiffonade, or 2 teaspoons dried basil

½ cup freshly grated Parmesan cheese, plus additional cheese for serving if desired

Put a large pot filled with a gallon of water on the stove to boil for the pasta. Add 1 tablespoon of the salt.

In a large skillet, melt the butter over medium heat. Lightly sauté the garlic and shallots for 3 minutes; stir constantly so that they don't brown.

Reduce the heat to low and stir in the cream, mustard, remaining ¼ teaspoon of salt, and pepper. Take the skillet off the heat and set it aside.

When the water is boiling, add the pasta and cook until it is done to your liking. Do not overcook it. When the pasta is nearly cooked, add the chicken, tomatoes, and basil to the reserved cream sauce in the skillet. Warm the mixture over low heat.

Drain the pasta well and stir it into the mixture in the skillet. Add the cheese and toss to mix well. Serve in warmed bowls and pass additional grated cheese separately, if desired.

✖ *Serves 4 as a main course, 6 as a first course*

Here is the technique for making and cooking ravioli. The pasta and the filling can be prepared a day or two ahead, but the ravioli must be shaped and cooked on the day you serve them. Jim liked these best in my homemade chicken broth (see Superior Chicken Broth, page 107). They are equally good when tossed with a mixture of melted butter and olive oil and Parmesan cheese, and, of course, you can also serve them with your favorite tomato sauce.

Basic Ravioli

▪▪▪▪▪▪▪▪▪▪▪▪▪▪▪▪▪▪▪▪▪▪▪▪▪▪

1 recipe Basic Pasta Dough (see page 135)
1 recipe Potato-Spinach Filling or Mushroom-Porcini filling (recipes follow)
1 quart Superior Chicken Broth (see page 107) or other homemade or canned chicken stock, or
   2 tablespoons butter melted with
   2 tablespoons olive oil
Grated Parmesan cheese

Cut dough into quarters. Work with one piece at a time, keeping the remaining dough covered with plastic wrap. Shape first piece of dough into a 3- by 5-inch rectangle. Knead the dough by passing it through the widest setting of a pasta machine three times. Between each time fold the dough into thirds, turn 180 degrees, and then roll through the machine again.

Continue passing pasta through machine, reducing the setting each time up to the second-to-last setting (so that the dough is about $\frac{1}{16}$ inch thick). The pasta will be about 4 to $4\frac{1}{2}$ inches wide.

Have ready a small bowl of water and pastry brush. Cut the band of pasta into two even lengths. Place on work surface. Onto one of the lengths, spoon or pipe two rows of $1\frac{1}{2}$-teaspoon-size dollops of the filling, about $\frac{1}{2}$ inch from the edge of the dough and spaced about 1 inch apart. Dip pastry brush in water and paint a strip down the center, then along the edges, and finally crosswise between the mounds. Lay the second band of dough over the first. Starting at one end, using one finger, push pasta down along the center so that it adheres. Press down crosswise between each mound and finally press down along the edges so that all the air is pushed out. Using a sharp knife or pastry wheel, cut into 2-inch squares. Place on a floured surface and repeat with remaining filling and pasta. If not cooking immediately, cover with plastic wrap.

When ready to cook, bring a large pot of water with 1 teaspoon salt to a boil. Working in batches, cook about 15 ravioli at a time. Cook ravioli for about 5 minutes. Remove with a slotted spoon to a cookie sheet lined with a clean towel to drain. Repeat with remaining ravioli.

If serving in Superior Chicken Broth, heat broth to boiling point. Ladle into shallow soup plates and add a few ravioli. Serve with Parmesan cheese. If serving with oil and butter, simply toss all together and serve with cheese.

✘ *Makes 4 dozen 2-inch ravioli*

Mushroom-Porcini Ravioli Filling

Dried porcini from Italy are full of robust earthy flavor. Just one-quarter ounce of them is enough to flavor three quarters of a pound of domestic mushrooms.

¼ ounce dried porcini mushrooms
½ cup boiling water
2 tablespoons olive oil
1 medium onion, peeled and finely chopped
 (about ½ cup)
1 clove garlic, peeled, minced, and smashed
¾ pounds fresh domestic mushrooms, with stems,
 finely chopped
2 tablespoons dry white wine
½ teaspoon dried basil
1 teaspoon kosher salt
2 teaspoons all-purpose flour
1½ tablespoons milk
2 tablespoons plain dry bread crumbs
1 egg yolk

Place the porcini in a small bowl and add boiling water. Allow to stand for 30 minutes. Drain, reserving liquid. Chop mushrooms and reserve.

Place 1 tablespoon oil and the onions in a large heavy skillet. Place over moderate heat and cook, stirring, for about 5 minutes, until soft and translucent. Stir in the garlic and cook 1 minute longer. Add remaining oil and chopped domestic mushrooms. Cook over high heat, stirring for about 3 minutes. Add the reserved porcini with

their liquid to the pan, along with wine, basil, and salt. Reduce heat and simmer uncovered, stirring occasionally, until the liquid has evaporated and mixture is quite dry. This should take about 30 minutes. Stir in flour and cook 2 minutes longer. Remove from heat and allow to cool.

Stir milk and bread crumbs together in a medium bowl. Allow to stand for 2 minutes to soften. Stir in egg yolk and mushroom mixture. Cover and refrigerate until needed.

✘ *Makes about 1½ cups*

Potato-Spinach Ravioli Filling

Fresh spinach adds a good flavor and color to hearty russet potatoes; with the addition of Parmigiano-Reggiano, a hearty vegetarian ravioli stuffing is created.

1 medium baking potato (about 8 ounces), peeled
 and cut into 1-inch chunks
Salt
½ pound fresh spinach, stemmed and washed
1 egg yolk
¼ cup grated Parmesan cheese
⅛ teaspoon freshly grated nutmeg
Kosher salt to taste
⅛ teaspoon freshly ground black pepper

Place potato in a small pan, cover with cold water, and add a pinch of salt. Over moderate heat, bring to a boil, and cook until tender. Remove from heat, drain, and cool to room temperature. Either pass through a potato ricer or mash with a fork in a medium bowl. Reserve.

Place spinach in a large pot with ½ cup cold water. Cover with lid and cook over moderate heat for about 3 minutes, stirring once, until just wilted. Drain in a strainer, pressing out most of the liquid. Finely chop spinach, either in a food processor or by hand, and reserve.

Stir egg into mashed potatoes with chopped spinach. Add remaining ingredients and blend well. Cover and refrigerate until needed.

✘ *Makes about 1½ cups (enough for 4 dozen 2-inch ravioli)*

Large Ravioli with Pepper Stuffing

▪▪▪▪▪▪▪▪▪▪▪▪▪▪▪▪▪▪▪▪▪▪▪

2 recipes Basic Pasta Dough (page 135)

3 tablespoons unsalted butter

1 medium onion, peeled and chopped

3 red bell peppers (about 1 pound), stemmed, seeded, roasted, peeled, and chopped

4 to 6 leaves fresh basil, chopped

1 medium potato (about 8 ounces), peeled and cooked

1 egg

¼ cup freshly grated Parmesan cheese (1 ounce)

¼ cup fresh bread crumbs (from 1 slice trimmed white bread)

Salt to taste

Freshly ground black pepper to taste

Goat Cheese Sauce (recipe follows)

Freshly grated Parmesan cheese, for serving, if desired

Using a pasta machine, roll the pasta dough into the thinnest sheets possible. Cut the dough into 3-inch squares, cover it with a clean towel, and proceed to make the ravioli filling.

In a medium skillet, melt the butter over medium-high heat, add the onions, and sauté until they are golden. Add the peppers and sauté them briefly.

Scrape the vegetables into the work bowl of a food processor. Add the basil, the potato, the egg, and the cheese and bread crumbs. Process the mixture to a smooth paste. Season it with salt and pepper and spoon it into a pastry bag fitted with a plain tip. Pipe about 1 tablespoon of the mixture in the center of half of the pasta squares. Cover each mound of filling with another square of pasta, and press the edges together to seal the package. If necessary, you can moisten the inside edges of the squares with water to help the squares of dough stick together.

Drop the ravioli into rapidly boiling salted water. Let them boil for 6 minutes (test one to see whether it is done), then drain them immediately. Arrange the ravioli on top of the Goat Cheese Sauce, either on a warmed serving plate or individual dinner plates. Sprinkle the ravioli with freshly grated Parmesan cheese and then run them briefly under the broiler to melt the cheese, if you like. ✖ *Makes 18 to 20 ravioli*

Goat Cheese Sauce

▪▪▪▪▪▪▪▪▪▪▪▪▪▪▪▪▪▪▪▪▪▪▪▪▪▪▪▪

2 tablespoons unsalted butter

1 scallion, trimmed and chopped

1 clove garlic, smashed, peeled, and minced

1 quart heavy cream

1 fresh sage leaf, or a small pinch of dried sage

Several sprigs fresh rosemary

8 ounces fresh goat cheese or Gorgonzola, cut into cubes at room temperature

Several leaves fresh basil, chopped

Salt to taste

Freshly ground black pepper to taste

In a large heavy saucepan, melt the butter over medium heat. Add the scallions and garlic and cook for 2 minutes, stirring frequently. Add the cream, sage, and rosemary. Cook, stirring occasionally, until the mixture has reduced and thickened.

Strain the cream mixture into a clean bowl. Add the cheese and whisk until the sauce is smooth. Add the basil and season with salt and pepper to taste.

PETER KUMP *was the original president of the Beard Foundation. Without him, it would not have existed. He has a cooking school in New York City that trains both professionals and amateurs. He is a past president of the International Association of Cooking Professionals and was a close friend of Jim's who visited Jim constantly when he was in the hospital. These ravioli get their own rather interesting dough. The ravioli are meant to be eaten as soon as made. They do not keep well.* ✍

Tirolean Raviolis

■■■■■■■■■■■■■■■■■■■■■■■■■■■

1⅓ cups rye flour
2 cups all-purpose flour
Salt
2 eggs
Cold water
1 medium white potato (about 6 ounces), peeled
    and cut into quarters
4 ounces unsalted butter
8 ounces onion, peeled and finely chopped
5 ounces farmer's cheese, or cream cheese, cut
    into small pieces
3 ounces Limburger cheese, or blue Castello, in
    small pieces
2 tablespoons minced chives
Freshly ground black pepper to taste

Place both flours, 1 teaspoon salt, and 1 egg in work bowl of food processor and pulse to combine. With the motor running gradually add enough water (about ⅔ cup) to form a stiff dough. Remove dough from work bowl, cover with plastic wrap, and allow to rest at room temperature for 30 minutes.

For the filling, place potato in a small pan, cover with water, and cook over high heat until cooked through. Drain and reserve potato.

Place half of the butter in a sauté pan and melt over medium heat. Stir in onions and cook until golden brown. Remove from heat. Pass the reserved potato through a potato ricer, or mash with a fork, and place in a bowl. Add half of the onions, the two cheeses, and half of the chives. Season with salt and pepper to taste. Reserve.

Knead the dough with the palm of your hands until it becomes smooth and elastic. Cut into 6 equal pieces. Working with one piece at a time (keep the remaining pieces covered so that they do not dry out), flatten dough slightly with fingertips. Roll the dough through a pasta machine, starting at the widest setting. Fold the dough into thirds, then pass through the machine at the next setting. Continue folding and rolling dough, each time at a narrower setting, until the strip is about 1/16 inch thick (about the next to last setting on the machine) and about 4 inches wide. Cut the strip across into 4 ½-inch pieces. Continue with the remaining dough.

Place the remaining egg in a small bowl with 1 to 2 tablespoons water and whisk to combine. Place a scant tablespoon of the reserved filling on one half of each pasta square. Paint egg wash around the edges of the pasta, fold in half, and pinch to close, removing most of the trapped air. As they are made, place ravioli on a towel until ready to cook.

Bring a large pot of salted water to a boil. Working in batches, cook about half the ravioli for about 10 minutes, with the water just simmering. Remove carefully with a slotted spoon to a warm serving dish. Repeat with the remaining ravioli.

In a small pan, melt the remaining butter until it just starts to brown. To serve the ravioli, pour over remaining cooked onions and browned butter. Sprinkle with remaining chives.

✖ *Makes 3 dozen ravioli*

ALICE WATERS *is one of the best known of American chefs. Her remarkable restaurant, Chez Panisse in Berkeley, was one of Jim's favorites. She has written several very popular books, trained quantities of chefs and so spawned generations of restaurants, and she has recognized talent in bakers, candy makers, florists, sausage makers, cheese makers, and a myriad of other specialties. She has found the people who help make her world unique and fostered their specialness so that they too make important contributions.*

Unfortunately, most of us don't have Alice's lush vegetable garden nor access to a grower like Tom Chino to supply us, so we used twelve regular garlic cloves in place of green garlic plants and the ravioli tasted fine. ✍

Green garlic, fresh garlic, is harvested at an early stage of its development. The texture is juicy and crisp. The cloves within the bulb are just beginning to form distinctly. The flavor is sweet, fresh, and very aromatic.

Green Garlic Ravioli

12 green garlic plants [or 12 regular garlic cloves, peeled, minced, and smashed]
4 to 5 tablespoons unsalted butter
8 ounces small new potatoes, peeled, halved, and cut into thin slices
Salt to taste
Freshly ground black pepper to taste
1 recipe Basic Pasta Dough (page 135)
1 cup chicken stock, homemade or canned

Cut the garlic bulbs from stalks, remove roots, and peel off outer layer of skin. Halve garlic

The James Beard Celebration Cookbook

and cut into slices. Cut green stalks in half, discard upper halves, trim lower halves down to tender center, and roughly chop them.

Melt 3 tablespoons butter in a sauté pan over moderate heat. Stir in potatoes and garlic. Cover and cook, stirring occasionally, for about 20 minutes, or until the mixture is soft enough to purée. Season with salt and pepper to taste. Transfer to work bowl of food processor and purée until smooth. Allow to cool and reserve.

Cut the pasta dough into three equal pieces. Working with one piece at a time, lightly flour the dough and roll through a pasta machine, starting at the widest setting and gradually working down to the next-to-thinnest setting. Lay the strip of pasta (this should be about 4 inches wide) on work surface and fold in half lengthwise to make a center crease to use as a guideline; unfold. Place a teaspoon of the filling every 2 inches on the bottom half of the pasta strip, just below the center crease. With a pastry brush dipped in water, lightly moisten the dough around each mound of filling. Fold the top half of the dough over the filling and press down firmly around each of the mounds. Cut between the pockets to form the ravioli either with a pastry wheel or a sharp knife. Place the ravioli on a floured baking sheet, cover, and finish with remaining pasta and filling. Refrigerate until ready to be cooked.

When ready to cook, bring a large pot of water with 1 teaspoon salt to a boil. Cook the ravioli in batches for about 3 minutes. Remove with a slotted spoon to a large serving platter.

In a small pan heat the chicken broth with the remaining butter to boiling point. Pour over the ravioli, garnish with black pepper, and serve hot. ✕ *Makes 30 to 35 ravioli*

SILVIA LEHRER *is a teacher who, like so many others, was once a student of Jim's. She owned Cooktique, a cooking school in Tenafly, New Jersey and published a book called* Cooking at Cooktique *in 1984.*

When we tested this recipe we found that—contrary to usual practice—it is better to make the pasta after the filling; otherwise the pasta tends to stiffen and crack. ✍

Beet Tortelli with Escarole and Hazelnut Butter

■■■■■■■■■■■■■■■■■■■■■■■■■■■

1 bunch escarole

2 tablespoons vegetable oil

2 tablespoons olive oil

1 medium red onion, peeled and cut into small dice

2 medium cloves garlic, smashed, peeled, and finely chopped

¼ pound pancetta, cut into small dice, optional

½ teaspoon salt

Freshly ground black pepper to taste

½ cup dry red wine

¼ cup finely chopped toasted hazelnuts

1 recipe Homemade Pasta Rossa (recipe follows)

□ *For the Sauce*

6 tablespoons unsalted butter

½ cup freshly grated Parmesan cheese

¼ cup finely chopped flat-leaf Italian parsley

Coarsely chopped toasted hazelnuts

Wash and soak the escarole. Spin or towel dry. Stack leaves and slice across into chiffonade about ¼ inch wide.

In a 12-inch skillet, heat vegetable and olive oil. Add onion and sauté over moderate heat for a minute or two. Add garlic and sauté for 40 to 50 seconds longer or until onions are tender. If you are using pancetta, add it with the garlic. Be careful not to allow the onions or garlic to brown.

Add escarole to the pan and cook, stirring frequently, until tender. Season with salt and pepper. Add red wine and cook, stirring occasionally, until moisture has evaporated. Taste and adjust seasoning if necessary. Add chopped

hazelnuts and stir to mix. Transfer to a bowl to cool and reserve. Stuffing can be made up to one day ahead.

Prepare pasta. Lay one thin sheet of the pasta across a cloth-lined table. Allow to dry for a few minutes. Place vegetable stuffing in 1-tablespoon mounds in a single row across half of the sheet of pasta. Dip a brush lightly in water and brush along both edges and between the mounds of stuffing. Fold over the pasta to cover the stuffing and press to seal around the edges and between the filling. Using a ravioli cutter, cut tortelli into approximately 2-inch squares. Repeat with remaining pasta and filling.

Line two cookie sheets with clean kitchen towels and sprinkle lightly with flour. Arrange the tortelli on the towels in a single layer, close together but not touching, or they will stick together. Set aside.

When ready to serve, place butter in large pasta bowl that can sit on top of the pot the pasta will cook in. This will keep the dish warm and melt the butter. When the pasta water is at a full rolling boil, remove serving dish. Add salt to the water and gradually put in the tortelli. Cover pot and quickly bring water back to the boil. Remove cover and cook pasta in briskly simmering water just until tender. Have a large colander in the kitchen sink to drain the tortelli the moment they are done.

Drain the tortelli, carefully shake the colander in the sink, and then transfer pasta to the serving bowl. Toss gently to coat with the melted butter and sprinkle over Parmesan, parsley, and coarsely chopped nuts. ✖ *Serves 6 to 8*

Homemade Pasta Rossa

■■■■■■■■■■■■■■■■■■■■■■■■■■

2 cups all-purpose flour
2 large eggs
1 tablespoon olive oil
Pinch salt
2 tablespoons finely chopped cooked beet (beet
    must be cooked until soft, peeled, then
    chopped extremely fine, wrapped in a clean
    kitchen towel and squeezed very dry)

Place flour in a mound on a large wooden board or other clean work surface. Make a well in the center deep enough to beat and hold eggs, oil, and salt. Add eggs to the well and beat carefully with a fork just to mix. Add oil and salt and beat until blended. Add chopped beets and stir to mix.

Gradually incorporate flour from inside of well, so the liquid does not seep out. When a heavy paste is formed, mix in as much flour as needed until the mixture becomes crumbly. Toss mixture back and forth with sides of your hands to make a soft dough that is no longer sticky. Gather dough into a ball and set aside. Scrape clean work surface with a pastry scraper. Sift any remaining flour through a sieve and use it to knead dough.

With clean hands, knead dough very gently with the heel of your hand by folding, turning, and pressing on a lightly floured surface. Knead until dough is smooth and supple, about 3 to 4 minutes. Any remaining flour should be passed through a sieve again and kept to coat the dough as you knead and thin the
pasta through the machine.

Cut dough in half and work with one piece at a time. Cover second piece with a clean kitchen towel to prevent drying. Flatten dough with fingertips and pass through the pasta machine at the widest setting. Lightly flour one side of dough, brushing off excess. Fold into thirds, floured side out, and press down to flatten. Pass dough between rollers folded-end first to squeeze out any air. Then repeat entire process 7 or 8 times as necessary until dough is smooth and elastic.

Adjust the knob on the side of the machine down one notch and pass dough through rollers. Continue in this fashion until you have passed dough through the Number 2 setting on the machine. Pasta is now ready for filling. Repeat with remaining dough. Do not allow pasta to dry, as sheets should be malleable and not brittle.

JIM FOBEL *has given of himself nobly to this book with recipes, testing, and with his interview on page 36 with James.* ✍

Here is my favorite version of the famous Italian pasta dish. On occasion I have substituted the tiny clams one can buy in Chinatown (using twice as many because they are twice as small) with more than excellent results. Following Marcella Hazan, I somewhat uncharacteristically use cheese and butter in this sauce.

Linguine with White Clam Sauce

▪▪▪▪▪▪▪▪▪▪▪▪▪▪▪▪▪▪▪▪▪▪▪▪▪▪▪▪

2 dozen small littleneck clams in their shells
¼ cup extra virgin olive oil
2 ounces finely chopped shallots or onion (about
   ½ cup)
2 cloves garlic, smashed, peeled, and minced
¼ teaspoon dried hot red pepper flakes
½ cup dry white wine
8 ounces dried linguine
¼ cup chopped Italian parsley, plus more for
   topping
¼ cup freshly grated Parmesan cheese, plus more
   for topping
2 tablespoons unsalted butter

Place clams in a large bowl of cold water, allow to soak for about 10 minutes, and scrub clean. Drain out the water and transfer clams to a large heavy pot. Cover tightly with lid and place over high heat. Cook for about 4 minutes, or until all clams are open. Remove from heat, uncover and allow to stand until cool enough to handle. With a spoon, over a medium bowl, scoop out clam meat and drain juices into bowl and reserve. Discard any clams that cannot be pried open.

In a heavy nonreactive saucepan, combine olive oil and shallots. Place over moderate heat and cook, stirring, for about 5 minutes or until soft and translucent. Stir in garlic and red pepper flakes and cook for about a minute longer. Pour in wine, bring mixture to a boil, and cook for 4 minutes or until sauce has reduced by about half.

Drain the clams, reserving the juice, roughly chop, and reserve. Add the juice to the sauce and simmer for about 3 minutes or until reduced by about a third. Remove from heat and reserve.

Bring a large pot of salted water to a boil. Add linguine and cook, stirring frequently, until pasta is al dente. Remove from heat, drain, and reserve.

Stir chopped clams into the reserved sauce and return mixture to a simmer. Remove from the heat and stir in parsley, cheese, and butter. Toss pasta with sauce and serve with additional parsley and cheese. ✖ *Serves 2 (amply) as a main course or 4 as a pasta course.*

PAUL MINNILLO *is the owner and chef of The Baricelli Inn in Cleveland, Ohio. He met Jim while studying at Peter Kump's New York Cooking School and then went on to work at the Dorchester in London. When you look at his recipe it may seem endlessly difficult. The flavor makes it well worth the fuss. Try it on a leisurely day with appreciative guests.*

Squid Ink and Calamata Olive Fettucini with Scallops, Prawns, and Goat's Cheese

□ *Pasta*

1 teaspoon squid ink (about 8 grams)

¼ cup warm water

1 cup pitted Calamata olives

¼ cup olive oil

4 cups all-purpose flour

2 eggs

□ *Sauce*

3 cups heavy cream

1 pound goat cheese

3 tablespoons olive oil

16 sea scallops

12 large shrimp (with heads on if possible), peeled

2 tablespoons all-purpose flour

Salt and freshly ground black pepper, to taste

1 tablespoon chopped chives

Stir squid ink and warm water together in large mixing bowl and reserve.

Place olives and oil in blender and purée until smooth. Stir into squid ink. Start folding in ⅓ of flour; when fully incorporated add 1 egg. Continue adding remaining flour and egg until all mixed. Add ¼ cup extra flour if necessary to achieve desired consistency for dough.

Turn dough out onto lightly floured surface and knead with hands for about 5 minutes. Divide into 8 pieces. Working with one piece of dough at a time, roll dough through a pasta machine starting with the machine's thickest setting and gradually working to setting number 3. Cut pasta into strips for fettucine. As batches of

fettucine are finished, place in parchment-lined sheet pans until ready to cook.

When ready to cook bring a large pot of salted water to a boil. Add pasta and cook for about 3 minutes, or until pasta floats to the surface and tastes cooked through. Drain through a colander and reserve.

Combine heavy cream and goat cheese in a medium pan. Bring to a boil over moderate heat, reduce heat to low, and simmer for about 20 minutes, stirring frequently, until sauce has reduced to about half.

When sauce is almost ready, heat olive oil in a medium skillet over moderate heat. Dredge scallops and shrimp with flour and sauté in skillet for about 4 minutes, until cooked through (time will depend on size of seafood).

To serve, toss pasta, sauce, and seafood together on large serving platter and season to taste with salt and pepper. Sprinkle with chopped chives. ✖ *Serves 10*

LIDIA BASTIANICH *is the chef and owner, along with her husband, of a fine restaurant, Felidia, in New York. Lydia comes from the disputed area along the Adriatic that joins Italy and Yugoslavia and centers on Trieste. It has been, at different periods, Austrian, Italian, and Yugoslavian and its cooking reflects all these traditions. Lydia's cooking leans more to the Italian influence, as her mother was Italian.*

Jim didn't like livers; but he might have been very tempted by this singularly rich and full-tasting sauce. ✍

Pappardelle with Duck, Livers, Mushrooms, and Bacon

▪▪▪▪▪▪▪▪▪▪▪▪▪▪▪▪▪▪▪▪▪▪▪▪▪▪▪

1 4½- to 5-pound duck, boned, excess fat removed, and cut into 1-inch pieces

¼ cup olive oil

Salt to taste

Freshly ground black pepper to taste

3 medium onions, chopped (about 2 cups)

⅓ cup finely chopped pancetta or bacon

½ cup coarsely chopped chicken livers

½ cup dried porcini mushrooms (1 ounce), soaked for 20 to 30 minutes in 2 cups hot water

2 bay leaves

1 small branch fresh rosemary or 1 teaspoon dried rosemary

4 whole cloves

1 cup dry white wine

3 tablespoons tomato paste

3 cups chicken stock, homemade or canned

Pappardelle (recipe follows)

¼ cup freshly grated Parmesan cheese, plus additional cheese for serving if desired

Pat the pieces of duck dry with paper toweling. In a large heavy casserole, warm the olive oil over high heat. Add the duck pieces to the hot oil and sprinkle liberally with salt and pepper. Cook over high heat, stirring often, until golden brown, about 10 minutes. Pour off about three-quarters of the fat in the casserole; discard it or keep it for another use.

Add the onions and pancetta to the casserole. Season again with salt and pepper. Sauté until the onions are lightly colored, about 8 minutes. Add the chicken livers and cook for 2 minutes, stirring constantly.

Strain the softened mushrooms, reserving the soaking liquid. Rinse off any grit and chop them coarsely; strain the soaking liquid through a fine sieve or a strainer lined with damp cheesecloth that has been wrung out thoroughly, and set it aside. Add the mushrooms, bay leaves, rosemary, and cloves to the casserole and cook, stirring frequently, for 5 minutes. Add the wine and cook, stirring constantly, until the wine has nearly evaporated. Stir in the tomato paste thoroughly and simmer for 2 minutes.

Add the stock and the reserved mushroom soaking liquid. Stir well and bring the mixture to a boil. Lower the heat and partially cover the casserole. Let the dish simmer for 45 minutes.

Discard the bay leaves and any visible rosemary stems. Skim fat from the sauce, and adjust the seasonings to taste. Cook Pappardelle (recipe follows); toss with Parmesan and about half of the sauce from the duck. ✖ *Serves 6*

Pappardelle

▪▪▪▪▪▪▪▪▪▪▪▪▪▪▪▪▪▪▪▪▪▪▪▪▪▪▪

3½ cups all-purpose flour

2 eggs

¼ teaspoon plus 1 tablespoon salt

1 teaspoon olive oil

¾ cup warm water

Mound 3 cups of the flour on a clean work surface and make a well in the center of the flour. Beat the eggs together with ¼ teaspoon of the salt. Pour the beaten eggs into the well. Using your fingertips, gradually stir the flour into the eggs. When about half of the flour has been incorporated, drizzle the oil over the egg mixture and stir it in.

The James Beard Celebration Cookbook

Clean your fingers of any sticky bits of dough (easily done by rubbing a little of the reserved ½ cup flour over them). Using your fingers, continue to incorporate flour into the egg mixture, alternating flour with dribbles of the warm water; work all of the flour on the work surface into the dough with just enough water to form a mass that is supple but not sticky.

Knead the dough until it is very smooth and silky, about 10 minutes. Add a little of the reserved flour if it becomes sticky, or a little warm water if it is too firm. Cover the dough and let it rest for 30 minutes.

Take one third of the dough and place it on a lightly floured board. (Cover the remaining dough so that it won't dry out while you work.) Roll out the dough on the board to a thickness of ⅛ of an inch and cut it into 5- by 1-inch papardelle strips. An easy way to do this is to roll all of the dough, starting from the end nearest you, around the rolling pin. Using a sharp knife, cut the dough down the length of the rolling pin into long, inch-wide strips, and then cut the strips into 5-inch lengths. The pasta is easily separated into individual pappardelles. Repeat with the remaining two thirds of the dough. Place the pappardelles on a tray lined with a lightly floured cloth and let them dry briefly, uncovered, in the refrigerator.

Bring 5 quarts of water to boil in a large pot and add 1 tablespoon salt. Add the pappardelles gradually, stirring them into the water with a wooden spoon. Let them boil vigorously, uncovered, until they are just tender, for 2 to 4 minutes. Drain the pasta well.

Return the pasta to the empty pot and pour over about half of the sauce from the duck and the Parmesan. Toss gently over medium heat. Serve immediately on warmed plates, generously topped with some of the duck and livers and more sauce. Pass additional Parmesan cheese separately, if you like.

Make this excellent dish only when you can get fresh sage—otherwise it doesn't taste right. You may find you only need half this quantity of sauce. Extra sauce can be frozen for another dinner.

Potato Gnocchi with Fresh Sage Sauce

6 large Idaho potatoes, boiled, peeled, riced, and
    allowed to cool completely
1 tablespoon salt
Freshly ground white pepper
2 eggs, lightly beaten
4 cups unbleached white flour
Fresh Sage Sauce (recipe follows)
1 cup freshly grated Parmesan cheese

Mound the cooled potatoes on a marble or wooden kitchen surface and make a well in the center of them. Stir 1 teaspoon of the salt and a dash of pepper into the eggs, then pour the eggs into the mound of potatoes. Using your hands, quickly work the potatoes and eggs to a smooth mixture. Gradually knead in 3 cups of the flour. Scrape the dough from the work surface occasionally with a knife and incorporate it. Try not to work the dough for longer than 10 minutes, as it will always take on additional flour and make the gnocchi heavier as it does so.

When the mass of dough has taken on 3 cups of the flour, it will still be sticky on the inside. Sprinkle it with some of the remaining flour and cut it into 8 equal pieces. Dust your hands, the work surface, and the dough again with flour. Take a lump of dough and roll it with your hands into a rope about ½ inch thick. Cut the rope into ½-inch-long gnocchi.

Roll out and cut the remaining dough, dusting your hands, the work surface, and the dough with flour as necessary. While shaping the gnocchi, bring 6 quarts of water to a boil with the remaining 2 teaspoons of salt.

Drop the gnocchi, a few at a time, into the

boiling water; stir constantly with a long-handled wooden spoon. Cook the gnocchi until they rise to the water's surface, about 3 to 5 minutes, or until cooked through. Scoop the cooked gnocchi up with a slotted spoon and transfer them to warmed serving dishes. Toss the gnocchi with Fresh Sage Sauce, add a grinding of pepper, and sprinkle with freshly grated Parmesan cheese.

✗ *Serves 6*

Fresh Sage Sauce

½ pound unsalted butter
8 fresh sage leaves, quartered
2 cups heavy cream
1 cup chicken stock, homemade or canned
Salt to taste
Freshly ground white pepper to taste

In a medium saucepan, melt the butter over medium-high heat. Stir the sage into the hot butter and let it cook for 2 minutes.

Stir in the cream and stock. Let the mixture simmer for 5 minutes. Season with salt and pepper.

These are the noodles I developed for a class in San Francisco, later published in *American Food and California Wine*, and which Jim used in *Beard on Pasta*. The recipe was developed to go with Daphne Engstrom's golden caviar from California Sunshine. Daphne was a great friend of Jim's and sometimes supplied caviar of various kinds, salmon and sturgeon, for sumptuous tastings in class. At that time, the golden caviar was brand-new and we realized that its slightly crisp eggs would not be destroyed or bleed into a hot sauce.

The idea for the noodles was a takeoff from blini. The beer was used to simulate the yeasty taste of blini without having the dough so risen that it would not roll.

Buckwheat Noodles with Golden American Caviar and Lemon Beurre Blanc

½ cup beer, at room temperature
1 teaspoon dry yeast
¼ cup buckwheat flour
1 cup all-purpose flour
¼ teaspoon kosher salt
½ cup plus 1 teaspoon fresh lemon juice
½ pound cold unsalted butter, cut in ½-inch
　　pieces
2 tablespoons golden American caviar

In a small bowl combine ¼ cup beer, yeast, and 2 tablespoons buckwheat flour. Cover loosely with a towel and place in a warm place to rise for about an hour.

Uncover and stir in remaining buckwheat flour, all-purpose flour, salt, and enough of the remaining beer to make a soft but firm dough. Cover dough loosely and allow to rest for 20 to 30 minutes.

Divide the dough into quarters. Working with one piece of dough at a time, begin to roll the dough through a pasta machine starting with the machine set on the widest opening. Repeat rolling the pasta, working down to the second or third thinnest setting. Dust lightly with flour if dough becomes too sticky as you work.

Hang the rolled dough up to dry slightly. Repeat with the remaining pieces of dough.

Take the first piece of dough and cut it for fettucine. Toss the cut noodles with a little all-purpose flour. Cut remaining sheets of pasta.

When ready to cook pasta, bring a large pot of salted water to a boil. Add pasta and cook until barely tender. Drain thoroughly.

To make sauce: Pour ½ cup lemon juice into a heavy non-aluminium saucepan and cook over moderate heat until reduced to about 1 tablespoon. Remove from heat, and when liquid becomes just cool enough to touch for a couple of seconds, quickly whisk in 2 pieces of the butter. When it is soft and creamy, but not melted, gradually whisk in remaining butter. As more butter is added and the pan cools, it will be necessary to return the pan to low heat for a short time.

When all the butter has been incorporated, add the remaining lemon juice and 1 tablespoon of caviar.

When both sauce and pasta are ready, spoon about 2 tablespoons sauce into each of 4 salad plates. Mound equal amounts of cooked pasta over sauce and spoon over remaining sauce. Top each plate with remaining caviar. ✘ *Serves 4*

is another of our fine chefs, like Mark Miller and Robert del Grande, who are escapees from academia. She was taking her degree in Chinese poetry of the Sung when she went to Taiwan to perfect her Mandarin. Her Chinese is fine, but what she really perfected was a love of China's food. She started to cater and write articles; then she moved to San Francisco to teach, write a big book, and open her own restaurant, China Moon. She first met Jim during her early days in California, when she was much in awe (page 223). I asked her if she would contribute a congee recipe since it was the only particular Chinese dish that Jim talked about having eaten at home as a child. She responds in her usual inventive fashion, Americanizing in a way James would have deeply approved. ✍

The classic southern Chinese breakfast is a steaming bowlful of white rice porridge, typically made from rice left over from the evening meal and embellished with salty, protein-rich condiments—wedges of purple thousand-year-old eggs, slivers of pressed duck, whole silvery fish embalmed in salt. At China Moon we indulge in a bit of heresy. We add wild rice and a rich, roasted-garlic-and-serrano-chili–infused chicken stock to the bowl, and crown it with house-smoked meat and a tangle of scallions and fried ginger threads. The result is a great anytime snack, perfect for a hangover or nursing a tired belly.

China Moon Wild Rice Congee

½ cup white rice, short- or medium-grain preferred

⅓ cup wild rice

5 cups rich chicken broth

1 tablespoon good-quality Chinese rice wine or good sherry

1¼ teaspoons kosher salt, if using unsalted broth

Freshly ground black pepper, if desired

1 cup finely slivered smoked ham, chicken, duck, or fish

⅔ cup finely slivered green and white scallion and/or coarsely chopped coriander

⅔ cup finely slivered fresh ginger, fried in 350° F. corn or peanut oil just until golden, about 5 seconds, and drained

Rinse the white rice in repeated changes of cold water until the water runs clear. Drain well. Rinse the wild rice once or twice with cold water. Drain well.

Combine the white rice, wild rice, broth, salt, and pepper in a heavy 2½- to 3-quart pot. Bring to a boil, stirring occasionally; then let bubble for 5 minutes.

Reduce the heat to maintain a simmer, cover tightly, and cook for 1 hour. At the end of the hour, the mixture will be soupy and the rice splayed at the ends. Taste and adjust seasoning, if necessary, then portion into heated bowls. Sprinkle with the toppings in the order listed and serve at once. ✖ *Serves 2 to 4*

SEPPI RENGGLI. *James lived in many restaurants as if they were extensions of his home. Surely, the most home-place was the Four Seasons in New York, created by Joe Baum in the Restaurant Associates days and then bought and polished by the present proprietors, Paul Kovi and Tom Margittai. Jim was a consultant to the original Four Seasons and even roped in Julia Child on the occasion of one spectacular dinner.*

The Seasons was so much home that, like a good mother, it sent food to the hospital during James's frequent incarcerations. You can imagine the astonishment of patients and hospital staff alike when a page attired in bright pink jacket if it was spring, leaf green if it was summer, arrived lofting an enormous tray replete with dome-covered dishes and with filled shopping bags looped over his arm. If Jim was on a special diet, the food was prepared to match its restrictions. Came the next meal period, came the next page.

By the time Tom and Paul were fully in charge, the extremely talented Swiss chef Seppi Renggli had taken over the kitchens. He would often make special dishes for Jim, and some of them ended up in Jim's columns. Seppi had been with Restaurant Associates for many years before joining Tom and Paul. The recipe he gives here is based on one done at La Fonda del Sol. A blind and brilliant cook, Elena Zelayeta, had been one of the consultants and Seppi made this dish for Jim in memory of Elena and the years the three of them worked together. ✍

This is a good dish to prepare in advance. If you want to bake it straight out of the refrigerator, set it in a 300° F. oven for 30 minutes, and then turn the heat up to 400° F. for 10 minutes longer.

Green Chili Rice

3 tablespoons lard or unsalted butter
1 small onion, peeled and chopped
1 cup long-grain rice, rinsed under cold running water and drained thoroughly
2 cups chicken stock, homemade or canned
1 cup white wine
2 medium jalapeño peppers, stemmed, seeded, and chopped
1 green bell pepper, stemmed, seeded, deribbed, and cut into ¼-inch dice
1 Anaheim pepper, stemmed, seeded, deribbed, and cut into ¼-inch dice
Salt to taste
1 stalk celery, trimmed, strung, and cut into ¼-inch dice
½ cup diced Monterey Jack cheese (cubes about ¼ inch)
½ cup diced sharp Cheddar cheese (cubes about ¼ inch)
½ cup diced Mozzarella (cubes about ¼ inch)
1½ cups sour cream
Unsalted butter, for the baking dish

Preheat oven to 350° F.

In a large oven-proof skillet, melt the fat and sauté the onions. Add the rice and stir until the grains are well coated. Add the stock, wine, all of the peppers, and salt. Bring the mixture to a boil and cover the skillet. Let the rice cook in the oven for 15 minutes, until the liquid has been absorbed.

Pour the hot mixture into a large mixing bowl. Fold in the celery, cheeses, and sour cream. Butter a 9-inch by 13-inch baking dish. Turn the rice mixture into the buttered dish, and place it in the oven. Turn the oven up to 400 degrees° F. and bake the rice for 20 minutes. The top should be a nice, golden brown. ✕ *Serves 4 to 6*

Wild Mushroom Risotto

■ ■

5 tablespoons unsalted butter

1 cup converted white rice

⅔ cup finely chopped yellow onion

1¼ cups chicken stock

¾ cup dry white wine or brut Champagne

6 ounces fresh wild mushrooms, trimmed and
      thinly sliced (about 2 cups)

⅓ cup heavy cream

Salt to taste

White pepper to taste

Pinch ground nutmeg

2 tablespoons finely chopped fresh parsley

Freshly grated Parmesan cheese, optional

     Melt 3 tablespoons of the butter in a
medium-sized heavy saucepan over moderate
heat. Stir in the rice and onion. Increase the heat
to medium-high and cook, stirring frequently, for
3 to 4 minutes until rice is translucent and onion is
softened.

     Stir in broth and wine or Champagne.
Bring to a boil. Reduce heat to low, cover and
simmer for 20 minutes.

     While rice is cooking, melt remaining butter

in a skillet and sauté mushrooms until
tender. With a slotted spoon, remove from skillet
to a plate and reserve.

     Remove rice from heat and allow to stand,
covered, for about 5 minutes, until all the liquid is
absorbed. Stir in reserved mushrooms, cream, salt,
pepper, and nutmeg.

     Spoon into serving dish and sprinkle with
chopped parsley. Serve with Parmesan cheese, if
desired. ✖ *Makes 4 cups; serves 6 as a side dish*

ANNA TERESA CALLEN *teaches Italian cooking at Peter Kump's New York Cooking School and at her own school. She has written some excellent books, is a devoted supporter of the Foundation, and is very active in Italian culinary organizations.* ✍

Risotto Fumo e Bolle

∎∎∎∎∎∎∎∎∎∎∎∎∎∎∎∎∎∎∎∎∎∎∎∎∎∎∎

(Risotto Smoke and Bubbles)

4 tablespoons unsalted butter
1 onion, peeled and finely chopped
6 cups chicken broth
1 cup spumante or other sparkling wine
1½ cups arborio rice
3 ounces smoked mozzarella, diced
Freshly grated Parmesan cheese

Melt butter over low heat in a casserole. Add onion and cook until soft and translucent.

Place broth in a pot and bring to the boil. Lower heat and keep at a simmer.

When onion is cooked, add a little wine and cook until wine evaporates. Add the rice and stir so that the rice is coated with the butter and onion mixture. Add remaining wine and continue cooking, stirring constantly, until wine is absorbed. Add broth, one ladle at a time, stirring constantly, until rice is done. Sprinkle over cheese and serve.

✗ *Serves 6*

BARBARA KAFKA. *For me this is a recipe rich in*
memories. As many people in this book mention, Jim was devoted to Olympia oysters. When it came time to create recipes for The American, a Joe Baum production in Kansas City, where we both worked as consultants, it seemed appropriate at the time to make a new American dish using Olympias. If you cannot— and most of us can't—get Olympias in the shell or shucked in refrigerated bottles, substitute a cup of any fresh oysters and cut them into quarter-inch pieces with a scissors. Later, we taught this in class. ✍

Risotto with Olympia Oysters

▪▪▪▪▪▪▪▪▪▪▪▪▪▪▪▪▪▪▪▪▪▪▪▪▪▪

9 tablespoons unsalted butter
3 tablespoons chopped shallots
1 tablespoon chopped parsley
1 cup arborio rice
1 cup shucked Olympia oysters, with 1 cup oyster
    liquor
1 cup chicken stock, homemade or canned
1 cup dry white wine
1 cup fresh or bottled clam juice
Freshly ground black pepper to taste
¾ cup freshly grated Parmesan cheese

In a 2-quart saucepan melt 3 tablespoons of the butter over medium heat. Add the shallots and cook, stirring once or twice, for 2 minutes. Add the parsley and rice, and stir to coat the rice with the butter. Add the oyster liquor, and shake the pan gently until the liquid begins to simmer. Lower the heat slightly. Using a wooden spoon, stir the rice until the liquid is almost completely absorbed. The rice will form a cohesive mass at this point.

Combine the chicken stock, wine, and clam juice. Add enough liquid to barely cover the rice. Continue cooking and stirring until the liquid is absorbed. Continue adding the liquid and stirring and cooking until all the liquid has been added. The rice should be creamy and firm but not hard. If not yet done, add more liquid. Season to taste with pepper. Whisk in the remaining 6 table-spoons butter with the Parmesan cheese and oysters. Mix thoroughly and serve immediately.

✗ *Serves 6*

CHRIS KUMP *is the owner with his wife, Margaret Fox, of Café Beaujolais, the restaurant they run in Mendocino and from which they ship specialty products by mail. Chris got a head start in cooking and in knowing Jim because he is the son of Peter Kump.* ✍

My first memory of Jim is from the week he spent with my father and me in Austria when I was sixteen: I baked a Dobostorte for him and he gave me a copy of *Delights and Prejudices*. Though I saved the book and cooked several of its recipes, I wasn't old enough yet to fully appreciate its wealth of reminiscences of a childhood in the Pacific Northwest. (I was too absorbed in the firsthand imprinting of my own young palate.)

Upon moving to Mendocino five years ago, I finally sat down with the text itself. And there it was—the sensibility to seek out the wild mushrooms, nuts, and berries, the seashore, the salmon, the clams and mussels, in all their indigenous glory; to see the beauty of one's own backyard and to celebrate the resources of one's own region— what the French call *cuisine du terroir*. To communicate through your food the love and respect you have for your home is the inspiration Jim left me with, and that's what I've

strived for cooking in Mendocino ever since that summer when I first read his book and climbed in the Mendocino surf to gather the urchins for this dish.

Sea Urchin and Clam Risotto

4 ounces sea urchin roe

1 cup crème fraîche

Juice of 1 lemon

3 dozen manila clams (or any other small clams), scrubbed clean

2 cups dry white wine

4 tablespoons unsalted butter

2 to 3 shallots, peeled and finely chopped

1½ cups arborio or pearl rice

2 to 3 cups homemade clam broth or bottled clam juice

3 tablespoons chopped fresh thyme (or 2 teaspoons dried)

½ cup minced fresh chives

1 cup freshly grated asiago or Parmesan cheese

6 chive blossoms and 18 thyme flowers for garnish, if available

If using whole sea urchins, carefully remove roe from the shells and reserve shells to use as serving bowls. Place roe in a blender or food processor and purée until smooth. Pass mixture through a fine sieve. You should have about ½ cup purée. Stir in crème fraîche and lemon juice. Cover and refrigerate until ready to use.

Place cleaned clams and white wine in a large pot. Cover and place over high heat. Cook for about 4 minutes or until all the clams have opened. Remove from the heat and remove clams with a slotted spoon. Strain cooking liquid through cheesecloth into a small saucepan and keep warm over low heat. Remove clam meat from shells and reserve. Discard shells.

Melt butter in a medium saucepan over moderate heat. Add shallots and cook for about 3 minutes, stirring, until shallots are translucent. Stir in rice and cook for about 3 minutes longer. Start adding clam cooking liquid in ½-cup increments, stirring with each addition until all the liquid has been incorporated. Continue until all the liquid has been added, stirring constantly. Then add clam broth in the same manner. After about 25 minutes of continual stirring over moderate to low heat, the risotto should have a creamy consistency with the grains distinct and al dente but not chalky or raw in the center.

Stir in the reserved sea urchin roe mixture and clams, with about three quarters of the chopped thyme and chives and one quarter of the cheese. Increase the heat slightly and stir risotto quickly to warm the clams and return the rice to its creamy texture.

To serve, pour risotto into 6 warmed soup bowls or the sea urchin shells. Sprinkle with remaining thyme and chives and half of the remaining cheese. Decorate each bowl with a chive blossom and 3 thyme flowers and serve accompanied by the remaining cheese in a bowl.

✗ *Serves 6*

FISH & SHELLFISH

JIM LOVED FISH AND SEAFOOD. HIS FAVORITE CRAB WAS ALWAYS THE DUNGENESS OF HIS YOUTH. SAN FRANCISCO'S PETRALE SOLE WAS A MUST ORDER WHEN WE WERE ON THE WEST COAST. HE SANG THE PRAISE OF

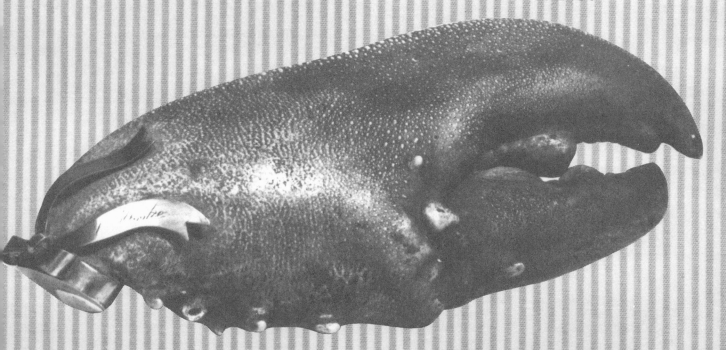

RAZOR CLAMS. MOST OF ALL HE WROTE A GREAT BIG BOOK, JAMES BEARD'S FISH COOKERY, IN 1954, LONG BEFORE FISH WAS A POPULAR ALTERNATIVE. HIS REVISION CAME OUT AS JAMES BEARD'S NEW FISH COOKERY IN 1976. IT WAS IN HIS INTRODUCTION TO THE REVISION THAT HE GAVE VOICE TO A GROWING CONCERN ABOUT THE ENVIRONMENT AND LOOKED FORWARD TO MORE AQUACULTURE.

IT WAS IN THE REVISION AS WELL THAT HE ESPOUSED THE CANADIAN COOKING METHOD FOR FISH, WHICH SAYS THAT FISH SHOULD BE COOKED FOR TEN MINUTES PER INCH OF THICKNESS OF THE FISH (MEASURED AT THE THICKEST POINT WHEN THE FISH IS ON ITS SIDE) NO MATTER WHAT THE COOKING METHOD, WITH ONLY THE PROVISO THAT FOR BAKING THE OVEN SHOULD BE AT 450° F. HE ADDS THAT FROZEN FISH SHOULD BE COOKED FROM THE FROZEN STATE FOR TWENTY MINUTES FOR EACH INCH.

ONE HAS ONLY TO LOOK AT JIM'S BOOK TO SEE HIS INTEREST IN THE WORLD AROUND HIM, ITS PROBLEMS, AND ITS PROGRESS, AND TO SEE THAT HE WAS A CONSUMMATE ADVENTURER INTO THE PAST—TO RETAIN THE BEST AND OUT OF CURIOSITY—AND INTO A WIDE RANGE OF CULINARY CULTURES—TO BRING BACK THE BOOTY OF THE BEST. LONG BEFORE THE POLYGLOT CUISINE OF TODAY, HE WAS INCLUDING SPANISH, ITALIAN, FRENCH, REGIONAL AMERICAN, RUSSIAN, AND CHINESE RECIPES. HIS TRAVELS AROUND AMERICA ALSO SHOW IN THE WIDE VARIETY OF FISH AND SHELLFISH HE USES. THE BOOK IS IN NO WAY PROVINCIAL.

HOWEVER, HE HOLDS FAST TO HIS DEAR FRIENDS; HELEN EVANS BROWN AND IRMA ROMBAUER MAKE THE TRIP FROM BOOK TO BOOK WITH HIM INTO JAMES BEARD'S NEW FISH COOKERY.

Irma Rombauer was surely beloved by thousands—or probably millions—of young Americans, and her cookbook, *Joy of Cooking*, is now edited by her daughter.

This fish pudding was one of Irma Rombauer's favorites as a child, and she has graciously passed it on to me. . . . It is a perfect way of using up leftover fish. This recipe is for 6 people. If you wish to serve 3, cut the ingredients in half and steam the pudding in a 1-pound coffee tin or small mold. [*JB*]

Irma Rombauer's Steamed Fish Pudding

2 cups flaked or ground cooked halibut or other fish
¾ cup bread crumbs
¼ cup melted butter
3 eggs, separated
2 teaspoons lemon juice or 1 teaspoon Worcestershire sauce
Salt
Paprika

Combine the fish, bread crumbs, butter, egg yolks, lemon juice, and seasonings. Beat egg whites stiff and fold them into the mixture. Pour into a well-buttered timbale mold or pudding tin and steam for 1 hour. Unmold onto a hot platter and serve with cream sauce flavored with Worcestershire or a mustard or tomato sauce.

✖ *Serves 6*

HELEN McCULLY *was a tartly opinionated woman who loved to gossip, which she and Jim did early almost every morning. Helen had been the first food editor of a major woman's magazine who was not a home economist and she had been attacked vigorously in her role. She never forgot that and continued to refer to it obliquely in the stage demonstrations that she gave with her young discovery, Jacques Pépin.*

As much as food was her work—she wrote several cookbooks, as well as being an editor—international education was her passion, and much of her time and money was spent on foreign students and on the IIE.

When, with Burt Wolf and brilliant graphic designer Milton Glaser, James started The Good Cooking School, whose most significant achievement may have been <u>The Cook's Catalogue,</u> *it was natural that he include Helen in a venture that was supposed to go on to have a permanent cooking school and be a culinary center in many of the ways the James Beard House has become. The Good Cooking School group did continue on long enough to produce several books and cooking classes around the country.*

Helen contributed the following recipe to the <u>Great Cook's Guide to Fish.</u> *Let's hope that Helen and Jim are eating fish and gossiping someplace still.*

Shad Roe Mousse with Sorrel Sauce

3 pairs small shad roe
3 cups heavy cream
3 egg whites
Salt
Freshly ground pepper
Paprika
Sorrel sauce (recipe follows)

Butter a 9-inch ring mold (not aluminum) very thoroughly and refrigerate.

Cut the pairs of shad roe apart and remove as much of the filmy skin as possible. Purée, about half at a time, in an electric food processor with a steel blade. Place the purée in a generous bowl with the cream, egg whites, and seasonings to taste. Beat steadily with an electric beater for about 10 minutes.

Pour the mixture into the prepared mold and place in the refrigerator for 30 minutes or so.

To bake, place the mold in a baking pan; pour in enough boiling water to reach two-thirds up the side of the mold. Bake in a preheated 350° F. oven on the middle rack for 1 hour and 15 minutes, or until a knife inserted in the center comes out clean.

While the mousse is baking, make the Sorrel Sauce, beginning with a Béchamel sauce (page 232). To serve, unmold the mousse onto a warm serving platter. Spoon some of the Sorrel Sauce over the ring and serve the remainder on the side. ✕ *Serves 6*

Sorrel Sauce

1½ cups Béchamel sauce
½ cup heavy cream
Salt
White pepper
½ tablespoon butter
¼ cup (approximately) fresh sorrel, cut in fine matchstick strips
2 tablespoons capers, well drained

Bring the white sauce to a simmer, then beat in the cream, a small amount at a time, until the sauce is lightly thickened. Season to taste with salt and white pepper. Set aside for the moment.

Melt the butter. When foaming, add the shredded sorrel and simmer for 5 to 6 minutes. Strain off any surplus juice and stir the sorrel into the cream sauce. Bring to a simmer again, then add the capers. Serve over Mousse.

JIMELLA LUCAS.

Jim got excited every time he discovered a new talent. The combination of a good young chef who was a woman and almost in his Gearhart backyard was really something to crow about and he did, both to his friends and, in print, to the world at large. ✍

One night, fourteen years ago, while chef at Jake's Famous Crawfish Restaurant in Portland, Oregon, I learned that James Beard would be coming to dinner. Needless to say, my anxiety level went to red alert. And if it weren't enough to have him there, he was bringing along local food editors!

Well, the evening came. And just as Murphy's Law dictates, the dining room got exceptionally busy just as the Beard party arrived. The meal unfolded, and I still recall the entree he ordered—Petrale Sole Meunière. And while I don't remember what the other guests had, I do retain the memory of how full my hands were that evening.

As the meal progressed to its conclusion, the waiter returned to the kitchen with table talk about food and product and to announce that Mr. Beard had asked who was in charge of the kitchen, and that further he had asked me to come out. Nervous as a cat, I walked out of the kitchen to introduce myself in person. I've forgotten what I had to say at the start; I'm sure, however, that I said about half my words backwards. What did stay with me was the man's gift for putting me at ease. I found his questions on food relaxing, and soon I felt I had connected with him.

The next day's food review was on a variety of Portland food places critiqued by Mr. Beard. I anxiously scanned the article and there, in a small paragraph, was the account of his meal at Jake's. That paragraph held what remains to this day one of the highest compliments of my career: "The kitchen is in the thorough hands of a woman, Jimella Lucas."

Then four years down the road, my partner, Nanci Main, and I opened our own restaurant on the Long Beach, Washington, Peninsula. One day we heard that a word or two from Yvonne Rothert, food editor of the *Portland Oregonian*, had encouraged Mr. Beard, who was teaching at nearby Gearhart, Oregon, to come for dinner.

Once again he liked our food: this time so much that he wrote a very complimentary column. Through the years he was to come over and over again. Nanci and I both know how very fortunate we were to have the friendship and support of Mr. Beard through the next five years. He had a way of inspiring and encouraging us to stay within our own sense of integrity to what we were; he had a lot to do with keeping alive our zest and reverence for food.

Moments we shared with him during that time come back often, moments that helped to cultivate and enhance our careers. All we had to do was recognize in his eyes the exhilaration stirred by what we were doing with food. He supported us as we accented the natural largess found on his beloved home turf, the Pacific Northwest. We remember, too, the deep compassion of those eyes when he appeared in the restaurant after Nanci and I had suffered a house fire; he brought a personally autographed copy of one of his cookbooks to start our culinary library again.

We cannot forget his wisdom and kindness as he advised us to make time for things other than work—I see him still, leaning against the bakery sink, spending a few moments after a meal at The Ark.

He inspired a kind of playfulness in us too: After he so generously did an introduction to our first cookbook, we decided not to send him a copy, but to deliver it by hand. We flew to New York to present it to him and to take him to lunch. Unhappily, his health wouldn't let him join us, but for three days, he shot us around that great city, finding the best chocolates, the sweetest butters, the finest sherries. Then, at the end of our stay, he called the Four Seasons with instructions to take good care of us when we came to dinner.

In 1984, when he came to visit, we were

struck by how carefully he chose from the menu; he was under doctor's orders. Then, suddenly, he told Nanci to change his order. He wanted all his old favorites: scotch on the rocks before dinner, panfried salmon cheeks with Cognac, bread pudding. Nanci and I knew this visit was a farewell.

We both remember vividly the end of the visit. We both ignored, for the moment, the frantic pace of our August operation. We stood with him for pictures, then it was time to say good-bye. We walked him to his car and stood there together watching him drive away. As his car turned the corner and went out of our sight, an overwhelming sense of fullness washed over us. It is that fullness that, even today, provokes the realization of how terribly we miss him.

These moments renew us in our passion to continue his work by encouraging, inspiring the people who aspire to our profession to maintain the same integrity, respect, and responsibility that he explained, asserted, and—the most important—exemplified toward what we in the profession do with food.

Sole with Pesto
■■■■■■■■■■■■■■■■■■■■■■■■

3 eggs
½ cup half-and-half or milk
4 fillets of petrale sole, each 5 to 6 ounces (can substitute flounder, lemon sole, or snapper)
2 tablespoons all-purpose flour
2 ounces clarified butter
⅓ cup dry white wine
3 tablespoons Pesto Sauce (recipe follows)

Lightly beat eggs with half-and-half in a shallow bowl or pie plate. Place the fish fillets in the egg mixture and allow them to stand for a few minutes, until they have absorbed some of the liquid.

Place flour on a plate. Remove fish from the egg mixture and lightly dust with the flour. Remove any excess flour from fish, as it will burn.

Heat butter in a large heavy skillet over moderate to high heat. Add the fillets and sauté for about 2 minutes. Turn the fillets over and cook for about a minute longer.

With a wide spatula remove fish to a warm platter and keep fish warm.

Place the skillet over moderate heat and deglaze with ¼ cup white wine, stirring to loosen the pieces on the bottom of the pan. Stir in the Pesto Sauce and remaining wine and simmer, stirring, for a few minutes to blend the sauce.

Pour sauce over warm fish and serve immediately. ✕ *Serves 4*

Pesto Sauce
••

5 cups cleaned, firmly packed fresh basil leaves
¼ cup chopped fresh parsley
9 cloves garlic, peeled and minced
½ cup pine nuts
½ cup freshly grated Parmesan cheese
1 teaspoon salt
¾ cup olive oil

Place basil leaves, parsley, and garlic in work bowl of a food processor and process to finely chop. Add pine nuts, cheese, and salt and process until fully incorporated.

With the motor running, add the oil slowly, in a steady stream. Continue to blend until mixture becomes a smooth green paste.

Scrape into plastic container with lid and store in the refrigerator. To freeze in plastic containers, pour about ½ inch olive oil on the top to form a seal.

MARION CUNNINGHAM *started out as one of James's most gifted students. As so frequently happened with such students, James made sure that she worked with him and that she developed a career in food. Marion taught with Jim in Seaside and San Francisco and went on to become the modern-day Fannie Farmer. She also has written other books as her own splendid self, taught, and written for newspapers and magazines.*

While Jim was alive, she assisted him far beyond the call of class. She chauffeured and she arranged. An early riser like Jim, she arose at the crack of dawn to cross the bridge into San Francisco and make sure that all of us were able to do our best.

For her own words on Jim, see page 355. ✍

The sauce that accompanies these fillets is quite thick—not a sauce that pours. It would be delicious with steak served with warm tortillas, too. This recipe makes about 1½ cups of sauce.

San Felipe Red Snapper

☐ *For the Sauce*

1 ripe avocado, peeled and pitted
6 tablespoons fresh lemon juice
3 cloves garlic, smashed and peeled
2 fresh Anaheim chilies, halved, seeded, and
    stemmed, or 1 canned Anaheim chile, rinsed,
    halved, seeded, and stemmed
1½ teaspoons salt
Hot red pepper sauce, to taste (optional)
½ cup fresh cilantro leaves
1 egg yolk
⅓ cup olive oil

☐ *For the fish*

2 tablespoons unsalted butter
2 tablespoons vegetable oil
⅓ cup all-purpose flour
6 red snapper or rock cod fillets (each fillet to
    make one portion), skin removed if desired
Salt to taste
Freshly ground black pepper to taste
Sprigs of fresh cilantro for garnish

For the sauce: Put the avocado, lemon juice, garlic, chiles, and 1 teaspoon of the salt in a blender or food processor. Process the mixture until it is smooth. Taste for salt, adding more if necessary. Add the cilantro and egg yolk, and process until well blended. With the machine running, add the olive oil in a thin, steady stream, and continue processing until thoroughly incorporated to make a thick sauce. If you would like a thinner sauce, beat in water, a little at a time, until the sauce is as thin as you like.

Put the butter and the oil in a large skillet and melt over medium heat. Lightly flour the fish fillets on all sides. When the fat is hot, place the fish in the skillet and season with salt and pepper. Fry quickly on each side until the crust is golden and the meat is just cooked.

Remove the fillets to a warm platter. Spoon some of the sauce over each piece of fish, and garnish with sprigs of cilantro. Pass extra sauce in a small bowl. ✖ *Serves 6*

Baum's Windows on the World at New York's World Trade Center. His version of leg of lamb with a delicious confit of tomatoes and olives is still on the menu. Joe is no longer at Windows on the World. Today, Hermann Reiner is the gifted chef. In Cellar in the Sky, a small elegant restaurant serving a fixed menu with an array of compatible wines, he prepares special dishes, one of which he shares here. Any of its several components could, on its own, be a welcome addition to a dinner. 🖎

Baked Red Snapper with Confit of Vegetables, Fried Onion Rings, Pepper Tartlets, and Two Pepper Sauces

Confit of Vegetables (recipe follows)
Green Pepper Sauce (recipe follows)
Red Pepper Sauce (recipe follows)
Fried Onion Rings (recipe follows)
Pepper Tartlets (recipe follows)
4 whole red snapper (about 1½ pounds each)
12 ounces White Fish Stock (recipe follows) or chicken stock
Salt
Freshly ground white pepper
1 ounce olive oil

Before preparing snapper, make garnishes. Preheat oven to 375° F.

Scale and fillet the fish if needed, but leave skin on. Save the bones for fish stock. Separate the two fillets of each fish.

Sprinkle over salt and pepper and rub with oil. Make White Fish Stock. Make the sauces.

Place snapper in a large flat pan and cover with stock. Bake for about 7 minutes or until tender.

To serve: Place 2 snapper fillets, skin side up, on each plate. Arrange vegetables in alternating and overlapping half circles—eggplant, tomato, zucchini, tomato, eggplant—on each side of the fillets. Spoon some Green Pepper Sauce and Red Pepper Sauce on each plate and top each with the contrasting colored Pepper Tartlet. Scatter Fried Onion Rings on top of fish. Pass remainder of each sauce separately in a bowl or sauce boat.

✗ *Serves 4*

White Fish Stock

2 pounds fish bones from red snapper or other white-fleshed, nonflat fish
2 quarts cold water
2 ounces shallot, peeled and chopped
4 ounces leek, washed and sliced
3 ounces celery, chopped
2 fresh mushrooms, chopped
1 fresh thyme sprig
2 bay leaves
5 white peppercorns
½ ounce salt
4 ounces dry white wine

Clean fish bones and cut into small pieces with a large knife. Rinse well under cold water to remove any traces of blood. Place in a 4-quart stockpot and cover with the water. Set pot over low heat and slowly bring to a boil. Using a skimmer or slotted spoon, remove fat and foam rising to the surface.

Add vegetables, herbs, spices, and wine. Lower the heat and simmer gently for 30 minutes, or until reduced to 1 quart.

Dampen a double thickness of cheesecloth and drape it over a fine-meshed sieve. Strain the stock and discard solids. Use warm or let stock stand until cool and store in the refrigerator.

Confit of Vegetables

1 medium zucchini (about 4 ounces)
1 small eggplant (about 4 ounces)
2 medium tomatoes (about 4 ounces)
3 ounces olive oil
1 fresh thyme sprig, chopped
Salt
Freshly ground white pepper

Preheat the oven to 375° F.

Cut the zucchini, eggplant, and tomatoes into thin slices. Layer the vegetable slices in an oven-proof casserole, alternating zucchini, eggplant, and tomatoes and sprinkling seasoning on each layer.

Bake in preheated oven for 10 minutes.

Green Pepper Sauce

1 pound green bell peppers
3 ounces shallot
2 ounces unsalted butter
2 ounces dry white wine
6 ounces White Fish Stock (see recipe above)
8 ounces heavy cream
2 tablespoons fresh lemon juice
Salt
Freshly ground white pepper

Wash the green peppers. Remove stems and seeds and dice. Chop the shallot. Or put the peppers and shallot in the food processor and finely chop.

In a 10-inch skillet, melt the butter. Add peppers and shallot and cook until shallot is translucent. Add wine and stock and simmer for about 10 minutes.

Stir in the cream. Reduce over high heat until it coats the back of a spoon. Transfer to a blender or food processor and blend until smooth. Strain through a fine sieve and season with lemon juice, salt, and pepper. ✗ *Makes 2 cups*

Red Pepper Sauce

1 pound red bell peppers
3 ounces shallot
2 ounces unsalted butter
2 ounces dry white wine
6 ounces White Fish Stock
8 ounces heavy cream
2 tablespoons fresh lemon juice
Salt
Freshly ground white pepper

Wash the red peppers. Remove the stems and seeds and dice. Chop the shallot. Or put peppers and shallot in food processor and finely chop.

In a 10-inch skillet, melt the butter. Add the peppers and shallot and cook until shallot is translucent. Add the wine and stock and simmer for about 10 minutes.

Stir in the cream. Reduce over high heat until it coats the back of a spoon. Transfer to a blender or food processor and blend until smooth. Strain through a fine sieve and season with lemon juice, salt, and pepper. ✗ *Makes 2 cups*

Fried Onion Rings

2 medium onions
2 ounces all-purpose flour (about ½ cup)
5 ounces vegetable oil

Peel onions and slice very thinly by hand or with the slicing disc of a food processor.

Place the flour in a large bowl. Add onions to flour and mix well to coat.

Heat the oil in a large deep skillet. Fry the onion rings until crisp. Remove to paper toweling to drain. Serve over fish.

Pepper Tartlets

1 red pepper, about 6 ounces
1 green pepper, about 6 ounces
2 ounces unsalted butter
4 ounces heavy cream
Salt
Freshly ground white pepper
☐ *Quiche Dough*
8 ounces unsalted butter, chilled
12 ounces all-purpose flour
Pinch salt
4 ounces cold water or milk

Finely dice the red and green pepper, but keep the colors separated.

In each of two skillets, melt 1 tablespoon butter. Sauté peppers (each color separately) until soft. Divide the cream between the skillets. Stir and cook until reduced slightly. Season with salt and pepper to taste.

Make the quiche dough: Cut the chilled butter into cubes. Place in a large mixing bowl with the flour. Rub butter in with your fingertips, working quickly and making sure butter pieces are coated with flour. Add the salt. Stirring with a fork, add water or milk just until the dough holds together when pressed into a ball. Wrap in plastic and refrigerate for at least half an hour before using.

Roll out dough and cut to fit 1½-inch tartlet shells. Bake the pastry shells for 8 minutes or until done.

Fill each of the shells with 1 tablespoon of either the red or green pepper mixture. Serve hot. (May be reheated.) ✘ *Makes 16 tartlets*

JIMMY SCHMIDT. *One of Jim's close food-friends was*
Lester Gruber of the London Chop House in Detroit. James met Jimmy Schmidt when the latter became the
chef of Lester's restaurant right out of training with Madeleine Kamman. Jimmy went on to open The
Rattlesnake Club in Denver, gave that up, and moved back to Detroit where he has his own Rattlesnake
Club. ✍

While James Beard was visiting the Lester Grubers, former proprietors of The London Chop House in Detroit, he brought along a giant shark fin for the making of that famous soup. Late after dinner one night, he decided to soak the shark fin, as required prior to making soup. Unable to locate a vessel large enough he decided to use the kitchen sink. Early the next morning everyone in the household was awakened by a bloodcurdling scream. The Grubers and guests raced about only to find the maid unconscious on the kitchen floor after meeting the mysterious beast in the pre-dawn light.

This salmon is a very dramatic presentation. Buy your smoked salmon already sliced, and use a very sharp, thin knife to slice the fresh salmon.

Flashed Salmon Carpaccio

¼ cup balsamic vinegar
¼ teaspoon salt
1 tablespoon coarse-grained mustard
1 tablespoon green peppercorns in brine, rinsed and finely chopped
⅓ cup capers, thoroughly rinsed and drained
¼ cup chopped fresh chives
½ cup olive oil
½ pound salmon fillet, skinned and cleaned of any fatty tissue
½ pound smoked salmon fillet, thinly sliced
1 cup diced jícama (¼-inch dice)
Seeds from 1 large papaya (about ¼ cup seeds), cleaned of membrane, rinsed, and toasted
16 croutons, made from thinly sliced French bread

Pour the vinegar into a medium bowl and stir in the salt. Add the mustard, peppercorns, capers, chives, and olive oil. Whisk to combine well, and adjust the seasonings. Set this sauce aside.

Heat the oven broiler to 450° F. Thinly slice the fresh salmon on an angle, so that it looks like the sliced smoked salmon.

Divide the fresh salmon among four plates, arranging the slices in two fans on opposing sides of each plate. Set the plates under the broiler, 4½ to 5 inches from the heating element, and warm the fish just until the surface becomes opaque, about 30 to 45 seconds.

Remove the plates from the oven. Arrange the smoked salmon on the remaining opposing quarters of each plate. Sprinkle the jicama over the salmon, and spoon the reserved sauce over all. Arrange four croutons in the center of each plate, and scatter the toasted papaya seeds over each serving. ✗ *Serves 4*

James really loved Alice Waters's restaurant, Chez Panisse, in Berkeley. It was the first place he took me to eat in San Francisco. Like a child with a napkin smoothed over his impressive front, he would settle himself at the table happily awaiting Alice's surprises. Her way with salmon here certainly would have pleased him.

Alice has a large charcoal grill in her kitchen that she often tends herself, but on nights when the load is heavy, she has been known to make another fire out of doors just outside the kitchen door. ✍

Here, salmon is served with a delicately flavored butter, perfect to make in late spring or early summer when the herb garden is in bloom and at its prettiest. A scattering of small petals from edible flowers, such as borage, calendula, nasturtium, viola, and roquette, over the fish makes a romantic and fanciful garnish.

Grilled Salmon with Herb Blossom Butter

☐ *For the Herb Blossom Butter*

6 tablespoons unsalted butter, at room temperature

2 tablespoons diced shallots

10 to 12 chives, finely cut

4 or 5 sprigs fresh chervil, finely chopped

1 tablespoon fresh basil, cut into ribbons

Salt to taste

Freshly ground black pepper to taste

Fresh lemon juice to taste

3 to 4 tablespoons herb blossoms, larger blossoms pulled into petals and lightly chopped (use such blossoms as roquette, thyme, sage, marjoram, savory, borage, calendula, nasturtium, and viola)

1 to 1½ pounds salmon fillet in one piece, preferably from the upper, collar section of the fish, rather than the tail end

Olive oil, to oil grill

Salt to taste

Freshly ground black pepper to taste

A small handful of petals from the same flowers as above, petals left whole if small, for garnish

Prepare a charcoal fire.

Make the Herb Blossom Butter: Stir the shallots, chives, chervil, and basil into the soft butter. Season to taste with salt, pepper, and lemon juice. Add the herb blossoms and blend well. Set this Herb Blossom Butter aside at room temperature until you are ready to serve the fish.

Holding a sharp knife at a 45-degree angle to the salmon fillet, cut the fish into eight slices of even thickness. Brush each slice with olive oil, and season with salt and pepper.

When the charcoal fire has died down and is no longer flaming, spread out the banked coals and lightly oil the surface of the grill. Cook the salmon for 2 to 3 minutes on each side, until just barely cooked; what you want is a dark pink, moist center. Transfer fish to warmed dinner plates, and spread each slice with a generous tablespoon of Herb Blossom Butter. Scatter petals over fish.

✘ *Serves 4 as a first course, 2 as a main course*

JOYCE GOLDSTEIN. *The warm and erudite Joyce Goldstein is now the proprietor-chef of Square One restaurant in San Francisco. For many years she was a cooking teacher. Then she helped Alice Waters to develop the upstairs café at Chez Panisse. Her son has joined her as the person in charge of wine at her restaurant. Her book with recipes from the restaurant has recently appeared. ✍*

Baked salmon can be as moist as poached salmon, and it tends not to fall apart as easily; but if you prefer, you may poach or grill the fish. For this dish you want each fillet to have a deep-pink center.

Baked Salmon with Ginger Sauce

☐ *Ginger Sauce*

¼ pound plus 4 tablespoons unsalted butter

8 to 10 shallots, finely minced (about ¼ cup)

Fresh ginger root, peeled and puréed in a food processor (about ½ cup purée)

½ cup dry white wine, slightly acid

1½ cups chicken or fish stock, or canned chicken broth

6 salmon fillets, about 6 ounces each

Salt to taste

Freshly ground black pepper to taste

1 tablespoon vegetable oil or unsalted butter, for the pan

For the Sauce: Melt ¼ pound of the butter in a nonreactive saucepan over medium-high heat. Add shallots and cook until they are transparent. Stir in the ginger root purée and cook for 2 minutes. Add the wine and reduce the mixture until nearly all of the liquid has evaporated.

Stir in the chicken or fish stock and reduce the liquid by one half. Remove the sauce from the heat, and swirl in the remaining 4 tablespoons of butter. Keep the sauce warm while you prepare the fish.

Preheat oven to 325° F.

Season each salmon fillet with salt and pepper to taste. Lightly oil a shallow baking dish or a broiling pan. Bake until just done, but still rosy in the center, about 8 minutes for thinnish fillets, 10 to 12 minutes for thicker ones.

Serve fillets napped with Ginger Sauce.

✖ *Serves 6*

FELIPE ROJAS-LOMBARDI. *Earlier recipes in this book have introduced Felipe Rojas-Lombardi and his relationship with Jim. Felipe, along with Helen McCully and a horde of Jim's friends—John Clancy, George Lang, Leon Lianides, Jacques Pépin, Alexis Bespaloff, Philip Brown, and Maurice Moore-Betty—were on the cover of* The Great Cooks Cookbook. *Many of them have contributed to this book, none more than Felipe.*

A 4-pound bass can measure as long as 22 inches from head to tail. For this recipe you will need a very long ovenproof platter, large enough to comfortably hold your fish and the cooking juices.

Baked Striped Bass

1 4-pound striped bass, scaled and cleaned, head left on
1½ teaspoons salt
Freshly ground black pepper
6 tablespoons unsalted butter
1 tablespoon olive oil
1 small onion, finely chopped (about ¼ cup)
½ pound fresh mushrooms, sliced
3 tablespoons chopped parsley
⅛ teaspoon dried tarragon, crumbled
12 black olives, pitted
2 tablespoons sherry or white wine
2 large tomatoes, peeled, seeded, and quartered
Dash of sugar
Lemon wedges for garnish

Preheat the oven to 400° F.

Go over the scaled bass once more to make certain that every single scale is removed. Wipe the fish with a wet cloth, remove any blood clots by holding the fish under cold running water, then wipe it dry. Rub the bass inside and out with salt, using about a teaspoon in all. Sprinkle with pepper.

Melt the butter in a large skillet over moderate heat. Brush the baking platter and the fish with about 2 tablespoons of the melted butter. Bake the fish, uncovered, for 15 minutes. Set a tablespoon of the butter aside and use it to baste the fish once or twice.

Add the olive oil to the 3 tablespoons of butter remaining in the skillet. When the fat is hot, add the onions and sauté over moderate heat, stirring frequently for a few minutes. Stir in the mushrooms, and cover the skillet to let the vegetables simmer for about 5 minutes, or until the mushrooms soften and release some of their liquid. Stir in 2 tablespoons of the parsley and the tarragon, olives, and wine, and cook briefly. Remove the skillet from the heat and add the tomatoes, sugar, the remaining salt, and pepper to taste. Stir gently to combine all the ingredients.

Remove the fish from the oven and reduce the temperature to 375° F. Surround the fish with the vegetables, piling some on top of the fish. Return the platter to the oven and continue baking for another 15 minutes. At this time, the vegetables should be soft, the tomatoes still intact, and the fish—if you gently lift the belly flap over the cavity—will look completely opaque and flake easily.

Sprinkle with the remaining tablespoon of parsley, garnish with lemon wedges, and serve at once. It should serve four amply, or five with modest appetites. ✕ *Serves 4 to 5*

PATRICIA UNTERMANN *is the chef-owner of the Hayes*
Street Grill in San Francisco and has been a newspaper restaurant reviewer as well. In her excellent,
informal restaurant is an open kitchen with grill. Originally, she contributed a recipe for this book—on page
120—that showed off West Coast foods. That was most appropriate to Jim; but she also agreed to send us
this recipe that can be made by cooks who don't have the special products she can get. ✍

This is one of the lightest, brightest, and most satisfying ways of preparing firm fish fillets like salmon, halibut, Atlantic cod, or sea bass. The fish is quickly poached, put onto hot plates, and then smothered in brilliant green watercress and spinach that has literally melted instantaneously into a little butter. Four tablespoons of light olive oil can be substituted for the 8 tablespoons of butter if cholesterol is a consideration.

Pan-Poached Halibut with Melted Spinach and Watercress

Court Bouillon

2 cups water
2 cups dry white wine
1 large onion (about 6 ounces), peeled and thinly sliced
1 bay leaf
2 sprigs fresh thyme or ½ teaspoon dried thyme
1 teaspoon salt
¼ teaspoon black peppercorns

4 8-ounce halibut fillets, about ¾ inch thick
2 bunches spinach, stemmed and washed (about 1 pound)
4 bunches watercress, stemmed and washed (about 1½ pounds)
8 tablespoons unsalted butter
2 teaspoons fresh lemon juice
Salt to taste
Freshly ground black pepper to taste

Make the Court Bouillon: Place all ingredients in a medium pan and bring to a boil over high heat. Reduce heat and simmer, uncovered, for 20 minutes. Strain liquid and reserve. There should be about 2 cups. Discard vegetables.

Dry spinach and watercress leaves thoroughly. Cut each separately into very thin chiffonade (about ⅛-inch thick strips). Toss together and reserve.

Pour Court Bouillon into a 10-inch frying pan with fitted lid. Bring to a boil over moderate heat. Reduce heat and add two fish fillets, cover, and simmer for about 3 minutes. Test thickest part of fish to make sure it is cooked through. Remove fillets to platter and keep warm. Cook remaining fish in same way.

Pour out Court Bouillon and add butter to pan. Melt over moderate heat. Add reserved spinach and watercress and stir to cook evenly. Cook for about 1 minute, so that spinach and watercress absorb butter and melt into a beautiful green sauce. Stir in lemon juice and season to taste.

Place fish on 4 dinner plates and cover each filet with melted greens. ✖ *Serves 4*

that I met before Jim. Joe Baum was a consultant to The American restaurant in Kansas City and I was helping out. Brad Ogden was the sous-chef. When the chef left somewhat precipitously, I suggested that he become the chef. Webs are generally more tangled than that even when we are being forthright. In fact, Jim was a consultant to that project and Brad used some of his recipes there. Later, Jim's good friend Bill Wilkinson left The Stanford Court and opened Campton Place. His chef at the brand-new hotel was Brad. Bill had met Brad when he came to San Francisco as part of the chefs' gala birthday party for James Beard and the benefit of the local public television station. Fine American food was indeed the interlocking world of James Beard.

Today Brad has his own Lark Creek Inn and tables are booked up for three months ahead. ✍

I feel that James Beard was truly the father of American cooking. He showed us how to appreciate the goodness found in the basic fresh foods that are so abundant in this country. He taught us to keep it that way, simple, and to always look for the extraordinary in foods that perhaps we had thought of before as anything but!

I remember cooking for him when he was hospitalized here in San Francisco. I was prepared to cook him anything, and his request: a perfectly roasted chicken. So simple, and so typically James Beard.

Baked Salmon Wrapped in Chicory with Chervil Broth
■■■■■■■■■■■■■■■■■■■■■■■

☐ *For the red wine butter*

1½ cups dry red wine

1 cup red wine vinegar

⅓ cup sliced shallots

3 tablespoons minced garlic

¼ pound unsalted butter, softened

☐ *For the chervil broth*

½ bunch chervil or ¼ bunch each tarragon and parsley

½ cup fennel leaves and stems

1 tablespoon minced garlic

¼ cup sliced shallots

½ cup dry vermouth

¼ cup white wine

2 cups fish, lobster, or crayfish broth

1 cup chicken broth

1 fresh tomato, cut in half

....

2½ pounds boneless, skinless salmon fillet, cut into 6 serving pieces

Kosher salt to taste

Freshly ground black pepper to taste

☐ *For the baking and finishing*

6 large leaves escarole

½ cup dry white vermouth

2 tablespoons unsalted butter

¼ each red, green, and yellow peppers, cut into ⅛-inch brunoise [dice]

1 baby fennel, peeled, and cut into ⅛-inch brunoise [dice]

1 small leek, white part only, cut into ⅛-inch brunoise [dice]

6 tablespoons chopped fresh chervil or 3 tablespoons each tarragon and parsley

2 tablespoons fresh lemon juice

Place the red wine, vinegar, shallots, and garlic in a saucepan and reduce down to ½ cup liquid. Let cool slightly. Stir in softened butter and whisk to combine. Place mixture in the refrigerator to chill and harden.

Combine all ingredients for the chervil broth in a large saucepan over medium heat. Bring to a boil. Lower heat and simmer for 15 to 20 minutes. Strain through a fine sieve and reserve.

Preheat oven to 400° F.

Season the fillets of salmon with kosher salt and black pepper. Blanch the escarole in rapidly boiling salted water until just wilted. Plunge into ice water to cool. Drain and pat dry. Top each salmon piece with 2 tablespoons of the red wine butter and wrap in a chicory leaf.

Arrange the salmon packets in a single layer in a baking dish. Pour the vermouth and ½ cup of the chervil broth over the packets. Place the dish in the oven and bake for 12 to 15 minutes or until the salmon is just undercooked. (It will continue to cook while you finish the dish.) Remove from pan and keep warm.

Melt butter in a large sauté pan over medium heat. Add the vegetables and sauté for 2 minutes. Add remaining chervil broth and chopped chervil. Bring to a boil and simmer for 1 minute. Add the lemon juice and taste for seasoning.

To serve, place a salmon packet in the center of each plate. Arrange the vegetables around the salmon, spoon over some of their juice, and serve immediately. ✖ *Serves 6*

CAROL GUIDICE *has her own cooking school, Carol's Cuisine, on Staten Island in New York. She is one of the many marvelous teachers around the country who have been paying their debt to Jim in full by helping to raise money for the Beard Foundation.* ✍

Shrimp Cakes

■ ■

3 cups Aromatic Poaching Broth (page 130)
1 pound medium shrimp
4 ounces Bermuda onion, peeled and finely
    chopped (about ¾ cup)
3 ribs celery, peeled and finely chopped
1½ cups self-rising flour
1 tablespoon chopped parsley
Salt to taste
Freshly ground black pepper to taste
1 egg
⅓ cup cold water
Vegetable oil, for frying

Pour poaching liquid into medium pan and bring to a boil. When boiling, add shrimp and cook for about 1 minute, or until cooked through.

Remove from heat and strain, discarding broth. Peel and devein shrimp and let stand until cool. Chop very fine either by hand or in a food processor. Place in a bowl and stir in onion and celery. Reserve.

Mix together flour, parsley, salt, and pepper in a medium bowl. Stir in egg and then water to form a dough-like mixture. Add the reserved shrimp mixture and mix well.

Pour ½-inch of oil into a large frying pan. Place over moderate heat. Test oil for heat by dropping in a little batter; if it bubbles, the oil is hot enough. Place heaped tablespoons of the batter in the oil and flatten slightly with the back of a wooden spoon. Keeping the heat at moderate to low, cook the cakes in batches until golden brown on one side, then turn them and cook the other side. Remove with a slotted spoon or spatula and drain on paper toweling. Repeat with remaining batter.

Serve warm with tartar sauce or cocktail sauce. ✖ *Makes 21 2-inch cakes*

JAMES NASSIKAS. *After James Nassikas made Jim Beard welcome to what was then Nassikas's hotel, the Stanford Court, in San Francisco—always one of Beard's favorite cities—Jim spent more and more time there and even considered living in San Francisco full-time. For several years, Jimmy Nassikas not only treated Jim Beard to the same corner suite overlooking the entire city, but also provided the elegant restaurant, Fournou's Ovens, for Jim's week-long morning cooking classes. Chuck Williams would haul all the impedimenta needed for the classes—pots and pans, burners, knives, and casseroles—out of storage and set it up. Much of the food shopping would be done by the Stanford Court.*

Jim would get up, as always, very early and knock on my adjoining door. We would chat in our bathrobes as he drank his fresh grapefruit juice and munched on whole wheat toast—not hot, always crisp, English style. We'd go down the staff elevator and meet with Marion Cunningham and any of the other loyal assistants who were going to do battle with the tumult of a participation class.

Sometimes Danny Kaye, another of Jimmy Nassikas's "cooker" (to use Danny's word) friends, would be staying at the hotel, and he would come down to class, invariably taking center stage at some point in the proceedings to show off his formidable skills with a Chinese cleaver.

All of us were at the sensational birthday party that Jimmy threw for Mr. Beard to benefit the local public television station. It was a complicated event, the first at which chefs from many different restaurants pooled their skills, each to make a dish for the over three hundred guests at the dinner. An extra ballroom was turned into a staging area and all the young cooks from the area's many restaurants worked as an assembly line to plate the food. Molly Chappellet, a great lady, an astounding beauty, wife of a vineyard owner, and longtime friend of both Jim and Danny, made extraordinary centerpieces for the large tables.

The centerpieces were about food and on Jim Beard's scale. Pigs' trotters were bunched together like mammoth white asparagus tied by a purple ribbon. With Jim Dodge, Molly filled a huge copper bowl with a giant whisk and meringue cooked long enough to be stable but also to stay white and look like a cloud of just-beaten egg whites.

If anybody festooned Jim Beard's last years with pleasure, it was Jimmy Nassikas. ✍

There are never two days that happen alike in the life of a hotelier. There is a new adventure around every corner, a new experience, a new personality with whom to laugh or to cry. Among the most agreeably memorable personalities who have ever entered my hotel life was James Beard. I don't know who, but some philosopher once categorized the human race into three parts: the lawn mowers, the well poisoners, and the life enhancers. Knowing James Beard has been a life-enhancing experience, not only for me, but for countless others.

James Beard first entered my life during my years at the Mayflower in Washington, D.C., in 1964. He had been invited by a local wine society to do a Cognac cooking demonstration in the Colonial Room. He was not well known then in comparison to what was to come through the '70s and into the early '80s. Among the cooking utensils which he brought with him was a little copper saucepan, not over 12 or 14 ounces in capacity, of exquisite French-built manufacture. He left it behind by mistake. My first reaction was to filch it, and I did! I'm not the type to do this sort of thing, but rather than wrap it up, go through the effort of researching an address, and mailing it, I decided I would return it to him once our paths would cross again. For some reason which I've never been able to explain, I just knew this would happen.

About the time I opened the Stanford Court in 1972, James Beard reenterd my life. He did not know the Stanford Court was mine, but I remembered him well since that Cognac demonstration eight years hence. Sheepishly, I returned the saucepan to my newfound Stanford Court guest, amongst guffaws of hearty laughter. In a sense, this fine old secondhand copper saucepan became a key which opened doors to nearly thirteen years of the most stimulating and rewarding experiences of all my hotel career.

This little copper saucepan led to the beginnings of a kind of salon which formed at the Stanford Court and at which Jim presided. Through this salon there passed a beguiling array of diverse personalities. James began spending extraordinary lengths of time in San Francisco, and I was so proud to have been able to contribute to his sense of doing so. I truly believe it was from this salon that James encouraged so many of the young people who have attained prominence in the American cuisine movement of today. He found so many, many of them out here in California, and he found them during this period of time. It became a crossroads of significant scale. I stood in awe in the presence of the rare brand of humility which he possessed, and rare was the occasion that James Beard would refuse to offer encouragement or a helping hand to anyone.

That little copper saucepan, wherever it may be and I wish I knew where . . . opened untold doors to the culinary euphoria which now prevails around us. He understood so well the joy of sharing success . . . because a shared success is the best success of all. Indeed, knowing him was a life-enhancing experience!

Rosemary-Lemon— Butter Shrimp

½ pound unsalted butter
3 tablespoons Worcestershire sauce
2 teaspoons freshly ground black pepper
1 tablespoon dried rosemary, crumbled
1 lemon, rind removed and cut across into ⅛-inch slices
1 teaspoon hot red pepper sauce
1 teaspoon salt
24 large shrimp (about 1 pound), in their shells

Preheat oven to 400° F.

Melt butter in a small saucepan over moderate heat. Add remaining ingredients except shrimp, and simmer over low heat for about 3 minutes to combine flavors. Remove from heat and reserve.

Arrange shrimp in a shallow baking pan large enough to hold shrimp in a single layer. Pour over reserved sauce.

Bake for about 10 minutes, or until shrimp are cooked through. Remove from oven and serve.

✗ *Serves 4*

MARK MILITELLO *is the chef of his own restaurant in Miami, the upscale, upbeat, highly successful Mark's Place. His cooking combines the best of Florida's wide range of ingredients, from seafood to tropical fruits and vegetables, and the ethnic influences of a widely diverse population.* ✍

Florida Lobster Enchiladas with Salsa Verde

□ *Salsa Verde*

1 pound fresh tomatillos, husked and well rinsed

1 serrano chili, stem removed

½ white onion, peeled and chopped

1 clove garlic, smashed, peeled, and chopped

1 bunch fresh cilantro, large stems discarded

2 tablespoons ground cumin

2 tablespoons granulated sugar

Salt to taste

2 cups seafood or chicken stock, homemade, or
    canned chicken broth

1 tablespoon unsalted butter

1¾ pound fresh Florida lobster, meat removed
    from tail, claws, and (if possible) legs and cut
    into ½-inch pieces

¼ cup sour cream

¼ cup heavy cream

Freshly ground white pepper to taste

4 corn tortillas

1 tablespoon vegetable oil

1 cup shredded Monterey Jack cheese

Lime wedges for serving

Chopped ripe tomatoes, red onions, pitted black
    olives, and scallions for garnish

Put the tomatillos, chili, white onion, garlic, cilantro, cumin, sugar, and salt to taste in a large stockpot. Add stock and simmer for 10 minutes. Pour into the work bowl of a food processor and purée. Set this Salsa Verde aside while you prepare the lobster enchiladas.

Melt the butter in a medium skillet over medium-high heat. Add the lobster meat and sauté until just cooked and opaque. Remove from heat and stir in the sour cream and heavy cream. Season to taste with salt and white pepper.

Preheat oven to 350° F.

Brush the tortillas with the oil. Roll each tortilla with some of the lobster filling and a sprinkling of grated cheese. Arrange filled tortillas snugly in a baking dish. Cover with Salsa Verde and sprinkle with the remaining cheese. Bake for 15 minutes. Serve with lime wedges and garnish with chopped tomatoes, red onions, black olives, and scallions. ✗ *Serves 2*

Waverly Place, not far from Jim's house, was literally a kitchen-away-from-home for Jim and his old friend and upstairs neighbor, Gino Cofacci. They spent many Thanksgivings and Christmases with Leon. After Jim died, Leon was extremely thoughtful and continued to invite Gino over for important meals. Jim enjoyed the marvelous Greek meals he had in Leon's home as well.

Try drinking a good American chardonnay with Leon's lovely lobster. His was one of the first restaurants in the country to have a large, strong California wine list to go with his American-based cooking. ✍

Lobster in Herb Sauce

■■■■■■■■■■■■■■■■■■■■■■■■■■■

2 carrots (about 3 to 4 ounces each), peeled, trimmed, and cut into 2-inch juliennes

1 large onion (8 ounces), trimmed, peeled, and cut into juliennes

½ cup white wine vinegar

1 tablespoon kosher salt

6 black peppercorns, cracked or coarsely crushed

½ teaspoon dried thyme

1 teaspoon chopped fresh parsley

1 bay leaf

4 1¼-pound fresh lobsters

¾ cup heavy cream

1 tablespoon chopped fresh chervil

1 tablespoon chopped fresh tarragon

1 cup Béarnaise Sauce (recipe follows)

Pour 3 quarts of cold water into a tall stockpot or a Dutch oven. Add the carrots, onion, vinegar, salt, peppercorns, thyme, parsley, and bay leaf. Let boil for 20 minutes. Add the lobsters and cook for 12 to 20 minutes, or until lobsters are cooked.

Strain cooking liquid (you will have about 2 quarts). Reserve 2 cups of the liquid; reserve vegetables. Place reserved liquid in a small saucepan. Add cream and half the chervil and tarragon. Cook until reduced by one half, about 20 minutes. Remove from heat and add the Béarnaise Sauce and reserved vegetables.

Split lobsters in half. Crack claws and remove meat from shells. Remove small sacs from heads, and pour sauce over the lobster. Sprinkle over remaining chervil and tarragon and serve. ✖ *Serves 4*

Béarnaise Sauce

••

12 tablespoons unsalted butter

⅓ cup dry white wine

¼ cup white wine vinegar or tarragon vinegar

2 tablespoons minced shallots

1 tablespoon chopped fresh tarragon

3 large egg yolks

½ teaspoon salt

Melt 10 tablespoons of the butter. Reserve the remaining 2 tablespoons in the refrigerator.

Place wine, vinegar, shallot, and tarragon in a small saucepan. Place over medium heat and bring to a boil. Boil until liquid is reduced to 2 tablespoons. Let cool.

Beat the egg yolks in a medium saucepan until thick. Strain in the wine-and-vinegar mixture and add 1 tablespoon of the cold butter. Place the mixture over low heat and cook, stirring, to thicken the egg yolks. When the yolks are thickened, remove from heat. Add the remaining 1 tablespoon cold butter to stop the cooking of the eggs.

Beat in melted butter bit by bit, as for a mayonnaise. Keep warm over a bowl of lukewarm water. ✖ *Makes about 1 cup*

JANE LAVINE *is co-owner of Abracadabra, a special event/party planning business in Boston. She is also a coeditor of the Zagat Restaurant Survey in Boston and a freelance restaurant consultant.* ✍

Jim Beard, not surprisingly, pioneered in the field of restaurant consulting. For thirteen years he made the train trip to Philadelphia to consult for Helen and Charles Wilson at their L'Auberge restaurant starting in the late '50s or early '60s. I had the honor of being one of his successors at this same job for five years, until 1986, when the Wilsons sold L'Auberge.

These filled mussel shells may be prepared and assembled several hours in advance. Simply place them under a preheated broiler just before serving to warm them through.

Open-Faced Fennel-Mustard Mussels

■■■■■■■■■■■■■■■■■■■■■■■■■■■■

2¼ pounds mussels, scrubbed and debearded
    (discard any that are cracked or broken)
6 tablespoons olive oil
¾ cup dry white wine
1 cup heavy cream
1 clove garlic, smashed, peeled, and minced
2 shallots, peeled and minced
¼ bulb fennel, cut into ¼-inch dice
¼ teaspoon crushed fennel seed
2 teaspoons Dijon mustard
½ cup fine, dry bread crumbs
Pinch cayenne pepper

Put the mussels in a Dutch oven or a casserole with a tight-fitting cover. Add 2 tablespoons of the olive oil and ½ cup of the wine. Over medium-high heat, shake the mussels in the covered dish until they open; the length of time it takes the mussels to open will depend on their size. When most of the mussels have opened, transfer the opened mussels to a bowl, and continue to cook the unopened mussels for 2 or 3 minutes. Discard any mussels that do not open after additional cooking.

When the mussels are cool enough to handle, pull them from their shells. Reserve the meat and half of the shells. Strain the mussel cooking liquid through a sieve lined with damp cheesecloth and reserve it; you will have about ¾ cup.

In a small heavy saucepan, reduce cream over medium-high heat to ½ cup. In a medium skillet over medium-high heat, warm 2 tablespoons of the remaining olive oil and sauté the garlic, shallots, and fennel until soft. Add the reserved mussel liquid, remaining ¼ cup wine, and fennel seed. Raise the heat and cook the mixture for 2 or 3 minutes, stirring occasionally. Lower the heat and whisk in the mustard and the reduced cream. Stir in the mussels, and take the skillet off the heat.

Heat the remaining 2 tablespoons oil in a small skillet over medium-high heat. When the oil is hot, add the bread crumbs and fry them until they are golden. Season them with cayenne pepper to taste.

Preheat the broiler.

Place a mussel and some sauce in each mussel shell. Cover with bread crumbs. Set the filled shells on a cookie sheet and warm the mussels briefly under the broiler, for 2 or 3 minutes. Serve the mussels immediately.

✖ *Makes about 40 mussels, to serve 10 as hors d'oeuvre, 4 to 6 as a luncheon dish*

Crab Cakes with Cracked Mustard Sauce

▪▪▪▪▪▪▪▪▪▪▪▪▪▪▪▪▪▪▪▪▪▪▪▪

☐ *For the cakes*

8 ounces bay scallops

1 egg white

7 tablespoons unsalted butter, at room temperature

½ teaspoon salt

¼ teaspoon freshly ground black pepper

⅓ cup heavy cream

1 small yellow pepper (about 6 ounces), stemmed, seeded, deribbed, and finely diced (about ½ cup)

1 small red pepper (about 6 ounces), stemmed, seeded, deribbed, and finely chopped (about ½ cup)

2 tablespoons chopped fresh parsley

2 tablespoons chopped chives

1 pound crabmeat, picked clean of shells (about 2¾ cups)

¼ cup all-purpose flour

☐ *For the sauce*

½ cup white wine

½ cup clam broth or juice

1 cup whipping cream

¼ cup coarse-grained mustard

2 tablespoons chopped chives for garnish

Place scallops and egg white in the work bowl of a food processor. Purée until smooth. Scrape into a bowl, cover with plastic wrap, and refrigerate.

In a large mixing bowl, beat together 4 tablespoons butter, salt, and pepper until smooth. Gradually add the chilled scallop mixture, stirring until well combined. Fold in the peppers, parsley, chives, and crabmeat. Form mixture into 8 cakes. Place cakes on parchment or wax paper, cover, and refrigerate for about 2 hours.

To make the sauce: Combine wine and clam broth in a medium pan and bring to a boil over moderate heat. Simmer, uncovered, for about 3 minutes until the liquid has reduced by about half. Stir in cream and simmer for about 10 minutes, or until sauce has thickened to coat the back of a spoon. Remove from heat and reserve.

Remove crab cakes from the refrigerator and lightly dust with flour. Melt remaining butter in a large heavy skillet over moderate to high heat. Add the crab cakes and cook for about 3 minutes on each side, until they become golden brown. Gently remove from pan and allow to drain on paper towels.

Return pan of sauce to a simmer and stir in mustard. Spoon sauce on serving plate, sprinkle over chopped chives, and arrange crab cakes in the center. ✗ *Serves 4*

CHICKEN LEA. *Your Favorite Things in Charlotte,*

North Carolina, is the cooking school that is home to Chicken Lea, an accomplished teacher. Like many of the teachers who responded to the making of this book, she was also a student of Jim's. While Jim never took a cooking class, he never stopped learning, and he could teach without condescending. Instead, we were all part of the wonderful world of food, together.

In my kitchen, we felt that Chicken Lea's rich dish could serve eight as a first course. We also made a food processor version of Hollandaise, not knowing exactly how Lea makes hers. Jim certainly used the food processor. ✍

My respect for Mr. Beard is enormous, but my affection became permanent when I was taking the Professional Masters course which he and Barbara Kafka were doing through Peter Kump's New York Cooking School.

When I asked for a dinner recommendation, he suggested the Quilted Giraffe and said that they had just gotten the first fresh morels of the season. A close friend and I went for dinner that night, and in addition to a fine meal, had lots and more than lots of fine wine. And I arrived at the next day's session feeling absolutely horrible. I was desperate enough to ask him what could salvage the day—or simply me! He said that Barbara would recommend "a little lemon juice," but he took a fillet of beef from the refrigerator, scraped a small portion from it with the back of a spoon, moistened it with bitters, salt, and pepper, rolled it into balls, and assured me the protein would quickly remedy my illness.

Whether it was his genuine kindness, or my awe and faith, I realized a miraculous cure and an everlasting fondness for James Beard.

If you like, you can serve the crabmeat and poached eggs over toasted bread for an even more substantial dish. Trim the crusts from good bread (or cut it out using a cutter, if you prefer), brush it on one side with a little melted butter, and bake it at 350° F. until golden brown, turning once. This is nice served with slices of melon and strawberries. Delicious crabmeat is readily available in our area, and this is a favorite Sunday brunch dish for my husband, Hurdle, and myself. We vary the seasonings, and use a little more lemon juice in the Hollandaise. I sometimes make brioche in a 46-ounce can to slice for the croûtes and it makes a good size and nice texture and flavor.

Crabmeat Délicieux

1 pound crabmeat, preferably lump blue
    crabmeat, picked clean of shells
¼ teaspoon salt
¼ teaspoon freshly ground white pepper
¼ teaspoon dry mustard
¼ teaspoon mace
Hot red pepper sauce, to taste
4 tablespoons unsalted butter
8 large eggs
¾ to 1 cup Hollandaise Sauce (recipe follows)
Fresh parsley for garnish, optional

     In a medium bowl, mix crabmeat well with
the salt, pepper, mustard, mace, and red pepper
sauce. Melt the butter in a medium skillet, stir in
the crab mixture, and warm it thoroughly over
medium-low heat.

     Poach the eggs. Divide the hot crabmeat
mixture among 4 warmed serving plates, and
nestle 2 well-drained poached eggs on each
mound of crabmeat. Pour some Hollandaise Sauce
over each portion, garnish with parsley (if
desired), and serve immediately. ✖ *Serves 4*

Hollandaise Sauce

BARBARA KAFKA

1 pound unsalted butter
3 egg yolks
½ teaspoon dry mustard
1 teaspoon kosher salt
¼ teaspoon freshly ground black pepper
2 teaspoons fresh lemon juice

     Melt the butter in a medium saucepan and
keep it hot over low heat.

     Place the egg yolks, mustard, salt, and
pepper in the work bowl of a food processor.
Process for 90 seconds. With the machine
running, slowly add the butter in a thin stream.
Add the lemon juice and continue processing
briefly.

     Scrape the sauce into a serving bowl and
serve immediately. If the sauce is to be held, keep
it warm in the top of a double boiler over
simmering water. ✖ *Makes 2 cups*

MICHAEL FOLEY *comes from a restaurant family—as traditional and compelling in its way as a theater family. He now has two award-winning restaurants in Chicago: Foley's Grand Ohio and Printer's Row.* ✍

Choose two crabs per person from your fish store. Make certain the crabs are fresh. Run your finger down the back to see if the crabs move; only take live soft-shells. Use the same day or day after they are purchased. Prepare the crabs by removing the lungs under each side of the top shell. Ask your fishmonger about how to do this—maybe this chore he will be glad to finish for you. The rest of the preparation you start just before eating. Serve this with an excellent-quality dry chenin blanc or Vouvray.

Soft-Shell Crabs with Bacon Butter

2 slices bacon, coarsely chopped
2 tablespoons all-purpose flour
Salt to taste
Freshly ground black pepper to taste
4 soft-shell crabs, cleaned
4 tablespoons unsalted butter
¼ cup white wine
1 teaspoon chopped fresh chives

Bring a very small pan of water to a boil over high heat. Add the bacon and cook for about 2 minutes to remove excess smoked flavor and fat. Drain and reserve.

Combine flour, salt, and pepper on a plate. Dredge crabs in this mixture.

In a medium, heavy skillet melt 2 tablespoons of the butter over moderate to high heat. When the foam subsides, add the crabs, shell side down, and cook for 1 to 2 minutes (depending on size of crabs). Turn and cook 1 to 2 minutes longer. Remove from pan and drain on paper toweling.

Add reserved bacon to the pan and cook over moderate heat until crisp, stirring. Add white wine and stir together, scraping up brown bits in the pan. Allow to cook for about 2 minutes until the wine has reduced to a light syrup consistency. Remove from heat.

Cut remaining butter into small pieces and whisk into pan with chives to make a light-colored, creamy-looking sauce. To serve, spoon sauce onto warm plates and place crabs over sauce.

✖ *Serves 2*

Since the days when Michael McCarty and James Beard first met, Michael has become a busy man indeed, with a Michael's in New York to join the original on the edge of Los Angeles and Adirondack Clubs in Denver and in Washington. ✍

My most memorable remembrance of James Beard occurred the first time I ever met him.

It was in 1979, shortly after I had opened Michael's in Santa Monica. Michael's had received enormous national press, funnily enough, even before it opened. This may sound bizarre, but having trained as a chef entirely in France, I had no idea who James Beard was.

Tom and Sally Jordan of Jordan Winery and I were throwing a weekend of "Great Parties" to celebrate the opening of the Jordan Winery. The guest list included many great food afficionados and James Beard was one of them.

The first night as I was running between the kitchen and the dining room, preparing the dinner, I bumped into someone, turned, and there it was, as I was to learn later, that unforgettable shape! He stared me in the eyes, then pronounced, "And I thought I was the only legend!" Figuring he was an overflow from the cocktail reception, I muttered "thanks" and rushed back to the kitchen. It was only after dinner, when we formally met, that I learned who "James Beard" really was.

As a footnote, someone named M.F.K. Fisher called me the next day to invite me to lunch. However, because I was too busy with the preparation and as well, not knowing who she was, I most unfortunately, as I now know, declined. *Ah, la recherche du temps perdu!*

Serve the following dish with shoestring potatoes.

Soft-Shell Crabs—Soft-Shell Crayfish with Giant Capers and Lemon and Parsley Butter

□ *Beurre blanc*

¼ cup Champagne vinegar

¼ cup chardonnay white wine

2 teaspoons minced shallots

1 teaspoon heavy cream

4 tablespoons cold unsalted butter, cut into pieces

1 teaspoon fresh lemon juice

Salt to taste

Freshly ground white pepper to taste

□ *Seafood*

¼ cup all-purpose flour

4 soft-shell crabs, cleaned

8 soft-shell crayfish, cleaned

2 tablespoons clarified butter

3 tablespoons giant Spanish capers

1 lemon, peeled and cut into segments

Juice of ½ lemon

1 tablespoon chopped fresh parsley

4 sprigs watercress

To make beurre blanc: Place vinegar, wine, and shallots in a small heavy nonaluminum pan and bring to a boil over moderate heat. Allow to boil about 4 minutes, until there is about 1 tablespoon liquid remaining. Stir in heavy cream and remove pan from heat. Whisking constantly, add cold butter, a few pieces at a time, adding more butter as each new addition blends into the sauce. Whisk in lemon juice and season to taste. To keep sauce warm, place pan inside a larger bowl or pan of hot tap water until ready to serve.

Dredge crabs and crayfish with flour. Place clarified butter in a large heavy skillet and set over moderate to high heat. Add crabs, shell side down, and cook about 1 minute. Add crayfish and cook 1 minute longer. Turn seafood over and cook 1 to 2 minutes longer, or until orange in color and cooked through. Remove from heat and keep warm.

Stir capers, lemon segments, lemon juice, and parsley into reserved beurre blanc.

To serve, divide watercress among four dinner plates. Arrange 1 soft shell crab and 2 crayfish over the watercress. Spoon beurre blanc around. ✗ *Serves 4*

MAGGIE GIN.
Jim had an ambivalent attitude to Chinese food. He thought it belonged in restaurants or should be made only by the Chinese. He took me to Maggie Gin's home and to her briefly open restaurant in Napa Valley. We enjoyed both feeds. Maggie has also written books, taught, and created her own line of Chinese cooking sauces. ✍

Whenever Jim came to San Francisco, which was at least twice a year, we would get together. Mostly, I would cook for him and gather some of the "foodie friends" together, like Loni Kuhn, Jim Nassikas, Chuck Williams, Marion Cunningham, Donn and Molly Chappellet and Danny Kaye. Jim loved to be around nice people from the food and music, especially opera, worlds. I took him to the San Francisco Opera on one of his visits and he thoroughly enjoyed Joan Sutherland in *The Merry Widow*. He called it a piece of fluff. He had never attended a performance in the San Francisco Opera House before this.

I will be eternally grateful to Jim Beard for the encouragement he gave me in starting my sauce business. The year was 1981, he came for dinner, and I prepared a very quick and easy Chinese meal using the sauces I had just put on the market. Jim thought the whole concept of enabling people to prepare Chinese food without fuss and getting consistent taste was great and wrote about my sauces within two months of being on the market. I didn't even realize this until a customer who saw me demonstrating my sauces at Bloomingdale's mentioned this to me. The next time I saw Jim, I gave him two extra kisses for the day.

On one of Jim's visits to San Francisco, he had a short stay at Presbyterian Hospital for his legs or feet. I came by one Sunday afternoon to visit him. I asked Jim if there was anything I could bring him . . . something he might be hungry for. "Yes," he said, "I'm in the mood for popcorn." "With butter?" "Of course!" Along with the popcorn, though he didn't ask for it, I brought along a bottle of his favorite Scotch . . . Glenlivet. When I arrived in his room, soon to follow down the hallway was another friend of Jim's, Chet Rhodes. We had a wonderful afternoon chatting, sipping Scotch, and eating popcorn.

Jim always ate his plate clean at the table. His favorite, I think, was seafood. I remember the first time I cooked him an all-Chinese seafood meal and one of the dishes was my stir-fry Dungeness crab. Jim thought the Dungeness crab was the best-tasting and -eating crab in the world. Here's the recipe.

Dungeness Crab with Lotsa Ginger and Garlic

■■■■■■■■■■■■■■■■■■■■■■■■■■■■

1 large, live Dungeness crab, about 2½ pounds
3 tablespoons peanut oil
3 green onions, cut into 2-inch lengths
8 thin slices peeled fresh ginger root
6 garlic cloves, smashed and peeled
1 tablespoon sherry or rice wine
1 tablespoon soy sauce
1 tablespoon oyster sauce
1 teaspoon Oriental sesame oil
Fresh cilantro sprigs for garnish

Bring a large pot of salted water to a boil. Add live crab, cover with lid, and cook for 2 minutes. Remove from heat, drain, and run crab under cold water to cool. Pull claws from body, crack them slightly, and reserve. Pull the body apart, remove the crab butter [tomalley and roe], and reserve. Discard the hard top shell, cut the meat part of the body into quarters, and reserve.

Heat peanut oil in a wok or large skillet over moderate to high heat. Add green onions, ginger, and garlic and stir-fry for about a minute to season the oil. Add the reserved crab pieces and stir-fry for about 30 seconds to coat with the oil.

Stir in reserved crab butter, sherry, soy sauce, and oyster sauce, blending well with the crab. Cover with lid, decrease the heat to low, and cook for 10 minutes.

Uncover and stir in sesame oil.

Serve garnished with cilantro sprigs.

✖ *Serves 3 to 4*

JEFF SMITH, *the Frugal Gourmet, is in many ways like Jim. In recent years, through television and a succession of books, no one has appealed to a broader American interest in food. Mr. Smith is of the American West. Strikingly like Jim, in recent years he has been establishing with an associate a series of in-store cookery shops providing his favorite utensils and giving information about them. You will notice his commendation of Jim's no-nonsense approach to food.* ✍

I must have forgotten how practical and basic Beard's recipes really are. We have all gotten so involved in nouvelle binges, in health fads that result in bland and colorless dishes, in dinner parties that are great displays of fancy decoration and food frou frou, that I was somewhat surprised to read again those dishes that the Grand Old Man of American Cooking first gave me.

The recipes that he sent me were for the sake of a fund raiser at our art museum in Tacoma, Washington. I was to prepare all of the food that he would demonstrate, and then we were to serve each of the 400 guests that came each night. I was a wreck! I knew the night would be a disaster since the museum had, at that time, a kitchen that consisted of a hot plate . . . a dirty hot plate at that. I installed ovens and had cabinets made, and then I waited for the letter of instruction. What came was a collection of terribly sensible and creative dishes, dishes that were basic and fresh and

filled with the seafood from Mr. Beard's beloved Pacific Northwest. I should not have worried. Beard hated the put-on and the pretentious. And he cursed and yelled about same often.

We were to have dinner together at a local restaurant. I arrived at his temporary residence to meet him for the first time. He stepped from the house wearing slippers since his feet were so swollen, and then he climbed into my Oldsmobile station wagon. That old car was built for action, but Beard was better built, and bigger. The tank nearly tipped over, but we were off to dinner, and to a grand friendship.

How that man loved to eat! I had been told that he was not to have any fat, salt, or alcohol, at the direction of his doctor. That night I watched him consume a double scotch, a spinach salad, fatty grilled lamb chops, and he closed out with a Chocolate Rum Mousse. He then fell asleep at the table. I was helpless but fascinated by this man who had caused America to finally accept the fact that we do have a cuisine of our own, and many regional cuisines at that. He changed the course of American eating habits, and I really believe that he would curse and yell again about the blandness of the health food set.

We met on several later occasions and I remember his patience with me as I pressed him for support or insight on one of my projects. *To this day I get letters from newlyweds asking me to recommend a cookbook or two that they must have. I don't recommend mine . . . I recommend The James Beard Cookbook.* It is filled with that basic and gracious insight that Beard continues to offer us . . . without all the frou frou.

The following is one of the recipes that Beard included in his letter of instructions. It could not be more simple, or more basic.

Gingered Scallops

6 tablespoons butter
1½ pounds bay scallops
2 tablespoons finely sliced fresh ginger
Salt and freshly ground black pepper to taste
2 tablespoons finely chopped parsley

Heat the butter until sizzling. Sauté the scallops and ginger briefly, just to heat scallops through and brown lightly on the outside. Season with salt and pepper. Sprinkle with parsley and serve. ✗ *Serves 4*

JOANNA PRUESS *has taught, catered, written for* **The New York Times,** *and written a book,* **The Supermarket Epicure.** ✍

Because of the lavish filling and its outstanding curry-flavored sauce, I prefer to serve this for more elegant cool-weather parties.

You can easily serve 12 appetizer-size portions from the casserole by scoring the crust into regular-shaped wedges, then spooning the filling over a small amount of steamed basmati rice served on plates or in the scallop shells often sold in markets. Replace the crust over the shellfish before serving, and sprinkle on thinly sliced scallions.

Curried Shellfish Pot Pie

1 live lobster, about 1¼ pounds
12 ounces carrots, peeled and cut into 2-inch sticks
6 tablespoons unsalted butter
½ cup all-purpose flour
1 cup clam broth
1 cup light cream or milk
¾ cup dry sherry
3 tablespoons fresh lemon juice
2 tablespoons freshly grated ginger
2 cloves garlic, smashed, peeled, and minced
2 tablespoons curry powder
⅛ teaspoon cayenne pepper
Salt to taste
Freshly ground black pepper to taste
⅓ cup chopped fresh parsley
1½ pounds large shrimp, peeled and deveined
1 pound sea scallops
4 ounces shiitake mushrooms, stemmed and cut into ¼-inch slices
1 10 -ounce package frozen "petite" peas, defrosted in a sieve under warm running water
1 16-ounce package frozen pearl onions, defrosted in a sieve under warm running water

1 cup slivered almonds, toasted
1 pound all-butter puff pastry
1 egg mixed with 1 tablespoon water for egg wash
Thinly sliced scallion greens for garnish, optional

Bring a large pot of water to a boil. Add lobster and cook over high heat for 5 minutes. Remove from heat and drain. Allow to cool until cool enough to handle. Remove lobster meat from tail and claws, coarsely chop, and reserve. Discard shells.

Bring a smaller pot of water to the boil, add carrots, and cook for 2 minutes. Drain and reserve.

Preheat oven to 425° F.

Invert a 3-quart casserole onto paper and trace the shape, allowing for a 1-inch border all around. Cut out the shape and reserve.

Melt butter in a large heavy skillet over moderate heat. Whisk in the flour, reduce heat to low, and cook, stirring, for 2 to 3 minutes. Gradually stir in clam broth, cream, sherry, and lemon juice so that there are no lumps. Slowly allow sauce to come to a boil, stirring, and cook for about 1 minute, until it becomes quite thick.

Remove from heat and stir in ginger, garlic, curry powder, cayenne pepper, salt, and pepper. Allow the sauce to cool for a few minutes, then gently fold in parsley, shrimp, scallops, mushrooms, peas, onions, and almonds, reserved lobster and carrots. Scrape mixture into the 3-quart casserole and smooth out surface with spatula.

On lightly floured surface, roll out puff pastry to about ¼ inch thick. Use paper template to cut out pastry to fit the casserole. Cut an X in the center (about 2½-inches across) as an air hole. With a pastry brush, brush rim of casserole with egg wash. Place pastry over casserole and press down edges with fingers to seal. Cut the remaining pastry into strips or shapes and decorate the top. (The pie may be prepared ahead up until this point and refrigerated for a day.) Brush the pastry with egg wash. To prevent sauce from boiling over onto pastry crust, roll a 3-inch-wide strip of heavy aluminum foil around the handle of a wooden spoon and insert it into the X to form a steam vent.

Place casserole on a cookie sheet and bake for 20 minutes. Reduce the heat to 375 degrees and bake for 20 minutes longer. Remove from oven and allow to rest, with the wooden spoon still in place, for about 10 minutes. Serve with mango chutney and steamed basmati rice.

✖ *Serves 8 to 12*

SUZANNE HOFFMAN *of The Kitchen Shoppe in Carlisle,*
Pennsylvania, tells her tale of Jim and sends us a recipe with a firm tradition in her Pennsylvania Dutch
area. The tale introduces an important character in the Beard ménage, Percy, a sand-colored pug. Stephen
Spector (page 140) found the dog for Jim. Somehow, no matter how many people made a fuss over Percy, he
always knew he belonged to Jim and obeyed him. ✍

On two different occasions I took my cooking school students to James Beard's home in New York for classes.

The first time, I wanted to take a little something along as a gift. . . . What food could I take for America's number-one cook??? After much thought I had a great idea—why not something homemade for *Percy* (gourmet dog treats)? So I tested and tested. Weeks later I had all kinds of canines at the back door.

The day of class, I made a big jar full of treats. Percy wouldn't even taste them.

I guess living with James Beard, he had his fill of gourmet treats. And preferred the store-bought dry tasteless dog treats.

Our classes with James Beard were most important to our students and our school. We sure do have happy memories of those classes.

Baked Oyster Pie

☐ *Pastry Crust*
2 cups all-purpose flour
4 ounces cold unsalted butter, cut into small pieces
1 teaspoon kosher salt
6 tablespoons cold water

3½ pounds boiling potatoes, peeled and diced
2 ribs celery, peeled and diced (about ½ cup)
1 large onion (about 8 ounces), peeled and roughly chopped
2 tablespoons unsalted butter
3 tablespoons all-purpose flour
2 cups milk
3 dozen shucked stewing oysters, drained, with their liquor reserved
3 hard-boiled eggs, peeled and roughly chopped
3 tablespoons chopped fresh parsley
Salt and freshly ground black pepper to taste
1 egg yolk
1 tablespoon water

Fish & Shellfish

To make pastry: Place flour, butter, and salt in the work bowl of a food processor fitted with steel blade. Process until mixture becomes like coarse meal. Add water and process until dough gathers together and forms a ball. Remove dough from work bowl and shape into a disk. Cover with plastic wrap and refrigerate at least 1 hour.

Place potatoes, celery, and onion in a large pan and cover with cold water. Place over moderate to high heat and bring to a boil. Cook, uncovered, for about 12 minutes, or until soft. Remove from heat and drain. Transfer to a large mixing bowl and allow to cool.

Melt butter in a medium pan over moderate heat. Stir in flour. Gradually blend in milk and oyster liquor. Cook, stirring, until mixture thickens and almost comes to a boil. Remove from heat. Add to potato mixture along with oysters, hard-boiled eggs, and parsley. Gently toss to coat and season to taste. Pour into a 14″ × 11″ × 2″ casserole dish and reserve.

Preheat oven to 350° F.

Place pastry on a lightly floured surface and roll out to a rectangle about ⅛ inch thick that will fit over the casserole dish. With a pastry brush wet the edges of the dish with water. Carefully cover the filled casserole with pastry and seal the edges with your fingers. With a sharp knife make a few slits in the crust so that the steam can escape. Mix together egg yolk and tablespoon water and brush over the pastry crust. Bake in the center of the oven for about 1 hour, or until crust is golden brown. Remove from oven and serve.

✖ *Serves 8 to 10*

JOHN CARROLL. *When I first met Jim, I envied him his luck with assistants. He always seemed to have who he needed when the need arose. I soon realized that it wasn't luck. Jim listened; he helped people; he encouraged their ambitions; he was enthusiastic and generous. It was no wonder people wanted to work with him—not just for the culinary learning and the career enhancement—for the human contact and learning.*

John Carroll was, in the last years, his assistant in California and at Seaside and made a great difference to Jim's life. John is a fine cook in his own right, has written one book, and is working on more. 🖎

In 1980 and '81 I spent several months with James Beard in Seaside, Oregon, after the regular summer cooking classes concluded. He loved to eat in what he fondly called "joints"— quirky places where local people gathered and the food was good and often a little greasy. James also had a passion for a few fast foods, especially Kentucky Fried Chicken, Original Version, and a Big Mac from McDonald's.

For lunch together, we'd often pick up a bucket of chicken from the Colonel, where people stared in disbelief (I think that's one reason he liked going there!). Then we'd drive to the beach and, depending on how he felt that day, either eat in the car or, if he was up to a walk, we'd sit on a big rock closer to the water.

One October, while driving from Portland to San Francisco, we stopped in Roseberg, Oregon, at Wendy's. He'd heard of the chain but never eaten there. We sat with our orders, and a young man came to the table and immediately struck up a conversation about bread. James cheerfully answered his questions, and as he left, the man said, "Boy, I can't wait to tell everybody I saw James Beard at Wendy's," and James responded, "I'll make a deal. I won't tell anybody I saw you here if *you* don't tell anybody you saw *me* here!''

We prepared this in the Oregon Coast classes on a morning when there was lots of leftover cooked fish from the previous day. It can also be made with fresh fish, or thoroughly desalted salt cod, added to the tomato mixture and simmered just until the fish is cooked through.

Seafood Chili

■■■■■■■■■■■■■■■■■■■■■■■■■■■

6 slices meaty bacon

2 large yellow onions (about 9 ounces each), peeled and thinly sliced (about 4 cups)

4 cloves garlic, smashed, peeled, and minced

1 to 2 jalapeño peppers, stemmed, seeded, and deribbed

3 tablespoons chili powder

6 cups canned Italian plum tomatoes, roughly chopped, with their liquid

1 teaspoon dried oregano

1 teaspoon ground cumin

1 tablespoon white wine vinegar

Salt to taste

1 4-ounce can green chilies, stemmed, seeded, deribbed, and cut into thin strips

2½ pounds boneless firm-fleshed fish (such as flounder), cooked or raw, cut into 1-inch cubes

Place the bacon in a large pan or Dutch oven and cook over medium heat until just crisp. Remove bacon with a slotted spoon and reserve, leaving rendered fat.

Add onions to bacon fat. Lower heat and cook, stirring occasionally, for about 30 minutes, or until they are very soft.

Stir in garlic, jalapeños, and chili powder and cook 5 minutes longer. Stir in tomatoes (with their liquid), oregano, cumin, vinegar, and salt. Simmer mixture for 20 to 30 minutes, until it thickens slightly.

Add the reserved bacon, green chilies, and fish. Simmer for about 5 minutes longer, or until the fish is cooked through. Serve hot.

✗ *Makes 11 cups, serves 6 to 8*

Make this with as much or as little shrimp as your pocketbook dictates. If you reduce shrimp below a pound, use an 8-ounce bottle of clam juice for the broth and add more ham. (I use sliced ham steaks from the market.) You can serve the jambalaya directly from the skillet, or mound it on a heated platter, garnished with lots of fresh parsley, to show off the glorious colors of the shrimp and vegetables. If you wish, reserve strips from one of the green peppers and half of the red pepper; sauté them separately in a little vegetable oil until they are crisp-tender, and scatter them around the jambalaya when you take it to the table.

Park Place Jambalaya

1 to 1½ pounds medium shrimp, in the shell
1 cup water
1 teaspoon dried thyme
1½ pounds mild Italian sausage, cut into bite-size
  pieces
1 tablespoon unsalted butter
1 cup finely chopped onion (about ¼ pound)
2 medium green bell peppers, stemmed, deribbed,
  seeded, and cut lengthwise into thin strips
1 medium red bell pepper, stemmed, deribbed,
  seeded, and cut lengthwise into thin strips (if
  red peppers are not available, use 3 green
  peppers and garnish the jambalaya with
  drained chopped pimientos)
1 to 2 stalks celery, trimmed, strung, and chopped
  (about 1 cup)
½ cup chopped fresh fennel (optional)
1½ cups raw long-grain rice
1 28-ounce can tomatoes, drained and coarsely
  chopped (liquid reserved)
2 cloves garlic, smashed, peeled, and minced
  (about 1½ tablespoons)
1 bay leaf
½ cup white wine or dry white vermouth
1 pound lean, good-quality ham, cut into bite-size
  pieces
½ teaspoon freshly ground black pepper
½ teaspoon hot red pepper sauce
Salt to taste
2 tablespoons chopped fresh parsley for garnish

Preheat the oven to 375° F.

Rinse the shrimp under cold running water, peel them, and reserve the shells. Cover the shrimp and refrigerate until needed.

In a medium saucepan, boil the water with the shrimp shells for 10 minutes, until the liquid is reduced to ½ cup. Strain and reserve the broth; discard the shells. Measure out 1 tablespoon of the broth and stir in the thyme. Set the thyme aside to soak.

In a large oven-proof skillet over medium heat, cook the sausage until it is lightly browned on all sides; this will take 10 to 15 minutes. Pour off all but 1 tablespoon of the fat. Add the butter and onions to the sausage in the skillet and cook over medium heat for 5 or 6 minutes, until the onions wilt. Add the pepper strips, celery, and the fennel, if desired. Continue to cook for 3 to 4 minutes longer. Stir in the rice. Cook, stirring frequently, until the grains of rice are coated and a milky color. Add the tomatoes, garlic, soaked thyme, and bay leaf. Mix well.

In a clean saucepan, heat the reserved shrimp broth with the reserved liquid from the canned tomatoes and the wine. When this mixture is hot, add it slowly to the sausage-and-rice mixture. Bring the mixture to a boil, stirring gently. Add the ham, cover the skillet, and bake in the lower part of the oven for 10 minutes.

Uncover the skillet and stir in the reserved shrimp. If the jambalaya seems dry, add hot water, chicken broth, or more wine. Cover and cook for 10 minutes longer, until the rice is tender.

Remove the bay leaf. Season with pepper, hot red pepper sauce and salt to taste. Garnish with chopped parsley. ✘ *Serves 6 to 8*

BEARD'S

BIRDS

After our first tumultuous disagreement, Jim and I disagreed about recipes and culinary technique very often; but the disputes seemed to

LEND SPICE, NOT ACRIMONY, TO OUR LIVES. ONE CONSTANT DISAGREEMENT HAD TO DO WITH HOW TO ROAST A BIRD— NOT ABOUT HOW GOOD A ROASTED BIRD COULD BE. WE BOTH THOUGHT ROAST CHICKEN ONE OF THE BEST FOODS IN THE WORLD. IT SEEMS HIS FRIENDS HAVE THEIR OWN IDEAS TOO, WHICH WAS CERTAINLY A HALLMARK OF JIM'S FRIENDS. A HALLMARK OF JIM WAS HIS LARGE FINGERS STRIPPING OFF THE CRISP SKIN TO EAT, LEAVING THE FLESH FOR THE LESS GREEDY.

WE ONCE DID A WHOLE DAY OF CHICKEN BECAUSE A GROUP OF CHICKEN PRODUCERS WERE IN THE CLASS. WE GOT COCKS' COMBS. I DON'T EVEN REMEMBER FOR WHAT CLASSIC DISH THEY WERE TO BE THE GARNITURE; BUT I DO REMEMBER THE CLASS LOYALLY SCRUBBING AWAY WITH TURKISH TOWELS AT THE COOKED COMBS TO REMOVE THEIR SKIN. THE COCKS' COMBS WEREN'T VERY GOOD—OLD, TOUGH, AND DULL IN COLOR.

JIM ACCOMMODATED HIS READERS BY HAVING TURKEY RECIPES IN ALMOST EVERY BOOK, BUT HE DIDN'T LIKE TURKEY—EVEN AT THANKSGIVING. IF HE FELT FORCED TO MAKE TURKEY, HE WOULD NEVER STUFF IT.

HE LIKED GAME AND WOULD HAPPILY EAT ALL KINDS OF GAME BIRDS. HE LOVED COMPOSED SALADS IN WHICH HE MIGHT, AS OFTEN AS NOT, THINK OF PUTTING COOKED OR SMOKED BIRDS. I HAVE SEEN SMOKED PHEASANT AND SMOKED DUCK SLIPPED ON TOP OF SALADS AT THE LAST MOMENT.

up to the present—has been welcomed for many years by Clay Triplette. Students and teachers alike had their way smoothed by Clay's unruffled way of running the house and the kitchen and by his faultless shopping for ingredients for classes.

Clay babied Mr. Beard and he loved it. When Jim was tired, Clay would make his Southern Fried Chicken. This was one time Jim didn't insist that the skin be crisp—the chicken is smothered at the end. ✍

Southern Fried Chicken

1 3½-pound frying chicken, cut into serving pieces
½ cup dried bread crumbs, preferably homemade
3 tablespoons all-purpose flour
2 tablespoons unsalted butter
6 tablespoons vegetable shortening
Salt to taste
Freshly ground black pepper to taste

Mix bread crumbs and flour in a plastic bag. Wash chicken but do not dry. Place chicken pieces into bag one at a time and shake until well coated with crumb mixture.

Melt butter and shortening in a deep skillet over high heat. Add chicken, skin side down. Cook for 4 to 5 minutes. Lower heat to medium and turn chicken. Cook for 10 minutes more. Turn again and cover pan. Cook for 20 minutes, until deep golden brown. Drain on paper toweling and sprinkle with salt and pepper to taste. ✘ *Serves 4*

Honey Fried Chicken with Thyme-Mint Cream Sauce

1 3½-pound chicken, cut into serving pieces (backbone, neck, and wings reserved for broth)
½ cup honey
2 tablespoons raspberry (or other fruit) vinegar
½ cup lard
½ cup vegetable oil
½ cup all-purpose flour
2 tablespoons whole wheat flour
1 teaspoon salt
¼ teaspoon freshly ground black pepper
½ cup dry white wine
½ cup chicken stock, homemade or canned
1½ cups heavy cream
1½ tablespoons chopped fresh mint
1 tablespoon fresh thyme leaves or 1 teaspoon dried
1 teaspoon lemon zest
Salt and freshly ground black pepper to taste

Place chicken pieces in a mixing bowl. Stir honey and vinegar together and pour over chicken. Marinate for at least two hours, stirring occasionally.

Heat lard and oil in a 12-inch frying pan over medium-high heat.

Preheat oven to 200° F.

Remove chicken from marinade and drain on paper toweling. Mix flours together. Sprinkle chicken with salt and pepper and coat with flour. Strain marinade and reserve 2 tablespoons for sauce.

Starting with the dark meat pieces, gently place chicken in hot fat, skin side down, and cook for 4 to 6 minutes until brown. Turn pieces and continue cooking, regulating heat so that the chicken browns evenly on both sides without burning. Turn once more and cook until well browned and tender when pierced with a fork. Cook dark meat a total of about 20 minutes, white meat for 10 to 13 minutes.

Keep chicken warm in oven while making sauce.

Pour off fat from frying pan, leaving browned bits on the bottom. Deglaze pan with wine and add chicken stock. Reduce by half over medium-high heat, about 3 to 4 minutes. Add cream, mint, thyme, zest, and reserved marinade and reduce until sauce is thick enough to coat the back of a spoon, about 5 to 6 minutes. Strain sauce and season with salt and pepper to taste. Serve with chicken. ✗ *Serves 4*

The pan juices are delicious, but don't pour them over the chicken because you want to keep that crispness; pour them around it. Serve with a salad and a good bottle of wine. You may also serve the chicken on a bed of rice or buttered noodles.

Chicken in Yogurt

1½ to 2 cups plain yogurt
1 clove garlic, smashed and peeled
½ teaspoon ground ginger
½ teaspoon salt
¼ teaspoon freshly ground black pepper
1 frying chicken, cut into serving pieces, or 8
    chicken legs, cut into thighs and drumsticks
½ cup all-purpose flour or corn meal
1 tablespoon vegetable oil, for the pan

In a large, shallow dish, combine the yogurt with the garlic, ginger, salt, and pepper (if you are cooking chicken legs rather than a whole chicken, use 2 cups of yogurt). Place the pieces of chicken in the yogurt mixture and let them marinate refrigerated, for at least 2 hours, turning them over once.

Preheat the oven to 350° F.

Remove the chicken from the marinade and scrape off any excess. Roll each piece of chicken in flour or corn meal until it is nicely, but lightly, coated. Arrange the coated chicken pieces in a lightly oiled baking or broiling pan. Bake them for 1 hour, until the chicken is tender and the coating is crisp and delicately browned.

✖ *Serves 6*

Jim Beard . . . the name brings a flood of memories of telephone calls with his relating some delicious gossip of the food world along with his always generous sharing of his tremendous wisdom about food and cooking. He always was so warm, so gracious and loving.

One memory of his special brand of graciousness stands out. It was planned as a gala evening to celebrate his birthday, which fell on a day when he was out of town, giving a talk at the Food Marketing Institute Convention. The birthday dinner, held at the convention city's most prestigious room, had been set up weeks in advance and, presumably, all would be perfect for the very special party.

Every food service place occasionally has off moments in the kitchen or service, but it all came together that evening to be a total disaster. No two people in the party were served the same course at the same time, with interminable waits between courses. The food reached heights of mediocrity. Jim was gracious as each disaster occurred, until the accumulation of disasters became ludicrous. It was finally climaxed with the restaurant bringing a liqueur cart to our table with the glasses falling from the cart smashing all around us. As hostess, I was devastated. Jim, the birthday honoree, made light of a horror situation, and had a great many chuckles about the evening.

If Jim were coming to my home for dinner, I would probably serve a simple Mustard Roast Chicken, a favorite which produces the crispy skin he so loved. I would accompany the chicken with a "signature" rice dish like Wild Mushroom Risotto (page 159) and the freshest, most interesting vegetables available, simply prepared. We'd splurge on the first course, served accompanied by a fine champagne.

Mustard Roast Chicken

1 4-pound broiler-fryer chicken
⅓ cup tarragon Dijon mustard
½ cup chicken stock, homemade or canned

Preheat oven to 450° F.

Remove giblets and neck pieces from chicken. Spread skin with mustard and place chicken in a roasting pan. Place in preheated oven and reduce heat to 350° F.

Roast chicken for about 18 minutes per pound until juices run clear and the legs move easily at the joint. After the first 15 minutes, baste with 2 tablespoons chicken broth every 10 minutes.

Remove from oven and allow to stand for 5 to 10 minutes before carving. ✗ *Serves 4*

MICHAEL MCCARTY. *Like Jim, Michael McCarty is a serious food professional, and, like Jim, there is much of the theatrical about him. Consider this festive treatment of chicken breasts. For more about Michael McCarty, see page 193.*

The Maui onions called for in the recipe are large and sweet, as are Vidalias and Walla Walla Sweets. ✍

Grilled Chicken and Goat Cheese Salad with Jalapeño-Cilantro-Lime Salsa

■■■■■■■■■■■■■■■■■■■■■■■■■

6 chicken breast halves, boned, with the skin left
    on and wing bones attached
1 8-ounce log California goat cheese, cut into
    ¼-inch slices
Salt to taste
Freshly ground black pepper to taste
3 medium red bell peppers, stemmed, seeded,
    deribbed, and cut into ¾-inch strips
3 medium yellow bell peppers, stemmed, seeded,
    deribbed, and cut into ¾-inch strips
1 large Maui or red onion, peeled and cut into
    ⅓-inch rings
2 tablespoons olive oil
1 cup Tomato Concassée (see page 293)
3 heads limestone (Bibb) lettuce, leaves separated,
    washed, dried, and torn into pieces
3 bunches mâche, leaves separated, washed, dried,
    and torn into pieces
2 bunches arugula, leaves separated, washed,
    dried, and torn into pieces
2 heads baby red leaf lettuce, leaves separated,
    washed, dried, and torn into pieces
1 head baby radicchio, leaves separated and torn
    into pieces
1 cup Jalapeño-Cilantro-Lime Salsa (see page 272)
1 bunch fresh chives, finely chopped

Preheat broiler or grill.

With your finger, make a pocket in between the skin and meat of each chicken breast, inserting your finger along the long side of each breast and leaving the skin attached along the other edges.

Slip goat cheese slices into the pockets, overlapping slightly, to stuff the breasts. Season with salt and pepper and reserve.

Brush pepper strips and onion slices with olive oil and season with salt and pepper. Reserve.

Place chicken breasts on the grill or under the broiler with skin side toward the heat for about 5 minutes, or until browned. Turn breasts over and cook about 6 minutes longer, or until cooked through. Remove from heat and reserve. Place pepper strips and onion slices on grill and cook for about 1 minute on each side. Remove from heat and reserve.

Combine salad leaves and divide among 6 large serving plates. Remove wing bones and cut each chicken breast across into 5 slices. Arrange chicken and grilled vegetables over salad in the center of each plate. Garnish each plate with about 2 generous tablespoons of Tomato Concassée and spoon Jalapeño-Cilantro-Lime Salsa over chicken. Sprinkle with chopped chives. ✗ *Serves 6*

FRANÇOIS DIONOT *is a highly respected cooking teacher in the Washington, D.C. area with his own cooking school, L'Académie de Cuisine, in Bethesda, Maryland. He has been the president of the International Association of Cooking Professionals [IACP].* ✍

Chicken Breast Salad with Green Beans and Quail Eggs

■■■■■■■■■■■■■■■■■■■■■■■■■

2 tablespoons vegetable oil
4 whole chicken breasts, skinned, boned, and split
½ pound haricots verts, stem ends snapped off
6 ounces slab bacon, cut into thin strips
Salt to taste
1 head leaf lettuce, washed and dried
3 tablespoons sherry vinegar
9 tablespoons hazelnut oil
1 tablespoon finely chopped shallots
Freshly ground black pepper to taste
12 hard-boiled quail eggs (or 4 chicken eggs),
     peeled and halved

Heat vegetable oil in a large skillet over moderate heat. Sprinkle chicken breasts with salt and pepper. Sauté in oil for about 4 minutes on each side. Remove pan from heat, cover with lid, and allow chicken to continue cooking in hot pan for 10 minutes longer.

Meanwhile, bring a small pan of salted water to a boil over high heat. Add haricots verts and cook for 4 minutes. Remove from heat, drain, and refresh under ice-cold running water. Drain and reserve.

Place bacon in a small pan and sauté over moderate heat, stirring, until crisp. Remove with a slotted spoon, drain on paper towels, and reserve.

Remove chicken breasts from pan and cut across into ½-inch slices. Add sherry vinegar, hazelnut oil, shallots, salt, and pepper to the pan and whisk together to incorporate vinaigrette completely.

To serve, line 4 plates with lettuce leaves. Arrange chicken slices on one side of the plate, green beans on the other side. Sprinkle bacon over plate and arrange pieces of egg to one side. Pour vinaigrette over salad. ✘ *Serves 4*

This is an absolutely delicious fricassee. Serve it over buttered noodles.

Chicken Fricassee

½ cup olive oil

4 whole large chicken breasts, skinned, boned, and cut into 1- by 2-inch strips

¼ pound unsalted butter

2 yellow onions, peeled and diced (about 1 cup)

½ pound mushrooms, trimmed and sliced ¼ inch thick

2 cups heavy cream

3 egg yolks

Freshly ground nutmeg

1 cup fresh peas, blanched, or frozen "petite" peas defrosted in a sieve under warm running water

Salt to taste

Freshly ground black pepper to taste

1 pound fresh egg fettuccine, cooked

Freshly grated Parmesan cheese, for serving

Heat the oil in a large skillet. Add the chicken and brown it quickly over high heat. When the chicken is nearly cooked through, remove it to drain on layers of paper toweling. Discard the oil.

Put the butter in the skillet and melt it over medium heat. Add the onions and cook until they are transparent, about 2 to 4 minutes. Add the mushrooms and cook for 2 minutes longer, scraping up any browned bits in the skillet.

Return the strips of chicken to the skillet. Whisk the cream into the egg yolks and add a pinch of nutmeg. Stir the cream mixture into the skillet, lower the heat, and cook for 4 to 6 minutes. Add the peas and heat the fricassee thoroughly.

Season the fricassee with salt and pepper to taste. Serve with cooked fettuccine. Pass freshly grated Parmesan cheese separately.

✘ *Serves 8 to 10*

as well as having a fine taste and ability in food. Jim enjoyed both sides of him. As with so many of Jim's friends, Christopher first turned up in class. At that time, he was a partner in the gloriously successful catering firm, Glorious Food. He left the firm and started writing cookbooks; now he has opened a restaurant in Manhattan called Ten Twenty-Two, which has much the air of a club and elegant versions of homey food like this chicken pot pie. ✍

Jim was standing in the kitchen preparing a single duck egg for his lunch—the first of many meals I would witness being cooked by him, and the first of many meals I would eat with him. He looked up and asked, "Do your friends invite you to dinner often?" I said no. He said, "Neither do mine.... You realize," he continued, "I'd be happy if they just invited me for a scrambled egg—anyone can scramble an egg. Well, almost anyone."

As he got older he preferred preparing and eating foods that were cooked simply. A litany of ingredients was not the mark of his lexicon of recipes. A ripe pear peeled and sliced with knife and fork was as thrilling to him as any that appeared poached in wine and standing in a pool of sabayon.

When I first cooked for him I had just returned from the kitchens of Paul Bocuse, and I adapted a chicken and vegetable dish with cubes of foie gras and a generous truffle sliced and pushed under the skin of the chicken. It was set in a tureen and sealed in puff pastry and baked till the chicken was tender and the pastry flaky gold. I remember how eager I was for his response. In the middle of the meal, he looked up and said, "This is quite delicious, but remember—you are an American. The foie gras and truffles can go." Thereafter, the foie gras and truffles were gone.

I continue to talk and reminisce about him with friends and pose imaginary questions to him when I am in doubt.

I miss him.

Chicken in Pastry Crust

■■■■■■■■■■■■■■■■■■■■■■■■■■■■■■■

1 chicken, about 3½ to 4 pounds
1 medium tomato
4 small white onions
2 cups chicken stock, homemade or canned
⅓ cup shelled fresh peas
4 ounces green beans
3 medium carrots, peeled and cut into 2-inch
    julienne (about 1½ cups)
1 small turnip, peeled and cut into quarters
1 head Bibb lettuce, washed and cut into quarters
7 tablespoons unsalted butter, cut into small pieces
Kosher salt and freshly ground black pepper to
    taste
1 pound frozen puff pastry, defrosted
1 egg lightly beaten, for egg wash

Preheat oven to 450° F.

Wash the chicken and pat dry with paper towels. Place it in a 3-quart oven-proof tureen.

Bring a medium pot of water to a boil, add the tomato, and blanch for about 2 minutes, or until the skin just starts to split. Remove with a slotted spoon and cool under running water. Leave the pot of water boiling on the stove. Core and peel tomato, cut into eighths, and remove seeds. Add to the tureen with the chicken.

Add onions to the boiling water and blanch for 2 minutes. Cool under running water and peel. Add to the tureen.

Pour water out of pot, add chicken stock and bring to a boil. Blanch the peas, beans, carrots, and turnip separately in chicken stock. Remove each vegetable with a slotted spoon, cool under running water, and add to the tureen. Stir in lettuce, butter, and one cup of the boiling chicken stock. Season to taste with salt and pepper.

Roll out pastry to fit the tureen with about an inch extending all around the rim. Brush the surface with the egg wash and place over tureen, with the brushed side down. Seal the edges by pressing the pastry lightly with your fingers. Brush the top of the pastry with the remaining egg wash.

Bake in the center of the oven for 10 minutes. Cover the crust loosely with aluminum foil and continue baking for 35 minutes longer.

Turn the oven off and leave the tureen in the closed oven for 15 minutes longer. To serve, remove crust to a plate with a metal spatula and cut into four pieces. Remove the chicken to a platter and carve. Divide chicken, vegetables, and broth among 4 heated soup plates. Place a portion of the crust on each portion. ✕ *Serves 4*

This was taken down from Jim Beard on the day of the choucroute feast in Henry's and my Paris apartment circa 1955. Eager but untutored, this is what I wrote. (I still have my original copybook pages of this simple, honest dish.)

Choucroute au Canard La Motte Picquet au Champagne
■ ■

3 pounds raw sauerkraut
½ pound sliced bacon
2 cloves garlic, peeled, minced, and smashed
Freshly ground black pepper to taste
8 to 10 juniper berries, crushed in a mortar and pestle or spice grinder
2 cups Champagne or white wine
1 duck, about 4 to 5 pounds, trimmed of excess fat
Salt to taste
1½ pounds small new potatoes (about 16), washed and halved
½ pound knockwurst sausages, cut across into ½-inch slices

Rinse sauerkraut in a sieve under cold running water and drain well. Arrange slices of bacon over the bottom of a large flame-proof casserole with tightly fitting lid. Scatter minced garlic over bacon and cover with drained sauerkraut. Sprinkle with 1 teaspoon black pepper and juniper berries. Pour in Champagne or wine. Cover with lid and bring to a boil over moderate heat. Reduce heat to very low and simmer for about 3 hours.

About an hour before sauerkraut is ready, preheat oven to 425° F.

Place duck on a rack in a baking pan. Sprinkle with salt and pepper. Roast for about 50 minutes or until juices run clear when flesh is pierced with a knife. Remove from oven and allow to stand for about 15 minutes.

Meanwhile, stir sauerkraut mixture (if mixture is very dry at this point, ½ cup water may be added) and stir in potatoes and sliced sausages. Recover with lid and cook for 20 minutes longer, or until potatoes are cooked through.

When duck is cool enough to handle, remove skin and fat, slice all meat from the bones, and cut into large pieces. Gently stir meat into the choucroute. Season to taste and serve with mustard and pickles.

✖ *Serves 6*

Duck and Wild Mushroom Gumbo

■■■■■■■■■■■■■■■■■■■■■■■■

☐ *Creole Meat Seasoning*

1 tablespoon salt

1 tablespoon granulated garlic

2 teaspoons paprika

2 teaspoons cayenne pepper

1 teaspoon black pepper

1 duck (about 5 pounds), trimmed of all excess fat

☐ *For the stock*

1 stalk celery, trimmed and cut into 1-inch pieces

1 medium onion, peeled and cut into quarters

½ head garlic, cloves separated and peeled

½ bunch parsley

2 quarts cold water

☐ *For the gumbo*

½ cup vegetable oil

½ cup flour

1 medium onion, peeled and diced

1 medium bell pepper, stemmed, seeded, deribbed, and diced

4 ounces assorted fresh wild mushrooms, trimmed and roughly chopped

1 stalk celery, trimmed and diced

3 cloves garlic, smashed, peeled and minced

1 teaspoon salt

½ teaspoon freshly ground black pepper

½ teaspoon cayenne pepper

Preheat oven to 375° F.

In a small bowl combine salt, granulated garlic, paprika, cayenne, and black pepper. Rub mixture over entire surface of duck. Place seasoned duck in a roasting pan and cook for 1 hour.

Remove duck from oven and allow to stand for about 10 minutes. Remove skin and all the meat from the duck. Reserve meat. Place the bones in a large pot with the stock ingredients. Place pot over high heat, cover, and bring to a boil. Uncover, reduce heat to moderate, and simmer for about 40 minutes or until the stock has reduced by about one third. Strain the stock and reserve. Discard bones and vegetables.

Heat oil in a large pot over moderate heat. Add flour and cook, stirring, for a few minutes until the mixture becomes a deep brown color. Stir in onion, pepper, celery, and garlic and cook for a few minutes, until the vegetables are tender.

Gradually add the reserved stock, whisking mixture until smooth after each addition. Stir in seasonings, reduce heat to low, and simmer for about 30 minutes. Add mushrooms and reserved duck meat and cook for 10 minutes longer.

Season to taste and serve.

✖ *Serves 6 to 8*

MARY HAMBLET, *James's oldest friend, still lives in Portland. A lively, witty, loving person she admits to being no cook; but does add that Jim did like her way with wild duck. James dedicated <u>Delights and Prejudices</u>, his most autobiographical book, to her and wrote movingly about shared times in Gearhart with her family.* ✍

Once when JAB and I were in Provence and we were about to rent a car, J. went ahead to the rental place where I was to meet him. Upon my arrival he announced he'd chosen the car—a deux cheveaux!

"James, you *can't* fit in that!"

"Of course I can, so long as I can expand in any direction."

Well, we had the deux cheveaux for a month. He sat tall—and we came to love it.

Wild Duck

2 fresh wild ducks, about 1¾ pounds each, or frozen ducks, completely defrosted
Salt to taste
Freshly ground black pepper to taste
1½ cups packaged stuffing mix
3 ounces yellow onion, peeled and finely chopped (about ½ cup)
2 ribs celery, peeled and finely chopped (about ½ cup)
2 tablespoons melted unsalted butter
½ teaspoon dried sage
½ teaspoon dried thyme
3 tablespoons cold water
2 slices salt pork, about 2½ ounces each

Preheat oven to 375° F.

Sprinkle each duck with salt and pepper over the skin and inside the cavity. Set aside while preparing stuffing.

Place stuffing mix in a bowl with onion, celery, butter, sage, thyme, and water and mix well together. Divide stuffing evenly between the birds and place them on a rack in a roasting pan. Place a slice of salt pork over each bird.

Roast for about 45 minutes, or until an instant-read thermometer inserted into the thickest part of the flesh reads 180° F. Remove from oven and allow to stand for about 5 minutes before carving. ✗ *Serves 4*

ROGER YASEEN *may be the most passionate food amateur—after Gregory Thomas—that Jim or I had ever met. For many years he headed and enlarged in membership and scope the Chaîne des Rôtisseurs. Today, he sponsors a yearly, mammoth tasting of American wines and food from great New York restaurants, called A View from the Vineyard. He and his wife Janet have welcomed some of the world's most notable chefs into their home and brought forth for their lucky guests precious bottles stored in what I am convinced must be the only temperature-controlled bedroom wine cellar.*

At one point Roger went on a search for perfect duck recipes with his characteristic enthusiasm and omniverousness. Here is one of the results. ✍

I consider myself a disciple of James Beard's and took many classes from him. For me, he was a mentor not so much of creative skills, but a teacher of the discernment of the accomplishments of others.

I recall with quiet pleasure private instructions on making a perfect omelette. Jim perched in a chair and "talked" me through six dozen two-egg omelettes until, satisfied with number seventy-three, he ate it—high praise.

We shared the experience of planning a menu for a gastronomic society's banquet at Paul Kovi and Tom Margittai's Forum of the Twelve Caesars. I was a neophyte; James, the teacher. Ably assisted by chef Seppi Renggli, the dinner, "Homage to Baby Lamb," using every part of that spring treat, took shape. We met a dozen times to plan, develop, and sample. Was the dinner successful? To many, it remains the standard for gourmet dinners—not my mother; she fainted when served the lamb's head accompanied by a neat diagram pointing out the edible portions.

I like to cook duck. Jim would have summarized, "Wash a duck; stick it in the oven at *any* temperature, and cook until done." Such lack of detail can make an amateur nervous. I obfuscate the intrinsic simplicity of preparing duck with a foolproof recipe that takes more time and makes more mess in the kitchen.

Although the simplest way to achieve crisp, richly browned duck is to cook it until all the fat has dripped away, this usually results in overcooked meat. The two-step preparation below guarantees the same desirable crispness outside but firm, juicy, and flavorful meat with a tinge of pink at the bone. If you prefer the meat more well done, reduce the heat to 350° F. after 20 minutes and cook for 30 minutes longer.

Perfect Roast Duck

■■■■■■■■■■■■■■■■■■■■■■■■■

1 duck
¼ cup hot water
2 tablespoons dark soy sauce
1 tablespoon honey

Prick duck skin all over. Do not truss.

Place a steamer or rack in a large deep pot and add 1 inch of stock or water. Set duck, breast side up, on steamer. Bring liquid to a simmer, cover, and steam gently for one hour.

Remove duck from pot and carefully pat dry, being careful not to tear skin.

Place an oven rack in the middle of the oven and a second rack in the lower third. Preheat oven to 425° F.

Combine water, soy sauce, and honey. Prick duck all over once more and brush on soy mixture. Place duck on cake rack on middle oven rack, or place directly on oven rack. Place a large pan to catch drippings on rack under duck. Roast for exactly 20 minutes.

Remove from oven and let rest 10 minutes before carving.

I was a shy novice in the land of cooking when we met, and to me James Beard was the Emperor. Everything about him was vast and terrifying, and I was totally cowed. His bulk was enormous. A Chinese-style jacket often stretched across his belly, and he wore Chinese cloth slippers on his huge feet. Perched on his thick finger was a ring fashioned with a gold mouse nibbling on a chunk of jade cheese; Beard, like me, was born in the Year of the Rat.

He inspired me with awe, he inspired me with fear. And like any Emperor knowing of his power, he inspired me with love.

Tremulously, I invited James Beard to dinner the day I met him. It was sheer bravado; I lived in a tiny cottage with a tiny kitchen and had never cooked a big-deal dinner. A duck was procured from nearby Chinatown, and I sat for a long while staring at its beady-eyed head and rosy webbed feet. I'd not cooked a duck before, but why not? I'd never cooked for an Emperor before, either.

Big-Deal Duck

1 large duck, preferably fresh
5 tablespoons kosher salt
¼ cup Szechuan peppercorns
¼ teaspoon black peppercorns
¼ teaspoon white peppercorns
½ teaspoon fennel seed
½ teaspoon coriander seeds
1 whole star anise, broken into eight points
2 2-inch pieces orange or tangerine zest, coarsely chopped
¼ teaspoon ground cinnamon
¼ teaspoon ground ginger
4 whole scallions, cut into 2-inch lengths
6 quarter-size slices fresh ginger
6 to 7 cups corn or peanut oil
½ cup all-purpose flour

Remove any visible fat from the cavity of the duck and clean thoroughly of any membranes, vessels, and innards. Flush duck inside and out with cold water, then pat dry. Press on the breast-bone to break it and flatten the duck.

Combine the salt, three types of pepper, fennel, coriander, anise, and zest in a heavy skillet. Stir over moderate heat until the salt turns off-white and the mixture is fragrant, 4 to 5 minutes. The Szechuan peppercorns will smoke; do not let them burn. Remove pan from heat, stir in the cinnamon and ground ginger, then grind the mixture in a clean spice or coffee grinder. Remove one third of the mixture and reserve.

Sprinkle remaining spice mixture over outside and inside of the duck, then rub the spice into the skin, including the hidden spots under the wings and legs. Smash the scallion and ginger with the broad side of a cleaver or chef's knife, then scatter them evenly inside and on top of the bird.

Place the duck, breast side up, in a Pyrex pie plate or heat-proof dish that will allow it to lie flat. Seal it airtight, then set aside to marinate for 6 hours at room temperature, or overnight in the refrigerator. Bring to room temperature before steaming.

Steam the duck on its plate over moderate heat in a Chinese steamer for 3 hours. If you do not have a Chinese steamer, place 2 inches of water in the bottom of a large stockpot. Place a custard cup in the middle and place dish on top of cup. Cover with lid, leaving it slightly askew. Replenish the steamer with boiling water as needed, and use a bulb baster to remove rendered fat and juices from the plate. The juices, skimmed free of fat, make a wonderful clear sauce for rice or noodles to accompany the duck; the seasoned fat is likewise terrific for sautéed greens. At the end of steaming, the duck will look fat-free and demoralized.

Let the duck cool undisturbed for 10 to 15 minutes, then tip the plate to remove any juices from the cavity. Carefully slip the duck, breast side up, onto a cookie rack and discard the scallion and ginger. Leave the duck to dry in a cool, airy spot for 4 to 8 hours. The skin will be crisper for the drying.

About 20 minutes before serving, bring the oil to 375° F. over high heat in a wok or wide heavy pot big enough to accommodate the duck. Be sure to allow three inches free at the top of the pot to allow for displacement and bubbling. While the oil heats, combine the reserved spice mixture with the flour and dust the duck liberally inside and out, including under the wings and legs.

Gently slide the duck, breast side up, into the oil; it will foam on contact. With a ladle, baste the duck as it frys until golden, 2 to 3 minutes. Carefully remove the duck—a large Chinese mesh spoon is the best tool—tip it over the pot to drain any oil from the cavity, then set it aside on paper toweling.

With the heat still on high, let the oil climb to 400° F. Then fry the bird a second time until it turns a nutty, deep brown, about 15 seconds. Tip the cavity dry and blot the duck with fresh paper toweling.

Chop the duck and bones into small pieces, discarding the backbone. For a Chinese mood, serve it alongside steamed rice or Chinese steamed bread, accompanied by an interesting stir-fried green such as mustard or Chinese spinach or red chard. Or, in a Western mood, serve the duck with fettucine tossed with the duck juices and a citrus-dressed salad of slightly bitter greens.

✖ *Serves 3 to 6*

Roast Quail with Polenta and Greens

■ ■

1½ cups yellow cornmeal
4½ cups cold water
1 teaspoon kosher salt
12 whole quail, cleaned
¼ cup cider vinegar
Kosher salt and freshly ground black pepper
12 sprigs fresh tarragon
Butcher's twine
5 tablespoons unsalted butter
6 to 7 tablespoons olive oil
2 tablespoons masa harina
1½ cups chicken stock
1½ cups rich veal stock
½ cup chicken glaze
1 pound mustard greens or kale, washed and dried
½ cup duck hearts and chicken giblets, trimmed and
    cut into ¼-inch dice

To make the polenta, put the cornmeal in the top of a double boiler and stir in 1 cup of water. Stir to mix well. Bring the rest of the water to a boil in another pan. Stir the boiling water into the cornmeal mixture and bring to a boil over a direct flame, stirring constantly. Add salt. Place pan back on the double boiler and bring to a simmer. Cover and steam for 40 to 50 minutes. Pour into a 9″ × 5″ loaf pan and chill until firmly set, about 3 hours.

Preheat oven to 500° F. Rub the inside of each quail with vinegar and sprinkle the cavity with salt and pepper. Stuff one sprig of tarragon inside each bird and tie the legs together with short pieces of twine. Press firmly on the back of each bird to crack the bones slightly, so that the legs will fit closely against the breast.

Remove polenta from pan and cut lengthwise into three slices. Using a 3-inch cookie cutter, cut two rounds from each slice. Over medium high heat, heat the butter and 3 tablespoons of the oil. Fry slices in one layer until crisp and golden on one side, about 4 to 5 minutes. Turn and fry other side for about 3 minutes. Remove from pan and place on paper toweling to drain for a few minutes.

Combine stocks and glaze in a 2-quart saucepan and bring to a boil. Place 1½ cups of combined stocks in a very large oven-proof sauté pan and bring to a boil. Add greens to sauté pan and braise until just wilted, about 2 to 3 minutes. Remove from heat. Add diced hearts and giblets to remaining stock in saucepan and braise for 3 to 4 minutes.

Place remaining oil in a skillet. Arrange birds in a circle in sauté pan and sprinkle with masa harina. Roast in preheated oven for 6 minutes. Remove pan and place on rack positioned 4 to 6 inches from the broiler. Broil until golden brown, about 5 minutes.

To serve, place one piece of fried polenta on the upper center portion of each of six dinner plates. Place a quail on either side of circle. With tongs, divide greens evenly among plates, placing them sparsely over the lower two thirds of each plate. Nap with ¼ cup of sauce per plate and sprinkle each serving with 1 rounded tablespoon of braised hearts and giblets. Serve immediately. ✘ *Serves 6*

LESLEE REIS *was the owner of Le Provençale in Chicago, where, with American ingredients, she made a basically French cuisine. Warm and generous, she was sure to be found where good works were getting done.* ✍

I have two vivid memories of Jim. The first time I ever saw him—up until then he was but a picture on a cookbook overleaf—was at a *tiny* table in a corner of The Box Tree Restaurant in New York by himself with a full linen napkin tucked at chin level and judiciously studying and enjoying every bite. He was in a direct sight line (every table must be, in that place) and I was fixated with his total enjoyment for a good two to three hours.

Secondly, in a class a student asked a question about blueberries. He pulled his stool over, sat down, and spoke eloquently for thirty minutes on the blueberry. It was magnificent! What an immense amount of knowledge in that one grand person—we do miss him.

Roast Wisconsin Quail Stuffed with Aromatic Vegetables

▪▪▪▪▪▪▪▪▪▪▪▪▪▪▪▪▪▪▪▪▪▪▪▪▪

12 tablespoons unsalted butter

1 pound leeks, whites only, cut into ⅛-inch brunoise [dice]

½ pound carrots, peeled and cut into ⅛-inch brunoise [dice]

½ pound celery, cut into ⅛-inch brunoise [dice]

½ pound fresh shiitake mushrooms, stemmed and cut into ¼-inch dice

4 cups chicken stock, homemade or canned

1 teaspoon chopped fresh tarragon

1 teaspoon chopped fresh rosemary

1 teaspoon chopped fresh parsley

Salt to taste

Freshly ground black pepper to taste

Cognac to taste

Balsamic vinegar to taste

½ pound mushrooms, roughly chopped

½ cup rich veal stock

¼ cup white wine

12 whole quail

Melt 4 tablespoons of the butter in a large sauté pan. Add leeks and sauté until soft. Add carrot and celery and cook until soft. Add shiitakes and cook for another 5 minutes. Stir in 2 cups of the chicken stock and cook until liquid just glazes vegetables, about 10 minutes. Stir in herbs, salt, and pepper. Then stir in a splash of Cognac and balsamic vinegar. Taste and correct seasoning. Divide this mixture in half, leaving half in the pan and reserving second half to stuff birds.

To vegetables in pan, add remaining mushrooms and cook for 5 minutes, or until soft. Add remaining chicken stock and veal stock. Cook over medium-high heat to reduce liquid to a sauce consistency, about 45 minutes. Strain through a fine sieve, pressing hard on the solids to extract all liquid. You should have about ½ cup sauce.

Preheat oven to 375° F.

When ready to cook, stuff each quail with a generous tablespoon of stuffing. Close by crossing legs through a small slash placed at the tip of each breast. Sprinkle with salt and pepper. Melt 4 tablespoons of the butter in a large sauté pan. Sauté quail, in batches if necessary, until browned on all sides. Transfer to a roasting pan and roast for about 5 minutes more, or until done.

Remove quail from oven. Place on a serving platter and keep warm. Deglaze roasting pan with wine. Add sauce and reduce until it is thick enough to coat a spoon. Stir in remaining 4 tablespoons butter. Add balsamic vinegar, salt, and pepper to taste. Serve 3 quail per person with some of the sauce spooned over. ✕ *Serves 4*

China by opening a series of restaurants in the Orient, first in Taiwan and then in Tokyo. Although raised in a world far different from the restaurant business, she had become a brilliant restaurateur by the time she established her two elegant, antique-embellished Mandarin restaurants in San Francisco and Los Angeles.

As we have seen, Jim had a sympathy with Chinese food from his days at home with Let and in restaurants with what he considered his second, Chinese, family. Johnny Kan, a member of that family, had a restaurant to which Jim went, almost as if going home, in San Francisco. When he met Cecilia, he admired her strength and food sense. Thus began his prolonged introduction to northern Chinese Mandarin cooking. ✍

In my fond memory, James was not only a good eater, but also a man with compassion for exotic food and endless new dishes. He loved Chinese food, especially the way the Chinese prepare pork dishes. He told me that, in his boyhood, the family's Chinese houseboy, named Let, used to cook Chinese dishes for him, and when he came to the Mandarin, he was amazed with the differences. He loved the minced squab the most. For those who find the squab too rich, a mixture of chicken and squab can be used instead.

I also had him to my home. I enjoyed cooking for him, even though I had to spend ten days preparing the meal, because he loved and appreciated every dish prepared for him. He was a great guest, always joking about the celebrities at the table.

Mandarin Minced Squab

12 dried black Chinese mushrooms
2 large squab, boned, with skin left on
1½ cups plus 4 tablespoons cooking (peanut) oil
1 cup dried rice noodles
1 large tomato
1 head iceberg lettuce
2 scallions, white part only, chopped fine
2 teaspoons peeled and minced fresh ginger
1 cup water chestnuts, minced
2 teaspoons minced Virginia ham
1 tablespoon rice wine or dry sherry
1 tablespoon oyster sauce
1 tablespoon soy sauce
½ teaspoon sesame seed oil
½ teaspoon sugar
¼ teaspoon ground white pepper

Soak the black mushrooms in warm water for approximately 20 minutes. Chop the squab meat and skin into fine pieces.

In a large wok, bring 1½ cups of oil to warm, not hot, temperature. Deep fry the rice noodles. Please note that these noodles puff up very quickly; be prepared to remove them from the oil within seconds. Allow to cool, and crush into medium-sized pieces. Spread crushed noodles out on a serving platter.

Cut the tomato into hollow wedges [seeded]. Place wedges around noodles on the platter.

Remove 8 to 12 large leaves from the head of lettuce and trim the edges to form neat lettuce cups. Put in refrigerator to create a contrast of texture with the lightly spiced squab.

Heat remaining 4 tablespoons of oil in a wok until hot. Add the squab and scallions; stir fry for 30 seconds. Add remaining ingredients and continue to stir fry for another 2 minutes.

Put a rounded mound of the squab mixture on the rice noodles.

Serve each person with squab and noodles spooned into a lettuce cup, which is meant to be picked up with the fingers. ✗ *Serves 2 to 4*

Aiguillettes de Pigeon Grillé Marocaine

☐ *For the couscous*

2½ cups water

1 teaspoon salt

10 tablespoons unsalted butter

8 ounces non-instant couscous (about 1⅓ cups)

¼ pound seedless black raisins (about 1 cup)

¼ cup pine nuts

2 tablespoons clarified butter

2 pounds spinach, washed, blanched, and drained

¼ teaspoon pepper

Nutmeg to taste

4 large squab (about 1 pound each)

2 cups pigeon stock [pigeon stock can be made with
    3 cups of chicken stock as a base and the bones
    from squab, cooked in a microwave oven for 20
    minutes]

1 cup veal stock

Salt to taste

Freshly ground black pepper to taste

In a small saucepan, bring to a boil ⅔ cup of the water, along with ½ teaspoon salt and 2 tablespoons of the butter. Spread out the couscous in a large baking pan and pour the mixture over it, working the grains with the liquid until it is absorbed. Let the couscous stand uncovered, stirring once or twice, for at least an hour to dry.

Steam the couscous over boiling water in the top section of a couscousière, covered, for 30 minutes. Empty the couscous into the baking pan again, spreading out the grains. Let them dry for at least 1 hour. Bring remaining water and 2 tablespoons butter to a simmer. Pour over couscous and separate grains as before. Let them dry for about 1 hour.

Split the squab down the back and remove breast bones and wings. Twist out leg bones (reserve bones for stock). Do not separate the halves. Flatten the birds slightly with the flat side of a cleaver. Reserve while making sauce.

Soak the raisins in ¾ cup hot tap water to soften them, and drain. In a small skillet, sauté the pine nuts in 1 tablespoon of the clarified butter until they are lightly colored. Drain and reserve.

Roughly chop the spinach. Melt 4 tablespoons of the butter in a skillet and add the spinach. Add raisins, ½ teaspoon salt, ¼ teaspoon pepper, and nutmeg to taste and cook until spinach is wilted and mixture is hot. Add pine nuts and toss to coat. Keep warm while finishing recipe.

Combine the pigeon stock and veal stock in a skillet. Cook over high heat until reduced to about 2 cups.

Sprinkle birds with salt and pepper and brush each with clarified butter. Broil, skin side down, for about 5 minutes. Turn over, brush with remaining clarified butter, and broil for 5 minutes longer or until skin is golden brown. Remove birds to a cutting board with a well and let sit for 4 minutes. Slice into long thin slices. Pour juice from well into reduced stock and cook until hot. Swirl in remaining 2 tablespoons butter.

Reheat couscous and spinach if necessary. To serve, mound the spinach in the center of a serving dish or individual plates. Arrange squab slices around spinach. Pour sauce over and around squab slices. Spoon a border of steamed couscous around the rim of the dish. ✖ *Serves 4*

Born in Ireland, with experience on a plantation in Africa and as an aide to Field Marshal Viscount Montgomery, this ex-military man, which he looked every inch with his erect posture and jutting jaw, would seem an unlikely cooking expert. Yet, before coming to America, he operated a very successful London restaurant.

After he came here, he had his own cooking school on the top floor of a carriage house in the Nineties of Manhattan, wrote for many magazines, and authored several books, among them The Maurice Moore-Betty Cookbook, from which the following recipe comes.

Maurice specialized in good no-nonsense food, but always done with enormous care, as with the flavoring of the milk for the Béchamel. Jim didn't like roast turkey—even at Christmas. He did like poached foods and this would, I am sure, have pleased him. ✍

Boiled turkey is delicious. It was a common-enough method of cooking the yuletide bird in Victorian times, but since then has fallen out of favor. It makes a welcome change from the eternal roasted and, more often than not, gargantuan turkey served at Thanksgiving.

Boiled Turkey and Celery Sauce

Parsley and Lemon Stuffing (recipe follows)
1 14-pound turkey
☐ *Stock*
4 medium carrots, sliced
1 turnip, peeled and sliced
1 rib celery, sliced
3 onions, unpeeled, stuck with 3 cloves each
15 black peppercorns
1 heaping tablespoon salt or to taste
2 bay leaves
4 sprigs thyme
Bunch of parsley stalks, left from the stuffing
Celery sauce (recipe follows)

Prepare the Parsley and Lemon Stuffing according to the recipe.

Stuff the turkey and wrap it in cheesecloth so that it can be lifted easily. Put it breast down on a small rack or trivet in a large pot with a lid.

Add all the stock ingredients and enough cold water to barely cover the bird. Bring to a boil and simmer gently for 2 hours, or until the turkey is cooked. The simplest way of judging this is to pull the bone end of the drumstick; if the leg moves easily from the body, the bird is done. Keep the stock for soup.

Place the bird on a heated platter and remove the cheesecloth. ✖ *Serves 8 to 10*

Parsley and Lemon Stuffing for Chicken or Turkey

1 loaf bread, grated to crumbs
Grated rind of 2 lemons
Juice of 1 lemon
Salt and freshly ground black pepper
1 teaspoon lemon thyme
1 teaspoon dried marjoram
4 ounces chopped fresh parsley
8 ounces butter, creamed
3 eggs, beaten

Spread the bread crumbs on a baking sheet and dry them in the oven. Do not allow them to color. Weigh out 8 ounces.

Mix the crumbs with the lemon rind and juice. Mix in the remaining herbs and parsley. Blend the mixture with the butter and stir in the beaten eggs.

Celery Sauce

1 head of celery
6 tablespoons unsalted butter
1½ cups Béchamel Sauce (recipe follows)
Salt and pepper
½ cup parsley sprigs, finely chopped

To make the sauce, wash, trim, and scrape the celery ribs. Cut them into strips about 3-inches long. Blanch them in boiling salted water for 5 to 6 minutes. The celery should be almost, but not quite, cooked.

Drain it well, place it in a pan with the butter, and cook, tossing the celery, for 2 to 3 minutes.

Add the Béchamel Sauce, stir to mix, and bring to the boiling point. Adjust the seasoning with salt and pepper; stir in the chopped parsley and pour into a heated vegetable dish.

Carve the turkey in the usual way and pass the sauce separately.

Sauce Béchamel

1 cup milk
1 slice onion
1 small piece bay leaf
6 peppercorns
1 tablespoon butter
1 tablespoon flour
Salt

Combine the milk, onion, bay leaf, and peppercorns in a saucepan; cover and simmer gently 5 to 6 minutes. Strain.

Melt butter in a heavy pan. Add flour and cook 5 minutes, taking care it does not brown.

Add half of the strained warm milk, mix, and add the remaining milk. Boil quickly for two minutes. Season with salt.

Note: By holding the quantity of the liquid constant and increasing the flour and butter, the result will be a thicker sauce.

The James Beard Celebration Cookbook

M E A T

We are at the heart of the matter. Jim loved meat. He liked to eat it, grill it, roast it, stew it, poach it, braise it, and praise it. He liked beef, lamb, pork, goat, and game. He liked the flesh, the fat, sometimes the skin, the blood, and the innards, even the prairie oysters. He liked meat fresh, pickled, and smoked.

When the weather was clement, Jim liked nothing better than firing up one of the grills he kept in the garden behind the house and having the

CLASS MAKE A REALLY RARE BUTTERFLIED LEG OF LAMB. HE CONTENDED THAT LAMB WAS AMERICA'S LEAST FAVORITE MEAT BECAUSE PEOPLE HAD NEVER EATEN IT PROPERLY COOKED. IT IS CERTAINLY TRUE THAT MANY STUDENTS WOULD BE STARTLED TO SEE THE BLOODY LAMB BEING SLICED AND THEN DELIGHTED BY ITS RICH, GARLICKY FLAVOR. HE COULD BE AS PARTIAL TO AN IRISH STEW WHEN SIMPLY AND IMPECCABLY PREPARED BY CHUCK WILLIAMS. HE ALSO LIKED POACHED LAMB AND THE CLASSIC MARINATED INJECTED LEG, KNOWN IN ALICE B. TOKLAS'S BOOK—SHE WAS ANOTHER FRIEND—AS GIGOT À LA CLINIQUE.

JAMES HAD A VIRTUAL LOVE AFFAIR WITH HAM. THERE WERE A FEW PRODUCERS AROUND THE COUNTRY WHO WOULD, FROM TIME TO TIME, SEND HIM AN EXAMPLE. IT WAS HIS IDEA OF A GREAT TREAT, AND HE WOULD LITERALLY TUG ME BY THE SLEEVE TO MAKE SURE I HAD A TASTE. HAM WAS HIS PREFERRED HOLIDAY MEAT WHEN HE COOKED AT HOME. HE BAKED WHOLE HAMS, POACHED WHOLE HAMS, ATE HAM SANDWICHES, AND SIZZLED IT UP TO EAT FOR BREAKFAST.

YOU HAVE ONLY TO LOOK ON PAGE 25 TO SEE HOW CAREFULLY HIS MOTHER PICKED BEEF AND HAD IT HUNG, AND ON PAGES 47–50 TO SEE THE MANY DIVERSE CUTS THAT PLEASED HIM, TO KNOW THAT HIS LIFELONG PASSION FOR A GOOD STEAK WAS NOT SIMPLY A COMMERCIAL ATTACHMENT TO OMAHA STEAKS, WITH WHOM HE WORKED FOR MANY YEARS, BUT WAS INSTEAD AN UNCONTRIVED DELIGHT.

PORK IN THE FORM OF A WHOLE SUCKLING PIG, ITS CRISP SKIN TORN OFF BY INSISTENT FINGERS, WAS

ANOTHER FAVORITE. THE NUMEROUS SAUSAGE FORMS OF PORK WERE CONSUMED WITH GLEE. WHEN HE AND I COULD SNEAK OFF FOR AN EVENING IN SAN FRANCISCO—RARE BECAUSE HE HAD SO MANY EAGER HOSTS—WE WOULD GO TO A SMALL BISTRO, LE CENTRAL, WHERE HE ALMOST ALWAYS STARTED WITH BLOOD SAUSAGES.

IT WAS THE FRENCH, ENGLISH, AND AMERICAN TRADITIONS OF MEAT COOKERY THAT PREVAILED WITH HIM. HE WOULD EAT EXOTIC CUISINES IN OTHER PEOPLE'S HOUSES; BUT FOR HIM THE GRILL, THE ROAST, AND THE STEW WERE SUPREME.

BETTINA McNULTY. *Bettina and Henry McNulty live in London. Their daughter is James's goddaughter. Bettina worked as an editor with* House & Garden *in the United States. Henry, a journalist, has written a first-rate book on drinks—but their affinity with Jim had to do with travel, eating, and pleasure in a no-nonsense way.* ✍

WITH JIM: AROUND THE WHIRL IN EATY DAYS.

Oh, the grace of the man! The grace of that glorious giant! Jim could relocate and reorient his impressive embonpoint to slip into our minutest Paris kitchen, one stolen from a cupboard between two rooms, and there perform a culinary Leonardo. On one occasion, it was a choucroute, very garni . . . with all those saucisson delights for which he had a passion, verging on phagomania, and which, no way, could he procure at home. Wasn't that the time he sank a split of Champagne into a huge platter of steaming choucroute and let it fountain and geyser at table?

You know how much space is allotted between the fixed table and the seats in the dining car of a French *wagon-lit* train, at least in the '50s version, for that's the time we're talking about. Jim measured it up and with not a shade of hesitation adjusted the not-so-mini dirigible tummy into place. Pinned in this state of only passable comfort (my phrase, not his, for he never complained), each morsel rose daintily from fork to lips with nary a flake escaping. A consummate napkin buff, his preference was for very large, very damask; he would touch his lips to the snowy surface after every few bites.

In those days meals on the SNCF were "worth a detour." The general gist could be a well-made pâté served with tiny sour cornichons and proper crusty French bread to start. The wine, of course, had been selected. Then came a fan of pink slices of *gigot pre-salé*, vegetables *printanier* (not forgetting baby turnips), and a ladle of *jus* from meat. To finish: *tarte aux quetsche*. Quite perfection. Jim was to take the limelight as an American superstar in Cognac that night. I should have recorded *that* evening's meal.

At picnics his elfin agility didn't escape my notice. In those thirty-five-years-ago days Jim simply folded down onto the spread blanket and with weaving arms poured a swaying bottle of friendly (sometimes great) *rouge* into stemmed glasses. Or, with stunning accuracy he would portion a tian of legumes into equal segments, not that he cared a fig about symmetry and never mind the fact that one partaker was a tiny Alice Toklas and another was a mammoth himself. I have often wondered if Alice would not really have preferred a bang-up lunch in Montfort-L'Amaury, just over the crest of those distant trees, at one of those manicured, hydrangea-ed places redolent with an aroma of high living you could almost taste. But for Jim, Henry, and me, in good weather, Sunday bliss was a scramble around the food markets, especially the amazing Rue Cler shops just around the corner from our apartment. If Jim was at the France et Choiseul, as he often was, he would probably pick up treats from Hédiard, Fauchon, or Androuët, whatever pleased his fancy for a *fête champêtre*.

We've picnicked together, on the banks of Maryland's Choptank, on a gargantuan salad of succulent nugget-lumps of Maryland crab, disarmingly ordered by Jim from the hotel the night before. This July Fourth weekend trip was planned so Jim could suss out a "dream" Inn-cum-Restaurant to buy. When we learned that the local tourist season folded not only proverbial tents but its boating gear, too, immediately after Labor Day, he capitulated and spent most of the rest of the weekend foraging for his favorite Royal Crown Derby.

Sometimes just Henry and Jim, and sometimes just Jim and me, but mostly together, the three of us as a happy trio, have rendezvoused in gleeful ways, in Bordeaux and Champagne, in Paris, in Cognac, in Plascassier, in London, Brighton, and Burford, in Palamos, in Oregon, in Maryland, California, and in the Big Apple. We are constantly nourished by our memories of Jim.

Jim and Henry shared a love for a good meatloaf. Ad lib, and long ago, Jim told Henry this one while I copied it down. [It is fairly exactly the one that he used in *American Cookery*.]

Meatloaf

■■■■■■■■■■■■■■■■■■■■■■■■■■■■■■■

3 cloves garlic, peeled and smashed

1 large yellow onion (about 8 ounces), peeled and cut into quarters

1 medium green bell pepper (about 6 ounces), stemmed, seeded, deribbed, and cut into 2-inch pieces

2 pounds ground beef

1 pound ground pork

1 cup dried bread crumbs

2 eggs

1 teaspoon salt

1 teaspoon freshly ground black pepper

½ teaspoon dried thyme

4 ounces sliced bacon (about 8 slices)

Preheat oven to 350° F. Line a 12″ × 15″ baking tin with aluminum foil.

Place garlic cloves in work bowl of food processor and finely chop. Add onion and green pepper and process to coarsely chop. Scrape mixture into large mixing bowl. Add remaining ingredients, except bacon, and knead together well with hands.

Arrange 4 slices of bacon next to each other on the base of lined baking tin. Mound the meatloaf mixture on top of the bacon and form into a loaf about 6″ × 12″ × 2″. Lay remaining bacon strips over meatloaf.

Cook in center of oven for 1½ hours. Remove from oven and allow to stand for about 5 minutes before slicing. ✖ *Serves 10 to 12*

Many countries have a version of this simple classic dish and all are delectable, for good boiled beef is one of the most satisfying of foods. To be good, it must be prepared with care and attention. The best cut for boiled beef is the brisket, and short ribs are the next choice. You may also use the rump and shin. Just be sure to get as lean a piece as possible. Boiled beef is equally delicious cold, so be generous when you buy. Leftovers are never a problem. [*JB*]

Boiled Beef

■ ■

4 to 5 pounds lean brisket
Salt
Freshly ground black pepper
Rosemary or thyme
1 onion stuck with 2 cloves
3 to 4 leeks
3 to 4 carrots
1 stalk of celery
1 sprig of parsley
Water
Cabbage, potatoes, carrots, or turnips

Rub the brisket with salt, freshly ground black pepper, and a little rosemary or thyme. Place it in a large kettle with the onion stuck with cloves, leeks, carrots, celery, parsley, and water to cover. Bring to a boil and boil for 5 minutes. Skim any scum that may have risen to the surface. Add 1 tablespoon of salt, lower the heat, and simmer for 2 to 2½ hours or until beef is tender. After 2 hours cooking time you may add additional vegetables to the pot if desired.

Remove brisket to a hot platter and surround with the vegetables. Serve with sharp horseradish sauce or mustard sauce. ✗ *Serves 6*

One of the best beef salads ever eaten used to be served in the historic old Astor Hotel on Broadway at 44th Street. In its heyday the Astor harbored the greats of the theater and music as well as the fashionable set. The food for many years was exemplary. The beef salad was long a favorite of mine before a matinee. It was similar to this salad. [*JB*]

Beef Salad

1 head romaine or 4 heads Bibb lettuce

4 1-inch slices lean cold boiled beef or corned beef, cut into ¾- to 1-inch squares

6 to 8 small new potatoes cooked in their jackets, peeled and sliced

4 tomatoes, peeled and cut into wedges, or 18 to 20 cherry tomatoes

6 hard-boiled eggs, halved

2 medium onions, cut into rings

1 tablespoon capers

2 tablespoons chopped parsley

¾ cup vinaigrette sauce flavored with thyme and garlic

Wash, dry, and crisp the greens. When ready to prepare the salad, tear the greens into manageable pieces and arrange in a bowl. Add the meat, potatoes, tomatoes, eggs, onions, and capers, and sprinkle all with parsley. Just before serving, add the vinaigrette sauce and toss.

James Andrew Beard's face was as familiar to many people from advertising photographs as from more hallowed sites. One of his long-time clients was Omaha Beef, represented by Fred Simon, who contributed the memoir below. He really believed in their products. Over the years, he developed many recipes for them and they have graciously permitted us to use some of them in this book. ✍

James Beard was a consultant to Omaha Steaks International from 1974 until he died. He believed in our product. He was employed by us to do two things: prepare recipes and endorse our product. He did both very well. One of the side benefits of our association was that Eve and I were able to dine several times a year with Jim in New York, so over the years we got to know him pretty well.

In addition to our professional interest in food, we have a strong interest in opera. Several years ago we became acquainted with Rose Bampton Pelletier, a mezzo-soprano who, in years past, had sung a number of major Wagnerian roles at the Metropolitan Opera and throughout the world. We knew of Jim's career and interest in opera, and we arranged a luncheon so that Jim and Rose could meet one another.

We arrived around noon at the Four Seasons restaurant. After Eve and I made appropriate introductions, we ordered lunch, Jim and Rose both ordered pasta with a sprinkling of white truffles, and then we sat for more than two hours and listened to Jim and Rose reminisce about her opera performances. We all know that Jim had a remarkable memory for taste, but we witnessed his extraordinary recall of very specific happenings in past performances. Rose was amazed . . . not only by Jim's knowledge and recall of events but the number of other performers who were Rose's associates at the time that Jim remembered in great detail. It was an enchanting afternoon. If I had known what was going to happen, I would have recorded every word.

Filet Mignon with Mushrooms [*JB*]

¾ pound firm fresh mushrooms
3 tablespoons butter
2 teaspoons flour
Salt and pepper
1 cup heavy cream, warmed
6 6-ounce Filet Mignons, thawed steaks
6 slices French bread
6 tablespoons butter
½ cup Scotch

Slice mushrooms and sauté in 3 tablespoons butter. Add flour and salt and pepper to taste. Blend well. Stir in warm cream. Keep well heated, in a separate skillet, while you sauté the filets in hot butter for 2½ minutes per side (for rare)*. Sauté bread slices in 6 tablespoons butter, turning often to prevent butter from being absorbed. Arrange bread slices in a ring on well-heated platter.

Top with filets, and arrange the mushroom sauce in the center. Stir the Scotch into pan juices, boil up for a minute or two, and spoon sauce over the meat. Additional sauce can be passed separately. ✗ *Serves 6*

*This will be extremely rare. For a medium-rare interior, sauté for 3 minutes per side.

For this Omaha Beef recipe, James wisely took advantage of the meat's arrival frozen. He allowed it to defrost in the marinade for more flavor. You will note that he gives indications only for rare beef. That's the way he liked it.

Marinated Heart of Prime Rib Roast [JB]

Heart of Prime Rib Roast
8 to 10 thick slices fresh ginger root
6 to 8 cloves garlic, split into thin strips
¼ cup oil
1 cup dry white wine or Vermouth
1½ cups soy sauce

Place frozen roast in a deep bowl or dish. Add ginger, garlic slivers, oil, white wine, and soy sauce. Marinate roast in this mixture for 1 day.

Turn it every time you pass the table where it is thawing. When completely thawed, cover with plastic wrap or foil and refrigerate until ready to roast. Just before roasting, make small gashes in the meat and insert garlic slivers and some slivered ginger root. (If you cannot obtain fresh ginger, use candied ginger, carefully washed free of all its sugar and cut into strips, for the same effect.)

For a very rare roast, preheat oven to 500° F. Place the roast on rack in shallow roasting pan and put in oven for 35 to 40 minutes. Remove roast from the oven and allow it to stand for 10 minutes.

has become famous as the butcher-man who writes about meat. Years ago, he took one of Jim's San Francisco classes. Jim always knew about his students, and when they had special knowledge he would let them take center stage, using them as assistant teachers, and so Merle showed the class how to cut meat. One thing is clear: Jim and Merle both loved a good steak. ✍

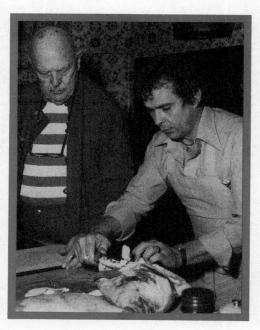

One of the most gratifying of all the gratifying things that have happened to me as a result of becoming involved in the "food world" was meeting and getting to know James Beard. I have been a fan, no, more than that, a student of James Beard's since the late 1950s when I bought my first copy of the *James Beard Cookbook*, which is to this day the most used, dog-eared, food-stained, and loved cookbook in my collection. But I did not meet Jim Beard, if you can call it that, until 1967 and that "meeting" almost cost me my job!

I was a television director at the time, directing among other programs the *News At Noon* on KRON-TV in San Francisco. Broadcasting out of a brand-new studio facility, which for some unknown and as yet undiscovered reason, had the studios on the second floor and the control rooms on the fourth, with an iron staircase going the two flights from one to the other.

One segment of the news program each day was devoted to what was listed in the log as "celebrity interview." A seven- or eight-minute segment of the program, buffeted on either side by a commercial break, was devoted to a one-on-one interview with the host of the show, Ed Hart, and some "celebrity," usually a visiting politician, musician, sports figure, or a "star" with a good figure up from Hollywood.

One day I saw listed on the log for the following day "celebrity interview—James Beard." So the next day I brought my dog-eared copy of Jim's book to work with me to get it autographed. The show was already on the air and I was therefore a little busy when Jim came into the studio two floors below me: "Ready one—take one—stand by Fl-roll—Fl-take! Ready ver-1—out cue 'David Brinkley in Washington' roll—take it—stand by on the floor—ready one—take one—Mike cue Ed." Jim was shown to his chair in the interview set and wired for sound in preparation for the interview. "Stand by in Master Control for the commercial break—take it MC."

During the seventy-two-second commercial break Ed crossed the studio from the news desk to the interview set, shook hands with Jim, clipped on his mike, and took his place. "Stand by in the studio—up on two—Mike cue Ed."

"Our guest today is James Beard, the dean of American cooking. . . ."

I directed the interview listening intently between "take one—take two" to every word. When it was over—"stand by in Master Control—take it MC"—I jerked off my headset and ran out of the control room, cookbook in hand. "Cover me, Tony," I shouted at my TD (technical director) as I started down the spiral staircase three steps at a time and out the studio door. I caught up with Jim just as he reached the elevator. "Mr. Beard," I panted, holding out his book, "could I please have your autograph?" "I'm glad to see you use this," he said with a smile, noting the book's rather ragged condition as he signed his name. "I love it. Thank you, Mr. Beard," I said, almost ripping the book out of his hands and heading back into the studio. I made it back up the two flights of spiral stairs and into the control room just in time to pant into the head set, "eh, up on one, eh, eh Mike, eh, cue Ed!"

When we hit the next commercial break Tony said, "Merle, what the hell's the matter with you? There've been presidents in this studio, kings, queens, and, last week, Raquel Welch, for Chris-sakes! You just sit there during a break and smoke a cigarette. What is it with this James Beard guy? You could get your can fired doin' something like that!"

"Tony," I said, lighting up a cigarette, "you wouldn't understand."

Here is a recipe for a dish I shared at one time or another over the years with Jim. It is from North Dakota, where we judged a beef cook-off together.

North Dakota South American Steak

■■■■■■■■■■■■■■■■■■■■■■■■■■■■■

⅓ cup North Dakota South American Steak Sauce
    (recipe follows)
1 rib or eye rib steak, about 10 ounces

Pour sauce over steak on a deep plate and allow to stand for about 10 minutes.

Either preheat broiler and cook steak on a pan about 3 inches from the heat, or cook on top of the stove in a cast-iron skillet over moderate heat for about 5 minutes on each side for rare meat. Remove from the heat and let stand about 3 minutes before serving. ✂ *Serves 1*

North Dakota South American Steak Sauce

■■■■■■■■■■■■■■■■■■■■■■■■■■■■■

1 20-ounce bottle soy sauce
1 10-ounce bottle Worcestershire sauce
1 10-ounce bottle A-1 Sauce
1 10-ounce bottle Heinz 57 Sauce
1 pound light brown sugar
2 teaspoons garlic powder
2 teaspoons onion powder
1 teaspoon ground black pepper
1 teaspoon celery salt
1 teaspoon freshly squeezed lemon juice
⅓ cup prepared mustard
2 teaspoons Tabasco sauce

Mix all ingredients together in a large glass or ceramic bowl. Pour into glass jars and refrigerate, covered, until ready to use.
✂ *Makes 2 quarts*

I can remember back to 1961 when I took a series of classes with Jim at his 10th Street apartment. One of the first tasks he turned over to me was the preparation of one of his favorite dishes, beef kidneys. I remember trimming the fat from the kidney, and splitting it in half before soaking it in milk. After praising me on my progress, he sent me to the broiler to cook them just long enough to brown the bread crumbs which covered their surface. I remember feeling a little faint on tasting the bloody-red kidney for the first time, and marveled as Jim devoured a whole half, saying it was the best beef kidney he had had in years. Although I have come to know that Jim was in the habit of lauding his students, at the time it made me feel very special, and of course that's one of the things that made Jim such a great teacher.

A steak au poivre is a thick slice of beef coated with cracked pepper, panfried, and flamed with Cognac. It is served rare to medium-rare with a cream sauce, potatoes, and watercress. Although there are many variations on this classic preparation, most of which include the use of a brown sauce and various other ingredients, none equals the flavor created by the combination of steak, pepper, Cognac, and cream.

Any good individual beefsteak can be used for this recipe, yet I prefer boneless shell of strip steak, and my second choice is a boneless sirloin. Both cuts have excellent flavor and texture.

Cracking the pepper is easy if you have a heavy-bottomed saucepan as a lever. Crush 8 to 10 peppercorns at a time, placing them under the portion of the pan nearest the handle. Holding the pan down at one end, use the handle to press down on the peppercorns to crush them. A coffee grinder also works well, but if you are not very careful you will have a very "hot" cup of coffee in the morning. Most other machines create partially crushed and partially powdered pepper.

When cooking the steaks, it is important to have enough oil in your pan to fry the pepper while cooking the steaks. If not fried, the amount of pepper used will be too hot to eat. Start with just enough oil to coat the bottom of your pan, and then add another tablespoon.

If it is your first time eating pepper steak, you may want to use commercially cracked pepper, or scrape some of the pepper off before serving it. Once you become a pepper steak lover, you will find yourself seeking pepper in spice stores in search of the ultimate aroma.

Steak au Poivre

■■■■■■■■■■■■■■■■■■■■■■■■■

¼ cup black peppercorns, crushed as above
4 individual steaks (each about 1¼ inches thick),
    completely trimmed of fat
2 to 3 tablespoons vegetable oil
Salt to taste
¼ cup plus 1 tablespoon Cognac
¾ cup heavy cream
1 bunch watercress, washed and stemmed

Place the crushed peppercorns on a large plate and coat both sides of the steaks, pressing the crushed pepper into the meat.

Place the oil in a heavy sauté pan large enough to fit the steaks comfortably. Heat over moderate-high heat, add steaks, and sauté for about 5 to 6 minutes on each side for medium-rare. Season to taste with a little salt and remove from the pan to a plate. Discard any remaining oil and return steaks to pan.

Add ¼ cup Cognac and flame the pan with a lit match; stand back from the pan while flaming. When the flames subside, remove steaks to a serving platter and keep warm.

With pan still over the heat, add cream to the pan and bring to a boil, stirring until cream has thickened to coat the back of a spoon. Stir in remaining Cognac and salt to taste. Spoon sauce over steaks and arrange watercress around dish.

Serve with baked or fried potatoes and a full-bodied red wine. ✕ *Serves 4*

SANDRA N. ALLEN *is a teacher of Brazilian and continental cooking at Peter Kump's New York Cooking School. She also teaches in Oxford, Connecticut, where she lives.* ✍

I remember many years ago, when James Beard went to a college in Monmouth County to give a lecture about "The Preparation of Food with Simplicity, but with Taste." Jim spoke calmly, with that twinkle in his eyes. The auditorium was packed with people, and all eyes were riveted on him. I was seated next to a very curious woman, and she said to me, "I never heard of James Beard before this seminar." I painfully had to take my eyes from Jim, and told her, "Yes, you had." She answered, very puzzled, "No, I haven't." I turned to her, and said with a very firm voice, "Yes, you had, that is why you are here today, and please keep it quiet."

James Beard was a terrific Master, a wonderful and kind human being. I am a better teacher today, because of James Beard yesterday.

Filet Mignon Paulista

¼ cup Madeira wine
1 clove garlic, smashed, peeled, and minced
1 small red onion (about 2 ounces), peeled and minced (⅓ cup)
1 teaspoon chopped fresh basil
1 teaspoon chopped fresh mint
½ teaspoon chopped rosemary
1 teaspoon freshly ground black pepper
Salt to taste
4 4-ounce pieces filet mignon, tied with string
2 tablespoons olive oil
3 tablespoons water (optional)

Stir together the first eight ingredients in a shallow dish large enough to hold the pieces of meat in a single layer. Add the filet and rub the marinade over both sides of the meat. Cover with plastic wrap and allow to marinate, at room temperature, for about 20 minutes.

Pour the oil into a 10-inch heavy skillet and place over high heat. Remove meat from marinade and pat dry with paper towels. When oil is hot, add the meat and cook over moderate to high heat for about 3 minutes on each side, for medium-rare meat.

Remove meat to a platter and keep warm. Add the marinade to the skillet and cook, stirring, over moderate heat. If there is very little liquid, the water may be added to make more of a sauce. Pour sauce over the pieces of meat. Serve with *pommes frites paille.* ✖ *Serves 4*

JAMES BEARD. *Although menu cookbooks have never sold as well as ones that are organized by category, James did write a successful one, James Beard's Menus for Entertaining, and always felt strongly about the importance of proper menu organization. When he was choosing the people for The Great Cooks Cookbook and deciding what chapters would be most appropriate for each, he took for himself the opening chapter, called "Menus." In the center of one menu, he placed Beef Stroganoff. It was a favorite recipe of his, following him with slight variations from book to book and even into latish classes. I think this is the last printed variation.* ✍

Beef Stroganoff

1½ pounds filet of beef, very thinly sliced
6 tablespoons unsalted butter
Olive oil
2 tablespoons chopped green onions, white part
    only
¼ cup white wine or dry vermouth
Worcestershire sauce
1½ cups sour cream
Salt to taste
Freshly ground black pepper to taste
Freshly chopped parsley

Melt 4 tablespoons of the butter and a bit of oil in a chafing dish or skillet over high heat without burning it. Sauté the beef slices in the hot fat very quickly, stirring. When they are lightly browned on both sides and done (this takes only 1 to 2 minutes), remove to a hot platter to keep warm.

Add remaining butter and green onions to the pan and cook for 1 minute. Add wine, Worcestershire, and sour cream. Stir well to heat through. Be careful not to boil, or the cream will curdle. Add salt and pepper to taste and pour over the beef. Sprinkle with parsley and serve with rice, if desired. ✖ *Serves 4 to 6*

DAN WYNN is a photographer. I don't think, despite the thousands of pictures he has taken, that there has ever been a subject as dear to his heart as Jim. He has a library of photographs of Jim from every stage of his professional life. Kindly, he has donated some beautiful ones to the Foundation.

A story such as Dan's about Jim's cooking is accurate, evocative, and frustrating. We would dearly love to know a little more about the precise recipes for those attractive ribs, those imaginative chilis. All I can suggest is that you use the recipe for Jeanne Owen's Chili below, from James Beard's Theory & Practice of Good Cooking. *It is a recipe Jim used in several books and then fooled around with for the variations Dan remembers. That would be very much in the James Beard spirit. He loved improvisation and variation.* ✍

Rita (Reet) Wynn with James Beard

The first time I set my eyes on Jim Beard was on Nantucket Island. This giant man was standing in front of a restaurant (Lucky Pierre's) he was managing for a friend of his. Instead of a belt, Beard had a rope in his trouser loops. Easier to let out. Reet, my wife, had read about him, and books by him, and wanted to attend his classes. We went into the restaurant for lunch. I, from California, missed spareribs. When I saw them on the menu, I ordered them, expecting decent ribs from an Eastern food master. They were fantastic! The memory of the taste haunted me all afternoon, so dinner found us back at Lucky Pierre's. The ribs were equally as good, or even better, but different! In our three-day stay, we ate lunch and dinner there except once (when we were disappointed at the highly recommended local tourist spot). I ordered ribs every time and they were wonderful! Every time! And each time they were different. On leaving the last night, I asked why he kept changing them. He said his friends all loved ribs and he felt they shouldn't be bored, so he devised different marinades and methods. Back home I had my wife's version—great and inspired but not Jim Beard's ribs.

The fondest recipe I have of Jim Beard's is his chili. For me it is not a recipe but a direction.

Jim did his recipe from scratch—he made or mixed his chili powder. He varied the cut of meat and how he cut the meat, that is chopped, ground, and sometimes scraped. He included two ingredients which I follow—almonds and hominy kernels. Jim might substitute walnuts but I love and always use almonds. Grind about two or three tablespoons to a two-quart pot. This is added at the end of the making of your own recipe for chili. Beside adding flavor it acts as a thickening agent.

The best hominy kernels are the dried if you can find them; otherwise a 16-ounce can will do. Of course the dried hominy kernels should be cooked first.

Bon appétit.

JEANNE OWEN *was an important character in James's personal pantheon. He spoke of her often. He met her when he was first starting to be a food professional. She worked with the Wine and Food Society and had a vague connection with* <u>Gourmet</u>*. For more on Jeanne Owen see page 64.* ✍

Our Southwestern chili con carne certainly qualifies as a braised beef dish, for it is, by definition, a stew. This recipe, while not for purists, is rather different and utterly delicious. It improves with aging, so make it the day before you serve it, and reheat. [*JB*]

Jeanne Owen's Chili con Carne

▪▪▪▪▪▪▪▪▪▪▪▪▪▪▪▪▪▪▪▪

⅓ cup olive oil
3 pounds lean round steak, cut into 1-inch cubes
2 onions, peeled and finely chopped
3 garlic cloves, peeled and finely chopped
Salt
4 cups boiling water
1 teaspoon caraway seeds
2 teaspoons sesame seeds
½ teaspoon oregano
2 to 4 tablespoons chili powder, or to taste
1 cup pitted green olives
2 1-pound cans kidney beans, drained and well rinsed

Heat the oil in a large sauté pan or 6-quart braising pan; add the beef, a few cubes at a time, so the pan is not too crowded, turning to brown on all sides. Add the chopped onions and sauté over medium heat for 2 to 3 minutes, then add the garlic. Season with salt to taste, add the boiling water, the caraway and sesame seeds, and the oregano. Reduce heat, cover, and simmer for 1 hour.

Gradually stir in the chili powder, tasting frequently until you achieve the flavor and hotness that suits your palate. Then add the olives, cover, and simmer for another hour. Taste and correct the seasoning, then mix in kidney beans and heat through. Toasted French bread, tortillas, or corn bread go well with this, and a crisp green salad. Beer is the only drink that can stand up to the spiciness of the chili. ✘ *Makes 6 servings*

JACQUELINE MALLORCA *is a formidable horsewoman who lives in San Francisco with her husband Juan, a serious collector of rare books, among which are many treasures in Jackie's food field. Jackie has written catalogues for Williams-Sonoma as well as food articles. It may well have been through Chuck Williams that Jackie and Jim first met.*

When José Wilson was no longer able to help Jim with the writing of his columns, he looked for a new aide. Several were tried, but despite the handicap of remote communication, it was Jackie who won the day. Partly it was her competence, erudition, and humor; but I think that her being an English lady helped as well. Their usual mode of work was for Jim to dictate a tape which was transcribed and sent to Jackie for polishing; but when they were both in the same city, the work was more collaborative, more the result of conversation. ✍

Although I knew James Beard in his later years, when his doctors had placed the most onerous restrictions upon his diet, he still had the most engaging curiosity about food, and would try at least one bite of anything. He was by no means a food snob, and could enjoy real country cooking every bit as much as the most sophisticated dish from the hands of a master chef. He loved barbecued foods and relished genuine cowboy cooking long before the Age of Mesquite and nouvelle Southwest cuisine. Cowboy cooks can wax quite poetic in an earthy kind of way when suitably inspired—Jim laughed for days when he came across a rhyme that went, as nearly as I can remember:

> Carnation Milk's the best in the lan'
> It comes to you in a li'l red can
> No tits to pull, no hay to pitch
> Jes' punch a hole in the sonofabitch!

I worked with Jim on his syndicated newspaper column, *Beard on Food,* and we were always looking for ideas. Coming up with a creative column once a week, year in and year out, was—as he put it, with mock despair—sheer drudgery. The only thing I could never get him to write about was tofu, though I did see him eat it once. Quite early on in our association, he invited me for lunch at a newly opened vegetarian restaurant in San Francisco. I arrived a little early and told the waiter I was with the James Beard party. This was a mistake. The poor man became so flustered that he "dusted" a perfectly clean chair before allowing me to sit down and then fluttered back and forth like a distracted butterfly. When Jim arrived with entourage, the kitchen rose to the occasion by sending out a little of everything to our table, including mesquite-grilled tofu and green bell pepper on skewers. Jim ate it very politely, but I don't think it was quite his style. He really preferred a nice piece of rare beef, and became very enthusiastic on one occasion when I made him a spur-of-the-moment dinner of steak with a Bourguignon sauce. The ingredients are almost the same as for a classic beef Bourguignon, but instead of everything being slowly stewed in the oven, the quickly assembled sauce is served over sautéed filet of beef. My husband liked it too, so the dish has remained part of the repertoire at home.

Beef Filet with Shallots, Mushrooms, and Burgundy

■ ■

4 slices beef filet, about 5 ounces each
2 strips lean bacon, each halved
1 tablespoon olive oil
1 tablespoon unsalted butter
16 small shallots, peeled
1 large clove garlic, smashed, peeled, and chopped
12 mushrooms (each about 1½ inches in diameter)
Salt to taste
Freshly ground black pepper to taste
1 teaspoon chopped fresh thyme or ½ teaspoon
    dried thyme
1½ teaspoons tomato paste
1 tablespoon Cognac
½ cup Burgundy or other full-bodied red wine
½ cup beef stock or canned beef broth
1 teaspoon cornstarch, dissolved in a little cold
    water

Trim the filets of all fat and membrane and let come to room temperature. In a heavy saucepan, cook the bacon until almost crisp. Drain on paper toweling, cut into ½-inch strips, and reserve.

Pour bacon fat from pan and replace with ½ tablespoon each of the oil and butter. Add shallots and braise over low heat, covered, until tender, about 10 minutes. Add garlic, mushrooms, a little salt and pepper, and thyme. Let cook for 2 minutes. Stir in tomato paste, Cognac, wine, and stock. Bring to a boil and simmer for 5 minutes. Reserve until needed.

When ready to serve, heat remaining oil and butter in a heavy skillet. Brown the beef on both sides for a total of 3 to 4 minutes for medium-rare meat. Turn several times, making sure to sear the edges of the meat.

Remove to warm plates and sprinkle lightly with salt and pepper. Discard fat in skillet and pour in sauce and reserved bacon. Stir well and bring to a boil. Stir in cornstarch mixture and bubble for a few seconds until the sauce thickens and clears. Taste seasoning. Spoon over beef, dividing shallots and mushrooms evenly among the plates. ✕ *Serves 4*

The James Beard Celebration Cookbook

Left to right: George Lang, James Beard, Julia Child, and Marilyn Hanson

Jim was wonderful fun to cook with. He had a free spirit, was always willing to try out new ideas, and was never difficult, overbearing, or egocentric— always genial and jovial and easy. The best kind of kitchen fun, for me anyway, is cooking with friends, and some of my best memories are cooking with Jim.

Our first joint spree was when he came to visit us in Cambridge, and we had invited a charming, somewhat elderly, food-loving musical couple who had taken a number of lessons with the fabled doyenne of French cuisine, Dione Lucas. They were dying to meet Jim. He and I agreed that we should do one of his favorite dishes, Chicken with 40 Cloves of Garlic.

Before their arrival he packed pieces of chicken with plenty of butter, wine, seasonings, and 40 large cloves of unpeeled garlic into a cas-serole, slapped on the lid, and into the oven it went. In due time in came the guests, and out came the chicken. Off with the lid, and the kitchen was filled with heady aroma of chicken and butter and wine and—those 40 cloves of garlic. They were so meltingly tender that Jim directed us to squish the pungent flesh out onto the pieces of our accompanying toast. We all, including a beaming Jim, munched them with lingering sighs of pleasure between bites of that wonderfully juicy chicken. Our musical friends were delighted, and Jim, always the fount of culinary gossip, enthralled them even more by recounting a goodly number of harrowing and hilarious stories about their mentor, Dione.

Another time Jim and I did a chowder duet for an annual meeting, in Boston, of the national newspaper food editors, using our PBS studio television set as a backdrop. We had prepared the chowders the night before—Jim's a spicy Manhattan-style brew with tomatoes, onions, garlic, and herbs. Mine was the traditional New England chowder with milk, potatoes, onions, and so forth.

We confidently transported them in big tubs to the studio, but when we took the lid off of mine the whole vast chowder was seething and bubbling in an ominous way. We should have waited until just before the event to add the crackers—since the tub was too big to refrigerate they had fermented overnight in the broth. By that time the audience of food editors had begun to arrive, and some were poking about in our mock kitchen. That didn't bother Jim. With a heave and a hearty ho ho, he picked up the offending chowder and dumped it all down the disposal. Of course they loved it, and we remade the whole thing during our demonstration—which we could well have done in the first place.

My husband, Paul, took a charming photograph of him during that demonstration, Jim in his blue cook's apron, his glasses on the end of his nose, reading the recipe for his chowder from an old cookbook.

Jim loved the south of France and several times either visited with us or took over our little house next to my colleague, Simca, in the back country near Grasse. One fall when Paul and Jim and I were shopping together at the open market in Grasse we got ourselves a mess of boletus mushrooms, those delicious edibles with the large brown caps and fat stems—*cèpes* in French, *porcini* in Italian. He remembered a recipe from somewhere that called for slicing the caps ⅜ inch thick, mincing the stems, and cooking each separately. He'd never tried it before, he said, but it sounded good to him.

First we must do all the prep for the dish, set the table, and be ready to dig in immediately they were done. We so proceeded, and Jim started out with an inch of our best olive oil in a frying pan. When it was hot, but not too hot, he slid in the sliced mushroom caps and let them cook slowly, bathed in the oil, for a good 5 minutes. Meanwhile, in a separate pan, he sautéed the

minced stems with parsley, garlic, and a sprinkling of fresh bread crumbs. When the sliced caps were lightly browned, he scooped them out onto paper towels to drain, tossed them with salt and pepper, and divided them among our hot plates. He strewed them with the garlic-scented stems, and we rushed them to the table.

I have never forgotten those mushrooms, the crisp exterior of the slowly browned caps with their tenderly moist interior, that crunchy pungent streusel on top, and the remembered sight of Jim's ample figure as he lovingly maneuvered each step. He really adored cooking, he looked well in a kitchen, and he was always experimenting on some new idea—often such homely items as a beer batter for fried zucchini flowers, or a new version of the Provençale fish soup, or a new stuffing for shoulder of lamb.

James Beard not only loved his work, he treasured his friends, and he wanted new friends to meet old friends. How kind he was to us when our first book came out in 1961, and we came to New York to launch it. It was Simca's first visit to America, and we ourselves had been living abroad for fifteen years, in the diplomatic service. Since the three of us knew no one in the American culinary field, our editor, Judith Jones, asked us whom we would like to meet. Simca opted for Dione Lucas, since they had mutual friends in France. I wanted to meet James A. Beard, and he invited us to come visit him in one of his evening cooking classes.

As we walked in the door, there he was roaring with laughter as he taught the class how to fold egg whites into the soufflé with his big bare hands. "You've got to get the feel of the thing," he explained to his pupils, "and this is the best way!" After demonstrating the technique, and wiping up, he held our book aloft and introduced us. When the class was over we sat with him over numerous glasses of Champagne, and gossiped. He invited the three of us to lunch with him the next day at The Four Seasons, and thus began our friendship.

Dione Lucas was so impressed with Simca

The James Beard Celebration Cookbook

that she decided, with kindness beyond reason, that she would give a dinner for fifty people in our honor at her restaurant. We would see to the guest list—inviting anyone we chose—we would help with some of the food, and we would provide the wines. Because our editors at Knopf knew only a handful and we knew none of the prospective invitees, we consulted Jim about the guest list and managed to send out invitations to everyone Knopf and we and he could think of. Jim also kindly offered to arrive early, thank heaven, to do the introductions. Everyone came, the food was delectable, and the party was a great success.

We kept up with Dione, by the way, seeing her almost every time we came to New York; we followed her ups and downs with affection and often dismay. After all her fame and public recognition, she should have been at least modestly well off, but she always seemed on the edge of despair. She worked hard long hours, but her hard-earned money seemed to slip through her fingers. The last time we lunched with her she was demonstrating cookery at a small gourmet shop in the east Fifties; she had had a double mastectomy, and her arms were painfully swollen. She was to take a little vacation with her sister in her native England, but she never returned. She died shortly after her arrival there. Dione Lucas was an inspiring and gifted cook, a great technician, one of the first of the modern cooks, as far as I know unless Jim Beard beat her to it, to do public demonstrations as well as television. She was a real culinary pioneer.

It was James Beard, however, besides his books and his great personality, who set the tone for the profession, as far as I am concerned. He always treated others in the business as colleagues and friends rather than rivals. He was a truly generous spirit.

This is the kind of recipe that Jim Beard would cook himself, I know, and one that I know he'd eat with gusto because he loved the creative use of leftovers, particularly those involving beef, pork, and lamb. This is an elegant solution, by the way, for the remains of a leg of lamb. There are only two ways with cooked lamb, however, and no half measures. Either you just warm it through, or it will be tough, or you simmer it an hour or more until it is tender. The following is the first approach, where you brown the bits of lamb briefly, remove them from the pan, make the sauce, and finally combine lamb and sauce to heat through just before serving.

This dish may be prepared in advance just to the point where the potatoes and lamb are added to the sauce. If you wish to hold the sauce for longer than thirty minutes, cover and refrigerate the lamb. Scrape the sauce into a smaller container, float a film of stock on top to prevent a skin from forming, and refrigerate. Then, reheat the sauce before continuing with the recipe.

Curried Lamb Hash

3 tablespoons unsalted butter, plus a little more if needed

1 tablespoon olive oil

2½ cups rare-cooked leg of lamb, cut into ½-inch dice

Salt

Freshly ground black pepper

1 cup minced onions

2 large cloves garlic, smashed, peeled, and minced

1 tablespoon fragrant curry powder

3 tablespoons all-purpose flour

1 cup lamb, beef, or chicken stock (plus a little more if needed), homemade, or canned chicken broth, brought to a simmer in a small saucepan

⅓ cup dry white French vermouth

½ cup heavy cream

1½ cups boiled potatoes, cut into ½-inch dice

Pinch of dried herbs: rosemary, thyme, or a mixture of both

A handful of fresh parsley, chopped

In a 10-inch no-stick frying pan, heat the butter and the oil over medium-high heat until the butter has melted and is no longer foaming. Add the lamb to the hot fat and toss it over the heat for 2 or 3 minutes, until the lamb pieces are lightly browned on the outside, still pink on the inside. Toss with a sprinkling of salt and pepper, and remove the lamb to a bowl.

Add the onions to the pan and sauté them until they are translucent, about 5 minutes. Stir the garlic into the onions and sauté it for a moment. Stir in the curry powder and sauté a moment longer. Sprinkle the flour over the onions and cook slowly, stirring constantly, for 2 minutes.

Remove the pan from the heat. When the mixture stops bubbling (about 1 minute or so), stir in the hot stock, then the vermouth and the cream. Return the pan to the heat and bring the mixture to a simmer, stirring constantly; cover the pan, reduce the heat to medium-low, and cook for 5 minutes. Season carefully with salt, pepper, and a big pinch of dried herbs. The sauce should be thick enough to coat a wooden spoon nicely; reduce it a little more if it seems too thin, or thin it with dribbles of warm broth if it seems too thick.

Fold the potatoes and the browned lamb into the sauce. Stir gently over moderate heat for several minutes until the dish is heated through, but do not overcook. Taste for seasoning again. Serve on warmed dinner plates with a salad of sliced tomatoes or halved cherry tomatoes and watercress, French bread, and a simple red wine such as one of the lighter zinfandels or a merlot.

✕ *Serves 4 amply*

JOHN FERRONE *is one of this country's most distinguished editors—not of cookbooks alone. After he and Jim became friendly, he worked with Jim on several of Jim's books—notably* American Cookery. *Jim felt strongly enough about John's contributions and friendship to name him as recipient of the royalties on all the books.*

John has a home in Bucks County and I often heard about the apples and the yellow tomatoes that he brought to Jim. ✍

When I arrived in New York in the early '50s I had the good luck to find an apartment a few doors away from James Beard, on 12th Street. A mutual friend brought us together, and soon I was a regular visitor at Jim's table. He lived alone in a brownstone studio apartment, painted forest green (like every other smart apartment in New York before white became the rage) and elegantly decorated with the help of his friend Agnes Crowther White. The beginnings of a lifelong majolica collection—cabbage leaves and turnips—were clustered around the mantel. And at one end of the long room stood a round marble slab on a pedestal, surrounded by Louis XV chairs.

The kitchen was ingenious, but it scarcely met Jim's professional needs. Part of it was carved out of a closet, and the rest intertwined with the bathroom. First came a small gas stove, then a toilet and a sink behind sliding panels, and finally a bathtub and shower. Opposite these were metal cabinets topped with marble, for storage of utensils and dishes. The washing up was done in the bathroom sink or under the shower in the bathtub, which also doubled as a giant wine cooler on gala occasions.

This arrangement would have intimidated a less resourceful cook, but I can remember Jim giving a dinner for eighteen people, with an elaborate main dish of lobster à l'américaine en croûte. An up-and-coming young food writer from Sunflower, Mississippi [Craig Claiborne], helped out with the puff pastry. This was one of those times when the bathtub glittered with ice and Champagne. Jim was possibly the first gastronome of his generation to understand that food was theater.

Despite his being the author of five books

and regarded as a leading food authority, he was years away from the universal acclaim as "the passionate pasha of food." In fact, he had to juggle a dozen jobs to make ends meet, writing food articles; serving as food editor for *Argosy;* doing demonstrations and tastings; making guest appearances on radio and TV; acting as consultant to an importer of wine and Cognac, to Restaurant Associates, and to several food corporations; and managing (one summer) a restaurant. He also gave private lessons and in the mid-'50s expanded into cooking classes. Still, he couldn't save a penny.

He entertained too handsomely, liked antiques, travel, the theater, and opera too well. And of course his food bills were astronomical, in large part due to kitchen testing. He would find himself roasting turkeys in August for the Christmas issue of a magazine or barbecuing in the dead of winter or doing twenty soufflés in a single day. He expected his friends to help him eat up his experiments, and that's where I came in. I was handy and could be summoned for dinner on short notice. In the beginning months of our friendship I was eating with him once or twice a week, ending up late in the evening with large drafts of Cognac or eau-de-vie. We once ate dessert at midnight. A flourless lemon soufflé had flopped, so Jim did it over again.

When he prepared batches of food for the camera, he would call up friends in the neighborhood to carry it off. I remember fetching an enormous paella studded with golden-brown chicken. It looked too good to be eaten in solitude, so I got on the phone and invited a friend to dinner. After putting the paella in the oven to heat through I presented it with a bit of a fanfare. My friend oohed and ahhed. But when we cut into the chicken it was completely raw. It had been cooked just long enough to look pretty for its picture.

After several months of Jim's cooking for me, it was clear that I would have to cook for him, and I suffered the stage fright that most of his friends probably experienced the first time around. I owned two cookbooks, I couldn't imagine inventing anything, and my repertoire was limited to a few run-of-the-mill Italian dishes. I fell back on the family's lasagne, done with tiny meatballs the size of marbles. Jim was not only gracious and encouraging but actually intrigued by the novelty of the meatballs. That taught me to try to come up with one fresh idea, however minor, whenever I cooked for him. I also learned to offer unpretentious food prepared as carefully as possible. We went on to cook for each other for the next thirty years.

For me it was always a nice challenge, especially when Jim began dieting in the '70s, but he was sure to succumb to fresh vegetables from the country garden, long-forgotten varieties of apples, exclusive white peaches, or a hearty Pennsylvania Dutch sausage.

For years we made a ritual of eating the first asparagus of the season with shad roe and new potatoes. During one of these dinners, twenty years after my cooking debut, I asked Jim how he felt about being entertained at home.

"It's very flattering," he said, "because people so often say, 'I couldn't think of cooking for you.' Well, I'm the least critical person in the world of anything that people prepare in their homes. (I can be critical in a restaurant, but that's another matter.) I enjoy it thoroughly whether it's a big dinner party or a tête-à-tête.

"Of course some people try to produce all of their specialties at one meal, which is crazy. And there are people who are too hospitable—who push things on you that you may not want to eat or who make a production, which isn't necessary. I'm uncomfortable if it's an elaborate, fussy meal. I feel that they've broken their backs to do this for me and that I'm obliged to avail myself of everything there. I can be

perfectly happy with bread and sausage and beer."

The New Year's Day menu I prepared for Jim and other guests in January 1973 began with a crabmeat coleslaw, followed by a peppery poached leg of lamb, adapted from a recipe of June Platt, and a gratin of potato and celery root. The dessert was a persimmon sherbet (page 379).

Spicy Poached
Leg of Lamb

■■■■■■■■■■■■■■■■■■■■■■■■■■

1 shank half of leg of lamb, 4 to 5 pounds
Water to cover
1 medium onion, stuck with a clove
1 large clove garlic, smashed and peeled
1 bay leaf
1 teaspoon dried rosemary
¼ cup black peppercorns
2 teaspoons salt

□ *For the sauce*

8 anchovy fillets, finely chopped
1 clove garlic, smashed, peeled, and crushed
1½ teaspoons Dijon mustard
1½ tablespoons capers, rinsed, drained, and
    chopped
¼ teaspoon Tabasco
Broth from the poaching

Trim the lamb of most of its fat and wrap in cheesecloth or a clean dish towel. Tie well in several places with butcher's string. Put enough water in a large pot to later cover the lamb. Add onion, garlic, bay leaf, rosemary, peppercorns, and salt and bring to a boil. Lower heat and simmer for 30 minutes.

Place a shallow rack or an inverted plate in the bottom of the pot. Arrange lamb on rack and bring liquid to the boil again. Simmer for 12 to 14 minutes a pound for rare lamb. Remove from broth, unwrap, and transfer to a carving board.

To make the sauce, combine anchovy, garlic, mustard, capers and Tabasco in a measuring cup or small bowl. Add enough of the poaching liquid to make ½ cup of sauce.

✕ *Serves 4*

recipe above and the recipe provided by Burt Wolf, Jim kept his recipes and their major ideas intact—here broth-poached lamb with a sauce based on anchovies—but a niggling exactitude of repetition was hardly his style. Feel free to try either the black pepper version above or this red pepper kind.

The shape of the pot determines the amount of water needed to cook the lamb—a round pot takes more and a large fish poacher takes less; adjust the seasonings accordingly. ✍

For a number of years in the mid–1970s, I had the pleasure of being partners with James Beard in a company called Beard, Glaser, Wolf, Ltd. We worked together on a number of book projects, the development of cooking equipment, and, at one point, a road company of great cooks who traveled around the country giving demonstrations. James had spent much of his youth developing his career as an opera singer and did not actually come into the food world until he was in his thirties. When he went on stage for a cooking demonstration, he brought with him his great sense of the theater. He once prepared the following recipe in a theater in front of an audience of one thousand people. The leg of lamb was held on a rope some fifty feet above the pot and slowly lowered into the stock while James talked about the drama of the kitchen.

Gigot à La Ficelle
∎∎∎∎∎∎∎∎∎∎∎∎∎∎∎∎∎∎∎∎∎∎∎∎

1 leg of lamb (about 7 pounds), boned and tied, with the bones
7 cloves garlic, smashed, peeled, and sliced
Water
3 tablespoons dried tarragon
4 tablespoons freshly ground black pepper
6 dried red peppers, crumbled with fingers
2 bay leaves
2 tablespoons salt
☐ *Anchovy Sauce*
  2 cloves garlic, smashed and peeled
  24 anchovy fillets
  24 black pitted olives, Italian or Greek
  2 to 3 hot peppers (fresh or pickled), stemmed and seeded

¼ cup olive oil
2 teaspoons fresh lemon juice
2 teaspoons grated lemon zest
1 cup strained lamb broth, reserved from poaching lamb

Roll the lamb in a linen towel or cloth and tie securely, leaving enough string at either end so that they can be tied to the handles of the cooking pot. Reserve.

Pour enough water to cover the lamb into a large pot with handles, add the lamb bones and remaining ingredients. Place pot over high heat and bring to a boil. Lower heat to medium and simmer, uncovered, for one hour.

Place the reserved lamb in the broth and tie the ends to the pot handles so that the lamb hangs clear of the bottom of the pan. If the meat is not completely covered with liquid add enough water to cover. Bring the broth back to the boil over high heat. Reduce the heat and simmer, uncovered, for 10 to 12 minutes per pound boned weight for rare lamb.

Carefully remove the lamb from the broth. Remove the towel and keep warm. Strain the broth and use 1 cup for the Anchovy Sauce.

For the Anchovy Sauce, place all the ingredients in a blender and process until smooth. Pour into a small pan and cook over medium heat until heated through. Slice the lamb and serve with the Anchovy Sauce.

✘ *Serves 8*

MAGGIE WALDRON, *an enthusiast for Jim, her other friends, and good food, is a publicist and doyenne of the food establishment in San Francisco. She once arranged a loving tribute from the Beef Industry Council for Jim. There was a splendid dinner in New York with many of Jim's California friends and a commemorative booklet,* <u>Dear James Beard</u>*, with memories and recipes. Jim was alight with pleasure.*

I remember a time when Jim and Maggie were in the hospital in San Francisco at the same time. They made it a social and loving time, visiting and sharing food sent by friends. They both laughed. ✑

Like a few other giants in their fields, Jim was exceptionally well suited to the pleasures of his work. I once wrote, "I love to eat with him in a restaurant—it's almost like a Broadway show, waiters and proprietors dancing around his table with delicacies not offered common mortals, which he shares with great gusto and style." He loved brasseries and bistros, the operatic waiters in San Francisco's North Beach, anything that smacked of theater.

But he was a man of simple tastes. I think he liked to cook outdoors best. He was doing the simple grills of his Oregon boyhood long before they became fashionable. He was inspired by the *feu de bois* in the South of France and the open hearths in Italy where the specialties were cooked over coals with pungent herbs and gnarled grapevines. He was intrigued with our funky houseboat in Sausalito where we once did a magazine piece together, barbecuing on every deck for the benefit of ourselves and the photographer. He was particularly fond of these Burn-Your-Fingers Chops rubbed with garlic and anchovies, which we did on the "hors d'oeuvre" deck and, as I remember, he snitched two or three of them before we got around to the photograph. Like most giants, he never worried about burning his fingers.

Meat

Costolette a Costaditi

(Burn-Your-Fingers Chops)

1 clove garlic, smashed and peeled
2 anchovy fillets
½ teaspoon salt
Freshly ground black pepper to taste
2 tablespoons olive oil
12 baby lamb chops (each weighing about
    6 ounces)
2 green bell peppers, stemmed, seeded, deribbed,
    and cut into 1-inch pieces

Finely chop the garlic and place in a small bowl. Add anchovies and salt and mash together with a small spoon. Stir in pepper and oil. Rub mixture over both sides of the chops and let stand, loosely covered, at room temperature for 2 hours.

Heat charcoal grill. Divide peppers and lamb chops among 12 metal skewers and string them on the skewers. When grill is hot, cook lamb and peppers for about 6 minutes on each side for rare-cooked meat. ✕ *Serves 6*

is an old friend of Jim's from Portland, an interior decorator who used to have an antique shop. It was to that shop that Jim sent most of his multi-colored glass wine rinsers when, as he periodically did, he decided to clean things out. Once when we were staying at the Stanford Court, Jerry arrived with bulky swatches of fabric so Jim could decide on the redecoration of the second—living—floor of the New York apartment. The swatches were draped over every piece of furniture. Jerry, Jim, and I pondered until Jim characteristically decided on an assertive mix of patterns with a vaguely Chinese feel. The colors were as bold as Jim and his clothes, but it worked when Jerry finally got it all in place.

Since the formation of the Foundation, Jerry has been a great help as we try to bring the house back to its former intimacy and energy. ✍

Jim Beard's marvelous palette and taste were not confined to the kitchen. I immediately recognized his sophisticated understanding of periods and design. He responded to color as he did to the food. When I suggested painting his library and living room Chinese red, he said, "Let's do it. It will be like sitting in a great bowl of *good* tomato soup." From then on it was a great romance of color and style with a bit of whimsical humor Jim could not be without.

Lamb Steaks with Pesto

3 tablespoons all-purpose flour
Salt to taste
Freshly ground black pepper to taste
4 lamb steaks, about ¾ inch thick and 10 ounces each, trimmed of all fat
1 tablespoon olive oil
1 medium onion (about 6 ounces), peeled and coarsely chopped
2 cloves garlic, smashed, peeled, and minced
4 ounces domestic mushrooms, wiped clean, trimmed, and thinly sliced
¾ cup red wine
2 cups tomato purée (Italian packaged in paper containers is best)
¾ cup pesto (page 137)

Preheat oven to 350° F.

Combine flour, salt, and pepper on a plate. Dust both sides of steaks with flour and reserve.

Place olive oil in an oven-proof skillet that is large enough to hold the steaks comfortably in a single layer. Place pan over moderately high heat. When oil is hot, add steaks and cook for about 3 minutes on each side, or until well browned. Remove steaks to a plate and keep warm.

Reduce heat to low and add onion and garlic to the pan. Cook until softened. Add mushrooms and cook for about 3 minutes more. Stir in remaining ingredients. Return steaks to the pan and spoon sauce over them.

Bake in the center of the oven for about 35 minutes. Serve with fettucine. ✗ *Serves 4*

JAMES BEARD AND HELEN EVANS BROWN. *Not for*
James Beard timidity of taste. As he and his beloved Helen Evans Brown described in The Complete Book of
Outdoor Cookery, *he loved the assertive flavor of mutton. He was always trying to get Joe Baum to put*
mutton chops on a menu. This book was written in the days when recipes were a good deal vaguer than
today, but no less evocative. ✍

Mutton Chops
■■■■■■■■■■■■■■■■■■■■■■■■

Mutton chops
Garlic
Melted unsalted butter
Salt and pepper to taste

The best mutton chops run very heavy, and
we like them better than lamb. There is a goodly
covering of fat, which should be well trimmed, as
mutton fat has a not too pleasant flavor. Rub the
chops well with garlic and brush with a little
melted butter. Grill over a medium fire, turning
the chops on the fat edge for a bit of their cooking
time, as well as on the two fleshy sides. Test for
doneness by cutting close to the bone. Salt and
sprinkle with pepper. We like a mutton chop with
potato and turnip casserole, string beans, and
stuffed olives. Also a great deal of ale.

✗ *Serve 1 chop per person*

GAEL GREENE *is a force of nature—she writes restaurant criticism for* New York *magazine as well as novels and she gives an overwhelming amount of her time to City Meals on Wheels, an organization to feed New York's homebound elderly on holidays and weekends or at any other time the public sector cannot provide. It is an organization that she and Jim helped to found after reading in a local newspaper that these people would have no holiday meals at Christmastime. Money was hastily raised to feed many. Over the years, constant fund raising with dinners, auctions, contributions, and galas has gone on, and Jim is still remembered in the name of the spring event which brings together chefs from all over the country to cook their food for partyers in Rockefeller Plaza—a grand night.* ✍*

Not long ago I was just a clumsy southpaw trying to learn how to swirl an omelette in James Beard's teaching kitchen. To help you get the feel of it, Jim would put his giant hand over yours . . . together you would swirl. And then . . . for me and for so many of the neophyte foodies who apprenticed with the Master would come the spark of recognition, affection . . . of shared mischief. Days of astonishing deliciousness followed and I came to feel very close.

What incredible evenings those were. We ate the best food in New York at the end of each class, and the miracle was we'd cooked it ourselves on Jim's maddening electric burners. No matter what disasters we committed, somehow, in the end, the food was delicious. The boned leg of lamb wrapped in a cheesecloth sling and poached in a peppery broth. The *gâteau chocolat* with raisins soaked in whiskey, the flourless soufflé deliciously boobytrapped with apricots and prunes soaked in vodka.

I remember one class where every dish was laced with garlic (except the perfect pear tart mounted on a glaze of chocolate) and I went home to bed with garlic oozing from every pore.

What a treasury of riches Jim's kitchen was, with its pewter ice cream molds and copper pig's head, the wild boar terrines, the magnificent majolica, the Guerlain cologne bottles filled with vanilla beans in Cognac and vinegars steeping. The bathtub was piled high with Imari. Even the toilet paper was special, pale peach, and it felt like silk, imported from heaven knows where.

James sat, feet splayed out to balance himself, on a tiny velvet stool, its seat about eight inches square, an amiable laughing giant in a blue denim tunic, sipping water from a Baccarat tumbler, telling stories . . . tasting.

I can close my eyes and see him forever at the end of one class, slicing a juicy, jiggling piece of beef brisket, picking up a piece of fat, and popping it into his mouth. "I'm just a fat boy," he said with a magical laugh. And that's what separates a born foody from the mere mortal. An appreciation of fat. A passion for leftover pasta cold the next morning. The ability to weep over the perfect ripeness of a Chambery peach, scarlet inside of its prim green skin. And that's the secret Jim brought us. What fun it is. How lucky we are.

Some food people have a great eye. Some have great hands. Some are brilliant scholars of gastronomy. A few are blessed with both taste and a taste memory. That James had, and with it . . . his insatiable passion. One day in class we were making his classic gateau of crêpes and duxelles and he picked up a Cognac and began pouring it into the batter. "Isn't that a lot of Cognac, Mr. Beard?" asked a classmate, Jane Freiman. And Jim raised his eye without raising his chin and gave her a Rabelaisian smile. "You can never have too much Cognac," he said.

Well, of course, we all did commit a few misdemeanors of excess. And who knows how many nutritionally myopic doctors tried to get Jim to cut down on salt. "If you can't eat what you want to eat what's the point of life?" he once observed to me.

My butterflied leg of lamb is dedicated to loving life. It's somewhat Greek, somewhat Moroccan, and scarcely original. And it has no salt. I served it at a barbecue in Amagansett once and no one, none of my salt-dependent friends, asked for the salt shaker.

Lemon-Yogurt–Grilled Leg of Lamb

1½ cups plain yogurt
⅓ cup fresh lemon juice
⅓ cup fresh lime juice
2 teaspoons ground cumin
2 teaspoons cinnamon
2 medium onions (about 6 ounces each), peeled and thinly sliced
1 whole butterflied leg of lamb (about 5 pounds)

Stir together all ingredients except lamb in a baking pan large enough to hold the lamb comfortably. Place the lamb in the pan and coat well with the mixture. Cover with plastic wrap and marinate for about 7 hours in the refrigerator, turning meat occasionally.

When ready to cook, bring meat to room temperature and preheat grill. Grill lamb for about 10 minutes on each side for rare meat. Remove from grill and let stand for about 5 minutes before cutting across into slices.

✗ *Serves 8*

BETTY ROSBOTTOM *has owned and run a cooking school in Cleveland, La Belle Pomme, and has put out an excellent book with the school's recipes. Betty also writes often for* Bon Appétit *and newspapers.* ✍

One day several years ago, while searching for information about brown rice, I looked through five or six cookbooks before discovering the material I needed in James Beard's *The Theory & Practice of Good Cooking.* As I was reading this book, my husband arrived home with the news that James Beard had died.

I was deeply saddened that one of America's greatest culinary talents had passed away. As a cooking teacher, I had used his books countless times for information and recipes just as I was doing on the day of his death. Beard was a living legend in the world of food. He was the first, and I think most ardent, advocate of American cookery.

His influence can certainly be felt today, for chefs and cooks are looking at our own heritage for inspiration just as the maestro did. He was as well a believer in simple robust dishes based on this tradition. The following is a recipe from my own repertoire and one which could aptly be described as hearty, unpretentious fare in the style of James Beard.

Serve this with Potatoes Baked with Chèvre and Thyme (page 308).

Mustard-and-Garlic–Marinated Lamb Chops

6 tablespoons red wine vinegar
¼ cup Dijon mustard
1 teaspoon salt
Freshly ground black pepper to taste
1 cup plus 2 tablespoons olive oil
4 cloves garlic, smashed and peeled
12 loin lamb chops, trimmed of excess fat (each
    about 1½ inches thick and weighing about
    5 ounces)

Whisk together vinegar, mustard, salt, and pepper in a medium bowl until well blended. Gradually whisk in oil. Add garlic cloves.

Arrange lamb chops in a large nonaluminum pan in a single layer. Pour marinade over chops. Turn chops to coat evenly. Cover with plastic wrap and marinate, refrigerated, for at least 6 hours or overnight, turning several times.

When ready to cook, bring lamb to room temperature and preheat grill. Cook the chops for 6 to 7 minutes on each side for medium rare. The cooking time will depend on type of grill and level of heat. ✕ *Serves 6*

J im always loved simple dishes, and, especially if it was pork, he could eat the whole thing.

Rôti de Porc Braisé aux Oignons

■■■■■■■■■■■■■■■■■■■■■■■

(Braised Pork Roast with Onions)

3 tablespoons olive oil
4 pounds pork roast (picnic cut)
4 large onions, peeled and cut into eighths
1 teaspoon salt
Freshly ground black pepper
1 cup water

Heat the olive oil in a Dutch oven or other large casserole with a lid. Add the roast and brown well on all sides.

Put onions around the roast along with salt, pepper, and water. Cover with lid and braise for 2 to 2½ hours, turning the roast occasionally and adding more liquid if necessary.

Transfer roast to a cutting board and cover with aluminum foil to keep warm. Let it rest for 15 minutes.

When ready to serve, reheat onions and degrease braising liquid to use as a sauce.

✖ *Serves 6*

Nothing could be more perfect with Liz Clark's loin of pork than piping-hot mashed potatoes.

Pork Loin with Apple-and-Mustard Cream

▪▪▪▪▪▪▪▪▪▪▪▪▪▪▪▪▪▪▪▪▪▪▪▪▪▪▪

4 pounds boned and rolled pork loin
Salt
Freshly ground black pepper
¼ pound unsalted butter
2 medium yellow onions, peeled and diced
6 medium Granny Smith apples, cored, peeled, and sliced
1 cup heavy cream
4 teaspoons Dijon mustard
Freshly ground nutmeg

Preheat the oven to 425° F.

Rub roast with salt and pepper and place it on a rack in a roasting pan. Insert a meat thermometer into the thickest part of the roast. Roast the pork for 30 minutes, then lower the heat to 375° F. and continue to cook until the meat thermometer registers 160° F. Remove the roast from the oven and keep it warm while you prepare the sauce.

In a heavy enameled saucepan, melt the butter over medium heat. Stir in the onions and cook until they are translucent. Add the apple slices and cook until soft, but not mushy. Stir in the cream, bring the liquid to a boil, and reduce it slightly. Add the mustard and stir well. Season the sauce with salt, pepper, and nutmeg. To serve, spoon about 2 tablespoons of sauce onto a warmed plate and place a slice of pork over.

✖ *Serves 8 to 10*

ELIZABETH LAMBERT ORTIZ *now has returned to*
England, but she has lived in many parts of the world and written about their food. She has written on
Mexico, the Caribbean, and Portugal as well as England. She was one of Jim's favorites, and he always
called her Lizzie.

I remember very vividly cooking this for Jim. Michael Field was also a guest and though I am a notorious chatterer I spent that evening listening. The two were deeply interested in the food from every possible aspect—history, which involved the Spanish conquest; food origins, which involved the birth of agriculture in the valley of Mexico about 7000 B.C.; geography, which involved the effect of altitude since this high-plateau dish would be cooked at almost eight thousand feet; and, of course taste, as the dish uses Old and New World ingredients in a rather exuberant mix. I think Jim knew almost all there is to be known about food. He did say to me, shortly before his death, that the thing he loved most about working in food is that he never stopped learning; certainly his enthusiasm never flagged.

Though he had a sharp wit, he was a deeply kind man. That night I remember I was a little worried about the wine my husband had chosen. "You need," he said, "a rather rustic and robust sort of wine for a very robust and rustic dish like this one." I forget now what the wine was. Anyway, all my guests that evening, Frances Field and José Wilson with Jim and Michael, enjoyed the meal.

As well as knowing all about food and wine, Jim was a very fine cook and yet I did not feel hesitant about cooking for him, though naturally I went to a great deal of trouble not to give him disappointing food. He once said of a mutual friend that he liked her better than he liked her cooking; but it was gently said, and, alas, was something we all agreed with. He had an adventurous palate so that it was possible to choose unfamiliar food for him knowing it would be appreciated. Finicky guests are a great bore and Jim was never that.

We were all rather spoiled when Jim was only a phone call away but there is comfort in the fact that his many books are no more than a hand's reach away on one's bookshelf.

This dish is typical of the exuberance of the Mexican Colonial kitchen when the Aztecs, who were considerable gourmets, combined their own foods with the foods brought in by the Spaniards. Jim liked its robust character.

Tapado de Cerdo

(Smothered Pork)

6 pasilla chilies

3 pounds boneless pork loin or shoulder, cut into 2-inch chunks

2 teaspoons salt

3 cloves garlic, smashed, peeled, and minced

5 tablespoons vegetable oil or lard

3 chorizo sausages, skinned and roughly chopped

4 ounces boiled ham, roughly chopped

¼ cup toasted slivered almonds

¼ cup pimiento-stuffed olives, halved

1 large onion (about 12 ounces), peeled and finely chopped

3 large tomatoes (about 1½ pounds), peeled, seeded, and roughly chopped

1 10-ounce can Mexican green tomatoes [tomatillos]

Salt and freshly ground black pepper to taste

½ cup dry sherry

Rinse chilies under cold water. Remove stems, seeds, and veins. Tear into pieces and place in small bowl. Cover with boiling water and allow to soak, stirring occasionally, for about 30 minutes, or until they are soft. Reserve in water while finishing recipe.

Place pork in a large pan and cover with water and salt. Bring to a boil over moderate heat. Reduce heat to low and simmer, covered, for about 2 hours, or until meat is tender. Remove pan from heat, drain the meat, and reserve in large heavy casserole. Discard the water.

Drain chilies, reserving the soaking water, and purée with garlic in a blender or food processor until smooth. If necessary, use a little of the water to make a paste.

Heat 2 tablespoons of the oil or lard in a heavy skillet over moderate heat. Add paste and cook, stirring constantly, for about 5 minutes. Remove from heat, cool, and stir into the reserved pork.

Heat 1 tablespoon oil in the skillet and cook sausage, stirring, over moderate heat for about 4 minutes, or until cooked through. Remove from heat, drain off fat and discard, and scatter over pork along with ham, almonds, and olives.

Heat the remaining oil or lard in the skillet over moderate heat. Cook onion for about 3 minutes until soft. Stir in the tomatoes and green tomatoes with their liquid. Cook, stirring occasionally, for 10 to 15 minutes until mixture is thick and smooth. Season to taste with salt and pepper. Pour sauce over meat in casserole and finish with sherry.

Cover casserole with lid and cook over moderate heat for about 25 minutes, shaking the casserole occasionally to prevent the meat at the bottom from sticking. Serve with rice, freshly made tortillas, and guacamole. ✖ *Serves 6 to 8*

Molasses-Barbecued Pork Sandwich

■■■■■■■■■■■■■■■■■■■■■■■■■■

2 sweet onions, such as Maui or Vidalia, 1 peeled and cut into chunks and 1 peeled and cut into ¼-inch slices

2 garlic cloves, smashed and peeled

1 small red bell pepper, stemmed, seeded, and cut into chunks

1 small green bell pepper, stemmed, seeded, and cut into chunks

1 jalapeño pepper, roasted, stemmed, seeded, and cut into chunks

2½ pounds pork tenderloin

4¼ cups good tomato-molasses–based commercial barbecue sauce

¾ cup molasses

¼ cup strong black coffee

1 lime, juiced

Salt

Freshly ground white pepper

¾ cup clarified butter

2 18-inch-long sourdough baguettes, or 6 6-inch-long sourdough rolls

2 bunches watercress leaves, coarsely chopped

6 tablespoons Jalapeño-Cilantro-Lime Salsa (recipe follows)

Start marinating the pork the night before you want to serve it. Place onion cut in chunks, garlic, and all peppers in a food processor and chop finely, or chop by hand. Combine vegetables with 4 cups of the barbecue sauce, molasses, coffee, and lime juice.

Place pork in a dish large enough to hold it in one layer with sauce. Pour over marinade. Cover with plastic wrap and place in the refrigerator overnight.

Preheat a grill or broiler.

Wipe marinade from pork and discard. Brush tenderloins with some of remaining barbecue sauce and sprinkle lightly with salt and pepper. Grill pork for 10 minutes on each side, basting frequently, or until medium rare.

About 5 minutes before pork is done, brush onion slices with butter and grill. Cut each baguette into 3 pieces and halve lengthwise. Brush the inside with butter and toast on the grill.

To assemble each sandwich, brush bottom half of bread with barbecue sauce and cover with watercress. Slice pork diagonally into ¼-inch-thick slices and arrange on top of the watercress. Spoon salsa over pork and arrange onions over salsa. Spoon more barbecue sauce over onions, slice each sandwich in half, and serve with a green salad, if desired. ✖ *Serves 6*

Jalapeño-Cilantro-Lime Salsa

■■■■■■■■■■■■■■■■■■■■■■■■■■■■■■■

2 jalapeño peppers, roasted, peeled, seeded, and finely chopped

2 tablespoons chopped fresh cilantro

1 cup extra virgin olive oil

Salt to taste

Freshly ground white pepper to taste

2 limes, halved

Stir together jalapeños, cilantro, and oil in a bowl. Season with salt and pepper to taste. Just before serving, squeeze the limes into the mixture and stir well. (The lime juice will turn the cilantro brown if added any earlier.) ✖ *Makes 1 cup*

MARK MILLER *is introduced on page 118. This recipe*
has lots of ingredients and takes a fair amount of work; but at the end you have a dish well worth the
bother. ✍

Pork with Manchamantel Sauce

■■■■■■■■■■■■■■■■■■■■■■■■

⅓ cup granulated sugar

1½ tablespoons salt

1 tablespoon dried thyme

½ tablespoon ground cumin

1 tablespoon broken-up bay leaf

1 teaspoon freshly ground black pepper

1 teaspoon dried oregano

2 tablespoons chile powder

4 allspice berries

4 whole cloves

1 stick cinnamon

6 cups water

4 double pork loin chops

Salt to taste

Freshly ground black pepper to taste

3 tablespoons olive oil

Manchamantel Sauce (recipe follows)

Combine all ingredients except pork, salt, pepper, oil, and sauce in a 5-quart container. Add pork, cover, and marinate overnight in the refrigerator.

When ready to serve pork, remove from marinade and bring to room temperature. Season with salt and pepper.

Preheat oven to 400° F.

Heat oil to almost smoking in a skillet over high heat. Reduce heat to medium and sauté pork in oil until browned, about 2 minutes per side. Remove from skillet and place in a roasting pan. Roast for 20 minutes or until internal temperature reaches 140° F. Alternatively, grill the chops over a medium-low fire. Divide sauce among four plates, place pork on top of sauce, and serve. ✘ *Serves 4*

Manchamantel Sauce

••

¼ pound whole dried ancho chilies

1 quart water

¼ pound Italian tomatoes

1 clove garlic, smashed and peeled

1 pound fresh pineapple, trimmed, skinned, cored, and cut into large dice (about 1¾ cups)

¼ pound ripe banana

½ large green apple, peeled, cored, and cubed

1½ teaspoons ground cinnamon

1½ teaspoons cider vinegar

Pinch ground cloves

⅛ teaspoon ground allspice

1 teaspoon salt

1½ teaspoons granulated sugar

1½ teaspoons peanut oil or lard

Preheat oven to 250° F.

Remove stems and seeds from chilies. Place chilies in a roasting pan and roast for 5 minutes. Place water in a medium pot. Add chilies to the water and bring to a boil. Lower heat and simmer for 30 minutes. Drain chilies. Taste liquid. If bitter, discard. If not, reserve and let cool.

Preheat broiler.

Roast tomatoes and garlic under the broiler or in a skillet for about 5 minutes. Place in a food processor along with chilies and remaining ingredients except oil. Purée until smooth. Add a little of the chile water if necessary to thin the sauce slightly.

Place the oil in a deep skillet. Heat until almost smoking and add sauce. Fry for 3 to 4 minutes, stirring constantly. ✘ *Makes 3 cups*

Once when Judith and I were spending a few days in Jim's company on the Oregon coast, he gave us a quick tour of the summer communities of Gearhart, Seaside, and Cannon Beach, where he'd enjoyed much of his childhood, and he got to talking about the two great influences of his life as master of culinary matters: his hotelier mother, and his travels that led to so many gastronomic discoveries.

As a youngster at his mother's side, he fell in love with the five-block-long public market on Yamhill Street in Portland, and always thereafter, wherever his travels took him, it was as important to him to tour the local outdoor market as it was to have dinner in the best restaurant in the vicinity.

He was already a devotee of the markets of London, Paris, and the Caribbean by the time, during World War II, that he was assigned to run an off-duty club for the American merchant marines in Rio de Janeiro. It was here, he recalled, that he learned a few tricks of shopping in preparation for cooking feijoada completa, the Brazilian national dish that is a combination of cured and fresh meats and black beans. He told us he considered it one of the most interesting feasts for a party, adding that he loved it particularly because its basic ingredients include some of his favorite things, such as pig's ears and tails.

When he came to dinner soon after we returned from the Oregon coast, we made haste to consult our apartment building superintendent. For years Ludovico Silva had been filling the lower hall with the good smells of his own cooking as he had learned the art of *cozinha velha* in São Paulo, where he'd been born. Yes, he knew of Mr. Beard's reputation; better, he volunteered to shop for us and bring the true ingredients from the New Jersey Portuguese enclave where most of his friends lived. Yes, too, he would write out the true Bahia recipe for feijoada completa.

Our friend Silva delivered the pig's ear and tails, and the carne seca, chourico, and linguica as well. For the accents that are imperative in serving this gaudy meal, we made sure we also had fresh kale and plenty of oranges to slice.

Feijoada Completa

4 pig's ears
2 pig's tails
Kosher salt
1 pound carne seca (sun-cured salt beef)
2 pounds raw smoked tongue
½ pound salt pork
3 cups dried black beans
½ pound chourico
½ pound linguica
2 tablespoons vegetable oil
2 onions, peeled and chopped
2 cloves garlic, smashed, peeled, and chopped
2 tomatoes, peeled, seeded, and chopped
Tabasco to taste
Salt to taste
Freshly ground black pepper to taste

Two days before serving, put the ears and tails in a container and sprinkle with kosher salt. Cover tightly and chill in the refrigerator.

One day before serving, place the cured beef, tongue, and salt pork in a large bowl and cover with cold water. Soak overnight in the refrigerator, changing the water several times. Wash the beans and soak overnight in water.

Remove ears and tails from the accumulated liquid and rinse well in cold water. Discard liquid. Place in a pot and cover with fresh cold water. Simmer for 1½ hours. Set aside to cool.

Drain beans and cover with fresh water and simmer for about 4 hours, or until tender. Drain ears and tails and add to the pot. Cook for 1½ hours longer.

Drain cured beef, tongue, and salt pork and cover with fresh water. Simmer for 1 hour. Remove cured beef and salt pork with a slotted spoon and add to the beans, leaving tongue simmering in pot. Add more water as necessary to the beans and continue cooking for 2 hours more.

Drain and cool the tongue. Peel it and remove bones and gristle before adding it to the beans, with additional water if necessary. Stir well.

Blanch sausages for 2 minutes and add to the beans. In a skillet, heat the oil. Add onions and garlic and sauté until soft. Stir in tomatoes, Tabasco, salt, and pepper and cook for 5 minutes. Stir into the beans and cook for 15 minutes more.

To serve, remove meat and vegetables from bean pot with a slotted spoon. Place on a platter with plenty of rice. Put the beans in a serving bowl and serve with separate dishes of hot cooked kale and orange slices. ✗ *Serves 10*

The "we" below is Philip and Helen Evans Brown. Jim respected and loved them as individuals and together. Few conversations with Jim about food were complete without a mention of Helen, whose approach to food Jim admired and whose sponsorship of the food of her home state, California, he respected. ✍

We were very close to James Beard. We traveled together in France, as well as touring a good portion of the West looking for cheese factories (we visited them all!), wineries, unusual food items, and Basque cooking. When he was in Southern California he always stayed with us, and we did lots of experimental cooking together. Jim loved to go marketing, and we spent many happy hours filling baskets with odd combinations of foods. After Helen's death in 1964, Jim and I did many cooking demonstrations together all over the country, and I did a couple of appearances at his New York cooking school. We enjoyed one another and could happily spend hours talking together about whatever the subject happened to be. I miss him. He was my friend.

To attempt to single out Jim Beard's favorite recipe would be an exercise in futility—he liked nearly everything, except cranberries. And while his name is a symbol of refined eating, he doted on simple foods such as sausages, fried chicken, lamb shanks, and so on. He demanded only that they be perfectly cooked. When he first came to our Pasadena house for dinner, Helen and I spent the day in the kitchen getting ready for the great man's arrival. I had never met him before, though Helen had. It was with a certain trepidation that I opened the door to that gentle giant of a man, but in five minutes we were fast friends and went on being so until his death.

That first dinner was in 1952, shortly after the publication of *Helen Brown's West Coast Cook Book,* which Jim greatly admired. As I recall, the menu was Mexican fare, whose mysteries Helen was unraveling at the time, and whose classic dishes Jim knew well. I do not remember the entire menu, but it was a huge success and lasted for hours—the first of many happy times together.

A couple of years later, Jim was in Pasadena for the Christmas holidays, and stayed with us. On New Year's morning, I had ready a large pot of menudo, the great Mexican restorative tripe stew, which is usually served on Sunday morning. Jim loved it and insisted on having it whenever he stayed with us.

Menudo

■■■■■■■■■■■■■■■■■■■■■■■■■■■

5 pounds tripe
1 veal knuckle, cracked
6 quarts water
4 cloves garlic, chopped
2 teaspoons salt
2 cups chopped onion
1 teaspoon ground coriander
1 tablespoon oregano
1 tablespoon chili powder, optional
Freshly ground black pepper
1 large can whole hominy (about 3 cups)
Chopped scallion for serving
Chopped fresh mint for serving

Cut tripe in 1- to 2-inch pieces and put in a kettle with the veal knuckle, water, and remaining ingredients except the hominy. Bring to a boil. Turn down heat and cook over low heat for about 6 hours, or until the tripe is very tender.

Stir in hominy and cook for 30 minutes more. Remove veal knuckle and taste for seasoning, adding more salt and pepper if necessary. Transfer to a large soup tureen and garnish with the scallion and mint. Serve with tortillas, if desired. ✘ *Serves 8 to 10*

FELIPE ROJAS-LOMBARDI. *On page 109, Felipe tells us about Jim's love of his food. He certainly adored picking at the crisp skin of the pig with his asbestos fingers.* ✍

To choose the perfect suckling pig, weight is of the utmost importance. The weight will indicate not only the age of the pig but the amount of meat you can get from it. Up to fifteen pounds, and even up to eighteen pounds, the little hams are full and plump with luscious meat, and the ribs also have succulent meat around the bones.

However, when a pig is over eighteen pounds, it is no longer a suckling pig and the animal has lost all of its muscle. The plump hams have become skinny and there is not much to eat, except skin and bones.

If the ideal weight of ten to fifteen pounds is not available, the second-best option is to obtain a pig weighing twenty-eight pounds or over. At that stage the animal has again filled out its muscles.

It is the crispy crackling skin that makes a suckling pig a smashing success. I find this good crispy skin absolutely irresistible.

To obtain an ideal crispiness, never baste the suckling pig with liquid of any kind before, during, or after roasting. As a matter of fact, wipe the skin dry and let the pig sit on the kitchen table for several hours before cooking so the skin will dry out. Another method is to apply plain lard or a flavored, colored oil [achiote oil] to the skin, and this should be done once at the beginning of the roasting.

To maintain a crispy skin after the pig has been roasted, pour no juices over the skin. Never cover the dish to keep it warm. If you cover it, the moisture released by the meat will be absorbed immediately by the dry skin which will make the skin rubbery and the marvelous crispiness will be lost. If you need to keep the suckling pig warm, keep it in a hot oven with the door slightly ajar, or place it under heat lamps.

A suckling pig weighing between ten to fifteen pounds and offered as a main course will serve about 8 people comfortably. For a buffet, serve smaller portions, and you can get twice the amount of servings from the pig.

The James Beard Celebration Cookbook

Lechon Asado

■■■■■■■■■■■■■■■■■■■■■■■■■■■

(Roast Suckling Pig)

1 suckling pig, weighing between 12 and 15
    pounds
18 cloves garlic, smashed, peeled, and finely
    chopped
1 tablespoon dried oregano
2 teaspoons ground cumin
½ teaspoon ground cloves
1 tablespoon freshly ground white pepper
½ cup fresh lime or lemon juice
½ cup fresh orange juice
¼ cup achiote oil
2 medium onions (about 12 ounces), peeled and
    sliced (about 2 cups)
3 large carrots, peeled and thinly sliced
1 bunch celery, peeled and sliced

Wipe pig inside and out with a damp cloth. Butterfly the pig by placing it cavity up on a work table. Open the cavity. With the help of a cleaver, crack the ribs on both sides of the backbone and press down on both sides of the rib cage to flatten. Set aside.

In a small bowl, combine garlic, oregano, cumin, cloves, pepper, and juices. Mix well and let stand at room temperature for 1 hour. Add the oil and blend thoroughly.

Rub the pig inside and out with the spice-oil mixture and let marinate for 12 hours at room temperature or 24 to 28 hours in the refrigerator.

In a roasting pan large enough to hold the pig, combine vegetables and arrange down the middle. Place the pig, cavity down, over the vegetables, making sure that all the vegetables are inside the cavity and the feet and head are contained within the roasting pan. If necessary, tie the hooves together to keep them inside the pan.

With small pieces of oiled aluminum foil, loosely cover the ears, snout, and tail to protect them from burning. With a clean dry towel wipe off the marinade from the surface of the skin and let the pig dry undisturbed for 4 to 6 hours.

Preheat the oven to 475° F.

Place the pig in the oven and lower heat to 450° F. Cook for 1½ to 2 hours, or until golden and crisp. (Do not baste.)

Remove pig from oven and let sit in a warm spot for 8 to 10 minutes before carving. (Do not cover.) Transfer pig with the vegetables to a big serving platter and serve. ✗ *Serves 8*

JAMES VILLAS *has written on food and restaurants for*
Town & Country and has written some smashing cookbooks. A witty, urbane man who likes real food and
drink, he and Jim Beard were natural friends. I will never forget a far-from-well Beard sitting in the
Stanford Court near despair. He had dictated the introduction to a Villas book and, with the perversity of
machines, the copy had arrived in New York unusable. With great effort, but great love, he sat down and
redid the whole thing. ✍

THE OPERATIC BEARD. "Hi kiddo," he had addressed me rather frantically one morning on the phone. "I really think these doctors are trying to kill me with this miserable diet, and I'm craving just a small juicy steak, and do you think the two of us could hop out this evening and talk a little opera?"

Shortly after 7:00 P.M., Jim Beard and I were perched around a table at The Post House in New York, Beard's looming presence, as always, creating the atmosphere of a papal audience for staff and customers alike. In his genteel style, he listened patiently while the owner of the restaurant volunteered what he was trying to accomplish at his new place; he sat quietly while the waiter described each and every item on the menu and wine list in minute detail; and he even tolerated an abrupt interruption by a total stranger eager to explain how *she* prepared fried chicken. After about twenty minutes of all this, Jim was noticeably nervous.

"God," he whispered while buttering the first of many rolls, "I'm definitely not allowed to drink any wine, but would you please get me a double malt whiskey on the rocks? And now, let's see, what should we eat? To begin, I think I'll have the lobster cocktail followed by a little clam chowder. Then, why don't you take the steak so I can have the double lamb chops, and don't you agree we should at least try the hashed browns and fried onion rings and creamed spinach, and . . . umm . . . maybe a portion of Caesar salad? For dessert, there's cheesecake, apple Betty, blueberry tart—hell, let's order all three just to sample."

That was going to be Jim's little steak dinner, and while I did feel a bit guilty for not protesting his illicit overindulgence, I wasn't about to dilute the joy of this man who, even in his final years, relished good food and drink like nobody I've ever known. Instead, I simply agreed to the vast array of dishes he wanted to order, sipped my Manhattan, and proceeded to tell him about the performance of Wagner's *Parsifal* I'd attended the night before.

Of course, what most of the world never knew about James Beard was that his true love was not really gastronomy but opera, and what people still find so ironic is that, just as the last topic Craig Claiborne and I discuss at table is food, virtually every meal I ever had with Jim (a frustrated tenor if there ever was one) was spent extolling the genius of Puccini or criticizing the upper range of Callas or analyzing the leitmotives in *The Ring*. On this particular memorable evening, one subject at hand was the Good Friday spell in the third act of *Parsifal,* one of the greatest moments in all opera, demanding the ultimate in interpretive ability from both the tenor and bass.

"Now, how did Hans Sotin phrase '*Das ist Charfreitags Zauber, Herr!*'?" asked Beard, cutting into the first pink lamb chop and washing down the bite with a slug of his second Scotch.

"Not much pause after '*Zauber,*'" I related while pouring Cabernet into my glass.

"Ah, that's wrong, so wrong," he reacted, taking a few fingerfuls of fried onions and buttering another hot roll. "Too bad you weren't old enough to hear Otto Edelmann's Gurnemanz. Here's how he handled that phrase." With which Jim, in his best basso attempt, leaned back in his seat, cleared his throat with whiskey, and sounded forth the line, emphasizing a long pause before "*Herr*" and causing a few heads close by to turn. "I remember it like it was yesterday," he added, stabbing at the platter of potatoes, "And . . . umm, good potatoes. . . . What a shame you never heard Melchior's Parsifal. You know when Kundry kisses Parsifal and he recoils with that incredible response '*Amfortas!—die Wunde!*'? Well, I can hear Melchior now at this dramatic moment of revelation, extending the second syllable in the name Amfortas so long you could almost feel the man's pain." Jim sat straight up, head very erect, holding a piece of meat up with his fork the way Parsifal holds up a sword. "*Amforrrrr-tas!*" he vocalized with trembling fervor, provoking a momentary hush throughout the restaurant to which he now seemed oblivious. "*Amforrrrrtas!—die Wuuuuunde!*" he repeated, raising the lamb high into the air.

And so it went for close to three hours, the two of us recalling and singing phrases and motives from maybe a dozen operas, picking casually at delicious charred meat, crisp onions, and sinful desserts, getting progressively smashed on booze, wine, and fine Cognac, and once again savoring a very private and meaningful world that Jim could share with so few people. No doubt we were utterly outrageous that evening, but today, I never sink my teeth into a thick sirloin or spoon creamed spinach on my plate that I don't still envision that wonderful great man of gastronomy grabbing his walking stick and my arm, humming ecstatically the final notes of some aria or another, and, with doggie bag in hand, making his way happily out of the restaurant like a gratified Wotan being escorted from the sacred halls of Valhalla.

Ham and Sweet Potato Hash

12 ounces cooked lean ham, cut into ¼-inch dice
1 pound sweet potatoes, cooked, peeled, and cut into ½-inch dice (about 3 cups)
4 ounces yellow onion, peeled and finely chopped (about ¾ cup)
3 ounces green bell pepper, stemmed, seeded, deribbed, and finely chopped (⅓ cup)
½ cup heavy cream
2 eggs
1 tablespoon chopped fresh sage or 1 teaspoon dried sage
Freshly ground black pepper to taste
3 tablespoons unsalted butter
4 to 6 poached eggs
Minced fresh parsley

In a large bowl combine ham, potatoes, onion, and green pepper. Whisk together cream, eggs, sage, and black pepper in a small bowl and add to the ham mixture.

In a 10-inch heavy skillet, melt 1½ tablespoons butter over high heat. When almost brown, add hash and press down with the back of a spoon to form a round cake. Lower heat to moderate and cook for 4 minutes, gently shaking the pan occasionally to loosen the bottom.

To brown the top, use one of these methods: Slide hash out onto a cookie sheet and invert onto a large plate. Melt the remaining butter in the pan and slide hash back into the pan. Cook as above for 5 minutes longer. Slide out into serving platter. Or, place pan under preheated broiler for 3 to 5 minutes to brown the top and slide out onto serving platter as above. Top each portion with a poached egg and sprinkle with minced parsley. ✘ *Serves 4 to 6*

FLO BRAKER *is one of the warmest and sunniest of people and a fine baker, teacher, and food writer as well. She writes for The San José Mercury News, has written a splendid baking book, and is at work on another one.*

As a student, she lit up every class that she was in. It is typical of her that, when I was having some trouble with one or another of the baking recipes for this book, she worked on them until they were perfect.

For Flo's own words and baking, see page 338. ✍

Ham Hocks Vinaigrette

■■■■■■■■■■■■■■■■■■■■■■■■■

20 meaty ham hocks (about 5 pounds)

2 medium onions (each weighing about 6 ounces), peeled and each studded with 10 whole cloves

12 cloves garlic, smashed and peeled

4 carrots (each weighing about 3 ounces), peeled and cut into 1-inch pieces

3 turnips (each weighing about 3 ounces), peeled and cut into 1-inch pieces

Cold water

☐ *Vinaigrette*

1 egg yolk

2 tablespoons fresh lemon juice

1 ounce finely chopped onion

1 clove garlic

½ cup olive oil

¼ cup fresh dill

2 teaspoons Cognac

Freshly ground black pepper to taste

2 teaspoons capers, optional

Place the ham hocks and vegetables in a large stockpot. Add enough water to cover. Bring to a boil over high heat. Reduce the heat to low and simmer, uncovered, for about 2 hours. During the cooking time skim the surface of any fat and scum that rises. Add 1 cup cold water from time to time to bring the fat to the surface and keep the hocks covered.

While ham hocks are cooking, place egg yolk, lemon juice, onion, and garlic in a blender. With the motor running, gradually add the oil in a thin stream. Add the remaining ingredients and process to combine. Scrape into a small bowl, cover with plastic wrap, and reserve in the refrigerator.

When ham hocks are cooked, remove from heat and let cool in their broth. When cool enough to handle, remove hocks and strain and reserve broth for another use. Remove the meat from the hocks and cut into ½-inch pieces, discarding skin, bones, and fat. Place in a serving bowl. Pour over vinaigrette, toss to combine, and serve.

✖ *Serves 10 or more*

JACQUES PÉPIN *has been a restaurant chef, a scholar, a teacher for professionals (at Boston University and at the French Culinary Institute as dean) and laity (cooking schools all over the country), a writer for The New York Times, an author of numerous definitive and charming cookbooks, and a strong supporter of the Foundation.* ✍

Jacques Pépin, third from left, in his kitchen

What amazed me the most about James Beard was his incredible food memory. He once described a meal that he had eaten many years earlier, in the 1940s, with Fernand Point; James went through the menu with me dish by dish, pointing out the specific taste and characteristics of each one. Yet, with all of his knowledge of food, he wasn't a snob; he loved country dishes, especially those containing pork in all forms: ham, sausage, pâté, and stew. I braised a Virginia ham once at the home of Helen McCully, my "surrogate American mother." James was a guest on this particular evening in the early 1960s, before the national obsession with cholesterol (not that he would have been bothered much by it, anyway) and I recall him eating most of the rind and a substantial part of the fat of that ham along with copious amounts of meat. He just kept picking away at it while he discussed the quality and availability of Virginia hams. This was Jim at his best as I remember him. I think this simple recipe would have pleased him and I hope you like it, too.

Although this recipe can be made with store-bought sausage, we made our own sausage mixture here with ground pork.

Meat

Potato-Onion-Sausage Stew

2 pounds coarsely ground pork

1 tablespoon plus 1 teaspoon salt

1 teaspoon freshly ground black pepper

¼ teaspoon cayenne pepper

½ teaspoon dried thyme

¾ cup red wine

1 head garlic, cloves separated and peeled

1 tablespoon olive oil

¾ pound large pearl onions, peeled, if fresh or
    frozen, defrosted in a sieve under warm
    running water if frozen

1½ pounds small new potatoes (about 12), cleaned
    and halved

1 teaspoon *herbes de Provence* (or mixture of dried
    thyme, oregano, and savory)

¾ cup water

1 tablespoon coarsely chopped flat parsley

In a mixing bowl combine pork, 1 tablespoon of the salt, ½ teaspoon of the black pepper, cayenne pepper, thyme, and ¼ cup of the wine. Peel one clove garlic, chop finely, and add to sausage mixture. Cover with plastic wrap and refrigerate for at least a few hours or, if possible, overnight.

When ready to cook, shape sausage mixture into 12 patties (each about 2½ to 3 ounces).

Place oil in a large heavy skillet or Dutch oven with a lid, and heat over moderate heat. Add sausage patties and brown for about 3 minutes on each side, working in batches, if necessary. When browned, remove to a large plate and reserve.

Add pearl onions to skillet and brown over high heat for 2 to 3 minutes. Stir in potatoes, remaining garlic cloves, *herbes de Provence*, water, remaining wine, salt, and pepper. Place sausage patties over vegetables and cover with lid. Reduce heat to low and simmer for about 25 minutes, or until potatoes and onions are cooked through.

To serve, arrange vegetables and meat on a large platter and pour juice over. Sprinkle with chopped parsley. ✗ *Serves 6*

Yucatán White Sausage

■■■■■■■■■■■■■■■■■■■■■■■■■

1¼ pounds pork butt with fat, cut into 1-inch
    cubes
¾ pound chicken breast, skinned, boned, and cut
    into 1-inch cubes
½ pound fat back, cut into 1-inch cubes
10 serrano chilies, stemmed, seeded, and coarsely
    chopped
¼ cup white wine
1 clove garlic, smashed, peeled, and minced
1 cup packed cilantro leaves
1 tablespoon granulated sugar
1 tablespoon salt
½ teaspoon ground allspice
1 egg
Sausage casing, optional

    Combine all ingredients except the egg in a
stainless steel bowl. Cover with plastic wrap and
place in freezer for about 1 hour. Meanwhile, chill
all parts of meat grinder or workbowl of food
processor.

    Remove meat mixture from freezer and
process together with the egg, or grind and then
combine with egg. Form mixture into patties or
force into casings.

    Heat a heavy skillet over moderate to low
heat, add patties or sausages, and cook for about 5
minutes on each side, until well browned and
cooked through. Drain on paper toweling and
serve hot. ✖ *Serves 6 to 8*

CARL SONTHEIMER *would have an altar in the pantheon of American culinary history if it were only for his introduction of the food processor to America's home kitchens. In the early years of proselytizing on behalf of his machine, he made friends with many of the foremost French and American cooking experts. Among them was James Beard, whom he met at the time of* The Cook's Catalogue. *In fact, the food processor ended up on our cover.*

At Carl's behest, Jim undertook—with the aid of Carl Jerome—the writing of a cookbook using the food processor. Jim was also on retainer for several years as a consultant to Carl's company.

They were both erudite men and shared a passion for rare cookbooks. Montagné, who is mentioned below, was a chef in Paris during Jim's earliest stay and that's when Jim missed him.

Like Jim, Carl at a certain point became concerned with the healthfulness of his recipes. As a scientist educated at M.I.T., he has carefully analyzed his adaptation of the nineteenth-century recipe. ✍

Jim Beard told me he regretted having had only one, missed opportunity to meet the celebrated French chef Prosper Montagné, one of the two co-authors of the original *Larousse Gastronomique.*

This delicious, easily made Veal Blanquette is surprisingly low in calories and fat. Only the thickening in this recipe differs from the original. Montagné used heavy cream and egg yolks.

Blanquette of Veal*
▪▪▪▪▪▪▪▪▪▪▪▪▪▪▪▪▪▪▪▪▪▪▪▪▪▪▪

1 medium leek (white part only), split and cleaned, about 4 ounces
5 sprigs fresh thyme
1 rib celery, about 6 inches
½ bunch parsley stems
3 pounds veal neck or shoulder, trimmed of fat and cut into 1-ounce pieces
Cold water
5 cups boiling veal or chicken stock, homemade, or canned chicken broth or water
2 bay leaves
3 medium carrots, peeled, sliced, and quartered (about 1 cup)
2 medium onions (about 4 ounces each), peeled and each stuck with a clove
Salt to taste
8 ounces pearl onions, peeled and left whole, or large onions, peeled and sliced (about 2 cups)
8 ounces white mushrooms, wiped clean and left whole if small or quartered if large (about 3 cups)
3 tablespoons cornstarch
¼ cup all-purpose flour
1 cup low-fat milk

Tie the leek, thyme, celery, and parsley stems together in a bundle with string and reserve.
Place veal in a large pan and add water to

*Adapted from *Le Grand Livre de la Cuisine* by Montagné et Salles.

just cover. Place over moderate to high heat, cover with lid, and bring to a boil. Remove pan from the heat and fill to the top with cold water to bring the fat to the surface. Remove excess fat and water. Repeat this process until almost all of the scum and fat has been poured off. Drain veal through a colander and rinse well. Wipe out pan and return to the stove.

Return meat to the pan with veal stock, bay leaves, carrots, whole medium onions, reserved herb bundle, and salt. Bring to a boil over high heat. Reduce the heat to low and simmer, covered with a lid, for about 1 hour and 20 minutes. Remove herb bundle and onions and discard.

If using sliced large onions, add at this point. If using pearl onions, cook veal 10 minutes longer and then stir them in. Add mushrooms and simmer for about 15 minutes.

In a medium mixing bowl combine cornstarch and flour. Gradually add milk, stirring so that there are no lumps remaining. Pour mixture into the veal and continue stirring until the mixture thickens. Allow to simmer over low heat for about 2 minutes.

Remove from heat and serve hot.

✖ *Serves 8; each serving contains: calories 288; saturated fat 1.65g.; total fat 6.55g.; carbohydrate 16g.; protein 40.5g.; cholesterol 142.5 mg.; sodium 186 mg.*

JASPER WHITE *is one of the most gifted of our younger chefs and one of those responsible for turning Boston from being "the land of the bean and the cod" into a first-class gastronomic adventure with his restaurant Jasper's. He has written a cookbook based on New England ingredients and dishes transformed with energy, taste, and imagination that is thoroughly usable by the home cook. He has taught and cooked at The James Beard Foundation.*

Since this recipe is time-consuming, you might want to know that it can be prepared up until the point when the oven is to be preheated. Refrigerate and then later top with pastry and bake off. ✑

Everyone knows that rabbit makes a great sauce. Rabbit Pot Pie makes an excellent rich supper for a cold night. At Jasper's we serve individual pies on our winter menu; this recipe is for one large pie that makes six hearty portions.

Rabbit Pot Pie
■■■■■■■■■■■■■■■■■■■■■■■■

1 plump fresh rabbit (at least 3 pounds), skinned
    and cut into 4 pieces
1 bottle hearty red wine (750 ml)
2 cups rich veal stock (chicken stock or water can
    be substituted but veal stock is far superior),
    homemade, or canned chicken broth
2 large bay leaves
6 sprigs fresh thyme
1 tablespoon whole black peppercorns
4 cloves garlic (unpeeled)
1 small onion, about 3 ounces, peeled and
    cut in half
3 tablespoons clarified butter or vegetable oil
4 tablespoons all-purpose flour
8 ounces slab bacon, cut into lardons (½ × 1 inch)
1 pint pearl onions (unpeeled)
2 medium carrots (about 4 ounces each), peeled
    and cut into rough triangular chunks, about
    ¾ inch in size
1 small rutabaga (about 12 ounces), peeled and cut
    into rough triangular chunks, about ¾ inch
    in size
Salt to taste
Freshly ground black pepper to taste
Lard Crust (recipe follows)

    Place rabbit pieces in a heavy 10-inch saucepan. Pour over red wine, stock, and enough water to barely cover the rabbit (about 2 cups). Place pan over moderate to high heat and bring to a boil, uncovered. With a large metal spoon, skim the surface. Add bay leaves, thyme, peppercorns, garlic, and onion. Reduce heat to low and simmer, partially covered with a lid, for one hour.

    While rabbit is simmering, make a roux by

The James Beard Celebration Cookbook

combining butter or oil and flour in a small pan. Cook, stirring constantly, over low heat for about 8 minutes, until mixture turns a light brown color (the mixture is *very* hot at this point). Remove from heat and allow to cool.

Place bacon in a large skillet and cook over moderate heat until pieces begin to brown, but do not cook until crisp. Remove pan from heat and carefully pour off about half the fat. Reserve the remaining fat with the bacon in the skillet.

Bring a medium pan of salted water to a boil, add pearl onions. Once water has returned to a boil, cook for about 5 minutes or until onions are cooked through. With a slotted spoon, remove onions to a bowl of iced water. Bring water back to a boil and add carrots and rutabaga. Once water has returned to a boil, cook for about 3 minutes. Remove from heat and strain through a colander. Reserve.

When onions are cool enough to handle, cut off both ends and remove peel. Reserve peeled onions with carrots and rutabaga.

When rabbit has cooked for 1 hour, remove meat to a plate with a slotted spoon and allow to cool. With the pan of broth still over a low heat, stir in the roux until completely smooth. Continue to simmer the sauce over a low heat.

Remove all the rabbit meat from the bones, picking the carcass for every edible morsel, tearing the meat into large (1-inch) chunks. Return the bones to the sauce and simmer for about 45 minutes longer. Reserve meat separately.

Strain the sauce through a fine strainer. You should have about 3½ cups of rich sauce. Reserve.

Return the skillet with the bacon to the heat. Add the vegetables and cook over moderate heat, stirring gently, until they start to brown. Stir in the reserved meat and sauce and allow to simmer together, over low heat, for 8 to 10 minutes. Season to taste with salt and pepper. Don't be shy with the pepper. Pour mixture into a round pie dish with a lip, about 9 inches across and 3 inches deep. Allow mixture to cool completely.

Preheat oven to 350° F.

On a lightly floured surface roll out the chilled pastry to a size slightly larger than the pie dish. Spread a little water around the lip of the dish and carefully cover the dish with the pastry. With your fingers, seal the edges as tightly as possible. Make air vents in the dough with the tip of a sharp knife. Place pie on a cookie sheet and bake for about 1 hour. The crust will be pale brown and the pie will be bubbling in the center.

Remove pie from oven and allow to stand for 10 to 15 minutes before serving. ✖ *Serves 6*

Lard Crust

1 cup pastry flour
Pinch salt
4 tablespoons cold lard, cut in small pieces
2 tablespoons cold unsalted butter, cut in small pieces
About 4 tablespoons iced water

Combine flour and salt in a mixing bowl. Rub in the fats with your fingers until the mixture is like coarse crumbs. Mix in the water gradually just until the dough comes together to form a ball. Cover dough with plastic wrap and refrigerate for at least 30 minutes. ✖ *Enough for 1 single-crust pie*

American chef who has appeared at the Beard Foundation. After making a national reputation at Arizona 206 and various consultancy projects with restaurants, he will open his own restaurant. Although over the years he has cooked almost every sort of food, he has a penchant for the seasonings of the Southwest. ✍

Grinding fresh cumin and coriander makes for a more aromatic chili. Ancho chili purée is slightly time-consuming to make, but will last in your freezer and may be used to add zest to other dishes (see page 299).

This dish develops wonderfully if prepared a day in advance and reheated. Use as many as you want of the garnishes listed below, or use them all. It's also fun with fresh sautéed chilies and peppers served on top.

Brendan Walsh's Four-Hour Venison Chili

2 tablespoons olive oil
2 cups finely chopped onion
¼ cup finely chopped celery
3 cloves garlic, smashed, peeled, and minced
1 jalapeño, stemmed, seeded, and minced (two or three for a burner!)
1 tablespoon brown sugar
2 teaspoons ground cumin
½ teaspoon coriander
⅛ teaspoon dried oregano
2 bay leaves
2 cups crushed tomatoes
12 ounces chicken or beef stock, homemade, or canned chicken broth
4 tablespoons ancho chili purée *or* 2½ tablespoons ancho chili powder
2 pounds 6 ounces venison leg meat, cut into ½-inch cubes (about 4 cups); you can substitute beef (deckle meat from the flap of rib eye)
3 cups cooked white navy beans
☐ *Garnish*
Chopped cilantro
Grated Monterey Jack cheese
Salsa
Sour cream
Corn muffins

Place oil in an 8-quart pot over moderate heat. When oil is just starting to smoke, add onion and celery. Cook, stirring, until lightly browned. Stir in garlic and jalapeño and cook for a minute. Add brown sugar and cook for a minute more.

Stir in cumin, coriander, oregano, and bay leaves and cook briefly. Then add tomatoes and cook for a few minutes to blend the ingredients and caramelize them. Add stock, chili purée, and venison and bring the mixture to a boil. Reduce the heat to low and simmer, uncovered, for about 3 hours.

During the last 30 minutes of the cooking time, stir in the navy beans. Season to taste with salt and pepper and serve with any or all of the garnishes. ✗ *Serves 6*

SALADS &

VEGETABLES

Aside from the onion family and his beloved
potatoes, I cannot claim this as one of James
Beard's favorite menu categories, although it is

MINE. THERE WAS, HOWEVER, THE MEMORABLE YEAR WHEN, AT A TASTE CLASS IN SAN FRANCISCO, WE ASSEMBLED A GOOD THIRTY VINEGARS AND ALMOST AS MANY OLIVE OILS AND SET OUR STUDENTS FREE TO DEVISE THEIR OWN SALAD DRESSINGS WITH ONLY SALT AND PEPPER AS AIDS. THE SADNESS OF THE EXERCISE WAS THAT MOST OF THE STUDENTS TRIED TO FOLLOW RULES OF PROPORTION AND AT BEST COMBINED THEIR FAVORITES AMONG THE OILS AND VINEGARS. MOST OF THE RESULTS WERE MISMATCHES THAT DIDN'T TAKE INTO ACCOUNT THE SUITABILITY OF ONE FLAVOR TO ANOTHER AND THE FACT THAT THE PERCEPTION OF ACIDITY IS NOT NECESSARILY THE SAME AS THE FACTS. A BALSAMIC VINEGAR WITH A VERY HIGH ACID OFTEN TASTES MUCH LESS ACID THAN THE FEEBLY ACID, PLAIN WHITE AMERICAN VINEGAR.

HERE, A FEW OF TODAY'S BEST COOKS TAKE ON SALADS AND VEGETABLES IN A MOST POSITIVE FASHION. TOWARDS THE END OF THE CHAPTER, YOU WILL FIND SOME EXCELLENT RECIPES THAT ARE NOT SIDE DISHES, BUT DISHES IN THEIR OWN RIGHT. THEY JUST FIT BETTER HERE THAN ELSEWHERE.

Good, ripe tomatoes, peeled, seeded, and chopped, are a favorite ingredient and garnish of mine. Sometimes I'll use them unseasoned in a recipe, but more often, I'll toss them with herbs, seasonings, olive oil, and vinegar, particularly when they're an element in one of my salads.

Tomato Concassée

4 medium tomatoes (about 4 ounces each), peeled, cored, seeded, and cut into ¼-inch dice
1 cup extra virgin olive oil
¼ cup sherry wine vinegar
1 small shallot, peeled and minced
2 tablespoons basil leaves, cut into thin strips
Salt and freshly ground white pepper to taste

Mix all ingredients together in a bowl. Cover and refrigerate for at least 30 minutes before serving. ✘ *Makes 2 cups*

MICHAEL FOLEY, *about whom more on page 192, from*
his eminent position in the Middle West, takes on a salad that uses the not-often-thought-of, but mono-unsaturated, avocado oil to great advantage in a brilliantly colored tomato salad. If you grow or can buy unsprayed nasturtium flowers, their gorgeous yellows, oranges, and reds will increase the glow. Don't use ordinary tomatoes, or the salad will get watery. ✍

Yellow and Red Plum Tomato Salad with Avocado Oil and Basil
■■■■■■■■■■■■■■■■■■■■■■■■■■■

3 yellow plum tomatoes, cored and cut into
    quarters
3 red plum tomatoes, cored and cut into quarters
½ cup avocado oil (or extra virgin olive oil)
6 leaves opal or green basil, cut into thin strips
Juice of half a lemon
Salt to taste
Freshly ground black pepper to taste
Lettuce, such as baby red leaf or oak leaf
Nasturtium flowers, optional

In a large bowl, toss together tomatoes, 1 teaspoon of the oil, and basil leaves. Cover and refrigerate for 1 hour.

In a small bowl whisk together remaining oil with lemon juice, salt, and pepper. To serve, place about 3 lettuce leaves on each of 6 salad plates. Divide tomatoes among plates and spoon a little dressing on each. Garnish with nasturtium flowers (these are edible and impart a slightly peppery quality to the salad).

✗ *Serves 6 as a side dish*

Wilted Spinach Salad

■■■■■■■■■■■■■■■■■■■■■■■■■■■■

1 large clove garlic, smashed, peeled, and chopped
4 tablespoons olive oil
2 tablespoons soy sauce
½ cup thinly sliced water chestnuts
Freshly ground black pepper to taste
2 tablespoons fresh lemon juice
1 pound fresh spinach, washed, dried, and left to
    "crisp" in the refrigerator for 20 minutes or
    longer
Salt to taste
2 hard-boiled eggs, coarsely chopped, for garnish

In a large stockpot, cook the garlic in the oil over medium heat for 2 minutes; do not let the garlic brown. Add the soy sauce, water chestnuts, and pepper. Cook for 1 minute, stirring frequently. Stir in the lemon juice.

Reduce the heat to low and add the spinach. Toss the spinach, just as you would for salad, for about 1 minute, until the leaves are slightly wilted. Taste the salad and adjust the seasoning, if necessary. Turn out into a large bowl and sprinkle with the chopped egg. Serve warm.

✗ *Serves 8*

Avocado and Papaya Salad with Sesame Dressing

■■■■■■■■■■■■■■■■■■■■■■■■■■■■

½ cup toasted sesame seeds

3 tablespoons granulated sugar

½ teaspoon dry mustard

¼ to ½ teaspoon hot pepper sauce

½ teaspoon paprika

½ teaspoon Worcestershire sauce

1 cup vegetable oil

⅓ cup fresh lime juice

Salt to taste

Freshly ground black pepper to taste

4 bunches watercress, washed and stemmed

2 ripe avocados, peeled, pitted, and sliced

2 ripe papayas, peeled, seeded (rinse and reserve half of seeds), and sliced

1 medium red onion (about 6 ounces), peeled and sliced across into very thin rings

Whisk together the first ten ingredients in a bowl and reserve.

Arrange a bed of watercress on a large serving platter. Alternate slices of avocado and papaya over watercress and scatter red onion and papaya seeds over all. Pour over reserved dressing and serve. ✖ *Serves 6 to 8*

JEREMIAH TOWER *is one of the most elegant of men and a longtime friend of Jim's. Jeremiah's stylish cooking, dressing, and Champagne drinking conceal a will of iron and a firm business sense.*

The first time I met Jeremiah he was cooking a feast for Jim at Marion Cunningham's. Sadly, I couldn't eat a bite. Knowing Jim's taste, the only thing on the table was the newly in-season Dungeness crab. I am violently allergic. The next day we went with Jeremiah to visit a down-at-the-heels and dirty Italian restaurant which Jeremiah had the most extravagant plans to take over and refurbish. That was in 1981. The plan seemed to die; but in 1984 Jeremiah opened Stars in that very same space. In the meantime, he had taken over Santa Fe Bar and Grill in Berkeley and been a consultant to several other restaurants. Since the sucess of Stars, he has opened an informal eating spot in an adjacent space.

There is a cookbook with recipes from Stars, and who knows what is being crafted for the future in that architect's brain?

Jeremiah and Jim met when Jeremiah was the first chef at Chez Panisse. Jim had great faith in him and even tried to get him a job in New York, I think, as much because he wanted Jeremiah to be closer as for Jeremiah's career.

Jeremiah returned Jim's favors in part by writing a moving introduction to the new edition of The Complete Book of Outdoor Cookery, Jim's book with Helen Evans Brown. ✍

Left to right: Jeremiah Tower, Marion Cunningham, and James Beard, picnicking on Big Sur

Could one ever claim to have known Jim unless one had seen the temper-induced flapping and flying of these weighty and ponderous jowls, their quivering building into a more serious seismic bodily event, all of this a preface to a stentorian roar, as people, or as in the case I am about to relate, waiters ducked for cover? Yes, Jim had a temper. But before the night we walked into a certain San Francisco restaurant, I had never seen it. I had visited him every morning in his hotel room at the Stanford Court for the weeks he had been in town; I had bandaged his startling legs suffering colorfully from poor circulation, had massaged his feet, rewrapped the bandages, took tea, heard the latest gossip, saw on the coffee table the latest unreleased cookbooks, and, generally daily, was caught up on what was going ON in the cooking world and its satellites.

It was on one of those mornings that I decided that I was going to take him out to dinner. There was a new restaurant opened in San Francisco, and he had some social debts to pay. We all gathered at the table after being oiled into the room by the maitre d'. The prostration of the owner and the staff went over the required limit for Jim and he was already nervous. Nothing went well. The food was mediocre, the guests fidgety. Jim was turning even pinker in his already rosy face. He started to quiver, but so far there were only little firefights of comments out of the side of his mouth.

Then his espresso arrived. He trembled. His body started an earthquake-like increase in tempo. He roared, *Who* asked for lemon zest in the *coffee*?" The waiter turned to water. I hid. Soon we left. His cane was found and he launched himself, Robert Morley–like, into the foyer. "And furthermore, the coleslaw was *terrible*!" I saw my chance. I stretched to a height and said "O.K., Jim, but which is better: your uncle Billy's, or my aunt's coleslaw?" He looked at me fiercely. The heaving of his body (some of it from gasping for breath) turned from jagged to softer rollings as a laugh built up. Tears appeared and he roared with laughter.

I think "My Aunt's" beats his "Uncle Billy's" (see *Delights and Prejudices*).

The whole key to the success of this dish, I was firmly but very gently told, is to cut the cabbage and tomatoes in large pieces and to soak the cabbage in iced water in the refrigerator for four hours. Then you have to peel and seed the ripe tomatoes, and the dressed slaw has to sit in the refrigerator for a couple of hours to achieve the perfect flavor and texture.

My Aunt's Coleslaw

1 head white cabbage (about 3 pounds)
½ cup mayonnaise
½ cup sour cream
1 tablespoon freshly chopped ginger
1 teaspoon powdered ginger
1½ teaspoons dry mustard
4 large ripe tomatoes (about 1½ pounds), peeled, halved, and seeded
Salt to taste
Freshly ground black pepper to taste

Discard any wilted leaves from cabbage. Cut cabbage in half lengthwise and cut out the core. Place each half cut side down on to a cutting board and cut across into ½-inch slices. Place in a large bowl, cover with water and ice cubes, and refrigerate for 4 hours.

Stir together mayonnaise, sour cream, fresh and powdered ginger, and mustard in a small bowl. Cut each tomato half into 6 pieces. Remove cabbage from refrigerator and drain through a colander. Toss cabbage, tomatoes, and dressing together in a serving bowl. Season with salt and pepper, cover, and refrigerate for about 2 hours. Serve very cold. ✖ *Serves 6*

BRENDAN WALSH. *For more on Brendan Walsh, who briefly worked for Jeremiah Tower at Stars, see pages 225, 290.* ✍

This is a wonderful fall recipe which I enjoy on its own or served with grilled fish such as salmon, or my chili-rubbed chicken, which has a crusty cornmeal coating that adds a fun texture to the plate. Use different types of fresh beans or substitute with frozen varieties, which work just fine. This dish is a variation on the one that the East Coast Indians showed the Pilgrims. There are as many variations as stories.

Fresh Bean Succotash

4 dried ancho chili peppers
1½ cups fresh beans, such as cranberry, lima, fava, or flageolet
4 tablespoons unsalted butter
2 cloves garlic, smashed, peeled, and minced
1 medium zucchini, cleaned and cut into ¼-inch dice
1 medium red bell pepper, stemmed, seeded, and cut into julienne
1 small poblano chili pepper, stemmed, seeded, and cut into julienne
1 cup chicken stock, homemade or canned
Kernels from 10 ears fresh corn
1 tablespoon chopped fresh sage
1 plum tomato, peeled, seeded, and diced
Salt and freshly ground black pepper to taste

Place ancho chili peppers in a medium bowl, cover with boiling water, and allow to stand until very soft. Remove from the water and mash through a fine strainer. Discard the skin and seeds and reserve the pulp.

Bring a medium pot of salted water to a boil over high heat, add the beans, and cook until just tender. Drain and reserve. Melt 2 tablespoons of butter in a large saucepan over moderate to high heat. Add garlic and zucchini and cook, stirring, for 3 minutes.

Add the red bell and poblano peppers and cook, stirring, for a few minutes until softened. Stir in cooked beans and chicken stock. When mixture comes to a boil, add corn kernels, reserved ancho chili purée, and sage. When it has returned to a boil, reduce the heat to moderate and cook for 4 minutes.

Stir in tomato and remaining butter, and season to taste with salt and pepper. Serve at once.
✗ *Serves 6 to 8*

ANNA TERESA CALLEN *not only is an Italian who teaches Italian cooking, writes Italian cookery books, is active in Italian culinary organizations, and has been honored by the Italians, she also has an Italian soul filled with warmth, generosity, and energy. She has been extremely generous in helping the Foundation. Her recipe would be an addition to any plate of grillings, from fish to beef, or could be used on its own as an antipasto.* ✍

These are best when made a day ahead.

Zucchini Scapece

■ ■

(Marinated Zucchini)

2 cups vegetable oil or very mild olive oil

6 small zucchini, washed, trimmed, and cut across
    into ¼-inch slices (about 3½ cups)

2 cloves garlic, peeled, minced, and smashed

¼ cup coarsely chopped fresh mint leaves (basil
    leaves can be used instead)

4 tablespoons red wine vinegar

Salt to taste

Pour oil into heavy 12-inch skillet. Place over medium heat until hot but not smoking. Add zucchini slices and cook, stirring occasionally, for about 15 minutes, until golden brown on both sides.

Remove zucchini slices with a slotted spoon to drain on paper towels. Lay slices in a 9″ × 5″ × 3″ terrine, in an even layer. In a small bowl mix together remaining ingredients. Pour mixture over zucchini slices. Cover with plastic wrap and allow to rest for at least 1 hour at room temperature, or overnight in the refrigerator.

Stir together gently and serve at room temperature. ✖ *Serves 4 as a side dish*

Caponatina

■ ■

7 tablespoons olive oil

1 clove garlic, smashed and peeled

6 baby eggplants or 2 medium eggplants (1¼ to 1½ pounds together), trimmed and cut into ½-inch cubes (about 8 cups)

3 stalks celery, trimmed, strung, and cut into short julienne strips (about 2 cups)

1 large yellow or Spanish onion (8 ounces), peeled and sliced ¼ inch thick (about 2 cups)

3 firm, ripe tomatoes, cored, seeded, and cut into small cubes (about 3 cups)

3 tablespoons white wine vinegar

1 teaspoon granulated sugar

2 to 3 tablespoons capers

¾ cup oil-cured olives, pitted

Salt

In a large skillet, warm 4 tablespoons of the oil over medium-high heat and add the garlic. When the garlic begins to fry, add the eggplant. Stir-fry the eggplant for about 10 minutes, until it is slightly brown and soft, but not mushy. With a slotted spoon, remove the eggplant to drain on paper toweling. Discard the garlic.

Add 2 tablespoons of the oil to the skillet. When the oil is hot, stir-fry the celery for about 5 minutes, until it is soft and translucent. Remove the celery to a bowl.

Add the remaining 1 tablespoon of oil to the skillet and heat. Stir-fry the onion until it is soft and translucent. Add the onion to the celery.

Add the tomatoes to the skillet and let them fry for a few minutes. Return all of the vegetables to the skillet and add the vinegar, sugar, capers, olives, and salt to taste. Continue to cook for 5 to 6 minutes, stirring occasionally. Take the skillet from the heat and let cool. Serve at room temperature. ✖ *Serves 6*

BURT WOLF. *In The Great Cooks Cookbook, Jim accompanied his Beef Stroganoff (page 247) with Onions Braised with Madeira. Here they are, with a note from Burt Wolf as to why he thinks they are so apposite for inclusion in this book.* ✍

James mentioned that one of his earliest food memories consisted of his eating an entire raw onion and enjoying it. The event seems to have given him a lifelong love of onions.

Onions Braised with Madeira

2 tablespoons olive oil

2 tablespoons unsalted butter

4 large yellow onions (each weighing about 12 ounces), peeled, cut across into 1-inch-thick slices, and split into rings

1 teaspoon salt

½ teaspoon freshly ground black pepper

¼ cup beef stock, homemade, or canned chicken broth

¼ cup Madeira

Place the oil and butter in a 10- to 12-inch heavy sauté pan over medium heat. When the butter is melted, increase heat to high and add the onion rings. Cook for about 3 minutes, stirring well.

Add the salt, pepper, and stock and turn the heat down to low. Cover and cook for about 10 minutes, or until softened. Stir in the Madeira and cook, uncovered, for 2 minutes. Serve hot.

✗ *Serves 6 to 8*

Spector's Le Plaisir. For more about him and the restaurant, see page 140. This mousse is a delicate accompaniment for a simply prepared fish or poached chicken, or it can be served on its own as a first course. ✍

James Beard, seated, with, left to right, Massa, Peter Josten, and Stephen Spector

Le Plaisir's Asparagus Mousse

■■■■■■■■■■■■■■■■■■■■■■■■■■

1 pound asparagus, approximately
8 thin carrot rounds, trimmed to look like flowers,
    blanched
4 large eggs
1 cup heavy cream
Salt and freshly ground black pepper to taste
Vin Blanc Sauce (recipe follows)

Preheat oven to 350° F. Bring a large pan of salted water to a boil.

Trim the woody ends from the asparagus and cut into 2-inch pieces. You can use the whole asparagus or reserve the tips for another use. Cook asparagus in boiling water until tender. Drain and refresh under cold running water. Drain and purée in a food processor (you should

have about 2 cups purée).

Add eggs and cream and process to combine. Season to taste with salt and pepper.

Place a carrot flower in the bottom of each of 8 buttered ½-cup timbale molds. Divide asparagus mixture evenly among the molds. Tap the molds against counter to settle and eliminate any air bubbles.

Place molds in a water bath and bake in the oven for 30 minutes.

Remove from oven and unmold molds onto serving plates. Spoon the sauce around the mousse on the plate. ✖ *Serves 8*

Vin Blanc Sauce
for Asparagus Mousse

2 tablespoons unsalted butter
½ cup chopped shallots
1 cup dry white wine
1 cup chicken broth, homemade or canned
1½ cups heavy cream
Kosher salt to taste
Freshly ground black pepper to taste

Heat butter in a small saucepan. Add the shallots and cook until soft. Add the wine and cook until reduced to a glaze.

Add the broth and reduce by half. Stir in cream and cook until sauce is thick enough to coat the back of a spoon. Strain sauce through a fine sieve, pressing on the shallots to release all their liquid. Season with salt and pepper and serve with asparagus mousse.

Creamy Hash-Browned Potatoes

■■■■■■■■■■■■■■■■■■■■■■■■

3 large baking potatoes (about 10 ounces each),
    scrubbed clean
2 tablespoons vegetable oil
2 tablespoons lightly salted butter
2 tablespoons minced onions·
¼ teaspoon minced garlic
Salt to taste
Freshly ground black pepper to taste
½ cup heavy cream
2 tablespoons chopped fresh parsley

Bring a medium pot of salted water to a boil over high heat. Add whole potatoes and cook for about 20 minutes, or until just cooked through but still firm. Remove from heat, drain, and cool under cold water. When cool enough to handle, peel off the skin with a sharp knife and cut potatoes into ½-inch cubes.

Heat oil in a large nonstick sauté pan over moderate to high heat. Add potatoes and toss gently. Cook for about 5 minutes, stirring occasionally. When they begin to brown, add butter and continue to cook for about 4 minutes longer.

Reduce heat to low and stir in onion, garlic, and salt and pepper. Cook for about 2 minutes. Transfer potato mixture to a baking sheet covered with paper towels to absorb any excess fat.

Return potatoes to the pan with cream and parsley. Place over moderate heat and cook for a few minutes to bring the cream to a simmer. Serve immediately. ✖ *Serves 4*

CARL JEROME *has gone on, as have many of Jim's assistants, to be a well-known food personality and consultant, newspaper and magazine writer, and book author. He lives in Washington, D.C., after time spent in London and Aspen. All of that came after the years when he was still quite young when he worked as Jim's assistant both in recipe development and class. They had a great affinity and I know James enjoyed having him work on* James Beard's New Fish Cookery. ✍

Everyone in the food world has a secret gastronomic passion, and James Beard was no different. His closet eating, however, wasn't popcorn or Oreos or any of the other childhood favorites that we refuse to admit to eating as adults.

About twice a month, James would look up from his desk; he'd drop his oversized Mont Blanc pen, push the calender out of his way, turn toward me, and say, "Let's go for a walk." There would be a smile on his face, the kind of smile a child would have on his face when he is about to do something wrong. I knew where we were going.

Slowly we would walk across 12th Street to the corner of Seventh Avenue. I would hesitate for just a moment (it was part of the game), then James would point his cane (he always called it a stick) to the right, and we'd saunter up Seventh Avenue—past the corner pharmacy, past the clothing shop, and we'd stop just before the end of the block in front of the candy store. It was an old-fashioned candy store, dimly lit, with a broken orange neon sign over the door.

James would peer into the window as though he were discovering the store for the first time. With a determined, slightly guilty expression in his eyes, he'd glance at me and say, "Let's go in."

Once inside, the charade stopped. He walked straight to the counter, looking down the shelf to the right of the cash register to see if his favorite was in stock. "Half a pound of candied ginger, please," James would say to the clerk, usually a teenaged boy too young to recognize him.

James would clutch the small white waxed bag tightly for about half the walk home, then he'd stuff it into his pocket and swear me to secrecy. Looking around to assure himself that the coast was clear, that no one had seen him with the candy in his hand, we'd turn the corner and we'd head back to the house.

Once home, James would hide the ginger in his sock drawer. He only ate a few pieces at a time, so a half-pound stash would last Jim for about a week.

In this very Beardian recipe, the sweet potatoes are microwave-cooked, then refrigerated overnight so that they will be firm enough to slice and sauté. The sauce should be made ahead so that the flavors will have time to mellow. The aïoli may be prepared while the potatoes cook in the microwave oven, then refrigerated overnight as well. Remember to take the aïoli from the refrigerator so that it can be served at room temperature.

This dish lends itself to many variations on a theme. You can make a Basil Aïoli (simply substitute fresh basil for the tarragon; this is delicious with beef or chicken) or, if you are feeling especially daring, serve the potatoes with Mint Aïoli as an accompaniment to lamb; again, just substitute fresh mint for the tarragon. You can serve the sautéed potatoes with red pepper jelly instead of an aïoli. (Use homemade or store-bought jelly, as mild or hot as you like; bring it to room temperature before passing it around.) This is particularly good with grilled lamb chops or a roast leg of lamb.

Sautéed Sweet Potatoes with Tarragon Aïoli

■■■■■■■■■■■■■■■■■■■■■■■■■■

4 medium, evenly shaped sweet potatoes (1¾ to 2
    pounds together)
¼ cup olive oil

Prick each sweet potato 3 or 4 times with a
fork. Arrange them on a glass or ceramic plate (or
directly on a microwave carousel) with the thinner
ends of each toward the center of the plate.
Microwave-cook the potatoes, uncovered, on high
power until they are just barely tender; test for
doneness by inserting a toothpick into the thickest
part of a potato. In a full-power microwave oven,
they will be ready in 12 minutes; a less powerful
oven will take somewhat longer.

Remove the potatoes from the oven and
place them, uncovered, in the refrigerator to cool.

Slice the cooled potatoes about ½ inch
thick. If you want to serve them as part of a rather
formal meal, you may peel them first, but it isn't
necessary.

Heat 2 tablespoons of the oil in each of two
large skillets over medium-high heat. (If you
prefer, you can sauté the potatoes in 2 batches,
keeping the first warm in the oven while the
second is in the skillet.) When the oil is hot, add
the potato slices in a single, uncramped layer.
Sauté the potatoes for 4 to 5 minutes, until they
are deeply browned, lowering the heat as
necessary to keep them from burning. Carefully
turn the potato slices over and brown them on the
other side; this will take 2 to 3 minutes, depending
on the size of the slices.

When the potatoes are browned on both
sides, take them from the heat. Serve them piping
hot, with the Tarragon Aïoli passed separately.
✖ *Serves 4 (makes 35 to 45 potato slices of varying size)*

Tarragon Aïoli

•••••••••••••••••••••••••••••••••••

1 egg
1 cup olive oil
4 large cloves garlic, smashed, peeled, and
    chopped
3 tablespoons fresh lemon juice
½ cup lightly packed fresh tarragon leaves
Salt to taste
Freshly ground black pepper to taste

Break the egg into the work bowl of a food
processor and process for 30 seconds. With the
motor running, very slowly add the oil in a thin
stream. When all of the oil has been added, add
the garlic, lemon juice, and tarragon leaves to this
thick mayonnaise. Process the mixture with brief
pulses until the tarragon is finely chopped.

Taste the aïoli and season with salt and
pepper. Scrape it into a small bowl and store it in
the refrigerator, tightly covered, overnight. Let
the aïoli come back to room temperature before
serving it. ✖ *Makes 2 cups*

Potatoes Baked with Chèvre and Thyme

3 pounds baking potatoes
1 tablespoon dried rosemary
1 tablespoon dried thyme
12 ounces Chèvre, broken or crumbled into small
     pieces
⅔ cup grated Parmesan cheese
Freshly ground black pepper to taste
2 cups chicken stock, homemade or canned

Preheat oven to 400° F. Grease a 14″ × 9″ × 2″ baking pan.

Peel potatoes and cut across into ¼-inch-thick slices. Arrange a third of potatoes in overlapping slices in greased dish. Sprinkle with a third each of rosemary, thyme, Chèvre, and Parmesan and a pinch of black pepper. Continue layering two more times. Pour over chicken stock.

Bake, uncovered, for about an hour, until browned and potatoes are tender when pierced with a knife. ✖ *Serves 6 to 8 as a side dish*

gave me was Prudence Hilburn. Prudence has lived in Piedmont, Alabama, all her life except for an extraordinary few years in New York. She has a warm, supportive, and extraordinary husband, Hughie. After their children were grown, Hughie, who knew that her dream—she was a fine cook and the winner of innumerable cooking contests although her job had been as a bookkeeper—had always been to study with James Beard, sent her to New York for one of his classes. Emboldened by her pleasure in that class, she went on to join one of Peter Kump's summer classes at Simca's in the south of France. Peter was so impressed he asked Prudence if she would consider working at his cooking school in New York. Saint Hughie thought it was a good idea, so she moved to New York. The plan was for her to work for Peter several days a week and at Jim's the rest of the time. Unfortunately, Jim was already quite ill and that is how Prudence came to shed joy in my life for several years.

Now, she has gone home as a cooking professional, the author of a weekly column, The Gourmet Touch, in The Anniston Star and a syndicated column called Southern Cooking in thirty-five papers. She also caters and is working on a book.

Her recipe could be an hors d'oeuvre, a luncheon main course, or a side dish with an omelet. ✍

Serve these rich little crêpes warm.

Miniature Vegetable Crêpes with Duxelles and Chipped Beef

½ cup all-purpose flour, sifted
¼ teaspoon salt
⅛ teaspoon freshly ground black pepper
2 eggs, lightly beaten
¾ cup milk
1 tablespoon unsalted butter, melted
2 tablespoons finely grated carrots
1 tablespoon finely chopped scallions (including some of the green)
Clarified unsalted butter, for cooking the crêpes
6 ounces cream cheese, at room temperature
½ cup finely chopped dried beef (if it is extremely salty, let it soak for 10 minutes in cold water before draining and chopping)
1 cup Duxelles (recipe follows)

In a medium bowl, toss together the flour, salt, and pepper until they are well mixed. Add the eggs and whisk until the mixture is smooth. Gradually add the milk, whisking until the batter is free of lumps. Stir in the tablespoon of melted butter and the carrots and scallions. Cover the bowl and let the batter rest for at least 45 minutes.

Heat a crêpe pan or small nonstick frying pan. Brush it lightly with clarified butter. Spoon about ½ tablespoon of the batter into the pan and spread it with the back of the spoon into a 2-inch circle. Cook the crêpe for 1 minute on one side, turn it over, and let it cook for about 30 seconds on the second side, until lightly golden. Cook the remaining batter. Stack the cooked crêpes between sheets of waxed paper or plastic wrap.

In the work bowl of a food processor, combine the cream cheese and dried beef. Process until the mixture is smooth and well blended. Spread each crêpe with ½ to ¾ teaspoon of the beef mixture. Spoon 1 teaspoon of the Duxelles onto one end of each crêpe and roll the crêpe tightly. ✕ *Makes 45 miniature crêpes*

This is included for Prudence's recipe, but it's also a good staple to freeze and keep on hand.

Duxelles

....

BARBARA KAFKA

¼ pound unsalted butter

1 pound mushrooms, wiped clean and finely
   chopped

¼ pound shallots, peeled (about 5 shallots)

½ cup tightly packed parsley leaves

2 teaspoons kosher salt

½ teaspoon freshly ground black pepper

Heat butter in a 1-quart soufflé dish, uncovered, at 100 percent power for 2 minutes in a 650- to 700-watt microwave oven. Add mushrooms and stir to coat. Cook, uncovered, for 5 minutes.

In a food processor, finely chop shallots and parsley. Stir into mushrooms. Cook, uncovered, for 8 minutes. ✘ *Makes 1½ to 2 cups*

Kompkin of Bobbi and Carole's Cooking School in Miami, Florida, kindly sent this dish that could accompany a light main course or could be a luncheon dish. ✍

T his simple dish is at its best when summer tomatoes are luscious and fresh basil is plentiful.

Tomatoes Stuffed with Mozzarella and Gruyère

▪▪▪▪▪▪▪▪▪▪▪▪▪▪▪▪▪▪▪▪▪▪▪▪▪▪

4 large or 6 medium ripe, firm tomatoes
Vegetable oil, for the baking dish
Salt
Freshly ground black pepper
3 tablespoons olive oil
¼ pound Mozzarella cheese (you may use a bit less for only 4 tomatoes), coarsely chopped
¼ pound (or less) Gruyère cheese, coarsely chopped
2 tablespoons chopped fresh basil or 2 teaspoons dried basil

Slice the top from each tomato. Using a teaspoon, scoop out the pulp and seeds. Turn the tomatoes upside down on a platter or sheets of paper toweling and let them drain for 15 minutes.

Preheat the oven to 375° F.

Oil a baking dish just large enough to hold the tomatoes upright. Arrange the tomatoes in the dish. Sprinkle the interior of each tomato with a large pinch of salt and a grinding of pepper. Drizzle 1 teaspoon of the olive oil into each tomato. Mix the cheeses together with the basil. Stuff the tomatoes with the cheese mixture, and brush the outside of the tomatoes with the remaining olive oil. Bake for 15 minutes, until the cheese has melted. Serve immediately.

✖ *Serves 4 to 6*

This is an all-American favorite of mine. It is usually prepared as an accompaniment for a roast or for grilled game. You had better make extra because everyone gets their spoon in it before it reaches the table! The perfect fall dish which is so easy to prepare. Add the baking powder for an even lighter corn bread.

Buttercup Squash Spoonbread

4 cups milk
4 tablespoons unsalted butter
1 tablespoon salt
2 cups yellow cornmeal
2 cups buttercup squash purée (see Note)
5 eggs
1 cup heavy cream
¼ cup honey
⅛ teaspoon ground cloves
1 teaspoon baking powder, optional

Preheat oven to 375° F. Butter a deep 12-inch round pan or pie plate.

Bring milk to a boil in a large saucepan over moderate heat, stirring frequently to prevent it from scalding. Stir in butter and salt. When butter has melted, add cornmeal slowly, stirring constantly. Remove from the heat and let cool slightly. Stir in squash purée.

Place eggs in a medium bowl and whisk until light. Stir in remaining ingredients and baking powder, if desired. Fold into the cornmeal mixture until well blended. Pour mixture into prepared pan and bake in the center of the oven for 25 to 30 minutes, or until the top is golden brown. Drizzle a little extra melted butter over the top if desired and serve warm.

Note: To make purée, cut 2 pounds squash into cubes and bake or boil until tender when pierced with a knife. Drain squash and scoop out flesh. Discard skin. Purée in a food processor or blender until smooth. ✗ *Serves 12*

B R E A D S

Beard on Bread—an inspired and orthograph-
ically inevitable title—tells the tale. Jim loved
to bake bread and a great compliment was when he
said of someone, as he said of his last testing
assistant, Richard Nimmo, "He's good; he really has
the feel of it; he can make bread with anything."
That is exactly what Jim did, not by using odd
seasonings, but by using different basic ingredients
in different proportions.

To have seen Jim knead bread was a sensational kitchen experience. His hands were so huge that he only used one of them and he would bring his whole weight and height to bear, lifting and turning the thoroughly obedient dough with the same hand.

So we start this chapter with a few bread recipes that Jim liked even before <u>Beard on Bread</u>. Both the Cuban Bread—one of the few breads meant to be eaten hot—and the one following, Mabelle Jeffcott's Graham Bread, are from <u>The James Beard Cookbook</u>.

Cuban Bread

■■■■■■■■■■■■■■■■■■■■■■■■■■

1 package active dry yeast or 1 cake of yeast
2 cups warm water, approximately 115° F.
1¼ tablespoons salt
1 tablespoon granulated sugar
6 to 9 cups all-purpose flour

Dissolve the yeast in the water and add the salt and sugar, stirring thoroughly.

Stir in flour, one cup at a time, beating it in with a wooden spoon. Add enough flour to make a smooth dough. When the dough is thoroughly mixed, cover it with a towel, put in a warm spot, and let rise until double in bulk.

Turn dough out onto a floured board and shape into long French-style loaves or round Italian-style loaves. Or shape into small individual loaves. Arrange on a baking sheet heavily sprinkled with cornmeal. Let rise for 5 minutes.

Slash the tops of the loaves in two or three places with a knife, brush them with water, and place in a cold oven. Set the oven for 400° F. and start it. Add a pan of boiling water to the oven and bake the loaves until they are crusty and done. This should take about 40 to 45 minutes.

✘ *Makes 2 loaves*

Mabelle Jeffcott's Graham Bread [JB]

1 large can evaporated milk
Equal amount hot water
¼ cup melted unsalted butter
3 tablespoons granulated sugar
1 tablespoon salt
1 package active dry yeast or 1 cake of yeast
½ cup warm water, approximately 115° F.
3 cups coarse graham flour
5 to 6 cups all-purpose flour

Mix the evaporated milk with hot water, butter, sugar, and salt. Let cool to lukewarm.

Dissolve yeast in warm water and add to the milk mixture. Add the graham flour, using an electric mixer with the dough hook or a wooden spoon. Add the white flour, enough to make a smooth elastic dough.

Put the dough in a bowl and cover with a towel. Place in a warm spot to rise until double in bulk. Turn onto a lightly floured board and divide into 2 or 3 portions. Shape into loaves and put into buttered bread pans. Cover and let rise again until 1½ times its original size.

Preheat oven to 375° F.

Bake bread for about 1 hour or until browned and done. The bread will sound hollow when thumped with a knuckle when done. Remove from oven and cool on a rack.

✗ *Makes 2 to 3 loaves*

Refrigerator Potato Bread

- -

1 package active dry yeast

½ cup plus 1 tablespoon granulated sugar

½ cup warm water, approximately 115° F.

1 cup warm milk or potato water (water in which the potatoes were cooked)

¾ cup unsalted butter, softened in the milk or potato water

1½ tablespoons salt

2 eggs

1 cup mashed potatoes (instant mashed potatoes can be used)

6 cups all-purpose flour, approximately

Dissolve the yeast and tablespoon of sugar in the water and let proof for about 5 minutes. Add the milk or potato water, butter, remaining sugar, salt, and eggs to the yeast mixture and stir to blend thoroughly.

Add mashed potatoes and stir well. Then add the flour 1 cup at a time, stirring well after each addition, to make a thoroughly stiff dough. (You may not need the full 6 cups.)

Turn the dough out onto a floured board and knead for 10 to 12 minutes, until the dough is very smooth and elastic. Shape into a ball. Butter a large mixing bowl and place dough in the bowl, turning to coat all sides with the butter. Cover tightly and refrigerate overnight.

Remove from refrigerator, punch down, and turn on to a floured board. Let rest for 5 to 6 minutes and then knead vigorously for 4 to 5 minutes and let rest again. Shape into two loaves and place in two well-buttered 9″ × 5″ × 3″ pans. Or shape into a ball and place in a 9-inch pie plate to make a single round loaf. Let rise in pan until doubled in bulk.

Preheat the oven to 375° F.

Bake loaves or single loaf for 40 to 45 minutes. Remove bread from pans and rap with a knuckle to test for doneness. If bread sounds hollow it is done. Return bread to the oven without pan and bake for several minutes more to crisp and brown the crust.

Remove from oven and cool thoroughly before slicing. ✘ *Makes 1 round loaf or 2 regular loaves*

Breads

JAMES BEARD AND CARL JEROME. *Even though James was a great kneader by hand, as he learned to work with the food processor on his way to writing* <u>Recipes with a Cuisinart Food Processor</u> *with Carl Jerome for Carl Sontheimer, he discovered that the machine did a splendid job on bread doughs and came up with this mildly spiced bread.* ✍

This is a great sandwich bread, especially good for cold meats. It is a wonderfully perfumed loaf with the aroma of mustard emanating not only from the oven during baking, but also from the bread itself in a sandwich. [*JB*]

Mustard Mixed-Grain Bread

■ ■

2 packages active dry yeast
¾ cup warm water
1½ teaspoons granulated sugar
1⅓ cups unbleached all-purpose flour
⅔ cup rye flour
⅔ cup whole wheat flour
1 teaspoon salt
3 tablespoons unsalted butter, cut in 3 or more
    pieces
½ cup Dijon mustard

Proof yeast in ½ cup warm water with sugar.

Place flours, salt, and butter into a food processor and process until butter is cut into small pieces. Add mustard and process until combined.

Add yeast mixture to processor and process until combined. With machine running, pour in remaining ¼ cup water slowly until dough forms a ball (all the water may not be necessary).

Remove dough to a greased bowl, turning to coat all sides. Cover and let rise in a warm place until doubled in bulk, about 1½ hours.

Punch dough down and knead several times by hand. Return to greased bowl and let rise again until doubled, about 1 hour. Punch down and knead for 1 to 2 minutes. Allow to rest for 10 minutes.

Preheat oven to 375° F.

Shape into a loaf and place in a 5-cup buttered loaf pan. Cover and let rise until doubled. Slash top with a sharp knife in two or three places. If desired, brush with a glaze made by beating together 1 egg white and 1 tablespoon water. Bake in a preheated oven for 35 to 40 minutes.

No-Knead Whole Wheat Loaves

■■■■■■■■■■■■■■■■■■■■■■■■■■

3 pounds stone-ground whole wheat flour

2 teaspoons salt

3 tablespoons plus 4 cups warm water,
    approximately 115° F.

3 packages active dry yeast

1 tablespoon black molasses

Mix flour and salt in a large mixing bowl.

Combine 3 tablespoons water and yeast in a bowl and stir to dissolve yeast. Add the molasses. When the mixture becomes spongy, spoon into a well in the flour and salt. Gradually add remaining water, mixing with your hand until the dough leaves the sides of the bowl and is rather rubbery. Kneading is not necessary.

Divide the dough among three warm, buttered 1-quart loaf pans. Cover with a clean kitchen towel and let rise for 30 minutes. The dough should come to within ½ inch of the top of the pans.

Preheat the oven to 400° F.

Bake for 40 minutes or until a toothpick inserted comes out dry. Cool on a rack.

✘ *Makes 3 loaves*

erve Suzanne Corbett's Herbed Wheat Bread warm from the oven with her creamy Spinach Potato Soup (page 113).

Herbed Wheat Bread

½ cup warm water (between 105 and 115° F. is ideal)
½ cup honey
2 packages active dry yeast
¾ cup chopped scallions, equal parts white and green (about 2 bunches)
⅓ cup vegetable oil
1 cup milk, warmed (between 105 and 115° F.)
½ cup finely chopped parsley (about 2 bunches)
2 teaspoons salt
1 teaspoon dried dill weed
2 cups whole wheat flour
2 to 3 cups all-purpose flour
3 tablespoons unsalted butter or vegetable oil, for the bowl and pans
1 egg white, lightly beaten, for a glaze, optional

Preheat the oven to 375° F.

In a large bowl, combine the water and the honey. Add the yeast and stir until it dissolves. Add the scallions, oil, milk, parsley, salt, dill weed, and whole wheat flour. Stir until the dough is smooth. Add enough of the all-purpose flour to make a stiff dough.

Turn the dough out onto a lightly floured surface and knead until it is smooth. Grease a large bowl with 1 tablespoon of the butter. Place the dough in the bowl, cover it lightly, and let it rise in a warm place until doubled, about 1 hour. Punch the dough down and shape it into 2 loaves. Grease two 9″ × 5″ × 3″ loaf pans with 1 tablespoon of the butter each. Fit the dough into the pans and let it rise, lightly covered, until doubled; this will take about 1 hour.

Brush the tops of the loaves with a little beaten egg white, if desired. Bake the loaves for 35 to 40 minutes, until the bread sounds hollow when tapped on the bottom. Remove the pans to a cooling rack; after 5 minutes turn the loaves out of the pans and let them cool completely.

✖ *Makes 2 large loaves*

starts the meals at her restaurant with hot focaccia, a flattish bread usually made with a pizza dough.
Lidia's dough is lighter and more elegant. ✍

Topped with sliced onions, olive oil, rosemary, and coarse salt before baking, this is a homey bread to break off in chunks and enjoy with a glass of wine (Italian, of course!). With a bowl of cherry tomatoes, and a chunk of Parmesan cheese to break off and nibble, this focaccia would make a light summer lunch.

Focaccia

■ ■

3 envelopes active dry yeast or 2 ounces
    compressed fresh yeast, crumbled
2 cups warm water (between 105° and 115° F.)
2 tablespoons granulated sugar
5½ to 6 cups all-purpose flour
1 tablespoon kosher salt
¼ cup olive oil
¾ cup thinly sliced onions
½ to 1 teaspoon dried rosemary, crumbled
½ teaspoon freshly ground black pepper

In a medium bowl, mix the yeast with the water and sugar. Let it stand (to proof) for 10 minutes, until foamy.

Mix 5 cups of the flour with 1½ teaspoons of the salt in a large bowl. Make a well in the center of the flour and pour in the foamy yeast mixture and 2 tablespoons of the oil. Stir the mixture, gradually incorporating the flour, to make a soft dough; if the dough becomes too stiff to mix with a spoon, use your hands.

Sprinkle a work surface with ¼ cup of the remaining flour. Turn the dough out onto the floured surface and sprinkle it with another ¼ cup of the flour. Knead the dough until it is smooth and elastic, for about 10 minutes, using a little of the remaining flour if the dough gets sticky.

Shape the dough into a ball. Place it in a large bowl greased with ½ tablespoon of the oil. Turn the dough over to coat it with oil. Set the bowl in a warm, draft-free place and cover it

lightly with a dampened dish towel or with plastic wrap. Let the dough rise for 30 minutes, until it has doubled in volume.

Punch the dough down and let it rise twice more, about 30 minutes each time. Grease a 15″ × 11″ baking pan with about ½ tablespoon of the oil. Press the dough into the pan, pushing and stretching it 1 inch up the sides of the pan. Using your knuckles, press little indentations over the flat surface of the dough. Cover the pan lightly and let the dough rest for 10 minutes.

Preheat the oven to 400° F.

In a medium bowl, mix the remaining tablespoon of oil with the onions, rosemary, pepper, and the remaining 1½ teaspoons salt. Uncover the dough and use your knuckles to press down on the dough; don't press the sides of the dough. Spread the onion mixture over the flat surface of the dough and brush the border with any oil left in the bowl. Bake the focaccia for 35 to 45 minutes. If it browns very quickly, cover it loosely with aluminum foil.

Remove the pan to a cooling rack. When cool, slice or break the focaccia into 12 pieces.
✗ *Serves 12*

JAN BIRNBAUM. *Bill Wilkinson of the Campton Place hotel (page 71) asked his chef to share these round and somewhat sweet loaves with us. They are very good.* ✍

Honey Bread

■ ■

1¼ cups heavy cream
1 cup honey
1 cup milk
¼ pound unsalted butter
¼ cup granulated sugar
¼ cup active dry yeast
3½ pounds bread flour
2 tablespoons salt
1 egg
2 egg yolks
2 tablespoons water

Combine cream, honey, milk, butter, and sugar in a heavy saucepan and cook over moderate heat, stirring, until butter is almost melted. Remove from heat and allow to cool to about 94° F.

Sprinkle yeast over cooled liquid and allow to stand for about 5 minutes, or until yeast has started to foam.

In a large bowl of an electric mixer with a dough hook, combine flour and salt. With mixer running, gradually add yeast mixture along with the egg and one of the yolks. Knead with dough hook for about 10 minutes, or until very shiny and elastic. Cover bowl with a cloth and set in a warm place to rise until dough has almost doubled in size, about 2 hours.

Punch the dough down and turn onto a lightly floured surface. Divide into 8 equal pieces and form each piece into a loaf about 6 by 3 inches. Place on a large baking sheet, cover, and return to warm place for about 1 hour.

Preheat oven to 300° F.

In a small bowl mix remaining egg yolk with water and brush over loaves. Bake for 35 minutes, or until they are golden brown and sound hollow when thumped with a knuckle. Cool completely on a rack before slicing.

✗ *Makes 8 loaves*

Writing about his own brioche loaf in <u>Beard on Bread,</u> *Jim said, "Not the classic brioche that one prepares for the little topknotted rolls, although similar to it, this is a loaf that is especially good for delicate sandwiches, such as the popular onion sandwich hors d'oeuvre I created years ago. It is also a delicious egg bread by itself, easy to make and pleasant in flavor." You will find those slightly controversial, but delicious, sandwiches on page 57.*

This is my own bread of the brioche order and it comes with a variation for a Pepper Brioche that can be used in Larry Forgione's recipe on page 100. Both of these breads can be sliced after cooling, the slices individually wrapped, frozen, and then unwrapped and toasted as needed. Of course, it is possible to make only one loaf of the Pepper Brioche and one loaf of regular brioche by dividing the dough, using half the quantity of the two peppers, and kneading them into only one loaf. ✍

Brioche Bread

▪▪▪▪▪▪▪▪▪▪▪▪▪▪▪▪▪▪▪▪▪▪▪

1½ packages active dry yeast
½ cup warm water approximately 115° F.
4 cups all-purpose flour
1 cup melted unsalted butter
2 teaspoons kosher salt
5 eggs
2 tablespoons milk

Combine the yeast and warm water in the large bowl of an electric mixer or any other large bowl. Mixing with the dough hook or by hand, add flour. Reserve 1 tablespoon of the butter and add the remainder to the flour mixture with mixer running. Add 4 of the eggs one at a time, waiting until each egg is incorporated before adding the next egg.

Coat a large bowl with the remaining tablespoon butter. Place dough in bowl, coating it well with the melted butter. Cover tightly with plastic wrap and place in the refrigerator overnight. Bring to room temperature before baking (this may take several hours).

Preheat oven to 400° F.

Punch down dough and shape into 2 loaves. Fit into buttered 8″ × 4″ × 2″ loaf pans and let rise again in a warm place until doubled in bulk, about 1 hour. Whisk together remaining egg and milk in a small bowl. Brush the loaves with egg wash and bake for about 30 minutes, or until the loaves are a deep golden brown and sound hollow when tapped with the knuckles. Cool on a rack.

✖ *Makes 2 loaves*

Pepper Brioche Variation

▪▪▪▪▪▪▪▪▪▪▪▪▪▪▪▪▪▪▪▪▪▪▪

1 recipe Brioche Bread
1½ teaspoons freshly ground black pepper
2 teaspoons whole green peppercorns in brine, thoroughly rinsed in a sieve under cold running water

After Brioche Bread is knocked down, but before it is formed into loaves, thoroughly knead in both peppers. Form, raise, and bake as above.

CAROLINE STUART *was an assistant of Jim's in New York in his last years. Since his death, she has given of herself selflessly to The Beard Foundation. She offers us a historical note by telling us that the Cranberry Raisin Pie in Judith and Evan Jones's* The L. L. Bean Cookbook *was the last recipe developed in the Beard kitchen and was inspired by a dinner James had attended at the American Harvest Restaurant in New York in a festival that paid homage to Amerindian foods.*

Caroline is a talented cook in her own right and sometimes assisted in class. These very special biscuits are uniquely her own. ✍

Sweet Potato Yeast Biscuits

5 cups self-rising flour
1 teaspoon baking powder
¼ cup granulated sugar
1 cup vegetable shortening
¾ cup cooked and well-mashed sweet potatoes
1 egg, lightly beaten
1 package active dry yeast, dissolved in a little
    warm water
1 cup buttermilk
Melted butter, for coating the rising bowl and
    brushing the muffins

Sift together flour, baking powder, and sugar and reserve.

Place shortening and sweet potatoes in the large bowl of an electric mixer and cream together until smooth. Add the egg and the yeast mixture and mix to blend well. Add the buttermilk and mix to combine.

Gradually add the reserved flour mixture, kneading dough enough to make a smooth ball. Place in a large buttered bowl and brush with additional melted butter. Cover with a kitchen towel and let rise for several hours or overnight at room temperature.

Remove dough from bowl and knead briefly. Roll out to a thickness of approximately ½ inch and cut with a 1½-inch biscuit cutter. Place on a greased pan and let rest for 1 to 2 hours.

Preheat oven to 400° F.

When ready to bake, brush biscuits with melted butter. Bake for 15 minutes or until brown.

✘ *Makes about 50 biscuits*

I f you are pressed for time, you may chop the bell peppers in a food processor, and melt the butter and shortening in the same pan.

Jalapeño Blue Corn Bread

7 tablespoons unsalted butter, 1 tablespoon at room temperature, remaining 6 tablespoons melted and cooled

1 cup all-purpose flour

1¼ cups blue cornmeal (use yellow cornmeal if blue is not available)

2 tablespoons granulated sugar

1 teaspoon salt

1 tablespoon baking powder

1 tablespoon olive oil or unsalted butter

3 fresh jalapeño peppers, stemmed, seeded, and diced

1 medium red bell pepper, stemmed, seeded, deribbed, and diced

1 medium green bell pepper, stemmed, seeded, deribbed, and diced

3 cloves garlic, smashed, peeled, and minced

2 eggs

6 tablespoons vegetable shortening, melted and cooled

1 cup buttermilk, at room temperature, mixed with a pinch of baking soda

3 tablespoons chopped fresh cilantro

Preheat the oven to 400° F.

Lightly butter an 8″ × 12″ baking pan with the tablespoon of butter at room temperature. Sift together flour, cornmeal, sugar, salt, and baking powder into a medium bowl and reserve.

Heat the oil in a medium skillet. Add peppers and garlic and sauté for 2 minutes. Remove from heat and set the vegetables aside.

Beat the eggs lightly and stir in the melted shortening and remaining butter. Add the buttermilk mixture and stir well. Pour into dry ingredients and mix lightly with a fork or spatula just until smooth. Do not overmix. Fold in the reserved vegetables and the cilantro.

Pour the batter into the prepared baking pan. Bake for 30 to 40 minutes, until the top is golden brown. ✕ *Serves 12 generously*

Serve these warm with butter or honey.

Cranberry Cornmeal Muffins

■■■■■■■■■■■■■■■■■■■■■■■■■■

¾ cup cranberries (fresh or frozen)

1 cup cranberry juice cocktail

1 tablespoon orange liqueur

1 cup all-purpose flour

1 cup yellow cornmeal

¼ cup granulated sugar

4 teaspoons baking powder

1½ teaspoons salt

2 eggs

1 egg yolk

½ cup milk

½ cup heavy cream

6 tablespoons unsalted butter, melted

Combine cranberries, cranberry juice, and orange liqueur in a small bowl. Allow to stand at room temperature for 30 minutes.

Preheat oven to 425° F. Grease muffin cups lightly.

In a large bowl mix together the dry ingredients. In a smaller bowl mix together the eggs, milk, and cream. Stir into the dry ingredients with the melted butter. Drain the cranberries and gently fold into the muffin batter. Discard the cranberry juice.

Spoon the batter into the cups and bake in the center of the oven for 14 minutes for tea-size muffins and 18 minutes for medium-size muffins. Remove from oven and allow to stand for a few minutes in the tin. Turn out onto a wire rack to cool. ✖ *Makes 12 medium or 24 tea-size muffins*

WOLFGANG PUCK, *that quintessential California chef,*
with Spago and Chinois on Main restaurants in Los Angeles and other ventures around California and
around the globe is originally from Austria. He has given us two bread recipes from his book, The Wolfgang
Puck Cookbook: Recipes from Spago, Chinois and Points East and West. *The first recipe seems to me to*
show his European background, the second the influence of his new American home.

Wolfgang has been indefatigable in raising money for worthwhile causes and his own charitable
foundation. Many of the fund raisings have been group events by chefs at Spago. ✍

This bread is fantastic toasted, with butter and marmalade for breakfast, or just grilled and served with ripe cheese and wine. The recipe works best in the large quantity given. It freezes well.

Pecan and Walnut Bread
■■■■■■■■■■■■■■■■■■■■■■■■■■■■

1⅓ packages (1 tablespoon plus 1 teaspoon) active
    dry yeast
3 cups lukewarm water
5 cups all-purpose flour
3 cups rye flour
4½ tablespoons salt
1 tablespoon honey
1 teaspoon chopped fresh rosemary or thyme
    leaves, or ½ teaspoon dried
7 tablespoons (3½ ounces) unsalted butter
1½ cups chopped walnuts
1½ cups chopped pecans

Dissolve the yeast in ½ cup of the lukewarm water.

Place the remaining water, both flours, and the salt, honey, rosemary or thyme, and butter in a mixer fitted with a dough hook. Mix for about 5 minutes. Add the dissolved yeast and continue to knead in the mixer for about 15 minutes. Add the walnuts and pecans and continue to knead until the nuts are well mixed into the dough. The dough should come together neatly into a ball.

Cover the mixing bowl with a damp towel and let the dough rise for about 45 minutes at room temperature, or until it approximately doubles in volume.

Knead the dough briefly by hand to remove any large air pockets.

Butter and flour three 10″ × 4″ loaf pans. Divide the dough in three parts, shape each into a 10-inch cylinder, and place them in the prepared pans. Let the loaves rise in the pans for about an hour, or until they at least double in volume.

Preheat the oven to 375° F.

Bake the loaves for about 20 minutes, or until they are nicely browned, then reduce the heat to 325° F. and continue baking for another 25 minutes. Remove from pans and let cool.

✖ *Makes 3 10-inch loaves*

Corn Muffins with Jalapeño Peppers and Fresh Rosemary

8 ounces unsalted butter, at room temperature

3 small jalapeño peppers, stemmed, seeded, and
finely chopped

Kernels from 1 medium ear of corn

2 teaspoons chopped fresh rosemary

2 packed tablespoons light brown sugar

1 egg

1 cup all-purpose flour

1 cup stone-ground cornmeal

1 teaspoon salt

1 teaspoon baking soda

1¼ cups buttermilk

Preheat oven to 425° F.

Melt 1½ tablespoons butter in a small pan. Brush medium-sized muffin tins with some of the butter and set tins aside. Add the jalapeño peppers to the remaining butter in the pan. Return to the heat and cook for 1 minute. Remove from the heat. Stir in corn and rosemary and reserve.

In the bowl of an electric mixer, cream the remaining butter with sugar. Add egg and mix well, scraping down the sides of the bowl as necessary. The mixture should be light and fluffy.

In a separate bowl, mix together flour, cornmeal, salt, and baking soda. Add a quarter of the flour mixture to the mixer, then a quarter of the buttermilk. Blending well with each addition, continue with alternate additions of flour and buttermilk until fully combined. Stir in reserved corn mixture.

Spoon the batter into the prepared muffin tins so that they are about three-quarters full. Bake in the center of the oven for 18 to 20 minutes or until a toothpick inserted in the center comes out clean. Let muffins cool in pans for 5 minutes. Remove to a napkin-lined basket and serve hot with fresh unsalted butter.

✗ *Makes 12 muffins*

D E S S E R T S

JAMES HAD AN ODDLY AMBIVALENT ATTITUDE TOWARDS
DESSERTS. I NEVER KNEW HIM TO ORDER ONE WHEN
WE WERE IN A RESTAURANT. SINCE I HAVE SEEN HIM EAT

CHUNKS OF CRISPED MEAT FAT, DIET WAS CLEARLY NOT THE ANSWER. IT JUST WASN'T HIS FAVORITE THING TO EAT. DESPITE THAT, HE WAS FASCINATED BY AMERICAN AND ENGLISH DESSERTS, THEIR HISTORY, AND THEIR NAMES. WE ONCE SPENT TWO DAYS TRYING TO FIND THE EARLIEST BRIDE'S CAKE RECIPE AND A REASON FOR THE NAME AND USAGE. HE LOVED THE SOUND OF GRUNT AND CRUMBLE AND SLUMP. HE ALSO ADMIRED THE TECHNICAL SPLENDORS OF THE PASTRY MAKER'S CRAFT.

CERTAINLY HIS BOOKS WERE RICH IN LAYER CAKES AND HE NEVER THOUGHT ABOUT DESSERT WITHOUT THINKING OF POUND CAKE. IT REPRESENTED TEATIME TO HIM.

IN HIS HONOR, MANY COOKS AND CHEFS HAVE SENT US DELICIOUS SWEETS. HE WOULD HAVE ADMIRED THE RECIPES AND TASTED—PROBABLY PICKING UP HIS SAMPLES WITH HIS FINGERS.

ONE KIND HE COULDN'T HAVE EATEN WITH HIS FINGERS WERE CUSTARDY DESSERTS. WE START WITH THOSE, SENT BY GOOD FRIENDS. WE GO ON TO THE MAINLY FRUIT DESSERTS, FORGE ONWARD TO CAKES AND TORTES, AND END UP WITH THE FROZEN PLEASURES; BUT DO NOTE THAT SINCE AN ACCOMPANYING ICE CREAM IS PART OF MANY OF THE DESSERTS, THERE ARE ICE CREAMS SCOOPED THROUGHOUT THIS CHAPTER.

Ginger and Passion Fruit Crème Brulé

■ ■ ■ ■ ■ ■ ■ ■ ■ ■ ■ ■ ■ ■ ■ ■ ■ ■ ■

4 cups heavy cream
1 cup half-and-half
20 egg yolks
1 cup superfine sugar
2 tablespoons vanilla extract
1 cup passion fruit purée (from about 30 passion
      fruit) or orange juice concentrate or peach
      purée
2 tablespoons Ginger Purée (recipe follows)
2¼ cups packed light brown sugar

Adjust oven rack to the lower third of the oven and preheat oven to 300° F.

Place cream and half-and-half in a medium pan over moderate heat. Heat until almost boiling. Remove from heat and allow to cool slightly.

In a large mixing bowl whisk together egg yolks, sugar, and vanilla with a wire whisk until color lightens and mixture thickens. Whisk in warm cream mixture, passion fruit purée, and ginger purée. Pour through a fine sieve into twelve 5″ × 1″ custard dishes and fill the dishes to about ¼ inch from the top.

Place custard dishes in a shallow pan large enough to hold them and place in oven. Pour enough water into the pan to reach about halfway up the sides of the dishes. Cook for 20 minutes, or until a skewer inserted into the center is hot to the touch. Remove from oven and transfer custard dishes to a cooling rack. Cook remaining custards as above.

When cool, cover with plastic wrap and refrigerate for at least 2 hours. When ready to serve, preheat broiler. Sprinkle about 3 tablespoons brown sugar over each dessert and place under broiler for 4 minutes, or until sugar caramelizes. Allow to cool for a few minutes before serving. ✖ *Serves 12*

Ginger Purée

● ● ● ● ● ● ● ● ● ● ● ● ● ● ● ● ● ● ● ●

½ cup grated fresh ginger
3 tablespoons water
1 tablespoon granulated sugar
1 teaspoon fresh lemon juice

Combine all ingredients in a blender and purée until smooth, scraping down the sides occasionally.

Scrape into a small heavy pan and place over very low heat. Cook for about 5 minutes, stirring constantly. Remove pan from heat and allow to cool. ✖ *Makes 3 tablespoons*

CHUCK WILLIAMS *was one of Jim's closest friends. Jim loved going to his house tucked into a back garden in San Francisco. We would sit happily in Chuck's beautiful, large kitchen as he turned out crystal-clear classics seemingly effortlessly.*

It comes as no surprise that Chuck has a glorious kitchen. He is the founder of Williams-Sonoma, which has been bringing a strong aesthetic sense to American kitchens for years. We have only to look at one of the many Williams-Sonoma stores that dot America or the striking catalogues to see what a sure eye and cook's intelligence inform Chuck's choices and the mise-en-scènes he creates.

The kitchen is the whole ground floor of the house. It is uncluttered because there are long double walls with storage behind them. Every place one looks the eye rests with pleasure due to whimsy or beauty.

Chuck set up James's San Francisco classes. He helped to find students and he stored the huge impedimenta that made the classes possible. He also actually assisted in the classes from time to time. He brought to James's attention new machines and equipment—such as the electric sorbet machine—that he knew James would love.

After dinner, James would ponderously climb the stairs to Chuck's cozy living room and would only leave when it was clear that Chuck would be too tired in the morning to work.

Chuck wrote a very good cookbook, The Williams-Sonoma Cookbook and Guide to Kitchenware. He provides us with a variant of a recipe from his book that is exactly the kind of thing that appealed to James, a variant on a homely classic that makes it splendid. ✍

Chuck Williams, James Beard, and, far right, Marion Cunningham

Bread and Butter Custard with Grand Marnier

■■■■■■■■■■■■■■■■■■■■■■■■■■■■

½ cup raisins

3 tablespoons Grand Marnier

2 cups milk

2 cups heavy cream

3 3-inch strips orange zest

1 loaf day-old French bread

3 to 4 tablespoons unsalted butter

3 whole eggs

6 egg yolks

½ cup granulated sugar

2 tablespoons sliced almonds

1 to 2 tablespoons confectioner's sugar, for serving

Put the raisins in a small bowl and sprinkle with the Grand Marnier. Let them macerate for 1 to 2 hours, turning them occasionally in the liqueur.

Preheat the oven to 325°F.

In a heavy saucepan, combine the milk, cream, and orange zest over medium heat. Bring the liquid to a boil; then immediately remove it from the heat and let cool for 5 to 10 minutes.

Slice and trim enough pieces of bread (½ to ¾ inch thick) to cover the bottom of a 2½-quart baking dish approximately 10″ × 8″ × 2″. Remove the bread, spread one side of each slice with some butter, and set it aside.

In a large bowl, beat the whole eggs and yolks with the sugar until light and lemon colored. Remove the orange zest from the warm milk-cream infusion and discard it. Stir the infusion into the egg mixture, then stir in the raisins and their liquid. Pour this custard into the baking dish. Gently float the slices of bread, buttered side up, on the custard and sprinkle the almonds over the bread. Set the baking dish in a large pan, and fill the pan with boiling water to reach halfway up the side of the baking dish.

Bake the custard for 40 to 50 minutes, until the top is golden brown and crusty and a knife blade inserted in the center comes out clean. Dust with confectioner's sugar. Serve slightly warm or at room temperature. ✕ *Serves 6*

JEANNE VOLTZ *is one of the real pros of food writing.*
Born in Alabama, she first worked for newspapers and won many awards and then moved on to be—for many years—the food editor of <u>Woman's Day</u>. *She is the author of numerous cookbooks, all of them focusing on the essentials of the American tradition. Jim said of her* <u>Barbecued Ribs and Other Great Feeds</u>: *"Jeanne Voltz has written a definitive book on barbecuing. It is eminently practical, altogether sensible, and wide in its scope. She has lived in various parts of the 'Barbecue Belt.' She understands the varying tastes and the techniques of each region she covers, and this is* <u>the</u> *book on barbecue. I love it."*
Jeanne was a close friend. They shared many good times. ✍

Jim Beard kept holidays happily, with "family." In the last few years of his life, my husband, until his death, our daughters, and I had Jim and Gino for Thanksgiving and we went to 12th Street for Christmas, English-style even to crackers from London. After popping the crackers, we put on the tissue hats. You can imagine a silly paper frill perched over Jim's magnificent brow.

His intimates knew that Jim was not for desserts, but adored custards and sweets remembered from childhood. I made fine pastry and good pumpkin pie, but the year that I serve floating island I knew it was right, a classic gone sophisticated, with Cognac in place of vanilla.

Our last Thanksgiving was sad, but sweet. His health was failing and his diet was cruelly restricted. He was sitting in the big chair in the office when I dropped by to invite him. His eyes warmed as he accepted and an impish twinkle flashed as he added, "Don't expect me to keep to the diet for Thanksgiving!"

Jim had dark meat of turkey, his preference, corn bread stuffing and trimmings, then dessert. I ladled the lake of custard from the crystal bowl into small dishes and floated an "island" on each. He ate his dessert quickly, then beamed like a child, a role he played so well.

Floating Island for Jim and Company

■■■■■■■■■■■■■■■■■■■■■■■■■

5 eggs
¾ cup granulated sugar
2½ cups milk
2 tablespoons Cognac or Grand Marnier
⅛ teaspoon salt
Candied Orange Peel (recipe follows)

Separate 4 of the eggs and place whites in a large metal bowl. Reserve yolks, covered closely with plastic wrap to prevent a skin from forming. Whisk egg whites until stiff peaks form. Gradually whisk in ½ cup of the sugar and continue to whisk until mixture is stiff but not dry. Reserve.

Pour milk and 1 tablespoon of the Cognac in a 12-inch deep skillet (milk should be about ¼-inch deep, and if a larger or small pan is used the quantity of milk should be adjusted accordingly). Place over moderate heat until bubbles just appear around edge of pan. Remove pan from heat.

Beat meringue for a few minutes to make stiff again. Working in two batches, drop large spoonfuls (using a large mixing spoon) of meringue into the hot milk to make 6 balls. Keeping the balls separate, return pan to low heat so that milk barely bubbles. Cook for about 1 minute or until meringue balls feel slightly dry. Carefully turn balls over and cook for about 1½ minutes longer. Remove from milk with a slotted spoon and drain on paper towels. Repeat with remaining meringue.

Remove milk from heat, strain through a fine sieve, and add more as necessary to make it up to 2 cups.

Beat reserved egg yolks and remaining whole egg in the top of a double boiler. Stir in remaining sugar, salt, and milk. Place over hot, but not boiling, water and cook, stirring constantly, for about 8 minutes, until custard thickens and coats the back of a spoon. Remove pan from heat, place top of double boiler in a bowl of iced water, and stir in remaining Cognac. Allow to cool. Place meringue "islands" and custard in refrigerator to chill.

To serve, spoon custard into shallow dessert bowls and float two "islands" on each dessert. Scatter candied orange peel over. ✕ *Serves 6*

Candied Orange Peel

1 thick-skinned orange
1 cup granulated sugar
1 cup water

With a vegetable peeler or sharp paring knife cut rind from orange into wide strips, making sure that you have none of the white pith. Cut the strips into very thin slices.

In a small heavy pan, combine sugar and water over moderate heat. Bring to a boil and cook for 3 minutes, uncovered, until it becomes syrupy. Drop orange rind into syrup and cook for about 3 minutes.

With a fork remove orange rind and place on waxed paper to dry. If not using same day, when dry, place in flat refrigerator dish, cover, and refrigerate overnight.

STEPHAN PYLES. *How Jim enjoyed such words as*
buckle, worth a long conversation and fingers dirtied by piles of books. Stephan Pyles (pages 129, 210, 325)
of Routh Street Café in Dallas has been a real supporter of the Foundation, coming to New York to appear
at the house and contributing generously to this book.

Serve this buckle still warm from the oven with vanilla ice cream.

Blueberry Buckle with Cinnamon-Whiskey Sauce

☐ *For the cake and filling*

½ pound plus 2 tablespoons unsalted butter

2 cups plus 2 tablespoons all-purpose flour

⅓ cup granulated sugar

1 egg, beaten

1 teaspoon baking powder

1 teaspoon baking soda

1 cup buttermilk

2 pints fresh blueberries (about 4 cups), tossed in ¼ to ¾ cup granulated sugar (depending on the sweetness of the berries)

☐ *For the crumb topping*

½ cup granulated sugar

½ cup dark brown sugar

1 cup all-purpose flour

½ teaspoon freshly ground nutmeg

¼ teaspoon powdered ginger or 1 teaspoon grated, peeled fresh ginger root

¼ pound unsalted butter, at room temperature

2 ounces pecans (½ cup), chopped

Cinnamon-Whiskey Sauce (recipe follows)

Preheat the oven to 350° F.

Grease the bottom and sides of a 9″ × 13″ pan with 2 tablespoons of the butter; dust it with 2 tablespoons of the flour, tapping the pan to shake off any excess flour.

Prepare the cake and filling: In the bowl of an electric mixer, beat the sugar with the remaining butter until it is light and fluffy. Add the egg and mix well. Set this mixture aside.

Sift together the remaining flour with the baking powder and baking soda. Add about one third of the flour mixture to the butter mixture and mix well. Add half of the buttermilk and beat well. Add half of the remaining flour mixture, then the remaining buttermilk, and finally the rest of the flour mixture, beating thoroughly after each addition. Spread the batter in the prepared pan and cover it with the blueberries.

In a medium bowl, combine all of the ingredients for the crumb topping. Use your fingertips to blend the mixture. Sprinkle the crumb topping over the blueberries. Bake for 1 hour.

When it is done, remove the pan to a cooling rack. Serve the buckle lukewarm with Cinnamon-Whiskey Sauce. ✕ *Serves 12*

Cinnamon-Whiskey Sauce

¼ pound unsalted butter, cut into bits

⅔ cup granulated sugar

2 eggs

½ teaspoon cinnamon

1 tablespoon very hot water

½ cup heavy cream

½ cup bourbon

In the top of the double boiler, melt the butter over simmering water. In the meantime, combine the sugar, eggs, and cinnamon in a medium bowl and beat the mixture with a hand-held mixer for 1 minute.

Stir the egg mixture into the melted butter. Add the hot water and cream. Cook the mixture, stirring constantly, until the sugar has dissolved and the sauce has thickened. Take the pan from the heat and let the sauce cool to room temperature. Stir in the bourbon and serve with Blueberry Buckle. ✕ *Makes 2 cups*

The James Beard Celebration Cookbook

(page 169) is famous for her homey desserts. ✍

If there's a perennial hit among the Ark desserts, it's this cobbler. We use local wild blackberries, picked for us from the woods around Willapa Bay, and serve it warm, topped with the French Vanilla ice cream. The biscuits for this cobbler are exceptionally light and delicate, a nice balance to the tart berries.

Wild Blackberry Cobbler
■■■■■■■■■■■■■■■■■■■■■■■■■■

8 cups blackberries (can substitute raspberries or
    marionberries)
1 scant cup plus 2 tablespoons all-purpose flour
¾ cup plus 2 teaspoons granulated sugar
Grated zest of 1 lemon
1½ teaspoons baking powder
½ teaspoon cinnamon
¼ teaspoon salt
5 tablespoons chilled butter, cut into small pieces
⅓ cup cold milk
1 teaspoon vanilla extract

Preheat oven to 400° F.

Place blackberries in a medium saucepan over moderate heat. Cook, stirring occasionally, for about 5 minutes, until berries are broken and mixture has come to a boil.

In a small bowl combine 2 tablespoons flour and ¾ cup sugar. Stir into the fruit with the grated lemon zest. Taste and add more sugar if desired. Cook for about 4 minutes, or until mixture has thickened slightly. Remove from heat and pour into a 13″ × 9″ baking dish.

Into a mixing bowl sift remaining flour and sugar with baking powder, cinnamon, and salt. Cut in 3 tablespoons of the chilled butter with two knives until mixture has the consistency of cornmeal. Make a well in the center and pour in milk and vanilla. Gently mix together with a fork until just blended. Do not overwork.

Dot the remaining butter over the blackberries. Form the dough into 8 biscuits and place them, evenly spaced, over the blackberries. Bake cobbler in the middle of the oven for about 25 minutes, or until the biscuits are cooked through and the cobber is bubbling.

Serve warm with French Vanilla ice cream.

You can reheat in the microwave by removing the biscuits first so that they do not become tough. ✖ *Serves 8*

of Perfect Baking, is a naturally gifted, enthusiastic baker who understands that details in baking make all the difference. Jim knew what he was doing when he challenged her to cheer on the cherries. In the San Francisco classes, whenever we had a tricky baking recipe, Jim always said, "Let Flo do it." ✍

Jim Beard's conviction that hands-on cooking was the best way to learn and his faith that his students could meet any culinary challenge provided me with one of my fondest memories.

One sunny morning in Seaside, Oregon, someone brought Jim a large basket of sour cherries. The assignment: Use them in an American pie and a French tart. And so I went to work to produce a juicy, not-too-sweet filling in a tender flaky pastry. The recipes demonstrate how each cuisine handles the challenge.

The fruit filling for an American pie is thickened, in this instance, with flour and baked in an all-Crisco pie crust. The French treatment tosses the fruit with the sugar in a bowl, and after 30 minutes the sugar extracts some juice from the fruit. The crust, part butter and Crisco, is pre-baked before returning to the oven with the fruit.

Cherry Tart, Seaside '78

□ *Pastry Crust*
1 egg
¼ cup cold water
1 tablespoon white vinegar
3 cups unsifted all-purpose flour
1 teaspoon salt
¾ cup vegetable shortening
4 ounces unsalted butter, cut into small pieces

□ *Filling*
4 cups pitted cherries
½ to ¾ cup sugar (depending on sweetness of cherries)
1 tablespoon Kirsch (cherry liquor)

In a small bowl mix together egg, water, and vinegar. Place flour and salt in a large bowl or work bowl of food processor. Add vegetable shortening, in small spoonfuls, and butter. Crumble or pulse until the mixture resembles coarse meal. Add egg mixture and mix just until pastry comes together to form a ball. Cover with plastic wrap and refrigerate for at least 2 hours.

On a lightly floured surface, roll out pastry to fit into a 10- to 12-inch pie plate or tart pan with about ¾-inch overhang around the edge. Prick the bottom 4 or 5 times with a fork. Place in freezer for 30 minutes to firm the pastry.

Adjust rack to lower third of the oven and preheat to 450° F.

Toss together cherries, sugar, and Kirsch and let stand at room temperature for about 30 minutes.

Remove chilled piecrust from freezer and line the pastry with a sheet of aluminum foil so that the edges are uncovered. Fill with pie weights or dried beans. Bake for 10 minutes, reduce heat to 375° F., and bake 5 minutes longer, or until pastry edges appears set. Remove foil and beans and cook for about 10 minutes longer, or until the bottom is almost cooked through. Remove from oven to a cooling rack. Increase oven temperature to 400° F.

Spoon cherry filling into crust, discarding most of syrup that has accumulated in the bowl. Bake tart for about 30 minutes. Serve warm or at room temperature.

Cherry Pie, Seaside '78
■ ■

☐ *Pastry Crust*
3 cups unsifted all-purpose flour
1 teaspoon salt
1¼ cup vegetable shortening (Crisco)
1 large egg
¼ cup cold water
1 tablespoon vinegar
☐ *Cherry Filling*
3 cups pitted sour cherries
1½ to 2 cups granulated sugar (depending on the tartness of the cherries)
½ cup unsifted all-purpose flour
3 tablespoons unsalted butter, melted
¼ teaspoon almond extract

Combine flour and salt in a large mixing bowl. Cut in the vegetable shortening with a knife or pastry blender. In a small bowl stir together the egg and liquids and add to the flour. Mix just until dough comes together to form a ball. Divide the dough in half, wrap each piece in plastic wrap, and refrigerate for at least 2 hours.

Adjust oven rack to the lower third of the oven and preheat to 400° F.

On a lightly floured surface roll out one piece of the dough to a circle to fit a 10-inch pie pan. Line pan with the dough and trim the overhang to about ¾ inch. Roll out the second piece of dough to form a 13-inch circle and reserve.

In a large bowl toss together cherries, flour, and sugar. Stir in butter and almond extract. Spread mixture evenly in the pastry-lined pan. Cut the reserved circle of pastry into ½-inch-wide strips with a long sharp knife or pastry wheel. Lay the strips over filling to form a lattice top.

Cut the overhanging strips even with the bottom crust. Lift the bottom crust and fold it over the ends of the strips, pressing with your fingers to form a seal and crimping the edges.

Place pie on a cookie sheet and bake for 45 minutes. Reduce oven temperature to 350° F. and bake for 15 minutes longer or until crust is golden brown and filling is bubbling.

Remove pie from oven to a cooling rack. Serve warm or at room temperature.
✘ *Serves 6 to 8*

PETER KUMP *has a cooking school in New York that trains both professionals and serious amateurs. As good as the people he trains are, this is not the sum of his contributions to his chosen field. (See page 145.)*

Peter has been a staunch supporter of Diana Kennedy and Simca as well. Many of the people who work for him have given generously of their time to the Foundation and to this book.

When Peter was starting his school, before he had permanent premises, he had Jim and me teach for a week and it was a well-organized pleasure.

Jim never seemed interested in sophisticated, sugary desserts. In fact, I rarely saw him eat many at all. But he loved fruit tarts and he loved plums. This tart is my version of one that is done in a little Bavarian village. The very long cooking allows most of the water in the plums to evaporate, concentrating their special rich flavor. I never made this for Jim, but it is definitely one that I would make if I had the opportunity to cook for him again.

Summary Plum Tart

Short Crust Pastry (recipe follows)
¼ cup strained plum preserves or jam, or a lightly beaten egg white
5 to 6 ripe Damson plums (or any other dark ripe plums), pitted and thinly sliced
1 cup granulated sugar

Preheat oven to 425° F.

Roll out chilled pastry to fit a 8- to 9-inch tart shell (preferably with removable bottom). Freeze or chill well.

Prick pastry shell all over with a fork, line with aluminum foil, and fill with beans, rice, or aluminum pie weights. Bake in the center of the oven for 10 minutes. Remove the foil and weights, prick all over again with fork, return to the oven, and bake for 10 minutes longer.

Warm plum preserves, if using, in a small pan over low heat. Paint the cooked tart shell with warmed preserves or egg white. Return tart shell to the oven and bake for 2 to 3 minutes longer. This will prevent the pastry from becoming soggy. Remove from the oven and allow to cool for a few minutes.

Arrange the sliced plums in the tart shell in overlapping concentric circles or rows. Sprinkle ⅓ cup of the sugar over the plums and place the tart on a cookie sheet with a lip, return tart to the oven, and bake for 20 minutes.

Reduce the heat to 375° F. Remove tart from the oven and sprinkle another ⅓ cup of sugar over tart. Return to the oven for 20 minutes longer. If the edges of the tart become too dark, cover the rim with pieces of aluminum foil.

Remove from the oven and sprinkle over

remaining sugar. Bake for a final 20 minutes.

Remove from the oven and allow to cool to lukewarm or room temperature before serving. Serve the tart as is or, to "gild the lily," serve with crème fraîche, sour cream, or unsweetened whipped cream. ✘ *Serves 8 to 12*

Basic Short Crust Pastry

1½ cups all-purpose flour
2 tablespoons granulated sugar
1½ sticks chilled unsalted butter, cut into small
    pieces
5 tablespoons ice-cold water

Place flour and sugar in work bowl of a food processor and pulse 4 or 5 times. Add pieces of butter and pulse a few more times to combine. Add water and pulse to incorporate. The dough should now be crumbly.

Remove dough to a clean smooth surface (counter top or marble slab) and squeeze into a ball. With the heel of your hand, "smear" the dough by pushing it away from you against the hard surface to incorporate the butter.

Re-form the dough into a ball, cover in plastic wrap, and refrigerate at least 30 minutes before rolling out.

JAN WEIMER. *Jim wrote and spoke about apples with real affection. We begin a large section of apple desserts with one by the gifted and imaginative food writer and editor Jan Weimer. For many years she was the food editor of* Bon Appétit. *Now, she has turned to book writing, which I'm sure will be a pleasure for all of us. You might think of her gratin as very sophisticated pie à la mode.* ✍

Poached Apple Gratin with Walnut Cinnamon Ice Cream

■ ■

2 cups sparkling nonalcoholic unsweetened cider

¾ cup granulated sugar

1 4-inch cinnamon stick

2 teaspoons vanilla extract

2 strips lemon zest, yellow part only (about ¾-inch long)

2 pounds small pippins or other tart apples, peeled and cut into 12 wedges (about ⅛ inch thick)

4 egg yolks, at room temperature

⅓ cup heavy cream

3 tablespoons Calvados or apple brandy

Walnut Cinnamon Ice Cream (recipe follows)

Place cider, sugar, cinnamon, vanilla, and lemon zest in a heavy, medium-sized saucepan. Place over low heat and cook until the sugar dissolves, swirling the pan occasionally.

Add the apples and adjust heat so that the liquid is barely simmering. Cover and poach apples for 6 to 9 minutes, or until apples are just tender. (The apples can be prepared 2 days ahead at this point, cooled, and then chilled.)

Remove pan from heat and strain apples through a colander into a bowl. Allow apples to dry for about an hour.

Divide apples among four 6- to 8-inch gratin dishes, overlapping the slices slightly to form a rosette pattern. Cover with plastic wrap and reserve.

Strain poaching liquid through a fine sieve back into the heavy pan and return to the heat. Discard cinnamon stick and lemon zest. Boil liquid over moderate to high heat until it has reduced to about ½ cup. (This can also be done ahead; it will solidify but can be remelted over low heat before continuing.)

Place a medium pan with about 2 inches of water over high heat and bring to a boil; reduce heat to low. Beat egg yolks in a large metal bowl until thick and pale yellow. Gradually stir in warm reduced poaching liquid and continue beating. Stir in cream and Calvados. Place bowl over gently simmering pan of water and continue beating until sauce thickens to custard consistency. (This can be done up to 6 hours ahead.)

Preheat broiler.

Uncover dishes of apples and spoon sauce over them. Place dishes on a baking sheet and broil 4 to 6 inches from the heat for about 2 minutes, or until the top is browned.

Remove from broiler and serve immediately with a scoop of Walnut Cinnamon Ice Cream.

✗ *Serves 4*

Walnut Cinnamon Ice Cream

2 cups heavy cream
1 cinnamon stick, about 4 inches long
7 egg yolks, at room temperature
½ cup sugar
2 teaspoons vanilla extract
2 tablespoons Calvados or apple brandy
½ cup walnuts, toasted and coarsely chopped

Place cream and cinnamon stick in a heavy saucepan over moderate heat and bring to a boil. Remove from the heat and cool to room temperature, about 2 hours.

Beat egg yolks and sugar in a large bowl until thick and pale yellow. Reheat cream over low heat. Remove cinnamon stick, squeeze out into the cream, and discard.

Gradually beat the cream into the egg yolks. Return mixture to the pan and place over low to moderate heat. Cook, stirring continually, until the mixture almost simmers and thickens enough to coat the back of a spoon. Do not allow it to boil.

Remove from heat and press mixture through a fine sieve into a bowl. Stir in vanilla and Calvados. Cover surface of mixture with a sheet of plastic wrap (so it does not form a skin) and chill, preferably overnight.

Pour mixture into an ice cream maker and freeze according to manufacturer's instructions. When ice cream is frozen, remove from machine and stir in the walnuts. Place in the freezer for several hours before serving to mellow.

✗ *Makes about 1½ pints*

The idea of apples and ice cream cannot be kept down and in the hands of a chef like Stephan Pyles it takes on a delicious freshness. ✍

This splendid dessert is somewhat involved to prepare, and worth every moment. It is a marriage-in-heaven of flavors.

Apple-Raisin Spice Cake with Caramel Sauce and Pecan Ice Cream

■■■■■■■■■■■■■■■■■■■■■■■■■■

1 cup cake flour

2 cups all-purpose flour, plus a few tablespoons for the baking pan

1½ teaspoons baking soda

½ teaspoon ground nutmeg

½ teaspoon ground cinnamon

¼ teaspoon ground clove

¼ teaspoon mace

¼ teaspoon ground ginger

½ teaspoon salt

1½ cups plus 1 to 2 tablespoons unsalted butter, at room temperature

2 cups granulated sugar

3 eggs

3½ cups chopped unpeeled apples, cores and seeds removed

3½ cups chopped toasted pecans

1 cup raisins, allowed to plump for 20 minutes or longer in just enough bourbon to cover them

Caramel Sauce (recipe follows)

Pecan Ice Cream (recipe follows)

Heat the oven to 325° F. Sift the flour with the baking soda, nutmeg, cinnamon, clove, mace, ginger, and salt. Set this mixture aside.

In an electric mixer, beat 1½ cups of the butter with the sugar at medium speed until light and fluffy, about 5 minutes. Add the eggs, one at a time, beating well after each addition. Gradually fold in the reserved flour mixture and combine thoroughly. Add the apples, pecans, and the raisins (drain them first) and stir the batter gently with a spatula.

Pour the batter into a 10-inch springform pan, greased with the remaining butter and lightly floured. Bake the cake for 1½ to 2 hours, until a clean knife inserted near the middle of the cake comes out quite dry.

Serve with Caramel Sauce and Pecan Ice Cream ✖ *Serves 16*

Caramel Sauce

⅓ cup granulated sugar
1 cup light brown sugar
¼ cup pure maple syrup
¼ cup dark corn syrup
1 cup heavy cream

Combine all of the ingredients for the sauce in a heavy-bottomed saucepan. Cook over high heat until the mixture reaches 220° F. on a candy thermometer. Remove the sauce from the heat.

Let the Caramel Sauce cool for about 20 minutes. Skim the surface of the sauce, if necessary, and drizzle over the Apple-Raisin Spice Cake.

Pecan Ice Cream

2 cups milk
1 cup chopped toasted pecans
1 vanilla bean, split in half lengthwise
⅔ cup granulated sugar
6 egg yolks
¾ cup cold heavy cream or crème fraîche

Combine the milk, pecans, and vanilla bean in a medium saucepan. Bring the milk to a boil over medium-high heat, then immediately remove the saucepan from the heat. Cover the saucepan and let the mixture infuse for 15 minutes.

Whisk the sugar into the egg yolks. Continue to whisk vigorously until the mixture becomes quite light in color. Bring the milk infusion back to a boil and slowly pour it through a strainer into the yolk mixture, stirring the yolks constantly. Discard the pecans and the vanilla bean.

Pour the milk–egg yolk mixture back into the saucepan and cook it over low heat, stirring constantly (a spatula is ideal for making sure that you scrape all around the sides and bottom of the saucepan). Cook the mixture until it has thickened

considerably and registers 185° F. on a candy thermometer. Immediately remove the mixture from the heat and place it over ice. Stir in the cream and let the mixture chill thoroughly.

Proceed to make the ice cream in an ice cream maker according to the manufacturer's directions. ✖ *Makes 1 quart*

LESLEE REIS *had an American restaurant in addition to her thriving French one. This dessert is rather distinctively American.* ✍

Caramelized Apple Spice Cake

1¼ cups granulated sugar

⅓ cup water

1 tart apple (about 10 ounces), peeled, cored, and cut into a medium dice

Juice of half a lemon

2 tablespoons Calvados or brandy

2 egg yolks

2 tablespoons melted butter

¼ cup milk

½ teaspoon vanilla extract

1 cup all-purpose flour

2 teaspoons baking powder

⅛ teaspoon ground ginger

⅛ teaspoon nutmeg

⅛ teaspoon cinnamon

¼ teaspoon salt

Preheat oven to 350° F. Grease four 3½-inch ramekins either with nonstick spray or a little butter and reserve.

Place ¾ cup sugar and water in a small saucepan and bring to a boil over moderate heat without stirring. Reduce heat to low and simmer, uncovered, for about 10 minutes until syrup just starts to turn caramel color. Remove from heat and pour a little into each greased ramekin. Working quickly, tilt the ramekins around to coat the base and sides with the caramel, then pour out any excess caramel. Reserve ramekins.

In a small bowl toss the apple with lemon juice and Calvados and set aside.

Place egg yolks and remaining sugar in a mixing bowl and beat together until sugar has disolved and mixture has thickened slightly. Stir in melted butter, milk, and vanilla. Combine dry ingredients together and gently stir into egg mixture along with chopped apple. Divide batter among ramekins and place on a baking sheet and bake for 20 to 25 minutes, or until a cake tester inserted into the center comes out clean.

Remove from oven and, while still hot, turn out spice cakes onto cooling rack and scrape out any caramel that might have stuck to the ramekins. Allow to cool for about 5 minutes.

Serve warm, with equal parts heavy cream and crème fraîche whipped together with a little sugar, if desired. ✖ *Serves 4*

Apple and Walnut Dumplings

3 tablespoons unsalted butter

2 tablespoons golden raisins

4 tablespoons brown sugar

1 teaspoon freshly ground nutmeg

1 teaspoon ground cinnamon

3 tablespoons coarsely chopped walnuts

Biscuit Dough (recipe follows)

2 red apples, peeled, cored, and halved

1 egg yolk mixed with 2 tablespoons cold water,
    for egg wash

1 tablespoon unsalted butter, for the baking sheet

Combine butter, raisins, sugar, nutmeg, cinnamon, and walnuts in a small bowl. Mix well to a paste. Roll Biscuit Dough out to a thickness of ¼ inch. Cut dough into four 4-inch squares.

Preheat the oven to 375° F:

Fill each cored apple half with some of the walnut paste. Arrange an apple half, core side up, on each square of dough. Brush the inside edges of the dough with the egg wash. Bring the corners of each square of dough up over the apples and fold them together to make a sealed package. Brush each apple dumpling with more egg wash and set the dumplings on a lightly buttered baking sheet.

Bake the dumplings for 40 to 45 minutes, until the dough is golden and thoroughly cooked. Serve with ice cream. ✖ *Serves 4*

Biscuit Dough

13 ounces bread flour

1 teaspoon salt

1 teaspoon granulated sugar

1 ounce baking powder

5½ ounces vegetable shortening

1⅓ cups buttermilk

In a medium bowl combine the flour, salt, sugar, and baking powder. Mix well. Add the shortening and stir until the mixture is lumpy. Add the buttermilk and stir to combine well.

Knead the dough briefly (do not over-knead), using a little extra flour if necessary to keep the dough from sticking to the surface of the counter or table. Roll and cut the dough as above for the dumplings.

SHIRLEY SARVIS, *Jim, and I had many good meals in her hometown of San Francisco. Shirley has written innumerable magazine articles—this recipe comes from one in* Bon Appétit—*and many books; but she has become better known in recent years for her interesting classes in restaurants in which she illustrates various pairings of wines with food, some expectable, some extraordinary and delicious.*

I feel quite qualified to think that Jim would have liked this, because it was a takeoff from one of Jim's own recipes. It seemed I could always find, from him, the balance of flavors and the power of flavor, along with the fetching textures, that were satisfying to me. For this recipe, I wanted those qualities plus enough complication to make a true dessert-dessert, one where we (eaters) knew we had encountered a fulsome finish which made no apology for being an old-fashioned American dessert (and sweet enough to have taste).

Lacy Apricot Apple Bette

½ cup plus 2 tablespoons unsalted butter
3 cups fine, soft crumbs from day-old farm-style white bread (1-pound loaf, crusts trimmed) or from French or Italian bread
1 cup granulated sugar
¼ teaspoon ground cinnamon
2 teaspoons grated lemon zest
1½ pounds tart green cooking apples (such as Granny Smith), peeled, cored, and very thinly sliced (generous 1 quart apple slices)
Apricot-Rum Sauce (recipe follows), for serving
1 cup heavy cream softly whipped with 1 tablespoon granulated sugar, 1 teaspoon dark Jamaican rum, and ¾ teaspoon vanilla extract, for serving

Preheat the oven to 375° F. Grease a 1½-quart soufflé dish with 2 tablespoons of the butter and set it aside.

In a large heavy frying pan, melt the remaining ½ cup of butter over medium heat. Sauté the bread crumbs in the hot butter until they are crisp and a deep golden brown. Set the crumbs aside.

In a medium bowl, mix together the 1 cup sugar with the cinnamon and lemon zest. Sprinkle one third of the bread crumbs in the bottom of the prepared dish. Cover the crumbs with half of the apple slices, and sprinkle the apples with one third of the sugar mixture. Repeat the layers of crumbs, apple slices, and the sugar mixture. Top with the remaining crumbs and finally with the remaining sugar mixture. Bake the dessert until the apples are tender and the topping is well browned, about 45 minutes.

Remove the soufflé dish to a cooling rack and let the dessert cool for 15 to 30 minutes. Serve it while it is still very warm, and pass Apricot-Rum Sauce and whipped cream separately.
✖ *Serves 4 to 6*

Apricot-Rum Sauce

¾ cup apricot jam
2½ teaspoons granulated sugar
2 tablespoons water
1 teaspoon dark Jamaican rum

In a small heavy saucepan, combine the jam, sugar, and water. Simmer over medium heat, stirring occasionally, for 5 minutes.

Strain the mixture through a fine sieve into a serving bowl. When cool, stir in the rum. Serve with Lacy Apricot Apple Bette. ✖ *Makes 1 cup*

Coconut Cake with Rum Buttercream

■■■■■■■■■■■■■■■■■■■■■■■■■■■

3 cups cake flour, sifted before measuring

3 teaspoons baking powder

½ teaspoon salt

¾ cup unsalted butter, at room temperature

1½ cups granulated sugar (½ cup may be light brown sugar)

3 eggs, graded large, separated

2 tablespoons grated orange zest

¾ cup coconut milk, made by steeping 1 cup coconut with 2 cups hot milk and straining

¾ teaspoon vanilla extract

¾ cup freshly grated coconut, or shredded dry coconut reconstituted in ½ cup boiling water

Rum Buttercream (recipe follows)

Sift the cake flour with the baking powder and salt.

Preheat the oven to 350° F. Butter and flour two 9-inch round cake pans.

In an electric mixer, cream the butter until light. Beat in the sugar and beat until light and fluffy. Beat in the egg yolks and orange zest. Add flour in three additions, alternating with the coconut milk and vanilla.

In another clean bowl, beat the egg whites until stiff. Fold egg whites and coconut into batter and divide mixture evenly between the prepared cake pans. Bake until a toothpick inserted in the center is clean, about 30 minutes.

Remove from oven and cool on racks. Frost with Rum Buttercream when cool.

✖ *Serves 10 to 12*

Rum Buttercream
•••••••••••••••••••••••••••••••••••••••

1¼ cups unsalted butter

6 egg yolks

⅔ cup granulated sugar

¼ cup water

2 to 3 tablespoons dark rum

Pinch salt

In an electric mixer, beat butter until creamy. Remove bowl from mixer and set aside.

Combine sugar and water in a small saucepan. Cook, without stirring, to the soft ball stage (236° to 238° F. on a candy thermometer).

In a clean bowl of an electric mixer, beat egg yolks until thick and pale yellow. Gradually add syrup with mixer running and beat until cool. Slowly beat in butter, rum, and salt.

style pie. If your custard gets away from you and curdles slightly, you may want to throw it into a food processor or blender to smooth it out. ✑

Butterscotch Pie

■ ■

4 tablespoons unsalted butter

1¼ cups light brown sugar

3 cups light cream

4 egg yolks

9 tablespoons all-purpose flour

¼ teaspoon salt

1 teaspoon vanilla extract

1 baked 9-inch pie shell

1 cup heavy cream, whipped, for serving, if
    desired

Melt the butter in a 2-quart saucepan over medium-high heat. Add the brown sugar and stir it thoroughly into the butter. Cook the mixture until it darkens and bubbles up. Slowly stir in 2 cups of the cream. Cook the mixture, stirring constantly, until it is hot, but not boiling. Remove from heat.

In a medium bowl, combine the egg yolks, flour, and salt. Beat the mixture until it is smooth. Add the remaining 1 cup cream and stir well. Stirring briskly, add the egg yolk mixture to the hot sugar mixture. Reduce the heat to medium low and cook, stirring constantly, until the mixture boils. Immediately reduce heat to low and cook for 2 minutes longer, stirring constantly.

Pass the butterscotch filling through a strainer into a clean bowl, and stir in the vanilla extract. Let cool to room temperature before pouring into the pie shell. Serve with whipped cream, if desired. ✖ *Makes 1 9-inch pie; makes 2½ cups butterscotch filling*

KARIN MOSER-DUFTNER. *Peter Kump tells us: "This hot cross between a pudding and a soufflé comes from Karin Moser-Duftner, owner of the Boglerhof Hotel in Alpbach, Austria. This village is often cited as the most picturesque in the Tyrol. Beard and Marion Cunningham came to Austria and visited with me at my family's home, which is outside of Innsbruck. I took them to dinner at this hotel's charming restaurant to sample some of the local specialties. The next day, Jim went back to sample more. He became friends with the hotel's owner."* ✍

I will never forget James Beard sitting in the Fuggerstube eating from 11 A.M. to 7 P.M., tasting through the entire menu. He even wrote up one of my recipes in his column.

Black Bread Pudding

4 ounces (about 3 slices) German pumpernickel
½ cup milk
3 large eggs, separated
2 tablespoons granulated sugar
2 ounces (4 tablespoons) butter
1 teaspoon lemon zest
Pinch of cinnamon
4 ounces (about 1 cup) ground almonds
1 teaspoon vanilla
1½ ounces (⅓ cup) confectioner's sugar
□ *For the mold:*
½ tablespoon butter
1 tablespoon sugar

Cut the bread into cubes and soak it in the milk to soften.

Cream the yolks, granulated sugar, and butter together. Add the lemon zest and cinnamon.

Mix the almonds and vanilla with the softened bread to make an almost smooth paste. Add to yolk mixture.

Preheat oven to 325° F. Bring a pot of water to a boil.

Beat the egg whites to the stiff peak stage. Then add the confectioner's sugar, 1 tablespoon at a time, while continuing to beat. Fold egg whites into the bread mixture.

Butter and sugar a 1½-quart soufflé mold. Fill mold with mixture. Place mold in a deep roasting pan and place in oven. Fill pan with boiling water to a point halfway up the soufflé dish. Bake for 45 minutes. Serve warm.

✖ *Serves 6 to 8*

GEORGE LANG, *that essential Hungarian, author of a fine Hungarian cookbook and a plethora of incidental pieces, is well known as a fine violinist, friend of art, collector of rare cookbooks and representations of asparagus, husband of Jennifer, and father, restaurant consultant, and owner of Café des Artistes. He also got caught up with Jim Beard and George's good friend and sometime professional associate Milton Glaser in the projects of Beard, Glaser, Wolf. George was a consultant to* The Cooks' Catalogue, *providing a wealth of information from his years of exposure to restaurant equipment. George wrote a notable soup chapter for* The Great Cooks Cookbook. *In earlier days, when George was working with Restaurant Associates, he got to know Jim at many restaurants.* ✍

AN EVENING WITH SIR JAMES.

Restaurantitis, the illness that affects otherwise relatively normal natives of these United States, has replaced the maladies of yesteryear. For instance, during the '20s, to aspire to become a famous singer was almost as much of an obsession in the United States as it was and still is in Italy. Jim, who apparently had a good voice, was not immune to temptation; as a young man he had a passionate desire to become a singer and studied with Maestro Tano, who had coached Caruso and other famous singers of an earlier time.

Jim and I had quite a few uncorking good times talking about the potato bread my mother baked every Friday and the sautéed chicken with bacon and cream his mother used to make, but the conversation often came back to an argument over the relative merits of Lauri Volpi, Benjamino Gigli, Mario del Monaco, and their ilk. It's more difficult to kill a fantasy than the reality, and I am convinced that, deep down, he was certain that he could have been a great opera star.

One day we were talking about the special drinks and diets of great singers, and he told me that Caruso, who always traveled with his cook, ate macaroni almost every day for his midday meal, but never on a day when he performed. Then, Sir James—as I always called him—took out a virtually unknown little book from his shelf, written by Enrico himself, titled *How to Sing,* and read me the following paragraph: "I incline towards the simpler and more nourishing food though my tastes are broad in the matter, but lay particular stress on the excellence of the cooking, for one cannot afford to risk one's health on indifferently cooked food, no matter what its quality."

Then he looked at me with his pixieish smile and said: "I always wonder what kind of a singer I would have been, but it's comforting to know that Caruso, my dear George, surely could not have replaced me in the kitchen." At that point he was expecting me to agree with the second part of his statement—which I did dutifully so that we could end the evening with a pleasant dinner.

He disliked zip code dining in restaurants where the maître d'hôtel was the best-dressed man in the place, so I took him to a—by now defunct—little Hungarian restaurant on East 79th Street called Debrecen. Aficionados visited this garden restaurant to be insulted by Uncle Simon, the irascible waiter-in-residence, to drink coffee that was so weak (and mixed with chicory) that it wasn't habit forming, and to eat the delicious Friar's Ears, a kind of jam-filled flat dumpling that I grew up on and that always reminded me that if a food is worth eating, it's worth overeating. (The name, by the way, comes from the shape, and from the fact that friars couldn't eat meat on Fridays—this was a satisfying meatless main course, as well as dessert.)

Friar's Ears

■■■■■■■■■■■■■■■■■■■■■■■■■■■■

1½ pounds all-purpose potatoes, scrubbed clean
½ teaspoon salt
1 cup all-purpose flour
½ cup apricot jam
12 tablespoons unsalted butter
2 cups fresh bread crumbs
1 cup vanilla sugar (see Note)

Place potatoes and enough cold water to cover in a large pot. Bring to a boil over high heat and cook until tender enough for a fork to pierce them easily. Drain the potatoes and peel them when cool enough to handle. Put through a food mill or potato ricer.

Place riced potatoes into a large mixing bowl and add salt. Slowly work in the flour with your hands until well blended. Knead until dough is smooth.

Roll out dough on a lightly floured surface to a ¼-inch thickness. Cut into 3-inch squares; you will have about 20. Place a generous teaspoon of jam in the center of each square. Press two opposite corners together on either side to make a triangle and pinch edges together firmly to seal. Refrigerate until ready to cook. (Recipe can be made up to 24 hours ahead up to this point.)

Bring a generous amount of salted water to a rolling boil in a large pot. Lower heat so water simmers slowly. Add dough triangles and cook about 2 minutes or until dough is cooked through. Remove with a slotted spoon to a large platter.

Heat butter over high heat in a large skillet. Add bread crumbs to the hot fat and cook until golden brown. Remove skillet from heat and put triangles into the crumbs. Mix carefully, just enough to coat them. They will never have a breaded texture, so don't worry if the breadcrumbs stick to only some parts of the dumplings, leaving bald spots here and there. Sprinkle liberally with vanilla sugar and serve immediately.

Note: Vanilla sugar is granulated sugar that has had a split vanilla bean buried in it to give it subtle vanilla flavor. ✗ *Makes 20 dumplings*

CLAUDIA RODEN *is a fine British writer, primarily on Middle Eastern food, of whom Jim made a firm friend as he did so many others—especially of Judith Jones's authors. Jim did make countless cocktail sandwiches before the war and discusses them in* Hors d'Oeuvre and Canapés. *Whether he also made them in London I do not know; but anything is possible when it comes to Jim.* ✍

I first met Jim almost twenty years ago in London when he invited me to tea at the Savoy. He said I looked much smaller than he expected and I said he was much bigger than I thought. He had just come out of a diet and chuckled, "We have to pay for our pleasures!" We had sandwiches and he explained how they made the cucumber filling—slicing the cucumber paper thin, sprinkling with salt and letting the juices drain, then moistening with cream and adding chopped chives. He told me he had spent some time in London before the war, learning to sing, and had paid his way by making sandwiches.

He offered to do my publication party for Judith Jones when Knopf brought out my *Book of Middle Eastern Food.* The party in his house was magical for me and it went on till the early hours of the morning with an endless supply of magnificent food. Jim had arranged for Middle Eastern delicacies to be prepared by a Lebanese friend, a garage owner who adored cooking. It was a warm night and the guests spilled out into the garden where the fountain gave an Oriental air. I had dinner with Jim and Judith and Evan Jones every time I went to New York. In every restaurant, people would call out "Hi, Jim!" and the chefs would come out to pay their respects. His incredible warmth, his kindness, his mischievous sense of fun, and his joy of living made it such an extraordinary pleasure and such a privilege to be with him.

Almond and Pine Nut Pastry

6 eggs
1 pound ground almonds
1 pound superfine sugar
7 fluid ounces milk
5 drops vanilla
2 ounces pine nuts
5 fluid ounces apricot jam to glaze, optional

Preheat oven to 350° F.

Combine eggs, almonds, sugar, milk, and vanilla in a large mixing bowl.

Line a large shallow baking tin or pie dish with foil. Butter the foil and pour in the mixture. Sprinkle pine nuts on top and bake for 1¼ to 1½ hours, or until the top is brown and the pastry feels firm. While it is still warm, melt the jam with a little water and brush it over the top, if desired.
✗ *Serves 10 to 12*

MARION CUNNINGHAM *had a unique place in Jim's life and affections. She is a tall, handsome woman whose life was transfigured by Jim's belief in her as a cook and baker. She started by going to class, continued by assisting in class, and went on to revise* The Fannie Farmer Cookbook—*at his suggestion—and to develop into a distinctive authority in her own right with excellent books, articles, and classes. She has also done work as a restaurant consultant.*

I first met Marion well into her relationship with Jim. I was an upstart. She had been assisting him with classes and there I suddenly was in San Francisco as another aide. She knew many of the dramatis personae of Jim's California world; I didn't. She made me feel welcome and continued to work to make each class a success.

As with many of us, the price we paid, more or less willingly, for his unconditional support was an unconditional caretaking. Marion met Jim at airports, rose at five in the morning to get into town in time to be of help and to tend Jim's battered legs when necessary, shopped, and wrote notes. Most of all she was a loving, caring, devoted friend who never forgot the debt of student to teacher that so many learn to ignore.

Sometimes Jim's demands—even thought they were expressions of faith—were hard to meet. There was the class in which James decided that Marion should cook the already somewhat tricky tomato bread that was on the schedule on the floor of the large baking cavities of Fournou's Ovens, the restaurant at the Stanford Court where we taught. She finally triumphed to James's cry of "Splendid!" but it was hardly easy. The grace and warmth with which she did these things is evident in her memoir of Jim and in her impeccable recipes with their clearly American tradition. ✍

Among my most pleasant memories of James Beard is the memory of watching him cook.

James cooked quietly, with so little motion that it seemed a miracle to have such good food from so little effort.

One evening he decided to make a pasta dish with a spicy Mexican sauce. He sat in his tall director's chair at the counter and chopped the tomatoes, garlic, onion, and chilies. As rhythmic as rocking in a chair, the knife went up and down, back and forth. He went to the stove and poured a little oil into a sauté pan; meanwhile, the water in a kettle was boiling and he salted it. Into the sauté pan went the garlic mixture; he stirred it once or twice, seasoned it, and returned to his chair. From that minute on, it was as though he could hear the water boil and see the cooking process in his mind. At the moment of doneness, like magic, he directed or did the final finishing of the dish.

Desserts

He often asked all of us bustling helpers why we stirred so much and so often.

Recently, twelve of us who had been James's students from his first cooking classes in Seaside, Oregon, in 1972 had a reunion. I again realized that James Beard had given us all much more than cooking classes.

Whole Wheat Sponge Roll

■■■■■■■■■■■■■■■■■■■■■■■■■■■

¼ cup whole wheat flour
¼ cup cake flour
½ teaspoon baking powder
½ teaspoon salt
5 eggs
½ cup granulated sugar
1 teaspoon vanilla extract, optional
¾ cup heavy cream
¼ cup confectioner's sugar
½ pint strawberries, washed, hulled, and roughly chopped
Confectioner's sugar to sprinkle over top of roll

Adjust rack to the middle of the oven and preheat to 350° F.

Lightly grease a 15½″ × 10½″ jelly roll pan and line with wax paper.

Combine whole wheat flour, cake flour, baking powder, and salt in a mixing bowl. Combine eggs and sugar in a large mixing bowl or the large bowl of an electric mixer. Beat by hand or with an electric mixer for about 4 minutes, until eggs thicken and become light in color. Sprinkle the dry ingredients and the vanilla, if using, over the egg mixture and gently fold together until completely incorporated.

Pour batter into prepared pan and spread with a spatula to make an even layer. Bake for 12 to 15 minutes or until the top of the cake is golden brown. Remove from the oven and allow to stand for about 2 minutes.

Meanwhile, spread a clean kitchen towel on a flat surface and sprinkle with confectioner's sugar. Invert the cake onto the towel. Remove the pan and peel off the paper. With the towel, roll up the sponge starting from the long side and with the wide side up. Leave the cake rolled until ready to fill. It may be kept like this at room temperature for 12 hours.

For the filling, whip the cream and confectioner's sugar until stiff; fold in the chopped strawberries. Unroll the sponge. Spread the filling over the inside of the sponge, leaving about ½ inch all around. Reroll the sponge and place on a serving platter. Sprinkle with confectioner's sugar, slice, and serve. ✖ *Makes a 15-inch sponge roll*

Angel Food Cake with White Mountain Frosting

1 cup cake flour
1½ cups granulated sugar
About 2 cups egg whites (12 to 13 large eggs)
1½ teaspoons cream of tartar
1 teaspoon vanilla extract
½ teaspoon almond extract, optional
¼ teaspoon salt
White Mountain Frosting (recipe follows)

Preheat oven to 350° F. Wash and dry a 10-inch tube pan, making sure it is scrupulously clean.

Sift the cake flour and ¾ cup of the sugar three times. Reserve.

Using an electric mixer with a whisk attachment, beat the egg whites for a few seconds or until foamy. Add the cream of tartar, vanilla, almond extract, if using, and salt. Beat just to blend, then turn speed up to high and slowly add the remaining ¾ cup sugar. Beat until all the sugar is added and the whites are softly stiff and shiny.

Turn the mixer off. Sprinkle the reserved flour mixture over the whites and beat on the lowest setting to fold the flour into the whites. Remove the bowl from the mixer and stir gently with a hand whisk to finish blending.

Spoon the batter into the pan. Draw a rubber spatula through the batter in toward the center, holding it upright and touching the bottom of the pan. Bake for about 50 minutes or until a straw comes out clean when inserted in the center. Remove from oven and immediately invert the pan on a bottle. Cool the cake completely upside down. Remove from pan. Frost with White Mountain Frosting (recipe follows).

✗ *Serves 8 to 10*

This frosting must be used while warm; it is unspreadable when cool.

White Mountain Frosting

1½ cups granulated sugar
½ cup water
¼ teaspoon cream of tartar
¼ teaspoon salt
3 egg whites (about ½ cup)
1½ teaspoons vanilla extract

Combine sugar, water, cream of tartar, and salt in a saucepan and set over high heat, gently swirling to mix ingredients. Let boil, swirling occasionally, until mixture is perfectly clear, about 4 minutes. Cover with a lid and cook for 1 minute. Uncover and test syrup—it should read 240° F. on a candy thermometer.

Meanwhile, start beating egg whites in an electric mixer. Beat until stiff peaks form. When the syrup is ready, add to the egg whites, beating continuously at medium-high speed until slightly cooled and of a spreading consistency. Stir in vanilla and use immediately.

called Haute Cuisine, where she also does demonstrations and food styling. If this light and inventive version of a fruit cake is a sample of her work, she must be a roaring success. ✍

S oak the fruit the night before you want to make your cake. That way, you will have plump and juicy chunks of fruit. This tea cake is delicious sliced and spread with soft butter. It is most easily sliced if baked ahead, and it freezes beautifully.

Dolores Snyder's Tea Cake

1 pound mixed dried fruit, such as currants, candied orange peel, and golden raisins
1 cup dark brown sugar
1¼ cups cold strong tea (Earl Grey is especially nice)
1 to 2 tablespoons unsalted butter, for the pan
2 cups plus 2 tablespoons all-purpose flour
1 egg
1 tablespoon orange marmalade
2½ teaspoons baking powder
1 teaspoon ground allspice

In a large mixing bowl, toss the fruit with the sugar. Pour the tea over the fruit and stir well. Cover the bowl tightly with plastic wrap. Let the fruit macerate at room temperature overnight.

Preheat the oven to 350° F. Butter a 9″ × 5″ loaf pan or a 7-inch deep round cake pan. Line the bottom of the pan with buttered parchment paper, and dust the sides and bottom of the pan with 2 tablespoons of the flour. Tap out any excess flour.

In a small bowl, beat the egg with the marmalade. Stir this into the fruit mixture. Sift the remaining 2 cups of flour with the baking powder and allspice over the fruit mixture and stir until the mixture is just blended. Pour the batter into the prepared pan. Bake the cake for 1½ to 1¾ hours, until a toothpick inserted into the center of the cake comes out clean. If the cake has browned deeply after an hour of cooking, cover the top loosely with aluminum foil.

Remove the pan to a cooling rack. After 10 minutes, turn the cake carefully out of the pan. Peel the parchment paper from the bottom of the loaf, and let the cake cool thoroughly before serving or wrapping it. ✂ *Serves 20*

This cake puffs nicely while baking, then sinks and cracks while cooling. Serve it plain as a tea cake or dress it up with raspberries and heavy cream whipped to soft peaks.

Chocolate Nut Loaf Cake
■■■■■■■■■■■■■■■■■■■■■■■■■■■■■■

1 tablespoon unsalted butter, for the baking pan
2 tablespoons all-purpose flour, for the baking pan
1 cup (6 ounces) toasted blanched almonds
5 ounces semisweet chocolate, cut into small pieces
¼ cup fresh orange juice, at room temperature
5 large eggs, at room temperature, separated
¾ cup granulated sugar

Position the oven rack in the lower third of the oven. Preheat the oven to 350° F. Butter and flour a 10″ × 4″ loaf pan, and set it aside.

Grind the almonds to the consistency of cornmeal, being careful not to grind them into almond paste; you will have about 1¾ cups of ground almonds. Reserve the almonds.

Put the chocolate in a medium bowl set over a pan of hot water. Add the orange juice to the chocolate and let sit for at least a minute, stirring occasionally, until the chocolate has melted and the mixture is smooth and well blended. If the water bath cools, replace the water with hot tap water. Set this mixture aside.

Beat the egg yolks in a deep 2-quart mixing bowl, gradually adding ½ cup plus 2 tablespoons of the sugar as you beat. Continue beating until the mixture is thick and pale yellow. Fold in the reserved almonds and chocolate mixture.

In a clean large bowl, beat the egg whites until they begin to foam. Sprinkle 1 teaspoon of the remaining sugar over the egg whites and beat them to soft peaks. Continue beating, adding the remaining sugar in a steady stream, until the egg whites are stiff and shiny, but not dry.

Fold half of the egg whites into the chocolate mixture thoroughly, to lighten it. Gently fold in the remaining egg whites. Pour the batter into the prepared pan. Bake for 45 minutes, or until the cake springs back when lightly pressed in the middle. Let the cake cool in its pan on a rack for 30 minutes. Unmold it carefully and let it cool completely.

Thinly slice the cake with a serrated knife.
✖ *Makes 1 10″ × 4″ loaf*

ELAINE SHERMAN *met Jim when she took a San Francisco class. At that time she had a cookware shop and cooking school in the Chicago area. With warmth and persistence, she got Jim to come and teach and Marion Cunningham to assist him. Elaine arranged, as she has for so many, that Jim meet the entire food world of Chicago.*

She was born to be a loyal friend, a superb organizer, and has an excellent palate. She has contributed to the Foundation some excellent photographs she had taken of Jim. ✍

It wasn't just studying with him or listening to him, fixing a luncheon for him at my home, or having him teach at my cooking school; it was his presence, his guidance, and his encouragement that made James Beard such a special person. To know James was to love him. His simple, direct approach to life was reflected in his approach to food. James loved flavors—deep, pure flavors. I will never forget the time, when at James's urging, I added a half a teaspoon of cinnamon to a vegetable soup I was preparing. It made all the difference in the world.

James was a great storyteller. His reminiscences about food were a delight to the ear. To sit at his feet and listen to his stories was an experience of a lifetime.

His thoughts and feelings about food shall be with me forever. His friendship was very special. As a teacher there was none better. He taught me well. His picture hangs above my desk ... I will never forget him!

I give you a recipe for a Chocolate Bundt Cake that James would have loved. It is a simple recipe using basic techniques. The cake is full of deep, dark chocolate flavor. It is a moist cake and has plenty of staying power. James would have loved it.

Chocolate Bundt Cake

1 cup Dutch process cocoa
2 cups all-purpose unbleached flour
½ teaspoon baking powder
½ teaspoon salt
3 tablespoons instant coffee powder
1½ cups unsalted butter, at room temperature
3 cups granulated sugar
2 teaspoons vanilla extract
5 large eggs
1 cup buttermilk
Chocolate Glaze (recipe follows)

Preheat oven to 325° F. Butter and flour a 10-inch Bundt pan (or 3-cup ring mold). Set aside.

Sift together cocoa, flour, baking powder, salt, and coffee powder into a bowl.

Cream butter in a large bowl with an electric mixer until light and fluffy. Add sugar and beat on high speed for about 5 minutes, until dissolved. With mixer on medium speed add vanilla and eggs, one at a time, beating well after each addition.

Add dry ingredients alternately with buttermilk, beginning and ending with dry ingredients. Pour batter into prepared pan. Bake for about 1½ hours, or until a toothpick inserted in the center comes out clean.

Remove cake from oven and allow to cool on a rack for 20 minutes. Turn cake out of pan onto rack to cool completely. Place cake on serving plate and spread cool glaze over. Do not refrigerate cake. ✘ *Serves 12 to 16*

Chocolate Glaze

¼ cup light corn syrup
3 tablespoons water
2 tablespoons unsalted butter
8 ounces bittersweet chocolate, coarsely chopped

Place corn syrup, water, and butter in a small pan and bring to a boil over high heat.

Remove from heat and add chocolate. Whisk together until mixture is shiny and cool. Cover cake as directed.

SIMONE (SIMCA) BECK *was one of the trinity with Julia*
Child who remade America's French cooking. She has continued to write on her own and to teach as well.
She certainly can provide us with the richest of French chocolate cakes as a celebration, or maybe she is still
listening to James's advice about the American public. ✍

I didn't meet Jim until after *Mastering* came out in 1962. Immediately I had a real closeness with him, a real warmth. He had spent a lot of time in France and knew the basis of French cooking. When he started teaching and writing in the '40's, American cooking was unsophisticated. He changed that, he started the revolution.

In New York, I didn't have time to get to know him. He always had lots of friends around and was always getting telephone calls. He'd say to me "Come along!" but there was never any time alone. I got to really know him only here in France. Here, he was alone. We could chat and I got to know him. He came to Bramafam [where her house is in Provence] three times for a week or longer; the last time was in 1981. We were good, good friends; but of course he was not my teacher. For me, he was easily the number one American. He had the best palate of any one I knew in America, without a doubt. He was very honest, very direct. If he didn't know something, he didn't pretend.

When we were together, we would talk more about the taste of the American people. "Americans like more sweets than French people," he told me. He gave me a lot of confidence in my own writing for Americans. When I was writing *Simca's Cuisine,* the first thing he told me was "make a lot of sweet desserts, don't make too many classic dishes; the classic dishes are a bit boring." So I made things that weren't so classic.

I never knew anyone I liked more. He was really exceptional. He was a generous man, happy to be alive, never complaining; he laughed very easily. He was looking at things; he spoke with his eyes as well as his tongue. His eyes would sparkle.

When we ate together he didn't want a lot, just a little that was very good—good quality, good flavor—it wasn't the quantity for him. He loved Provence, he liked the scenery, the light, the trees, the hills. He often talked about St. Rémy. He liked the simple tastes, he seemed more interested in seeing women cook, cook the cuisines of Provence, rather than the professional chefs.

Le Chocolat en Fête à la Framboise

■■■■■■■■■■■■■■■■■■■■■■■■■■

(Chocolate Feast Cake with Raspberries)

5 ½-pint containers fresh rasberries (about
    2½ pounds)
4 envelopes powdered gelatin
2½ cups cold water
1 cup granulated sugar
14 ounces good-quality unsweetened chocolate
2 cups heavy cream
Confectioner's sugar

Line a 9″ × 3″ cake pan with plastic wrap and reserve.

Purée 4 containers of rasberries in a food mill fitted with fine disk. Remove ½ cup purée to a small bowl, stir in gelatin and set aside.

In a small pan bring 2 cups water and sugar to a boil. Allow to boil over moderate heat for about 15 minutes or until syrup has reached the soft ball stage and the bubbles are large. Stir in raspberry purée and simmer for 2 minutes. Remove from heat.

In a medium saucepan melt chocolate with ½ cup water over low heat, stirring until completely smooth. Add rasberry mixture, stirring until very smooth. Stir about ½ cup mixture into softened gelatin and whisk back into chocolate and raspberry mixture. Let stand until cool but not set, stirring occasionally.

When chocolate mixture is cool, whip cream to soft peaks. Fold into the chocolate mixture until completely blended. Pour into lined pan and cover top with another piece of plastic.

Refrigerate for at least 3 hours or overnight, until completely set. When ready to serve, unmold cake onto serving plate. Peel off plastic and garnish with remaining raspberries. Sprinkle with confectioner's sugar just before serving. ✗ *Serves 12 to 16*

Marquise au Chocolat avec Meringue et Chantilly

■■■■■■■■■■■■■■■■■■■■■■■■

10 ounces good-quality semisweet chocolate, in small pieces
¼ cup strong coffee
4 eggs, separated
6 ounces unsalted butter, cut in small pieces
Pinch salt
¼ cup plus 1 teaspoon cold water
4 ounces sugar cubes
1 cup heavy cream
½ teaspoon vanilla extract
2 tablespoons confectioner's sugar, optional

Combine chocolate and coffee in heavy-bottomed saucepan and place over low heat. Cook until chocolate is melted, stirring constantly.

Add the egg yolks to the melted chocolate, one at a time, stirring to incorporate each before adding the next. Return pan to very low heat and cook, stirring constantly, until mixture thickens. Do not allow it to boil. Remove from heat and add butter, stirring until fully melted. Transfer to a bowl to cool and set aside.

Place egg whites in a large bowl, preferably copper. Add a pinch of salt and 1 teaspoon water. Beat until white and frothy and set aside.

Combine sugar cubes and ¼ cup water in a small heavy pan and place over moderate heat. Allow sugar to dissolve completely and bring to a boil. Continue to boil until syrup reaches 220° to 225° F. on a candy thermometer (the "thread stage"). Remove from heat. While beating egg whites vigorously, pour in the syrup in a steady stream. Continue to beat until meringue is firm and shiny.

With a large metal spoon fold the chocolate mixture into the meringue. When completely combined, pour into a stainless steel mixing bowl.

Cover with plastic wrap and place in freezer for about 6 hours or overnight.

About 10 minutes before unmolding, place cream, vanilla, and confectioner's sugar (if using) in a mixing bowl set over a larger bowl of ice. Beat until stiff. Transfer to a piping bag fitted with a large star tip.

To unmold the Marquise, set the bowl over a larger bowl of very hot water for about 45 seconds. Remove and wipe off excess water with a cloth. If necessary, run a spatula around the inside edge to loosen the sides. Invert out onto serving plate. Pipe the chantilly cream decoratively over the Marquise. Serve immediately or return to the refrigerator until ready to serve.

✘ *Serves 8 to 10*

Chocolate Sherry Cream Bars

▪▪▪▪▪▪▪▪▪▪▪▪▪▪▪▪▪▪▪▪▪▪▪▪▪▪

☐ *For the base*

2 ounces unsweetened chocolate

½ cup unsalted butter

2 eggs

1 cup granulated sugar

½ teaspoon vanilla extract

½ cup all-purpose flour

¼ teaspoon salt

☐ *For the filling*

2 cups confectioner's sugar

4 tablespoons unsalted butter, at room
    temperature

2 tablespoons heavy cream

2 tablespoons dry sherry

½ cup chopped walnuts or pecans

☐ *For the topping*

½ cup (3 ounces) semisweet chocolate chips

2 tablespoons water

2 tablespoons unsalted butter

Preheat the oven to 325° F. Grease and lightly flour an 8-inch square baking pan.

Place chocolate and butter in a small pan and melt over low heat, stirring. Remove from heat and allow to cool slightly.

Place eggs in a large bowl and mix lightly. Add sugar and whisk until mixture becomes pale yellow and thick. Stir in melted chocolate, vanilla, flour, and salt and mix well to combine.

Scrape batter into prepared pan. Bake in the center of oven for 25 to 30 minutes, or until a cake tester inserted into the center comes out clean. Remove from oven and allow to cool on a wire rack. When cool, turn out onto a large plate and reserve.

Make the filling while the base is cooling. Place confectioner's sugar and butter in a bowl and beat together until creamy. Add cream and sherry and beat until light and fluffy. Stir in chopped

nuts. Spread over cooled chocolate base and chill in refrigerator.

Place all ingredients for the topping in a small saucepan and melt over low heat, stirring until melted. Spread evenly over the filling and chill to harden chocolate.

Trim the edges and cut into bars. If desired, they can be decorated with candied violets, rose petals, mimosas, or cinnamon red hots according to the season.

✖ *Makes about 32 bars (about 1" × 2")*

NICK MALGIERI *is a consummate baker who has written many articles and an excellent book. He has also taught for Peter Kump and worked for Joe Baum at Windows on the World—or should we say he worked as so many in the James Beard world, but with his own talents.*

Jim would have loved the candied violets, a childhood treat to him. ✍

I first met James Beard through Richard Olney in November 1974. At that time I had just returned from working in Switzerland and France and Mr. Beard offered to find me an interesting job making desserts in New York. He asked me to submit a list of the desserts I could prepare, then I made up some samples and brought them over in early December 1974. After lamenting the fact that his diet would prevent him from tasting any of the desserts, Mr. Beard asked to see them. He had a small taste of each, then decided that he would like to keep another small piece for his dessert at dinner later on. Between the tasting and saving, there was very little left! Throughout the course of the next few years, he encouraged me to continue pursuing a career as a pastry chef, and I owe a great deal to his kindness and support.

This elegant cake is chewy and creamy. Serve it with whipped cream, if you must. Chestnut desserts are especially appropriate to the holiday season. The chestnut buttercream combines well with the chocolate in a result neither too rich nor too sweet.

Chocolate Chestnut Cake
■■■■■■■■■■■■■■■■■■■■■■■

1 to 2 tablespoons plus ¾ pound unsalted butter
4 eggs
Pinch of salt
⅔ cup plus 4 tablespoons granulated sugar
⅓ cup cake flour
⅓ cup cornstarch
3 tablespoons cocoa powder
2 pinches of baking soda
4 ounces semisweet chocolate, broken into small pieces
½ cup heavy cream
1½ cups Crème de Marrons
7 tablespoons kirsch
½ cup water
1 teaspoon vanilla extract
Chocolate shavings for garnish
Crystallized violets for garnish

Preheat the oven to 350° F. Using 1 to 2 tablespoons of the butter, grease the sides and bottom of a 9- or 10-inch springform pan. Line the bottom of the pan with lightly buttered waxed or parchment paper.

In the bowl of an electric mixer, whisk together the eggs, salt, and ⅔ cup of the sugar. Place the bowl over a pan of simmering water and whisk until the mixture is lukewarm. Set the bowl in the base of the mixer and beat the mixture until it is cool and has tripled in volume. Sift together the cake flour, cornstarch, cocoa powder, and baking soda and add this gradually to the beaten egg mixture, folding it in gently. Pour the batter into the prepared pan and bake for 50 to 60 minutes, until the cake springs back when lightly pressed in the middle. Unmold the cake and let it cool on a rack.

Place the chocolate in a small bowl. In a small heavy saucepan, warm the cream over medium heat to boiling. Pour the hot cream over the chocolate. Let the mixture stand for a minute, then whisk until it is smooth. Strain it into a clean bowl and let this glaze cool to room temperature.

In a medium bowl, beat ¾ pound of the butter until it is soft and light. Beat in the Crème de Marrons and continue beating until the mixture is very smooth. Gradually beat in 3 tablespoons of the kirsch. Set this buttercream aside.

In a small heavy saucepan, combine the water with 4 tablespoons of the sugar over medium-high heat. Bring the mixture to a boil, then remove from the heat. Let this syrup cool, then stir in 4 tablespoons of the kirsch and the vanilla extract.

Slice the cooled cake horizontally into 3 layers. Place the bottom layer on a serving plate and moisten it with one third of the syrup. Spread the layer with one quarter of the reserved buttercream, and top with the second cake layer. Repeat the layers, then frost the sides of the assembled cake with most of the remaining buttercream, reserving some for decoration. Spread the cooled chocolate glaze on the top of the cake. Press chocolate shavings into the buttercream around the sides of the cake, and pipe the remaining buttercream through a pastry bag fitted with a star tip to decorate the top. Decorate the border with crystallized violets.

Jim was the honored guest at a small sit-down supper in my home perhaps fifteen years ago. I was then filled with the pleasures of the cuisine of Portugal, so the menu bore that motif, albeit in my interpretation and rendering. Jim ate with energy all through the supper, and gave his particular—and gratifying—approval to the almond dessert.

Don't overbake this cake. It must be moist to have its distinction. It is likely to settle as it cools or as you cut it; don't be alarmed. The crackled crisp top against the moist sturdier base is as it should be. Cover the cake and refrigerate it after baking, if you wish; with chilling, the cake is more confection-like and easier to slice.

Almond Torta

1 to 2 tablespoons unsalted butter, for the pan
6 eggs, separated (2 egg whites reserved for
    another use)
1¾ cups granulated sugar
1½ teaspoons almond extract
⅛ teaspoon vanilla extract
¼ teaspoon cream of tartar
2 cups blanched almonds (8 ounces), ground
2 cups heavy cream, softly whipped, for serving
Ground cinnamon, for serving
Amber Candy Shatters (recipe follows), for serving

Position an oven rack in the lower third of the oven. Preheat the oven to 400° F. Lightly butter a 10-inch springform pan.

In a large bowl, beat the egg yolks until they are light. Add 1 cup of the sugar and continue beating until the mixture is thick and lemon-colored. Add the almond and vanilla extracts and blend well. Set this mixture aside.

In the large bowl of an electric mixer, beat the 4 egg whites with the cream of tartar until soft peaks form. Continue beating, adding the remaining ¾ cup of sugar about 2 tablespoons at a time. Beat until the sugar has dissolved and the egg whites are stiff.

Gently fold the egg yolk mixture and the almonds into the egg whites. Do not overmix. Turn the batter into the prepared pan and smooth the surface. Bake the cake at 400° F. for 10 minutes, then reduce the temperature to 300° F. and bake for 40 minutes longer, just until the cake is barely set.

Remove the pan to a cooling rack; let the cake cool completely in its pan. (You may tightly cover the cooled cake, still in its pan, and keep it in the refrigerator until serving.) Remove the cake to a platter. Slice the cake into wedges and top each piece generously with whipped cream, a light dusting of ground cinnamon, and a sprinkling of Amber Candy Shatters. ✖ *Serves 10 to 12*

Amber Candy Shatters

2 tablespoons unsalted butter
1 cup granulated sugar

Butter a large shallow pan. Set it aside.

In a heavy frying pan, melt the sugar over medium heat, stirring constantly. When all of the sugar has melted and the syrup is deep amber, pour it into the prepared pan. Set the pan aside and wait for the candy to harden.

When the candy is perfectly cool and hard, break it into pieces. Smash the pieces with a mallet or a rolling pin.

PAULA WOLFERT *is one of our foremost food writers in magazines and newspapers and, more importantly, in a series of authoritative cookbooks that started with* Couscous and Other Good Foods from Morocco, *went on through* The Cooking of South-West France, *and whose most recent addition has been* Paula Wolfert's World of Food, *from which she has given us this charming anecdote and recipe.*

In the anecdote, one sees Jim's characteristic way of thrusting heavy challenges at people he thought had talent. Later he similarly pushed Paula to work at Chillingsworth as a chef. She always rose to the challenge, just as she made the recipes she worked with her own. ✍

Very early in my career, I went to see James Beard. I had served a year's apprenticeship under Dione Lucas and was looking for a job. Mr. Beard asked me to cook for him. I did, and apparently he was satisfied, for shortly thereafter he kindly recommended me as caterer for a luncheon that Mrs. Joshua Logan was giving for 150 people in her Connecticut home. I was a little scared; I'd never cooked for so many people before. But Beard calmed my fears: "Don't worry. Call her up, discuss the menu, then just follow your recipes."

I phoned Mrs. Logan, and she asked for a lunch of Quiche Lorraine, Boeuf Bourguignon, Fish in Aspic, and for dessert "a delicious cake"—a rather extraordinary menu, it seems to me now, especially for a lunch in May. In any case, I studied the menu carefully and assured myself I could bring it off. I did remain a little worried about the cake, as desserts were not my strong point, so I went back to Beard for advice. He gave me this recipe for a walnut roll. "It's easy," he said, "and it always works. You can triple it, quadruple it, multiply it as many times as you like. It will freeze. It will keep for days. It's delicious." I took his advice and made fifteen rolls for the party.

When I got off the train at Stamford station, with my walnut rolls, there wasn't anyone there to meet me. I was getting worried when a man with a chauffeur's cap tentatively approached. "Are you Mrs. Wolfert?" he asked, and when I nodded, he shook his head. Apparently he had questioned every mature woman who had gotten off the train and, finally desperate, had come up

to me, though, as he told me, "You seem so young."

At the house, Mrs. Logan took one look at me, became very upset, and took to her bed. Her words, according to her cooks, were, "Why have they done this to me? Sent a child to cook the lunch!"

Undaunted, I sent up a portion of the walnut roll, which restored Mrs. Logan's confidence. The lunch went well, all the dishes were a success, and when I departed Mrs. Logan told me she was very pleased.

Years later, when I found the recipe for this dessert in *The House & Garden Cookbook,* it brought back memories of my first professional culinary foray. Since then I have prepared the walnut roll in various forms, turning it into a yule log with meringue mushrooms for Christmas and a birthday cake for my children. It has been my favorite cake for twenty-eight years, so how could I not include it?

Walnut Roll

■■■■■■■■■■■■■■■■■■■■■■■■■■■

☐ *Cake*

1 ounce unsalted butter, at room temperature

5 eggs, yolks and whites separated

½ cup sugar

Pinch of salt

5 ounces finely ground walnuts (about 1¼ cups)

½ teaspoon baking powder

☐ *Walnut Filling*

6 ounces ground walnuts (about 1½ cups)

½ cup hot milk

¼ pound unsalted butter

⅔ cup sugar

2 tablespoons Cognac

1 cup heavy cream, whipped

½ cup confectioner's sugar

·Preheat oven to 375° F. Line an 11″ × 17″ jelly roll pan with wax paper, leaving a 1½-inch overhang at each end. Butter the paper and set the pan aside.

In a large bowl, beat the egg yolks, sugar, and salt until light in color. Stir in walnuts and baking powder. In another bowl, beat the egg whites until they form stiff peaks. Using a spatula, fold the egg whites into the yolk mixture.

Pour the mixture into the prepared pan, spreading evenly with the spatula. Bake in the center of the oven for 15 minutes, or until a cake tester inserted into the middle of the cake comes out clean. Remove from oven, cover with a damp kitchen towel, and place in the refrigerator for 30 minutes.

Prepare the filling: Place walnuts in a bowl and pour over hot milk. Allow to cool. In a large bowl cream together the butter and sugar until light and fluffy. Beat in the nut mixture and Cognac. Fold in the whipped cream. Reserve.

Remove cake from refrigerator. Sprinkle the surface with confectioner's sugar and place a 20-inch-long piece of wax paper over the cake. Invert the cake and pan onto the wax paper. Remove the pan and peel the paper from the cake.

Spread the reserved filling evenly over the cake. Holding on to the second piece of wax paper, roll up the cake like a jelly roll. Cover with foil and refrigerate until firm. Dust with confectioner's sugar before serving. ✖ *Serves 8*

teaching classes and catering. She has given endless time to organizing the rental of the Beard House for special events and fund raising. ✍

This is a fresh-tasting dessert, ideal to finish a gala brunch. Pass Chinese almond cookies on the side, if you can find them. Says Ross, "Of all the Chinese flavorings, James Beard loved the taste of ginger. In his honor, we developed this light orange dessert which ends a Chinese meal perfectly. Special thanks to Johanna Staray, our professional student, who tested this recipe 'in a hurry.'"

Gingered Oranges

3 cups water
1½ cups granulated sugar
5 slices fresh ginger root, peeled and cut into slivers
6 oranges
Crème Anglaise (recipe follows)

Measure the water into a medium saucepan, add the sugar, and stir until it dissolves. Add the slivers of ginger and place the saucepan over medium-high heat. Bring the syrup to a simmer, lower the heat, and let simmer for 15 minutes. Strain the syrup into a clean saucepan and discard the ginger.

Using a vegetable peeler, remove several strips of zest from one of the oranges, for the garnish. Cook the zest briefly in the syrup over low heat. Remove the zest and set it aside. Let the syrup cool.

Peel the oranges and remove as much of the white pith as possible. Slice the oranges crosswise. Slip the slices into the warm syrup and let them sit for 30 to 45 minutes. Strain them and place them in the refrigerator to chill thoroughly. Serve the orange slices with Crème Anglaise.

✗ *Serves 6*

Crème Anglaise

1 cup milk, heavy cream, or a mixture of both
3 egg yolks
¼ cup granulated sugar
2 to 4 teaspoons Grand Marnier or other orange-based liqueur

Warm the milk in a heavy saucepan over medium heat. Beat the egg yolks and sugar with a whisk until the mixture falls in a ribbon when the whisk is lifted. When the milk is warm, pour half of it into the egg mixture and whisk to combine thoroughly. Whisk this mixture into the remaining milk in the saucepan.

Cook the mixture over low heat until it thickens, stirring constantly. Take care not to curdle the eggs. When the custard is thick enough to coat the back of a spoon, take it from the heat. Strain the custard into a bowl and add the liqueur to your taste. Cover with plastic wrap and refrigerate until you are ready to serve it poured over the Gingered Oranges.

recipe that shows James's influence in the poaching of fresh fruit—a favorite—and the use of candied violets. The recipe may be prepared in steps on separate days and assembled just before dinner. ✍

You may poach the pears up to several days in advance. Let them cool to room temperature in the syrup. Store them in the syrup in the refrigerator. When you are ready to assemble the dessert, drain the pears well. Fragile almond or pistachio tuiles would be lovely with the pears.

Poires Maxim's
■ ■

2 cups granulated sugar
8 cups water
1-inch piece vanilla bean, split lengthwise
6 large firm-fleshed pears
9 egg yolks
1½ cups confectioner's sugar
½ cup Grand Marnier
2 cups cold heavy cream, plus additional cream for
    serving
Vanilla ice cream, for serving
Candied violets, for serving

In a heavy saucepan large enough to hold all of the pears comfortably, combine the granulated sugar, water, and vanilla bean over medium-high heat and let boil for 5 minutes.

Peel, halve, and core the pears; a quick way to core them is to use a melon baller to scoop out the center core, then a paring knife to cut out the stem in a neat "V."

Slip the pear halves into the hot sugar syrup and poach them over medium heat for about 20 minutes, until they are cooked through but still firm. Remove them from the syrup and let them drain on paper toweling. Place them in a bowl, cover them, and chill thoroughly.

In the top of a double boiler set over simmering water, beat the egg yolks with about one third of the confectioner's sugar until the mixture is smooth. Gradually add the remaining confectioner's sugar, beating thoroughly after

each addition. Continue beating until the mixture is thick and falls in a ribbon when dropped from the beater. This will take about 10 minutes. Remove the top of the double boiler from the heat and continue to beat the mixture until it has cooled. Stir in the Grand Marnier and set the mixture aside.

In a clean bowl, whip 2 cups of the cream until it is stiff. Fold the whipped cream into the sugar-egg mixture. Spoon this mousse into a large serving dish and chill thoroughly.

When you are ready to serve the dessert, arrange the pear halves on top of the chilled mousse, core side up. Fill each pear with some ice cream, and decorate the dessert with additional whipped cream piped through a pastry bag and candied violets. ✖ *Serves 12*

Desserts

JANE FREIMAN *has written a seductive book on entertaining. She writes restaurant reviews for* New York Newsday *and other articles for other publications. She gifts us with this recipe remembered from one of Jim's classes—a sort of child's dream.* ✍

An apple tart with applesauce filling, a strawberry tart with a chocolate-lined pastry, plain vanilla ice cream, and a chocolate Bavarian cream were among the desserts I loved best in Jim's classes.

This Christmasy recipe appeared in the second lesson of a fall series taught in the house on 10th Street, and I never look at a candy cane without remembering the wonderful and strange combination of peppermint and cream. While the recipe suggests unmolding the dessert, we actually prepared it in a glass soufflé dish (one of the lightweight rimless variety) and decorated the top with whipped cream and candy.

Apart from soup and dessert, the menu for this lesson was uncharacteristically French. It began with Oyster Purée, and continued with Côtes de Veau en Brioche and Courgettes Rapées.

James Beard's Peppermint Candy Bavarian Cream
■ ■

1 tablespoon unflavored gelatin
¼ cup cold water
3 whole eggs
1 egg yolk
¼ cup plus 1 tablespoon sugar
⅓ cup pulverized peppermint candies
1 teaspoon cornstarch
⅛ teaspoon salt
1¼ cups milk
1¼ cups heavy cream
1 drop red vegetable coloring
Whipped cream and crushed peppermint candies, for decoration

In a small bowl soften gelatin in cold water and reserve.

Separate whole eggs, reserving the whites in a large mixing bowl.

Combine yolks with 1 extra yolk and ¼ cup

sugar in another mixing bowl. Beat until mixture becomes very thick. Fold in pulverized candy, cornstarch, and salt.

Place milk in a 2-quart pan and scald over moderate heat. Remove from heat and quickly stir into the egg mixture. Pour mixture back into pan and cook over low heat, stirring constantly, until the mixture thickens and coats the back of a spoon.

Stir in the reserved gelatin until completely dissolved. Cool slightly.

Beat reserved egg whites until soft peaks form. Add remaining sugar and continue to beat until fully incorporated.

Gently but thoroughly fold whites into still-warm custard. Allow to cool completely.

Whip heavy cream until stiff; fold into cooled custard. Add red coloring and mix well to form a streaked effect. Pour mixture into a mold. Place in refrigerator and chill until quite firm.

Unmold onto a chilled serving platter and surround with whipped cream piped through a pastry tube, then sprinkle with crushed candy. Or decorate the Bavarian in its own mold and serve directly from there. ✗ *Serves 6*

a fine French restaurant in Philadelphia. ✍

If you like, you can serve this dessert with the raspberry sauce over the mousse, rather than swirled through it. It would be pretty garnished with chocolate triangles or a dusting of cocoa powder, too.

Parfait Glacé au Chocolat Blanc et Framboise

■■■■■■■■■■■■■■■■■■■■■■■■

¾ cup water
¾ cup granulated sugar
6 ounces best-quality white chocolate, cut into
    small pieces
3 eggs
2 cups heavy cream
10 ounces fresh raspberries, some raspberries
    reserved for garnish, if desired
Superfine or granulated sugar to taste, for the
    raspberries
Heavy cream for garnish, optional
Fresh mint leaves for garnish, optional

Combine water and sugar in a medium saucepan and bring the mixture to a boil over medium-high heat. Boil for exactly 1 minute, then remove from heat. Place the chocolate in the work bowl of a food processor or blender. With the motor running (at low speed, if you are using a blender), add the hot sugar syrup in a thin stream. Add the eggs and continue to process the mixture for 1 minute. Scrape the mixture into a stainless steel bowl and refrigerate, covered, until cold.

Whip the heavy cream until stiff. Fold it into the cold chocolate mixture. Spoon or pour the mixture into tall, chilled parfait glasses, filling each to within 1 inch from the top. Place in the freezer for at least ½ hour, until firm but not frozen solid.

Pureé the raspberries and pass the purée through a fine-mesh sieve to remove the seeds. Sweeten the purée to your taste with a little sugar. When the glacé is firm, pour 1 tablespoon of raspberry purée over the top of each parfait. Using a clean larding needle, ice pick, chop stick (or whatever else might do the job), swirl the purée down through the glacé.

Return the parfaits to the freezer for about one hour or longer. Serve garnished with fresh raspberries, whipped cream, and fresh mint leaves, if desired. ✖ *Serves 6*

No frozen dessert tastes creamier. Semifreddo is a very easy recipe, with delightful results.

Semifreddo

¾ cup finely crushed amaretti (Italian almond macaroons, about 1¼ cups whole amaretti)

2 teaspoons brandy

4 eggs, separated

¾ cup granulated sugar

A few grains of salt

2 cups heavy cream

Line a 9″ × 5″ × 3″ loaf pan with aluminum foil.

Place the amaretti crumbs in a small bowl and sprinkle them with the brandy. Set the crumbs aside.

In the bowl of an electric mixer, beat the egg yolks with ½ cup of the sugar at high speed for 3 minutes. Set the egg yolk mixture aside.

In a large clean bowl, whip the egg whites with the salt to soft peaks. Continue beating the egg whites, gradually adding the remaining ¼ cup sugar, until they form stiff peaks. Set the egg whites aside.

Whip the cream to soft peaks and fold it gently into the reserved egg yolk mixture. Fold in the beaten egg whites.

Sprinkle half of the crumb mixture over the bottom of the prepared pan. Pour in half of the cream mixture and sprinkle the surface evenly with the remaining crumbs. Top with the remaining cream mixture. Cover the pan tightly and freeze overnight. ✗ *Serves 10*

This is a lovely, sparkling, sweet granité. Don't pull out your best champagne for this; ordinary champagne is perfectly delicious with the cider. Accompany the granité with a plain shortbread cookie.

Cider Granité

1 cup granulated sugar
1 cup water
1 strip orange zest
1 strip lemon zest
1 ounce Calvados
2 cups cold, filtered apple cider
2 cups cold Champagne
Fresh mint leaves for garnish

Put the sugar, water, and zests in a medium saucepan. Stir the mixture over medium-high heat until the sugar dissolves, and bring it to a boil. Take this syrup off the heat and let cool to room temperature. Strain.

In a medium bowl, stir together 1 cup of the cooled, strained syrup with the Calvados, cider, and Champagne. Pour the mixture into a shallow pan and place it in the freezer. Stir the granité occasionally, every half hour or so, to break up the larger frozen blocks as they form. After 2 to 3 hours, the granité should be frozen sufficiently in chunks the size of small peas. Serve garnished with fresh mint leaves, if you like.

✗ *Serves 8 to 10*

smoother, more French in inspiration. ✍

This dessert was served with fresh raspberries and *langues du chat* that had been baked and then half-dipped in bittersweet chocolate at a dinner to honor James Beard.

Poire William Sorbet

■■■■■■■■■■■■■■■■■■■■■■■■■

6 ripe pears (about 6 ounces each), peeled, cored, and cut into 1-inch pieces, or 1 2-pound 2-ounce package frozen pear purée, defrosted
¼ cup fresh lemon juice
⅓ cup water
⅔ cup granulated sugar
¼ cup Poire William (pear brandy)

Place pear pieces in a blender with lemon juice and purée until smooth. Or, if using defrosted purée, place in blender with lemon juice and blend briefly to combine.

Combine water and sugar in a small saucepan over moderate heat. Cook until sugar has dissolved and syrup is almost boiling. Remove from heat. With motor running, add syrup to pear purée in processor, along with Poire William. Process to combine.

Pour mixture into ice cream maker and freeze according to manufacturer's instructions. Transfer to covered container and freeze for several hours before serving. ✘ *Makes about 5 cups, serves 6 to 8*

American Cookery *and sends us this American version of a frozen dessert.*

Sherbet is of course the American version of the Italian granita, the French sorbet. American persimmons would be the logical ideal; but we tested this with the new, less bitter Israeli persimmons and it was delightful. The color is pure Italian mural painting, lush but not sharp. The result is so voluptuous it is hard to believe there is no cream hanging around. If you add the egg white, you will have a more stable and creamier-seeming result. ✍

This sherbet can also be made with 3 large ripe Anjou pears and 1 large ripe persimmon, with a tablespoon of eau-de-vie replacing the tablespoon of kirsch.

Persimmon Sherbet

4 medium or 3 large *very* ripe persimmons
¾ cup granulated sugar
2 tablespoons fresh lemon juice
1 tablespoon kirsch
1 egg white, optional

Cut the persimmons into quarters, and remove cores and pithy centers. Scoop out pulp into the work bowl of a food processor. Add sugar, lemon juice, and kirsch and purée until smooth and fully combined. Add egg white, if using, and process to combine.

Pour into an ice cream machine and freeze according to manufacturer's instructions, or pour into a stainless steel bowl and freeze for several hours until the sherbet is firm, stirring at least three times. ✘ *Makes 3 cups, serves 4*

JANE MONTANT *was a good friend of Jim's. They loved to have good, gossipy lunches and they both valued good, plain American food highly. Their friendship was not impinged on by the fact that, as the editor in chief of* Gourmet, *she worked for Mr. MacAusland, the magazine's founder, a strong and crusty man who managed with ease to get into a long fight with Jim, who could be no small-time fighter himself. After the founder's death,* Gourmet *passed to Condé Nast and Mrs. Montant could once again talk to Jim about printing his work.*

The recipe, one of Mrs. Montant's personal favorites, is set out in the style of Gourmet *at that time, before the format of all recipes came to resemble each other.*

Pink Grapefruit Sorbet

In a small saucepan combine 1⅓ cups each of sugar and water, bring the mixture to a boil over moderate heat, stirring, and cook it, stirring, until the sugar is dissolved. Transfer the syrup to a bowl and chill it for 1 hour. Into another bowl squeeze and strain the juice from 3 large grapefruits (or enough to make 2½ cups strained juice) and chill it for 1 hour. Add the syrup and 1 tablespoon grenadine and chill the mixture for at least 2 hours. Freeze the mixture in an ice cream freezer according to the manufacturer's instructions. Arrange 2 scoops of the sorbet in each of 6 dessert glasses. ✕ *Serves 6.*

Serve these with a liquid dessert made of equal parts Kahlua and milk in an old-fashioned glass over ice cubes, sprinkled with cinnamon.

Polvoronnes

(Bride's Cookies)

1 cup all-purpose flour
¼ cup powdered sugar, plus extra in which to roll baked cookies
½ cup unsalted butter, cut into small pieces
Pinch salt
½ cup finely chopped almonds
2 teaspoons vanilla extract

Preheat oven to 325° F.

Place all ingredients in a mixing bowl and with fingers, rub together to mix completely.

Using about 2 tablespoons of dough for each cookie, form into small crescent shapes. Place on a cookie sheet and bake for about 18 minutes, or until cookies are a pale gold color.

Remove from oven and allow to cool slightly on the cookie sheet, then transfer cookies to a wire rack. When completely cool, sift extra powdered sugar onto a plate and roll the cookies in it to coat heavily with the sugar.

✖ *Makes about 15 cookies*

Sesame Cookies

∎∎∎∎∎∎∎∎∎∎∎∎∎∎∎∎∎∎∎∎∎∎∎

8 cups sifted all-purpose flour
1½ cups granulated sugar
3 teaspoons baking powder
1 teaspoon salt
1½ sticks unsalted butter
6 ounces vegetable shortening
2 large eggs, slightly beaten
1 cup milk, plus a little extra in a bowl
1¼ teaspoons vanilla extract
1 pound sesame seeds, rinsed in a fine strainer and
    kept damp

Preheat oven to 325° F.

Sift together flour, sugar, baking powder, and salt into a large bowl. With a pastry blender or two knives cut in the butter and shortening until mixture is like lumpy cornmeal.

Add eggs, milk, and vanilla and stir all together with a large spoon.

With your hands, work the dough just until it comes together to a ball. Take a handful of dough, squeeze it together with your hands, and roll it out with your fingers to make a sausage about ½ inch thick. Cut dough into 2-inch logs.

Dip logs in bowl of milk and then roll in the damp sesame seeds. Place on cookie sheets, allowing enough space between the cookies for expansion.

Bake in the center of the oven for about 45 minutes, until golden brown. Remove from oven and cool on a wire rack.

When completely cooled, place in an airtight container. They will keep, refrigerated, for a few weeks, or in the freezer for even longer.

✘ *Makes about 6 dozen cookies*

MATT KRAMER. *As we have seen, wherever Jim went, he looked for kindred spirits and tried to involve them in his world of food. In his home town of Portland he found a sympathetic soul in Matt Kramer, who has matured into the full-time wine and food writer that James hoped for. He writes twice weekly for* The Oregonian, *every other issue for* The Wine Spectator, *for his syndicated radio commentaries, and from time to time for the wide variety of local and national magazines. He is also the author of* Making Sense of Wine *and* Making Sense of Burgundy. ✍

Jim Beard had an enormous number of friends, acquaintances, and hangers-on. I was one of the hangers-on. I met Beard because I was—still am—a food and wine writer in Portland, Oregon, which, of course, was Beard's hometown. He had many authentic friends in Portland, among them his childhood chum Mary Hamblet (I used to live two houses away from her); his longtime interior decorator and pal Jerry Lamb; and above all, his friend Richard Nelson. Beard used to stay with Dick Nelson whenever he came to Portland, which was at least once a year. Dick was a faithful assistant to Beard in numerous cooking demonstrations and then, with Beard's blessings (and occasional misgivings, for Beard was like that), Dick went out on his own.

I met Beard in my capacity as a food writer. I interviewed him multiple times, with tape recorder in hand. Beard was wonderfully quotable and quite salty. Writers for family newspapers would have to edit, but I worked for a weekly that had no such inhibitions. Beard liked being quoted in full. I think that he chafed a little at the prissiness of food writing in daily newspapers.

It's fair to say that we hit it off. I have always loved history. In Jim Beard, I had history on the hoof. (Far from taking offense, he would have loved being described as "history on the hoof." He liked earthiness and could take it as well as dish it out.)

The first time I interviewed him was in San Francisco in 1977. He was holed up in the Stanford Court hotel, recuperating from one of his innumerable death-defying illnesses. We talked about:

• *Portland, Oregon*—"Portland has always been a city of pleasant homes and what I might call 'reactionary living.'"

• *Food writers*—"A lot of them use canned stuff. You know the public relations people provide them with material all of the time, and photographs. A lot of newspapers use that all the way through."

• *Fruits and vegetables*—"The trouble with produce here is that it's handled too much. And the Europeans are doing exactly the same thing: They're growing for shelf age and they're also putting stuff through those gas chambers. They're doing the same damn thing with chickens. All a chicken has to do now in France is get off the truck and walk through Bresse and it become a *poulet de Bresse*."

• *Restaurant reviewers* (of which I was one at the time)—"This is not to be taken personally at all, but restaurant reviewers can ruin a restaurant faster than anything in the world because they will go and review it and give it a half-assed review before the restaurant has a chance to get itself settled."

• *His forthcoming books*—"I'm going to do another book of memoirs. And I'm going to tell *all*."

Beard was a generous soul, especially to those only beginning to make their way. I was one. For example, only a few days after I returned to Portland after having interviewed Beard that first time, I got a telephone call from Michael Batterberry, who had founded *Food and Wine* magazine and was then its editor. He had seen Beard in San Francisco and Beard had sung my praises to him, urging Batterberry to get me to write for *Food and Wine*. And he did. I wrote some pieces for the magazine, thanks to Beard's generosity and credibility.

A number of years later, Beard renewed his desire to write a sequel to *Delights and Prejudices*, his 1964 memoir of growing up in Portland and of his early years in New York. It's easy to forget that Beard didn't even begin writing about food until he was thirty-seven, with his first book, *Hors d'Oeuvre and Canapes,* published in 1940. His soon-to-evolve career began only when he was in what was then considered midlife. It's a lesson and an example well worth recalling, as I do from time to time.

One of the pieces that I had written about Beard, titled "Recollections in the Round" (which Beard thought vastly amusing), probably led him to decide that he wanted me to work with him on his anticipated sequel to *Delights and Prejudices.* Because of my liking for history, I had by then absorbed most of the writings of Beard's contemporaries, all of whom he outlived. I suppose that he found it surprising to be asked about such now-forgotten food figures as G. Selmer Fougner. ("He had been a streetcar conductor for most of his life," recalled Beard. "And he ended up being one of the great food and wine authorities in the country. He wrote for the *New York Sun* and he was really the first food and wine critic around New York who was serious about what he was doing.")

Or about Clementine Paddleford, a better-known name: "Clementine Paddleford's columns in the *New York Herald-Tribune* were like nothing else that ever happened before or since. They were the most exhaustive collection of flowery prose that you've ever read in your life. Clementine could write a two-column story every day, and yet"—here he paused for a roaring laugh—"and yet she didn't know a goddamned thing about food!"

Or about his one-time mentor and later nemesis, the food writer and head of the New York Wine and Food Society, Jeanne Owen: "I would say that Jeanne did a great deal for me, and that started in 1938. Then, strangely enough, around 1950 or so, she decided I was getting too famous. So she decided to cut me off. After that, I was everything from an SOB to a thief to just about everything else. And yet, all those years that she hated my guts, and spent no small amount of time spreading around what she thought, she

would call up friends of mine and say, 'Now, I don't think Jim looks very well. You'd better tell him to be careful. Tell him to see a doctor if he hasn't.' "

Knowing my interest in, and passing knowledge of, these and other food-world figures of his day, Beard decided that he wanted me to work with him to assemble his memories that would begin where *Delights and Prejudices* left off, essentially post–World War Two. (The book never materialized.) He liked how I was able to help him collate long-unused strands of memories. And I think that he wanted to help me out, too. I was flattered, of course. And delighted, as I genuinely enjoyed interviewing him. By then I knew him well enough that we would sit together and talk as acquaintances.

One of our conversations concerned fruitcake. Beard always loved fruitcake. Its disparagement was setting in even then, but he was unperturbed. Beard had seen too many fads and fancies come and go. (Once, when I asked him if any of the latest food trends surprised him, he did admit that he never expected to see home bread-baking revived.) In *Delights and Prejudices* he recorded the best fruitcake recipe that I know, which he called "My Mother's Black Fruitcake." He agreed that it was the best fruitcake that he, too, had ever eaten.

My Mother's Black Fruitcake [JB]

First preparation: Cut into thin shreds ½ pound citron, ¼ pound orange peel, and 1 pound candied pineapple, and halve and pit ½ pound cherries. Combine these with 1 pound seeded raisins, ½ pound sultanas, and ½ pound currants. Add to this mixture 1 cup cognac and let it sit, covered, in the refrigerator for two days. Toast ½ pound filberts in a 350-degree oven for 30 minutes. [This is too long. Instead, toast for just 10 minutes. *M.K.*] Chop them coarsely or leave them whole, as you wish.

On the day you bake the cake, remove the fruit from the refrigerator, sprinkle ½ cup flour over it, and blend the mixture well. Add the nuts and mix again.

Sift 1½ cups flour and then measure to exactly 1½ cups. Combine the flour with 1 teaspoon cinnamon, a pinch of ground cloves, ½ teaspoon mace, and a touch of nutmeg. Add ½ teaspoon baking soda.

Cream together ½ cup butter and 2 cups sugar—you may use part brown sugar if you wish. Add 6 lightly beaten eggs, 3 ounces unsweetened grated chocolate, another ¼ cup cognac. Blend all this very firmly with the flour, which you should add a little at a time. When it is perfectly blended, pour over the fruit and nut mixture and mix well with your hands.

Line a pan or pans with silicon paper or brown paper. If you use brown paper you will need to butter the pans first. For fruitcake I like to use 9-inch bread pans or one large square pan or two 9-inch spring molds. The cakes should be baked at 275 degress. If bread pans are used, only 1½ hours' baking time is required. Cakes baked in the square pan or spring molds take about 2½ to 3½ hours. If you use a very large spring mold, the cake should bake about an hour longer.

Let the fruitcake stand for an hour or more after it comes from the oven.

When it was just warm Mother used to add a bath of cognac and put the cakes in tins to rest till they were to be used. She would make five times this recipe every year and often keep the cakes through the year with towels dampened in cognac wrapped around them, and in airtight containers, of course.

DRINKS & SUCH

IF YOU HAVE READ THIS FAR, YOU WILL REALIZE THAT JIM'S FAVORITE TIPPLE WAS THE GLENLIVET. EVEN AFTER HE GAVE UP WINE,

HE SOMEHOW FELT SCOTCH COULDN'T HARM HIM. CERTAINLY, THE FIRST CHAPTER OF HIS FIRST BOOK, <u>HORS D'OEUVRE AND CANAPÉS,</u> BASED AS IT WAS ON THE COCKTAIL PARTY, WAS FULL OF HINTS ABOUT HOW TO SERVE LIQUOR.

IT SEEMS APPROPRIATE AS WE APPROACH THE END OF THIS LONG TELLING OF LOVE STORIES TO INCLUDE A FEW DRINK RECIPES THAT HAVE BEEN INCLUDED AND TO INTRODUCE THEM WITH A TALE BY CLARK WOLF, WHO, FIRST IN SAN FRANCISCO AND THEN IN NEW YORK, WAS TO SHARE LONG GOSSIPY SESSIONS AND AFFECTION WITH JIM.

CLARK STARTED OFF WITH A SMALL CHEESE STORE TO WHICH JIM FOUND HIS WAY. THAT WAY—AS ALWAYS—INCLUDED A KEEN INTEREST IN THE DEVELOPING CAREERS OF NEW FRIENDS IN THE FOOD BUSINESS. WHEN CLARK BECAME THE MANAGER OF THE OAKVILLE GROCERY, ALSO IN SAN FRANCISCO, WE BEGAN TO SHOP THERE FOR OUR CLASSES. WHEN I OPENED MY SHORT-LIVED STORE, STAR SPANGLED FOODS, IN NEW YORK, IT WAS JIM WHO URGED ME TO BRING CLARK TO NEW YORK AS ITS MANAGER.

SINCE THEN CLARK HAS BECOME A CONSULTANT TO RESTAURANTS AND FOOD STORES AND WRITES ON FOOD FOR NEWSPAPERS AND MAGAZINES AND APPEARS, MOST AMUSINGLY, ON TELEVISION.

MY FIRST TIME. With little deference to Campari ads, *my* first time with James was, as for so many others, really quite memorable.

There I stood, in my little cheese shop at the base of Nob Hill, when, at once, the door did in fact darken. Before me, draped in a floor-to-heavens black leather trench coat, with collar flipped skyward and head gleaming, stood either a color Xerox negative of Darth Vader, or the legendary James Beard.

With a softly bellowed "Good afternoon" (how did he manage to affect both?), he ordered wedges of Appenzeller, St. Nectaire, and Compté, and then predicted his doctor's likely disapproval, eyes sparkling, eyebrows reaching.

It was some years before I was to again gather over foodstuffs with James.

Now, his assistant was a dear friend of mine who never tired of telling James of our adventures and exploits.

"He'd like to meet you," came the declaration. "We'll have drinks and dinner at The Stanford Court, but don't be surprised if we're dismissed and home before eleven. He tires so easily these days."

Sometime just before two A.M. we sat, we three, having our second or third after-dinner Glenlivet, when my friend finally admitted defeat and announced his intention to go home, and so to bed.

James, who had been merrily retelling stories, some of which I later learned were actually true, leaned over and winked.

"Clark," said he in that muted bellow, "why don't you come around tomorrow morning for breakfast, about 7:30. Then," he stage-whispered, "we can have a really good gossip."

MARK MILLER. *This may seem like more work than you want to go to for a drink. I thought so, but it is well worth it. These daiquiris could be the very soul of a party. Jim mentioned daiquiris in* Hors d'Oeuvre and Canapés, *and as he served in Brazil during World War II, I think he might have liked these.* ✍

Brazilian Daiquiri

■■■■■■■■■■■■■■■■■■■■■■■■■■■■■

1 cup Bacardi light rum
1 cup Bacardi dark rum
¾ cup Myers's rum
2 teaspoons vanilla extract
1 Mexican vanilla bean, split lengthwise
1 large sweet ripe pineapple, peeled, cored, and
    cut into eighths
2 ounces piloncillo or light brown sugar

Combine all ingredients in a clean glass jar, cover tightly, and leave to sit at room temperature for 48 hours. Strain out the pineapple (this is wonderful served with vanilla ice cream) and vanilla.

Put the rum mixture in the freezer until very cold. Serve in shot glasses or martini glasses.
✗ *Makes 12 cocktails*

Sangría

■■■■■■■■■■■■■■■■■■■■■■■

1 bottle dry red wine
¼ cup superfine sugar
¼ cup Cointreau or Orange Curaçao
1 large bay leaf, cracked
1 lemon, thinly sliced
1 orange, thinly sliced
¼ cup brandy
2 cups club soda
Ice

In a large pitcher, stir together wine, sugar, and Cointreau until the sugar has dissolved. Add bay leaf and sliced lemon and orange. Cover and refrigerate for at least 8 hours.

When ready to serve, mix with brandy and club soda and serve in tall glasses over lots of ice.

ENVOI
M.F.K. FISHER

It seems foolish to me to try to write anything about James Beard, especially since everybody else who ever knew him is puzzling over this same problem.

I can truthfully say that he is the only man I ever met whom I loved without question or doubt, and forever. I don't think we ever even held hands or exchanged a mild pat, avuncular on his part at least, and yet I could talk with him with complete confidence, and about any subject in the world, including the condition of his enormous feet, as well as "the state of our immortal souls." This lack of personal contact is without a doubt one of the real reasons for my inability to think of a recipe of any kind in connection with this most famous of all living cooks, for he is still living to me as well as to every other person who ever knew him, even vicariously.

I know that Jim cooked often for me, and I could pretend to know how he prepared the dishes, and say that I had often followed his behavior myself, and I could even say that I had prepared things for him from my own recipes. But this would be cheating, and he himself is and always was beyond that, at least in my memory of him.

The James Beard Celebration Cookbook

The James Beard Celebration Cookbook

GRATEFUL ACKNOWLEDGMENT IS
MADE TO THOSE PHOTOGRAPHERS
WHOSE WORK APPEARS ON THE
FOLLOWING PAGES:

Louis Wallach: all photographs of James Beard's
bow ties

Adam Anik: 37, 38, 39, 40, 46

Richard Bowditch: 98

Walt Chrynwski: 242

Corning, Inc.: 121

John Garetti: 107

KKing: 350

Harold Naideau: 109

Geoffrey Nilsen: 338

Len de Pas: 94

Art Rodgers Photography: 71

Stuart Rodgers-Reilly Photography: 159

Lozi Skpaz: 160

Dan Wynn: 52, 53, 63, 146, 157, 241, 248, 253, 283,
297, 303, 315, 342, 389

Many of the contributors have also kindly supplied
pictures of James Beard and of themselves from their
personal collections.